# ROWING BACKWARDS

# ROWING BACKWARDS

*A World War II Memoir*
*...And Beyond*

*to Liz, with love —Julia*
*Enjoy!*

## Julia "Jay" Jones Hensley

**To order additional copies of this book, contact:**
Xlibris Corporation
1-888-795-4274
www.Xlibris.com
Orders@Xlibris.com
50315

# CONTENTS

Acknowledgements ........................................................................11

We Were Summer People ...............................................................15

## PART 1

1—D.O.'s Party, Summer 1942 ........................................................19

2—Back to the City .........................................................................27

3—About My Family ......................................................................47

4—July Days with Pierre, 1943 ......................................................60

5—A Bolt of Lightning....................................................................78

## PART 2

6—Off to College............................................................................82

7—Rendezvous in Missouri.............................................................89

8—Summer 1944 in Ashfield ..........................................................92

9—A Week in Malden......................................................................97

10—Back to Penn State .................................................................101

11—Stopping by the Post Office, 1945 .........................................106

12—Roll of Honor .........................................................................110

13—A Life without Pierre .............................................................112

# PART 3

14—Summer's End ..................................................................114

15—My Last Two Years of College.....................................117

16—Philadelphia Interlude and Sagamore Summer.....................122

17—My Job at UMass ........................................................126

18—My Postgraduate Studies..............................................129

# PART 4

19—Breakfast at Mrs. Doty's and My Dream Job.........................136

20—An AshfieldWedding....................................................144

21—The Pammel Court Years...............................................150

22—The Unraveling..........................................................157

23—Encounter on I-75 and Citizen Jay .................................184

# PART 5

24—On My Own Again........................................................188

25—Early Years on the Creek ...........................................195

26—Return to Apple Valley...............................................219

27—My Job at UK, 1969-78 ...............................................230

28—A Rider in the Wilderness..........................................239

29—My Freelance Career...................................................242

30—The Trouble with My Cars and Truck ..............................250

31—Sleeping Scared.........................................................254

# PART 6

32—Meeting Claire, 1983 ....................................................260
33—Our Lives in the 1980s ................................................265
34—Broke-back Afternoon ..................................................291
35—West Coast Doug .........................................................294
36—Eva Horton and Me .....................................................299
37—Our Lives in the 1990s ................................................304
38—Selling *SNEWS* .........................................................319
39—My Years with the Chimney Sweeps ..........................322
40—My Letters to Pierre ....................................................339
41—Scotty, Night Visitor ...................................................344

# PART 7

42—Leaving the Jessamine Creek .....................................350
43—Summer of Loss, 2003 ................................................356
44—Gatherings of the Clans, 2005 ...................................367
45—Stopover in Saratoga Springs .....................................376
46—Remembering Ernie Jordan ........................................388
47—A Brief History Lesson ...............................................391
48—Imagining Pierre in France .........................................398
49—Reminiscing ................................................................400
50—Solace .........................................................................403
51—Thoughts upon Turning Eighty ..................................414

*For all my children,
grandchildren,
great-grandchildren
and their families*

Cover photo, circa 1933: My sister Pauline
(black cowboy hat) hitched up our pony Midget and took
us for an outing through the village. That's
me and little brother Phillips behind her. Next to her
are my friend Anne Smith and her brother David.

# ACKNOWLEDGEMENTS

## *and the Observations of a Time Traveler*

W hat began as a World War II memoir has morphed into a chronicle of my life. Albeit briefly summarized in some chapters, the essence of my journey is here. So many of those who might have assisted me in my remembering are gone. But I have mined magazine columns, journals, Christmas letters, and years of personal correspondence to jog my memory and keep me honest.

"Autobiographies are some of the best fiction out there," my friend and fellow writer George Strange tells me. But I have tried mightily to write down the truth of my life as I experienced it, realizing that people remember things differently and that there will be some who take issue with my version of the past.

I have become a time traveler. I work on this memoir in my head as I fall asleep at night, as I gather pinecones for kindling down by the pond, as I take a walk at sunrise and sunset, as I drive somewhere . . . Brushing my teeth, I am startled by my own reflection in the bathroom mirror. Where is the sixteen-year-old girl I have been all day as I relive that year of my life in rich detail?

It has been a daunting seesaw of writing intensely for months at a time, then losing momentum for long periods as other demands overtake me.

Now almost finished, I keep adding this and that to the narrative as strands of memory work their way through the labyrinth of my brain, picking up details along the way, and burst out upon me full-blown. These often come to me in the night or in the early morning while I'm still abed. I must scribble them down or boot up my computer and get to work before they fade away. I have discovered that the more I write, the more I remember.

This is not a tell-all book; for my children, my friends, and I all deserve our privacy in some of the struggles and sorrows that have come our way. And of necessity, a few names have been changed.

There are many people who have helped make this book possible.

After my mother and then my sister died, most of the letters I'd sent them found their way back to me. And when my high school pal Anne Alevizon Mitchell cleared out house and attic prior to moving to a retirement complex in Vermont, she bundled up and returned all those very candid letters I'd written to her through the years. (I don't know how she could bear to give them up. They were right entertaining!)

My brother Phillips remembers more clearly than I some of our shared past; also my cousins Murray Reed and Steve Fitzsimmons and my longtime Kentucky friend Peg Payne Taylor, who is like a sister to me. Her suggestions as she critiqued my first version of the book and later as she read through new and revised copy were always right on the mark.

George Strange, published author and teacher of writing, critiqued and diligently line edited my first version of *Rowing Backwards*. Book in hand, he came in my door one cold December evening, saying, "Jay, I think you have something here!" As we sat in front of the fire, he went over every chapter with me and suggested an effective new sequence for the last five.

Dick Lilly, knower of all things Ashfield and my brother's nephew by marriage, has been invaluable in sharing bits and pieces from his lifelong experience with Ashfield people and places. I discovered upon meeting him by phone when he called me from New York City, where he works at the Strand Bookstore, that I once knew his mother. When Ann Nye was a little girl of about six or seven, I took her for walks down our narrow tree-shaded lane and for picnic lunches in the woods below our pond.

Grace Lesure from the Ashfield Historical Society and my friend Norma Day Harris have also been helpful with their knowledge of early Ashfield and its residents. So too has Martha Townsley of Apple Valley. And my nephew Aaron Clark scanned old photographs into his computer and put them on a disk for me. A recent source of inspiration has been the *Tales of Apple Valley* memoir published by Barbara Clark Graves when she was ninety.

My friend Carol Rickwald, who teaches writing at Eastern Kentucky University, hit upon the perfect title for my book after reading the first chapter.

I am also indebted to Claire Cournand, Pierre's sister, whom I met in the Clark Orchards in 1983. Her friendship, encouragement, and old family photos have been a tremendous help in coaxing this memoir onto the printed page.

Cousin Murray and me playing
Indians down by the pond.

# WE WERE SUMMER PEOPLE

Slide the tape into the VCR, hit the Play button, and the past unfolds. A generation of family movies cobbled together.

The year is 1934. There I am, jumping onto my pony bareback and wheeling around into action, elbows flapping, heels pounding against her ribs. The big girl with me astride her own horse is my sister Pauline. In those days, she was sometimes mean to me. She'd say, "You can't do anything right!"

But there on the screen, giving lie to her words, is a fetching little girl of eight. Julia . . . long tangled brown hair, blue eyes in an animated face, an agile body, and a sure hand with her fractious old pony Midget, who gallops with neck outstretched and ears flat back.

My sister's animosity didn't last. We became good friends, shared our hopes and dreams, and I loved her all her long life.

There now on the screen is my beloved four-year-old brother, Phillips, peering gleefully over the head of a squirming cat held tight in his arms.

We were "summer people," the John Paul and Helen Jones family from Brooklyn, New York. "City kids" . . . but not really. We marked off the days on the calendar 'til our escape from the city in late May, stared out the car windows, sobbing, in September as we headed back into exile. For the Shattuck Place we rented on South Street, overlooking the village of Ashfield in the Berkshire Hills of Western Massachusetts, was the gateway to our *real lives*.

We swam in our pond, rode horseback through the village and way beyond to explore dirt roads and old logging trails. In the early years, we took our horses to be shod by old Adolphus Handifield in his leather apron at the village smithy behind the Sandy's garage across Main Street from the Episcopal Church.

Ashfield folk called him Dolphie. We never tired of holding a horse for him and watching him work. I remember the smell of singed hoof as he tested for fit the shoe he'd heated in red-hot coals and pounded into shape on the anvil.

We played tennis on the courts down by the Big Pond (Ashfield Lake) at the edge of the village, Kick the Can on summer evenings at the Page family's White Homestead next to the Congregational Church on Main Street, and softball on their big side lawn on summer afternoons.

In our teens, we attended parties there too as well as at Little Switzerland—the Walker place overlooking upper Apple Valley—and Snake Rock Farm, the Williams's place on Steady Lane a few miles outside the village.

We sweated our way exuberantly through the Saturday night square dances and polkas at the town hall, ate ice cream and danced to the jukebox tunes at Mike's place on the lake. We played Monopoly on our big front porch on rainy afternoons or ping-pong in the old milk room at the other end of the house. In our late teens, Pauline and I competed fiercely in gymkhanas, those contests on horseback held at various county fairs.

On winter vacations, we skied down the hill from the orchard, ice-skated on the pond, built a fire on the shore, and roasted hot dogs. Afterward, snug and warm in our living room we munched handfuls of hot buttered popcorn by the glow of a bed of hot coals over which we had jostled the corn into explosive life.

Oh, we did our share of chores too. For Pauline and me, that meant housework, cooking and baking, plus canning blueberries, pears, cherries, and the produce from Daddy's big garden. For Phillips, it was yard work and helping Daddy keep the house and barn in good repair.

We all took turns cranking the ice cream freezer and pulling the crosscut saw across from Daddy as he worked up firewood for our five fireplaces and wood-burning cookstove. And roused by Daddy while it was still dark, we picked wild blueberries in dew-soaked places just after sunrise, returned home a few hours later to eat blueberry pancakes or muffins for breakfast.

In my dreams, I still ride my bike "downstreet" to collect our mail at the post office next to the feed store. About once a week, I tie my pony to the hitching rock in front of the library across Main Street from the post office. An hour or two later, I head for home with a gunnysack full of books—fairy tales, mythology, horse books and poetry. Later on, I also read swashbuckling tales like *The Three Musketeers*, historical romances such as *Janice Meredith*, and, in secret, a pile of the Western pulps hidden under my bed.

The pulps came from Irene, a friendly curly-haired young woman who worked for us one summer. She had a tough, lively little horse named Queenie that she rode to work one day so that we could see her.

Harold and Bob Pichette, town kids a few years older than my sister and me, were our friends. In their teens, Harold and Pauline were sweethearts.

In 1938, after a fire that routed us one August night did considerable damage to the roof and water damage to the whole house, Daddy bought the property—house, barn, pond, and fifteen acres of fields, woods, and apple orchards.

In New York City, Mr. Shattuck collected his insurance money and let the whole estate go for a pittance. Unable to settle on our own grand name for it, we finally just called it the Place.

Daddy was the benevolent family dictator, Presbyterian minister, civil rights activist, matchless storyteller—a combination of intellectual, earthy do-it-yourselfer, and sometime clown. I adored him but stormily rebelled against him, much to the horror of my siblings. Family outings with Daddy were always fun.

Mom was the loving and compliant wife, the conscientious mother. Her only athletic pursuits were swimming and ice-skating. She swam with strong strokes around the pond in her one-piece black wool bathing suit. Afterward, she pulled off her white bathing cap, turned her head to one side, and shook out her long thick dark hair. In winter, she skimmed across the ice wearing her colorful wide-striped Hudson's Bay Company jacket.

With its eclectic assortment of framed prints and oil paintings on the walls, hundreds of books, secondhand furniture, an old upright piano in the dining room, a large assortment of classical records, and a pond to swim in, our place was a magnet for friends and relatives. They flowed through it all summer long. I spent many a long cozy evening curled up in a living room chair, listening to the grown-ups telling their stories, discussing ideas and books and current events.

Daddy kept a tight rein on Pauline and me when we reached our teens. We had to be in by a certain time, were not allowed to ride in boys' cars outside the confines of the village, except with special permission. My brother was accorded far more freedom to come and go, which outraged me.

Once, Norm Walker drove me home from the square dance. Holding me captive, he was determined to collect a good-night kiss. But I was fifteen and stubborn. The clock ticked away. Finally, defeated, he said, "The boys in town call you the Little Puritan up on the Hill!" Set free at last, I slammed his car door and stormed into the house.

And in September of 1942 as World War II flung its deepening shadow across the land, I connected with Pierre. I had just turned sixteen. Much of what follows next is excerpted from my tattered diary. It keeps our brief time together more than sixty years ago as achingly fresh as yesterday.

# 1

# D.O.'s Party, Summer 1942

## *Pages from My Diary*

### *Wednesday, Sept. 8, 1942, Ashfield, Mass.*

This afternoon Daddy felt like going on a spree, so we all hopped into the rattletrap [1931 Chrysler] and went over to Hamp [Northampton]. There weren't any good picture shows there, so we went to Greenfield and saw "Tombstone" and "Calling Dr. Gillespie." I was almost scared out of my wits by the time I got out of that place! We had supper over there and then came home.

We'd forgotten all about D.O.'s party. Harold and Bob were supposed to call for us at about 8:00 and we didn't get home 'til 9:00. But they soon came to fetch us. Harold, Bob, Normie [Walker] and D.O. arrived at 9:30 and drove us back up to D.O.'s. There was Pauline with Harold, D.O. with Bob and little Julia with Normie . . . Was I happy when who should walk in but Pierre Courneau. I could have thrown my arms around his neck and kissed him! (Well, almost.) From then on everything perked up and I had a wonderful, wonderful time.

Finally Bob came in, dragged me out of my chair, handed me my coat and said it was 12:30 and he was going home, and was I coming with him or not? And if so, I was to get moving.

Pierre: "Stay a little later, Julia, and I'll ride you home on my bike."

Me: "Okay. Bye, Bob!"

So Bob, Plinkie and Harold left, and about 15 minutes later we did, too . . . It was raining and awfully dark outside, and was I glad Pierre was taking me home.

What wild, crazy fun it was to go speeding down those hills in the darkness and the rain. He had a flashlight, but we turned it out. He thought I'd be scared, but I wasn't. He told me to keep leaning to the right. I was leaning against his arm and it seemed silly to be afraid.

I think he liked it, too, even with my hair blowing in his face. He sang a little in his deep musical voice—some of those boisterous, hearty Gilbert and Sullivan songs: "Da-da-da-da-da in the Queen's Navy!"

I guess I probably won't see him again until next summer. He's awfully nice and goodlooking, too, especially when his hair is all windblown and tousled and he has a pair of jeans on . . .

### Thursday morning

I've been thinking about last night and how excited I felt when I went to bed, and how strongly he shook my hand when he said goodnight and that he hoped he'd see me again before we both left. And I keep remembering how quiet and reserved he used to be when he first came here [his family had a summer place in South Ashfield on Bird Hill Road where the old Camp Ashfield for kids once was] and how he used to just suffer through some of those dances and parties last summer.

He's changed since then. I remember Bob saying that he loosened right up as soon as he went to work for a couple of weeks in the orchard with the other kids [probably the Don Howes Orchard in the upper Apple Valley]. Bob said Pierre taught them some French and Spanish and that the fellows all think the world of him.

Darn it anyway. He's probably forgotten all about Wednesday night and doesn't even know I exist.

I think I'll go to the dance stag tomorrow night since I had such a wonderful time at the last two dances, what with Ralph Townsley bringing me home the first time and those two R.A.F. lads turning up the next time . . . Well, I have to dust and sweep rugs now.

### *Sunday, September 12*

Gosh, a lot of things happened last night. I drove down to the dance with Plink and Harold, and Harold insisted on paying for me. He's always doing things like that. As soon as I got inside a square started and Ralph Townsley came running over and asked me for it.

I danced all the dances except one or two when I was too tired. I finally met the girl I'd been wanting to meet all summer, Janet Burdett. She comes from Charlemont and she's working at The Georgianna. She's swell . . . I'm going down to meet her at The Georgianna at 2 o'clock, this afternoon . . .

Ed Fuller brought me home [a farm boy from South Ashfield] . . . He's been hanging around at the dances watching me all summer . . . It's hard to believe that he's 20—he seems more like 17. He never danced with me or said more than three dozen words to me all summer, and then last night he suddenly came over and danced the last three dances with me . . . Ralph Townsley saw me with him, thought we were going to go around together again, gave me a rather forlorn look and left before the dance was even over! . . .

At the end of the last dance Ed said, "How you going home, walking?"

Me: "Yes, I guess so."

Him: "I'll drive you home."

Me: "Hmmm—O.K."

He helped me on with my raincoat and grabbed his big warm sweater and pulled it over his head, mussing his hair all up . . . In his car he starts out in the wrong direction. Oh, gosh . . .

Me: "What's this, the long way home?"

Him: "Yes. Don't you like the long way home?"

Me: "Yes, sometimes. No, turn around!" [I was remembering when I dated him the summer before, and he kept trying to kiss me.]

Him: "Nope."

Me: "But—Oh, look, there's Jimmy Walker."

Him: "Hop in, Jimmy, and we'll drive you home. You don't feel like walking three miles, do you?"

*After we took Jimmy home, Ed pulled off to the side of the road on the way home, stopped, put out the lights, and gave me a hard time. Well, I wouldn't let him kiss me, and he finally took me home. I did like him but wasn't ready for that. He was really nice about it, which I appreciated.*

### Tuesday, Sept. 14

Janet came up to the house yesterday afternoon. We played ping-pong and walked down to the pond and fooled around with the horses and stuff. She's 17 and she's going to Mass State this fall. She saved up more than $100 this summer. She said it's kind of fun to be out on your own, that is if you like the place you're working at and meet some nice kids . . . She's going to major in chemistry.

We went for a walk this afternoon, up to the Ashfield Lake and around the village. We were going to play tennis, but for some reason the tennis nets have been taken down and the bath houses have been closed up, too . . .

Mother's birthday was Sept. 12 and we gave her a fireplace set, a nut chopper and some salt and pepper shakers . . .

This afternoon I made a cake for Plink's birthday tomorrow. I got her a billfold and Mother's going to put a 5 dollar bill in it. I wouldn't mind having 5 dollars; all I have right now is 23 cents. Harold came up tonight with a big package and said, "Happy birthday, Plink!"

She: (blushing and surprised) "Why Harold, you naughty boy, you shouldn't have done that!"

He: "Tell me if it doesn't fit, and I'll have it exchanged."

### Thursday, Sept. 16

I could write pages and pages on all that happened yesterday!

Janet and I decided to go swimming at the Paddy Hole [the Ashfield Lake beach for local residents], so we put our bathing suits on under a skirt and blouse, and after we got down there we left our clothes on the bench and went swimming. The water was cold as ice, but it was fun after we got in. We hadn't been there more than 15 minutes before some boy rode up on a bicycle. He went behind the boys' bathhouse and soon emerged in his trunks.

It was Pierre. Yippee! He seemed very glad to see me. I introduced him to Janet and we all swam over to the big two-story raft at Mike's Place.

Janet had to leave at 5 o'clock, so Pierre took me rowing. He rowed for about 10 minutes and then asked me if I'd like to try for a while. I'd told him I could row before, so I took over the oars. Well, the last time I went rowing was up at Lake Winnipesauke [at a Presbyterian Church camp] with Robin about two or three months ago, and then I only rowed for about 5 minutes.

So I started to row, trying to look as though I'd been rowing all my life. But the oars felt awfully clumsy and awkward. Pierre was looking at me in the funniest way—I couldn't figure out why. He said, "You're . . . Oh, Hell, you probably know."

Me: "What?"

Him: "You're rowing backwards!"

Me: "Oh!"

And then we both burst out laughing. He just sat there, threw back his head and roared. I like the way he laughs.

Then I started rowing again (frontward!) and I splashed him with my oar, pretending I was angry because he'd laughed at me. He gave me a charming smile and then drenched me from head to foot with that icy water! I didn't splash him again.

He said he knew of a nice place way over at the other end of the lake where there was a stone bench under some pine trees, so we headed for there. He pulled the boat up on shore and we sat under the trees. The stone bench was too hard, so we sat on the pine needles instead and talked. We still had our bathing suits on.

I kept looking at my watch—I was supposed to be home by six to help with dinner, because we had company. Pretty soon he said, "Stop looking at that watch. You look like a slave of civilization!"

Me: "Well, I am."

Him: "No, you're not. Give me that watch."

So he set the watch back and then kept it. I didn't want to go home for dinner anyway.

I said something about getting blisters on my hands from rowing and he said, "Here, let me see" and ran his fingers across my hand.

Then he laughed—"Blisters! Look at my hands." I did and they were very brown and strong looking and the skin on his palms and fingers was as tough as leather.

He told me how he had been making a log cabin this summer, how he'd chopped down the trees for it, and everything else. No wonder his hands are like that. He said he had it all finished but the roof and was staying up two days longer so he could finish it altogether.

Then he looked at my fingernails, very long, with bright red polish on them. He told me I looked like a savage. For the first time I started to make excuses about my nails. Me! Who was always so stubborn about my fingernails and didn't give a damn whether anyone liked them or not. I'm disgusted with myself.

*From the time I was a little girl and up until a little more than a year earlier, I had always bitten my nails right down to the quick. The way I had finally beaten this horrible, unbecoming habit was to paint bright red polish on one nail at a time, not bite that one, add another red off-limits nail the next week, and so on until they were all bright red and growing. Those ten long shiny bloodred nails had become a symbol of my triumph.*

I can't possibly remember all we talked about. We were there for two hours, the sun went down and it got dark. All I know is that it was perfect, and we both forgot all about supper and what time it was, and the rowboat pulled up on the shore below us.

I felt as though I'd known Pierre for ages and ages. There's something very masculine and rugged about him. But I can't quite fathom his character—sometimes he's very quiet and thoughtful and other times, like Wednesday night, he seems reckless and daring. There's always a certain strength about him. You can see it in his face. I'd trust him anywhere.

He loves music and has hundreds of records. I mean classical music, of course. I love it, too. He said he'd come down to New York and take me to a concert sometime . . .

What's the matter with me? I'm only just turned 16 and he's only 18 and here I've been writing all these things about him . . . I've been reading too many novels!

Well, to go on—I was suddenly cold sitting there in my wet bathing suit and my teeth started chattering. Finally Pierre said, "Hey, are you cold?"

Me: "N-n-n-n-no."

Him: "We'd better be getting back." He stood up, pulled me to my feet and laughed. "And you were the one that wasn't going to get cold until after I did."

Me: "I'm n-n-n-n-n-not!"

Well, I decided to get him worn out rowing, so I kept saying, "Faster, Pierre, faster!" and he kept going faster and faster. Pretty soon he was rowing just as fast as he possibly could and I sat there fascinated, watching him. The wonderful muscles in his arms and shoulders kept working back and forth smoothly, rhythmically. What beautiful broad shoulders, and what a tan. Sigh!

He kept that pace up for almost one third the length of the lake and only stopped when I begged him to. And then he wasn't even breathing hard. He banged my hand across the knuckles with the oars once. He said he was sorry, but that's all. But later, when we'd taken the boat in and he paid for it and we were walking back towards the Paddy Hole, he took my hand and looked at it.

Him: "I didn't hurt your hand, did I?"

Me: "No. Look, the cars have their lights on already."

Him: "Yeah, and they must be saying, 'Humph, these late bathers!'"

We both laughed.

Me: "Do you usually get home this late when you come up swimming?"

Him: "No, I usually get home before the moon's out . . . Would you like to play tennis tomorrow? We can get the nets from Mr. Edward's."

Me: "What about your cabin?"

Him: "Oh, I forgot all about it!"

We got dressed—he went behind the bathhouse again—and when we got on our bikes I said something about my bathing suit being wet.

Him: "Oh, you still have your bathing suit on, don't you?"

Me: "Yes, don't you?"

Him: "No."

And then I burst out laughing. He hadn't known the bathhouses were closed, so he'd brought his trunks along wrapped up in a towel. When he found the bathhouse closed, he just went behind it and changed! Ha, ha!

When he said good-bye he asked for my address. He said if both our families came up to Ashfield Christmas vacation, maybe we could go skiing together. Then he left. He didn't have a light for his bike, or a flashlight, either, and he had almost 5 miles to go, part of it on a winding dirt road. But he loves it.

I rode Babs over to Plainfield this morning and Edgar Gould came and got Nonnie in his truck a little while ago . . . [Both horses were going to their winter homes]. I went down and helped Janet pack her things. I'll miss her. I have to do all my packing now. Tomorrow this time we'll be on our way back to the city.

Pierre in the summer of 1941

# 2

# BACK TO THE CITY

*F*rom kindergarten on, Pauline and I attended Shore Road
*Academy (SRA), a small progressive private school that I, for one,*
*loved. My sister was one grade ahead of me. The school complex*
*was situated on Shore Road, overlooking the Narrows, where we*
*could see the ships coming and going. It was coeducational through*
*fourth grade. My brother started out at SRA and then went on to*
*Polly Prep, a boys' private school.*

*The school was run by two Unitarian ladies, Ms. Reading and*
*Ms. Goldsmith, who lived in an apartment on the third floor in the*
*elegant big tile-roofed mansion of stucco and red brick that had*
*been converted to a school. At Shore Road, I learned to bowl; play*
*tennis, basketball, and softball; and work out on the parallel bars.*
*I took French every year and made the varsity basketball team my*
*freshman year of high school.*

*Our tuition was free because Ms. Reading and Ms. Goldsmith*
*had such great admiration and respect for Daddy and the liberal*
*causes he championed. Otherwise, we could not have afforded to*
*attend.*

*Classes met around long oval tables in what had once been*
*bedrooms. We had nicknames by which we addressed our teachers,*
*had from four to eleven students in each class. Ms. Lewis, our gym*
*teacher was Lou-Lou, with short white hair and skin as dark and*
*leathery as an Indian's.*

*At the end of my sophomore year, one of the headmistresses died, and the school was closed down. Not being able to complete high school at Shore Road Academy was devastating for me. Among other things, I would miss being part of that wonderful graduation ceremony where seniors in their lovely dresses walked carefully single file down the steps of the fire escape.*

*The next year, Pauline and I attended Friends School in downtown Brooklyn. It was a good school. But we had to take the subway there and back every day, which was a big drag! Now when we returned from Ashfield, we learned that the capable principal we'd liked so much was gone. A teacher we didn't respect had replaced him. We rebelled and decided not go back.*

*Daddy agreed with our decision, so we ended up attending a new public school, Fort Hamilton High. It had opened the year before, just a few blocks from us. Pauline was to take one more course there before attending college.*

*It was a big modern school with large classes, and the crush of students in the hallways reminded us of subway crowds in the rush hour. But Fort Hamilton had fine teachers; and my best friends, Anne Smith and Libby Shannon, were students there. I had a week's homework to make up, so I got started right away! But I missed my classmates at Friends.*

### Saturday, Sept. 26, 1942, Bay Ridge

I've been reading over my diary and I just remembered something that should have been included on Sept. 15:

After I got back from rowing with Pierre, I did an unforgivable thing. I cut my nails! I took the nail polish off and cut them just as short as I could. I was furious with myself afterwards and I still am. Just because Pierre didn't like them, I'd cut them off.

And what's more, today, Sept. 26, is the first day I've worn any polish since then. I'll never understand me. I'm just impossible.

I had hoped Pierre would write, but he hasn't. Maybe he's forgotten my address. Why did he ask for it anyway? I wish he hadn't.

Goodnight, I talk too much, I mean write too much.

### Tuesday, October 4

I'm so excited and flabbergasted that I could burst. Today, right after our chemistry test, Plinkie handed me a letter and said, "Here, Julia, it came this morning, I didn't give it to you before the test because I knew you'd be so excited you'd probably flunk it!"

I looked at the envelope blankly. It was from Andover, Mass. and in a strange handwriting. Then I looked at the back, and it said, "Cournand, P.B.R., Park House, Andover, Mass."

Suddenly it dawned on me that it was from Pierre! I hadn't known where his school, Phillips Academy, was or that his last name was spelled like that.

Well, my knees almost gave way and my hands began to shake. I shoved the letter in my notebook and galloped down the to the cafeteria and practically screamed at Libby, "I got a letter from Pierre!"

I couldn't eat any lunch, and I swear, I read that letter over three times before I calmed down enough to understand what it was all about.

He has swell handwriting—you know, the kind you have to decipher. It was a very nice letter, and seasoned with his wonderful, half-hidden sense of humor. It sounded exactly like him. He ended it like this: "Tell me what you are doing, if between classes and exams you find a few minutes of free time.—Your friend, Pierre."

I was so happy I felt like singing for the rest of the day and I could hardly keep from answering his letter as soon as I got home . . .

*Shortly thereafter, I received a letter from Robin, a delightful teenager I'd met at a Presbyterian summer camp at Lake Winnipesaukee, New Hampshire, early that previous summer. He lived in Darien, Connecticut, and wanted to come down to see me ASAP.*

### Monday, October 12

I wrote a letter to Pierre. It was one of the hardest letters I've ever written. I can usually rattle off a letter in ten or fifteen minutes, but in Pierre's letter I got all tongue-tied. What a nut I am.

I finally finished it and I think it's a pretty nice letter. It ought to be, after all the time I spent on it.

### Wednesday, Oct.

I finally broke down and wrote to Robin, asking him to come down some beautiful fall weekend to pass the time of day with his "Dear Little Miss Jones."

### Saturday, November 17

For three weeks now I've been working on a poetry project for English. I named it "Poems of Childhood," and have found a lot of adorable poems, six by Milne. If I don't get a wonderful mark on it after all my work, I'll be very mad.

I haven't heard from Pierre in ages. Since the first letter he's only sent a booklet about his school . . . I've started to have a lot of misgivings, so here's hoping!

### Sunday, November 29

I got a wonderful mark in my poetry project and Miss Stock put it up in the library on display . . .

### Sunday, December 27

Christmas has come and gone, New Year's is just around the corner and a lot of things have happened.

I went to the Blare Reunion [a get-together of teenagers from different churches]. Brownie was there [a boy I'd met previously], I had lots of fun and he brought me home. Two other boys wanted to bring me home, surprise!

That shows what I can do if I'm really in the mood and nobody that knows me is around. [I felt inhibited and self-conscious about being the minister's daughter in my own church group!]

After supper Brownie and I helped with the dishes, and believe me, 300 kids can get a lot of dishes dirty. The other kids were in the auditorium listening to a long drawn-out speech about something or other.

The Reunion ended at 10:00 and I didn't get home till 1:00 a.m. A whole bunch of us went to a little place and had something to eat, then we all went over to Penn Station. One of the girls had to take a train, so about 16 of us decided to see her off.

We were at Penn Station about an hour and a half raising Hell. We ran down the up escalator, slid down the long banister, pushed each other along in the baggage carrier (to the amusement of one of the guards on duty) and finally entertained everyone by doing folk dances under the superb leadership of Arthur Bonner, one of those cut-ups who has fun anywhere. Everybody in the Station gathered around us in a circle and laughed and clapped.

Once two of the girls chased a soldier around the place, finally caught him and brought him back to give us drilling practice. He was a rather grouchy-looking lieutenant, but pretty soon we had him smiling and laughing.

What a night! . . .

I got an Xmas card from Brownie and on Xmas day he called up and wanted me to go out with him New Year's Eve . . . So I have a date for New Year's Eve.

Robin came down to see me the first Saturday in December. I met him at the train station, we had lunch over there, I brought him over to Bay Ridge and he stayed for supper. Mother and Daddy took a great liking to him, he kissed me very much against my will and very thoroughly, I got so angry I almost cried, we had a long argument in the library, then made up, and finally he left, unwillingly, at about 10:00 pm.

Pauline has had influenza for the last month or so and just got over it last week. She heard Robin talking as we came down the street and jumped out of bed and looked out the window. When she saw me a little later, she said, "Boy, Julia, is he cute!"

He is much "cuter" and even nicer (and just as crazy) than I remember him as being. That's why I can't understand why I got so mad when he kissed me. I just did, that's all. He got sort of mad, too, and said, "Now look, Julia, you can't blame me, can you? I haven't seen you for five months!"

Why the Hell is life so complicated sometimes!

Well, he evidently liked his visit, because he wrote me three letters in a row before I even answered one of them. In the first of the three he cut loose and told me everything he felt and why he likes me. I wish he'd never written that letter. It made me feel like two cents. He called me up long distance on Xmas Eve, wished me a Merry Xmas, asked me why I didn't write and said he wanted to come down again on Jan. 9.

So, I wrote a letter today and told him to come on down. What else *could* I have said?

I got a letter from Pierre Nov. 21 and I answered it the next week. I haven't heard from him since and he didn't even send me a Christmas card. I don't understand . . .

### Monday, December 28

Pierre Cournand just called up from New York. He's coming right over!

(Later) We went to the movies and then walked down to the shore and talked for about two hours in the rain. We saw Jack Benny in "George Washington Slept Here."

To tell you the truth, I was rather disappointed. I guess Pierre will always seem to me as though he belongs in the country with a pair of old jeans on and his hair tousled by the wind. He seems out of place down here in the city, and he'd just had a haircut.

Things seemed a little strained between us for a while—until we went down on the shore and talked. I wanted to hear him sing again, but I just couldn't seem to ask him to.

He's very set on joining the Free French Army as soon as possible, but I think I persuaded him to get a deferment from regular army induction and then join the Free French in June, after graduation.

I probably won't ever see him again, since I don't graduate 'til late in June and he won't be able to come to Ashfield this summer. It's amazing when I begin to think how little I really know about Pierre Cournand.

*For several months that spring, I dated a sailor stationed at the Brooklyn Navy Yard. Artie Gould was the personable and lots-of-fun-to-be-with brother of Edgar Gould, who was keeping our horse Nonnie for us that winter.*

### March 12, Friday

It's 2 a.m. I just got home . . . Well, Artie came over and went to church with me and then stayed for dinner . . . By the way, he's 20, 6 feet tall, and being a country lad has a nice physique . . . Along about 2 o'clock Paul Meon, a boy in my history class at school, came over and I had the hardest time getting rid of him! He's tall with dark curly hair and very good-looking in his own way. I thought he was pretty nice until that Sunday afternoon, and then I took a sudden dislike to him.

He and Artie didn't get along at all. They stood and glared at each other for a few minutes and then Paul would make a lot of biting little remarks.

After we got rid of him, Artie and I went over to Central Park, where we spent the afternoon, walking, talking and feeding peanuts to the squirrels. I had told Artie about my winning a medal for my work in French a few years ago, so he thought I must be pretty good at speaking French. The truth is that I've forgotten more than I remember! Well, to go on, he suddenly hailed three French sailors with "Parley-vous Francais?" (which is the limit of his knowledge of French) and turned them over to me with a few gestures.

They gleefully descended on me, pouring out volumes of French. Gee, I wanted to turn and run for all I was worth. After a few minutes I stopped being embarrassed and began to talk to them very haltingly. We stood there talking for half an hour. I had them in hysterics—me and my mixed-up tenses and limited vocabulary. One of them, about 22 or 23, was very good-looking and reminded me a lot of Pierre. They were from the Richelieu and seemed to be enjoying themselves in New York.

That's an experience I won't ever forget. I told them about Pierre . . .

*March 29, Monday*

Artie and I went to Radio City Music Hall a few weeks ago and saw "Keeper of the Flame." It was pretty good . . . I went out with him a couple of times more before he shipped out, and I promised to write to him. He wants my graduation picture.

*April 30, 1943*

Robin's in the Army now and has been since April 5th. He came down to Bay Ridge Saturday, April third.

The rest of the family was up in Ashfield, so I stayed with the Smiths. Mrs. Smith said that, sure, she'd like to have Robin down, so I told him he could come. He said he'd been planning to come on the third anyway, whether I said he could or not!

We had a wonderful time together that afternoon . . . After supper I called up home to see if the family had arrived yet. They had, so we dashed over to see them. It was bitter cold that night, so before I could stop her, Mom invited Robin to stay overnight. He said yes right away, and that was that.

I didn't want him to stay over till Sunday because I had so much homework to do. But afterwards I was glad she'd asked him.

Saturday night we went to the movies, "The Amazing Mrs. Holiday" with Deanna Durbin. Robin didn't leave till 4 o'clock Sunday afternoon. He wanted to kiss me, but I walked him up to the corner so he couldn't. He'd brought along an instrument called a recorder, which looks and sounds quite a bit like a flute. The last I saw of him, he was walking up towards third avenue playing his recorder.

I stood and watched him, and I suddenly wanted to run after him and call out, "Robin, wait for me!"

Golly, I hated to see him go. I like him so much. The more I see him, the more I like him, and each time I discover something different about him.

Jessie and Clay [Hamlin, close longtime friends of the family] were here for Sunday dinner and Jessie was just crazy about Robin as soon as she met him. The Smiths think the world of him, too.

That's what seems to happen wherever he goes . . . I wonder if I'll ever see him again. Oh, what a horrible thought! . . .

Am still writing to Pierre and Artie, but get the most fun out of writing to Robin. He writes to me practically every day, and nice long letters, too. I don't know how he does it. He loves it down at Miami Beach [boot camp], but wishes that he didn't miss me quite so much. He says, "There's a little corner of my heart that keeps aching, Julia. I can't stop it, and I think you know why." . . .

### May 8
. . . All week I've been swamped with college catalogues I think Bucknell would be wonderful, but I can't go there because it's too expensive. I sent in applications to Mary Washington, a women's college in Virginia, and Penn State. Penn State's co-ed and they're doing some training of our armed forces there. It's beautiful and has lots of mountains and trees around.

### May 23
I was accepted by both Penn State and Mary Washington. I've decided on Penn State and I'm awfully excited about it. It doesn't start until Oct. 5, so I'll have a nice long summer . . .

### May 24
In my last letter I asked Robin for a picture. I'd already sent him a pretty good one of me. He said that naturally he had to show it to the fellows, since they'd been bragging about their girls. "They didn't have a thing to say," he wrote, "when they took one look at the sweetest girl in the world."

I just got a letter today and in it was a picture of him—in his gas mask! Was I mad!

In his letter he said, "Now, look Julia, you wouldn't want a picture of a tow-headed soldier with cropped hair, would you?" He said he'd send me one as soon as they let his hair grow out. But I want a picture of him NOW. I bet he looks darn cute in spite of the haircut.

### Wednesday, May 26

Artie's back in port. We went roller skating last night and it was quite a bit of fun. Artie isn't any too graceful on skates. He has such long legs . . .

### May 30

We went to Coney Island and I went on exactly one ride, "The Cyclone," and screamed all the way. It scared the living daylights out of me! And I'm not kidding. I all but shinnied up Artie's tie—oh, he liked that part of it all right. From then on we took in the milder aspects of the place, 'though Artie wanted to go on some more rides—he's got absolutely no nerves at all and he loves those things. It was really lots of fun . . .

When we got home Artie wanted to kiss me, but I wouldn't dream of letting him. I wonder if I'll ever meet a man that I really want to have kiss me. Of course, I know I will . . .

*School was very difficult that year as we were being prepared for the Regents examinations all seniors in high school were required to take in New York State. I had to buckle down and spend a lot of serious time doing homework. But one or another of the cute boys I flirted with in some of my classes usually walked me home from school, and I decided public school was okay.*

### My New Friend

I met Anne Alevizon in algebra class. It would become an enduring friendship based on the premise that opposites attract. We had little in common except that we liked spending time together. Years later, she told me she always considered me "a child of privilege"—living in our big three-story house on Eighty-second Street (the manse) and then dashing off to our summer "estate" in the Berkshires when school let out in late spring.

Anne was the daughter of Greek parents who immigrated separately to this country before World War II. Her father was a skilled cabinetmaker. They built a house in rural New Hampshire, had four children, moved to Brooklyn during the Depression in hope of a job and good schools for their kids, who all grew up bilingual. By the time I met Anne, her parents had moved back to New Hampshire; and she was living in an apartment with her sister Rita, whose serviceman husband had died of cancer, detected in the first year of their marriage.

**Christmas Vacation, 1941**

We often spent a week at Ashfield during Christmas vacation. We did so in 1941, when I was fifteen, and had a wonderful time. Ashfield kids joined us to skate on the pond, shovel out a wheel with spokes for playing fox and geese on the snow-covered ice, build a fire on the bank, and roast hot dogs and marshmallows over it. After dark, we trooped up to the house to fix popcorn and eat it with buttery fingers in the warm and cozy living room.

Dippy was one of the kids who came that year. He was a "state kid" who lived with a farm family—the Mowrys, I believe, on Steady Lane, a mile or two outside the village.

State kids were orphans taken care of by the State. They were often spoken for by families who needed a good worker and could offer the youngster a family life. I got the impression that the Mowrys worked Dippy very hard and didn't feel at all like family to him. But he liked Ashfield, and he had many friends among his classmates at Sanderson High.

He was a nice-looking fellow, fairly tall, with dark eyes, black hair, and a strong build. As we watched our hot dogs bursting and sizzling on our long sticks over the fire by the pond one afternoon, he invited me to go to the senior prom! Delighted, I said yes.

Dippy was shy, and we were both rank amateurs when it came to dancing. I have no idea what I wore, but 'twas great fun to be at the dance with him among so many of the kids I knew.

He caught me completely by surprise at my door when he said good night to me in the pale moonlight. My hand on the breakfast-room doorknob, I was looking up at him, starting to tell him what a wonderful time I'd had, when he said, "Oh, I just gotta kiss you," leaned down, and kissed me on the mouth.

This was my second kiss . . . and I wasn't at all sure I liked it.

## Leaving for Ashfield

On the morning of our departure from Brooklyn in early June, Daddy would awaken the household while it was still dark, shouting, "Everybody up! We leave for Ashfield at the crack of dawn!" Oh, it was an exciting, wonderful event.

After breakfast, he would supervise the hauling of blankets, pillows, suitcases, food, various household items, and personal possessions out to the driveway next to the car. He would study this array with a practiced eye, then start loading. The suitcases went into the car's small trunk. Most of the rest Daddy layered on the floor up to the level of the backseat, covering it all with blankets so that we three kids traveled with our legs outstretched.

The box of food went into the front seat for Mother to oversee—we would be stopping for a picnic lunch beside a favorite stream, followed by double-decker ice cream cones from a Howard Johnson's nearby. Tucked in last of all were books, crayons, and sketch pads, plus a cardboard box containing a batch of new kittens and their mama. We always had fun playing with the kittens on the way to Ashfield.

One morning, when I was about nine years old, a small band of neighborhood children appeared on the sidewalk as we started to pull out of the driveway. They shrieked, "We're glad to see you go! We're glad to see you go! We hope the heck you never come back! We're glad to see you go!"

You could tell they'd been practicing.

I was in tears. Little Phillips—eyes crossed, tongue out, thumbs jammed into his ears, and fingers flapping—made faces at the brats out the car window. And Pauline, observing them with a jaundiced eye, said, "Oh, they're just jealous!"

## A BAY RIDGE GIRL

Although we felt that Ashfield was our real home, I was not actually unhappy in the city. My best friend, Anne Smith, lived only seven blocks away. I loved school, and there was always something to do.

I liked our big roomy brown-shingled house. The backyard was tiny but tree shaded; and it contained a sturdy double swing, the perfect spot to wile away an afternoon, daydreaming or reading a good book. We also held solemn family funerals there for the birds and baby squirrels that invariably died after I rescued them from our cat.

Pauline was mostly sad and discontent in Bay Ridge. By the time she was ten, she had grown into an early and uneasy adolescence, was head and shoulders taller than me for years, thought she was too fat, was not that fond of school, and longed to be in Ashfield. She kept goldfish up in her room on the third floor and raised little white rats in cages in the cellar. Those tiny naked pink newborn rats held no appeal for me.

Even though she took good care of her pet rats, I once watched her feed little newborn mice to a barn cat up in the hayloft at Grandpa Jones's farm in Missouri. She dangled each one by its tail as the cat gobbled them up. I was horrified, but she just said, "Oh, they don't even know what's happening to them."

One event Pauline and I both enjoyed in Bay Ridge was the polo matches we attended at Fort Hamilton where her Shore Road Academy (SRA) classmate Sara Cavender's father was stationed. We'd show up there whenever possible for an exciting afternoon, spellbound as we watched these riders and their amazing horses compete.

On a balmy Sunday in the springtime, Anne, Libby Shannon, and I pedaled our one-speed bikes along Shore Road to the Sixty-ninth Street Ferry, planning to ride it to Staten Island and back for an afternoon's adventure.

We loved feeling the salty wind in our faces, watching the other boats and ferries come and go, seeing the Statue of Liberty, and observing closely how our captain maneuvered the ferry ponderously into the wharf at Staten Island.

When we discovered we had to get off and buy another ticket for the return trip, we were dismayed. It took us so long to find where to buy the tickets, then wait in line to do so, that we missed the next two ferries. I think the fare was only a dime in those days and a nickel for the subway.

Another time, Anne and I packed picnic lunches and spent the afternoon riding all over Staten Island on our bikes. It was very rural then, with lots of farms and pretty countryside. We had a vigorous workout, pumping our way up those hills until we were out of breath and our legs felt wobbly.

At one of the high points on the island, we stopped for lunch and viewed the East River, Brooklyn, and the skyscrapers of Manhattan laid out below us. By the time we arrived home, it was almost dark, and we were completely exhausted.

We often went to the movies on a Saturday afternoon, back when the feature was followed by a *Perils of Pauline*, *Buck Rogers*, or Tom Mix episode and the black-and-white newsreels. Libby's father was so strict with her that she couldn't go to the movies with us and missed out on many of our adventures.

Our parents warned us not to go down to the shore because of the hoboes, those bearded, unkempt, ragged, homeless, and scary men who hung out there. But we avoided going anywhere near them and raced down the grassy hill to the sidewalk at water's edge. There, we sat on benches, saw the ships come and go on the East River, and watched the loud-crying seagulls dive down right into the water to catch fish.

Once, I went horseback riding in Central Park with Mary Fields, a Shore Road Academy classmate. Her family's dignified tall dark-haired chauffeur Howard drove us there, paid for our rides, and waited for us. Mary managed to fall off her horse. I was disgusted with her, and the whole episode wasn't much fun!

Pauline, Phillips, and I all loved our family's forays into the city to visit the Museum of Natural History. Huge dinosaur skeletons awaited us there; and we saw scene after scene of lifelike—were they made of wax?—cavemen and their families, American Indians in their buffalo-hide teepees, an Eskimo family in their igloo, kings and peasants in their natural habitat, and all sorts of other slices of life from the past. It was a thrilling experience that plunged us back into history and into other lands, making us marvel at the ways different people lived.

One day, we traveled up, up, up the elevator to the very top of the Empire State Building and gazed out across the city. Afraid of heights, I had to screw up my courage to do this.

## My Night Ramblings

When I was about nine or ten, my restless spirit sent me on adventures into the night. I was supposed to be asleep in bed; but when the house was quiet, I climbed out of my window onto the roof, scrambled down a tree next to it, and wandered the dark streets.

One night, as I roamed the streets, pretending I was riding my horse through a medieval town, I noticed that a man wearing a dark hat and long black coat was following me. Alarmed, I walked faster and faster until I came to Daddy's church where I climbed the wide steps leading up to the heavy double doors to the vestibule.

"God, please keep me safe here," I implored, standing with my back against the tall doors. I looked down toward the sidewalk. The man stood silently looking up at me, his face glowing an eerie white from the streetlight nearby.

*He's dangerous*, I thought. And I realized that God, whom I didn't much believe in anyhow, wasn't going to protect me. It was up to me to make my escape! I walked slowly down the steps, then suddenly bolted past the startled man and bounded like a scared rabbit down block after block.

I never looked back. I took a roundabout route home, up and down several streets, to throw him off my trail. Hearing only my own footsteps and the pounding of my heart as I sped under one streetlight after another, I finally reached home, my shirt soaked with sweat. I scurried up the tree and was soon safe in bed.

Thus ended my nocturnal ramblings.

On rainy weekends, I read books and drew pictures with a soft-lead black pencil—mostly of horses, dogs, and all sorts of wild animals from *National Geographic* magazine. I copied some of the horse illustrations in books by Will James too, stories about cowboys, ranches, outlaws, and a horse named Smoky.

In "my dragon period," I drew and painted fierce dragons and had fantasies about taming them and riding them through the night skies. Years later, I found one of my very best dragons. I had painted it in black and red and green on brown wrapping paper.

He was breathing fire, but the brittle paper was now tattered and torn. After carefully pasting this fragile masterpiece onto black construction paper, I bought a golden frame for it. A reminder of my artistic past and deep affinity for fairy tales, it hangs on my wall below the charcoal drawing of a fencer.

Like city kids everywhere, we chalked a pattern on the sidewalk for playing hopscotch. We did a lot of jump-roping too, solo or with two kids manning the rope while the rest of us took turns, counting how many jumps we could do before tripping up. We chanted songs over and over to establish the beat of our jumping, but I don't remember the words to any of them.

And we had fun on roller skates, using the kind you fastened to your shoes and tightened up with a key. Daddy wouldn't let us skate in the street, so we used the sidewalks at times of day when there was otherwise little traffic. I always had scabby knees from spills on those rough sidewalks; then I picked the scabs off and had bloody knees.

Daddy liked to listen to the opera on the radio. We kids sure didn't share his enthusiasm and considered it just a bunch of fat ladies singing. Pauline and I mimicked them with gusto on Sunday afternoons as we washed the big pile of dinner dishes. We sang at the top of our lungs, and I'm sure people could hear us clear down the block—those crazy Jones girls!

Next door to us lived the Griffiths, a Catholic family with lots of children. When I was about seven, I had a crush on one the boys, Warren. But as we played spin the bottle one day, Warren's bottle came to a stop, pointing at me. In panic, I jumped up and ran home. Another time, he pulled back the elastic waistband of my sunsuit and blew his hot breath down onto my bare bottom! I screamed bloody murder and once more ran for home.

Daddy subscribed to the *New York Times*, which had no Sunday comics. So on Sunday morning after breakfast, often with my little brother in tow (although Phillips doesn't remember this), I knocked on the Griffiths' front door and asked plaintively, "Could we come in and read the funny papers?"

Happy to see us, they let us in, and all of us kids spread the comics out on the living room floor and gave them our rapt attention. The only funnies I can remember were *Li'l Abner* and *Blondie*. We also spent many a rainy afternoon in their cellar where the old newspapers were stacked high and read all the comic sections again.

Sometimes we were sick, missed school, and had to stay home in bed. Daddy made stubby tables from cardboard boxes that bridged our laps so that, propped up against pillows, we could eat from trays in bed.

For entertainment, we listened to the soap operas: *Stella Dallas* is the only one I remember, plus the trials and tribulations of a hillbilly girl who married Lord Somebody-or-Other from a hoity-toity wealthy, upper-class family in England.

**Radio Night**

Sunday evening was our radio night. Armed with slices of crisp, cold apples, glasses of milk, and a huge crock full of buttered popcorn, we climbed the stairs to the third-floor radio room and listened to our favorite programs: *The Green Hornet*—which opened with its theme song, "The Flight of the Bumblebee"—*The Shadow, The Lone Ranger, One Man's Family*, and *Inner Sanctum*, a spooky mystery series introduced by a door opening slowly on squeaking hinges.

We were lucky not to have television in those days because the radio helped us develop our imaginations. I conjured up colorful pictures in my head of the Lone Ranger, Tonto, and all those other characters from my favorite shows.

**The Milkman and the Iceman**

I awoke in the early mornings to the sound of a horse's hooves clopping on the street, then stopping for a while at each house where the milkman made a delivery. I listened to him load his clinking

bottles of milk into a metal carrier and unload them at our back
stoop, then heard his quick footsteps back to the milk wagon.

One morning, I heard the clop-clopping speed up; and then the
milkman was running down the street, hollering, "Whoa!" Was he
breaking in a new horse, or did his usually trustworthy workmate get
frisky and decide to run off?

Mom carefully poured the cream off the top of the milk, saving
it to whip and serve on desserts—pies, fruit cobblers, and chocolate
or butterscotch puddings she made with milk from a Jell-O mix,
cooked on the stove, poured into small tin molds to set, then put in
the icebox. She also made a delicious icebox cake with chocolate
wafers both stuck together and then iced with whipped cream. It was
one of the first desserts she taught me to make, that and chocolate
brownies.

The iceman arrived every week, coming in the back door, bent
over under a big block of ice he held with huge tongs against the piece
of thick leather on his shoulder. We liked to watch him chip away at
the block with his ice pick until it would fit in the top compartment
of our icebox. We gathered up those splinters and chunks of ice to roll
around on our tongues and crunch with our teeth.

## The Great Depression

The main thing I remember about the Great Depression in the
1930s was the down-and-out men who turned up at our front door
and asked humbly for something to eat. If Mom or Dad wasn't home,
Pauline and I were instructed never to let the man in the house.
Instead, we were to send him with a friendly smile to the back door
to wait while we fixed something for him to eat.

What we usually came up with was a few sandwiches—one to
eat and another wrapped in wax paper to go—plus an apple or an
orange, a glass of milk or a cup of coffee, some cookies, and a paper
napkin. With haunted eyes, he would thank us and sit on one of the
back steps to eat it.

After a while, so many men were coming that Daddy arranged
with some local restaurants to print tickets for a free meal, which
Daddy, or maybe it was the church, paid for at reduced rates. We

would give a ticket to each hungry man who made his way to our door.

Stories circulated about men who couldn't find work, lost hope, and became so desperate that they committed suicide. This made me terribly sad, and I always wondered what happened to their wives and children.

Daddy used to kid around about "keeping the wolf from the door." When I was little, I thought he meant a real wolf, and I had some bad dreams. Later on, I realized the wolf stood for hunger and poverty, but I felt safe and secure because I knew Daddy would always look after us.

When we were old enough to be allowed to ride the subway by ourselves, we made an adventure of it. Walking quickly through the train to the very end of either the last car or the first car, we watched the dark tunnel rapidly receding behind us or stretching out before us as we rocketed along.

## Going to Radio City

Once, Pauline and I rode the subway with Sarah Cavender all the way to Radio City in downtown New York City to attend the radio broadcast of a skinny young man whose clothes were too big for him. His name was Frank Sinatra.

He had a real nice voice, but girls our age in the audience kept screaming "Frankie!" and crying and carrying on something fierce. We couldn't figure out why. It embarrassed us to see them making such fools of themselves.

In spite of all the interesting things to see and do in the city, I sorely missed Ashfield and our horses. Along with Pauline and Phillips, I could hardly wait 'til school was out for the summer or for Christmas and spring vacations, which we often spent at Ashfield.

In the meantime, I dreamt about the make-believe horse we named Gypsy and kept in the garage. We'd converted it into a little barn and had fenced in the backyard so he could eat grass there.

At night, I rode our frisky little black horse on the streets of Bay Ridge and along the wide, sweeping expanse of Shore Road. I dreamt that I rode Gypsy to school one morning, and the other SRA students gathered around me in wonder. But there was no place to keep him there, so I had to ride him back home again.

## The Good Humor Man

One of my happiest early-childhood memories is of the Good Humor Man. The jinglejangle in the street from his white ice cream truck's bell on warm Saturday afternoons in the spring signaled the most exciting event of the day.

"The Good Humor Man, the Good Humor man!" we shouted and went running to Mother, begging for a nickel. She never failed to come up with three nickels. She must have had a pile of them stashed away. Then we raced down the sidewalk after the truck and joined a crowd of neighborhood kids clustered around the smiling Good Humor Man in his white uniform.

We waited our turns for that scrumptious chocolate-covered vanilla ice cream on a stick that he handed out. When one of us uncovered a stick with Lucky printed on it in red ink, entitling us to a freebie, the Good Humor Man seemed delighted too. This was a wonderful job for a man who loved children.

In those prerefrigerator years, ice cream was a special treat, mostly in the form of ice cream cones, sodas, and milk shakes at the local drugstore's soda fountain, or, in Ashfield, a dish of ice cream at Mike's place on the lake.

It was a staple at family birthday celebrations. Daddy fetched it in a quick trip to the store between dinner and dessert and served scoops of it on top of each piece of birthday cake, almost always a chocolate cake with chocolate icing. At Ashfield, especially when we had company to help, Mom mixed up our own ice cream; and we took turns churning it in our hand-cranked ice cream maker.

# 3

# ABOUT MY FAMILY

*There is no cure for a happy childhood.*
*It hangs about your neck like a rainbow for the rest of your days.*
—Author unknown

Lady Luck, that mysterious force in the universe, dealt me an exceptional family:

**Daddy**—that complicated, outrageous, brilliant, brave, charismatic, affectionate, and earthy man who made my childhood so memorable. Of solid build, with keen blue eyes and a wide face, he had wavy reddish brown hair that stayed thick and turned golden, then gray in his later years.

My sister did not share my adoration of him and grew up disliking him. But as an adult, she said, "I've gotten so that I can stand him!" She was the oldest child, and he was a very different father to her than he was to me.

My cousin Murray has a mental picture of Daddy "standing by a fireplace, one elbow on the mantle, toying with his pipe while he held his audience with an actor's skill and minister's way of connecting those present to larger issues and memories."

Daddy was a liberal, a progressive thinker and peace activist, ahead of his time and often in hot water. He counted among his friends Norman Thomas (socialist and perennial presidential candidate), Lester Granger (president of the Urban League) and his wife "Lefty," author Norman Cousins, and Bernard Herman (conductor of the New York Philharmonic). Plus many others, including Doug Wallop, who wrote *The Year the Yankees Lost the Pennant* as a potboiler, and his wife, Lucille Fletcher, who cowrote the thriller *Sorry, Wrong Number* with Alan Ullman and then went on to write the screenplay for the movie. Lucille, in particular, was my parents' close friend; and I remember her well.

For many years on the board of the American Civil Liberties Union, Daddy protested the internment of Japanese-American citizens during World War II, protested the McCarthy hearings, befriended homosexuals and their right to their own private lives, and counseled conscientious objectors. As president for several years of the Euthanasia Society of America, Daddy received much hate mail.

*LIFE* magazine (circa 1939) ran a photo feature about Daddy, covering his reenactment during a Sunday morning service of the 1937 arrest of Martin Niemoeller by Nazi storm troopers. Niemoeller was a Lutheran pastor whose fiery sermons had championed religious freedom in Germany. After his own "arrest," Daddy went on to preach his sermon behind the bars of a beaverboard replica of the walls of Sachsenhausen, the concentration camp where Niemoeller had just begun his second year in solitary confinement.

When the San Francisco Conference convened in 1945 to draft the fifty-nation charter that established the United Nations, Daddy served as a consultant to the United States delegation. His experiences there fulfilled for him the ambition of a lifetime.

**Mother**—that durable, resilient, gracious, loving woman. She was well educated, with a bachelor's degree in domestic science and a master's in nutrition, I believe. She was also beautiful, with gray-green eyes and her thick dark hair usually done up in a loose chignon. Most of her adult life after about fifty, she dealt valiantly with rheumatoid arthritis.

Murray's recollection of my mother: "At times, I thought of her as having an almost mystical serenity. Her calm, poised, gracious self; her ready and gentle laugh; and her portrait-quality beauty made an equally strong impression."

Mom taught Pauline and me to cook, starting off with brownies, moving on to blueberry pie, muffins, and complete breakfasts. Under her guidance, we learned to clean the house to a background of classical records played loud and to sew on our Singer treadle machine—our first projects were colorful broomstick skirts we could wear to the square dances.

When it was my turn to cook dinner, Mom once told me, I shooed everyone out of the kitchen and said, "Leave me alone!"

It was Daddy who taught me to iron and was very particular about his white dress shirts with their starched collars and cuffs. Mom was the one who usually read to us at bedtime, for in the city Daddy was often "out crawling on people" as he told us. At Ashfield, however, Daddy often read to us in the evenings. Sometimes it was whole chapters from a book in which he was engrossed. I particularly remember dazzling excerpts from *The Once and Future King* by T. H. White.

**Pauline**—the practical, determined, quietly vulnerable sister who became so dear to me and who shared my love of horses and rural life. When she was little, she had an imaginary friend who went everywhere with her, and she was mean to me. Called me "an ugly freckle-faced little brat!"—and I believed her. But she got over that, and we became close friends.

When I asked her many years later why she had once treated me so badly, she said with chagrin, "Because you were the smart, pretty one." (Her perceptions were flawed. This was not true!)

After she married, Pauline made quite a name for herself in New England as a breeder and trainer of Tennessee walking horses. She bought her own stallion, Ike's Bombardier, as a two-year-old, trained him, and handled him herself.

**Phillips**—the beloved little brother, four years younger than I. When he was little, we shared a room at our house in Bay Ridge, jumped up and down on our twin beds for the pure joy of

My mother and father in 1941
during their courtship days.

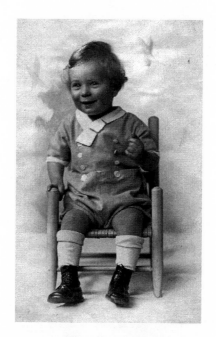

Our little brother Phillips.

My sister Pauline and me, Troy, New York; circa 1930.

it until the mattresses turned lumpy from broken springs. One day, we discovered Spud having kittens (all our cats were female, black-and-white and named Spud) in an open drawer in our walk-in closet. By the time the kittens were a few weeks old, we were pulling them into bed to play with us.

I often looked after little Phillips and sometimes read to him at bedtime. By the time he was ten, he had amassed a huge collection of comic books, which he arranged neatly in tall stacks. An Erector Set became his favorite toy. One of his more-elaborate structures was a windmill powered by a small electric motor.

By his early teens in Ashfield, Phillips had become a familiar sight in the village. Working for Reggie Billings, he mowed people's yards up and down Main Street with a sweat-powered push lawn mower. He *always* had money in the bank and was generous about lending it to me. This happened often as I was usually penniless. (Daddy would not allow my sister and me to get part-time jobs and was uncommonly frugal with his occasional handouts.)

My brother hoarded his chocolate Santa Clauses until they turned white. I often ferreted them out and ate them before this could happen.

Pauline and I thought Phillips was destined to be a farmer, but Mother recognized his scientific bent early on by what he sent for with breakfast-cereal box tops. In one such mail-order project, he made a still-picture projector with a cheap lens and cardboard tube, then slid funny paper strips through a slot to project on the wall for his audience.

He ran another experiment trying to build a barometer using water instead of mercury, a project fraught with difficulties. As he grew older, his curiosity led him into more complex realms of science and physics.

So it was no surprise to Mother when Phillips earned a PhD and became Dr. Jones, an atomic-physics professor at the University of Massachusetts. He and his graduate students were involved in several significant research projects.

Come to think of it, Phillips was a born teacher. When he was about five, he started collecting jokes and was eager to tell them. Afterward, he'd say, "Want me, want me, want me to 'splain it to you?" and launch blissfully into an involved description of why it was so funny. He could not be stopped!

After retiring from UMass, Phillips missed teaching. On my last two visits, I was his captive student for a physics lesson. I concentrated mightily and understood some of it but protested that I did not have the prerequisite courses. No matter; as in the old days, he could not be stopped.

**My Uncle Dave**—Daddy had five brothers and one sister. Anna and George, the two oldest, died in their late teens; she from a tonsillectomy, and he from appendicitis. A few years later, Daddy had a close brush with death due to a burst appendix. These dire events inspired Russell and David to pursue medical careers.

Anna's and George's deaths left Daddy as the oldest of five siblings. He was a take-charge kind of a fellow; and being big brother to Russell, Harry, David, and Joe suited him. My uncles were all fun to be with and were great storytellers. We never tired of hearing about their many adventures growing up on Grandpa's farm near Holliday, Missouri.

In the 1930s, my uncles often turned up to celebrate Christmas with us in Bay Ridge. I loved them all, but Uncle Dave was to become my favorite. In his early twenties, while still a bachelor and attending medical school, he started spending a month with us every summer at Ashfield. I was about ten, and we became buddies. Small of stature, like Grandpa Jones, he was a sandy-haired energetic fellow with lively blue eyes and fair skin, his nose a tad large in a face sunburned from our outdoor pursuits.

We rode horses, played ping-pong and tennis, tried to outdo each other diving off the raft into our pond, played cards, listened to records, picked wild blueberries, and ran along the cow paths in the pasture up beyond the rock wall behind our apple orchard. Years later, he admitted he'd had a devil of a time keeping up with me!

He liked to tell people about the time we were cantering along Briar Hill Road, and I made an unexpected right-angle turn onto an obscure path through the forest, a shortcut that would take us to

Bird Hill Road in South Ashfield. I looked back to see Dave nearly come off his horse as she scrambled over a tumbledown stone fence in her haste to follow us.

Once we were both married and had children, we kept visiting back and forth, wrote long letters to each other, and turned up at all the Joneses' family reunions. He remained dear to me until he died at ninety-four after a long and active life.

Tweedums and Skipper—In addition to our perennial mama cat Spud, we had two dogs. Tweedums was my sister's little long-haired black dog of indeterminate breed; and Skipper, a German shepherd, was mine. They set up a chorus of barking in the night with her shrill *yap yap yap yap yap* and his booming *ruf ruf ruf ruf ruf*! My parents were amazingly tolerant of all this racket.

We found Tweedums in a litter of puppies needing a home. Pauline saw no puppy to her liking until told there was a scared black one hiding under the bed. She crawled under the bed and gently extracted Tweedums.

As for Skipper, he followed me home one afternoon from the Big Pond where I had befriended him. He was so skinny and pitiful. At our house, he crashed through the screen door after me, then grabbed a raw slab of pot roast off the kitchen table. Startled, Mom stood there and watched him gulp it down.

"He acts half-starved!" she observed and fixed something else for dinner.

That night, I slept out in the barn with him, and he was my dog forever after. Daddy replaced the screen in the door; we soon fattened Skipper up, and he learned to wait patiently for me outside whenever I was in the house.

Tweedums and Spud went back to the city with us every fall, but until our return in late spring, Skipper lived with the T. P. Day family, our neighbors on South Street. He loved to chase cars up and down Main Street, and in later years, he often hung out at T. P. Day's store (Phillips called it Wigwam Day's) in the village.

When Pauline married, Tweedums went with her.

## Mom and Dad's Courtship Days

Mother was the eldest daughter of Dr. E. E. Reed, president of Westminster College, a prestigious men's college in Fulton, Missouri. One evening, he brought a promising student home to dinner with him. And John Paul Jones, a young farm boy who worked part-time in the local brick factory, started paying court to Helen Agnes Reed, known around campus as the beautiful unattainable daughter of the president.

Grandma Reed had managed to drive away all former suitors and one fiancé, determined that Helen, as the oldest daughter, would be the one to look after her parents in their old age. But Grandma was no match for Daddy.

One time that winter, Daddy rented a horse and sleigh, called for his lovely lady, handed her up onto the seat, and tucked a blanket around her. Off they glided at breathtaking speed as he demonstrated his horsemanship. Alas, they took a curve too fast; the sleigh tipped over and dumped them in a snowdrift.

Mom was twenty-seven and he was twenty-three when they married. She told me once that she would not have chosen to marry a minister, but she loved Daddy, and he was the architect of her escape from this tyrannical, moralistic mother who was soon widowed and lived to be 103.

Because she obviously disliked and disapproved of my father, I never warmed up to Grandma Reed. My cousin Murray thinks I am perhaps too hard on her.

His own young mother died within a few years of Grandfather Reed's death. By then, my grandmother was living in her own apartment in Cincinnati where she could be close to her son Ellery and family. She moved in with them during her daughter-in-law's fatal illness and upon Gertrude's death became the children's surrogate mother. Murray was only five years old, and his sister Lucy was eight.

About a year later, Uncle Ellery married Ella, a dedicated career woman who traveled frequently. My grandmother found that she was still very much needed and filled in for Ella whenever she was away.

Murray reports that "Grandma was warm and caring with me, and I think made a crucial difference in my younger days."

## Memories of Daddy

Some of my earliest and best childhood memories are of my times with Daddy. To this day, a certain piece of classical music will transport me back to 179 Eighty-second Street in Brooklyn to that three-story, brown-shingled manse on a one-way street in Bay Ridge. There I sit, a little blue-eyed blonde, snuggled up next to Daddy on the living room couch, listening to this same piece of music pouring forth from our Victrola. One of my favorites back then was the *William Tell* Overture. His right arm around me, his feet resting on a maroon leather footstool, Daddy is reading, the deeply ingrained habit of a lifetime.

I would fall asleep next to him, awaken the next day in my own bed in my room next to the green-tiled bathroom on the second floor. About five o'clock in the morning, I would hear Daddy doing his exercises—thumping sounds, a grunt or two. I would usually go back to sleep until Daddy roused me for the day with "Dearheart, time to get up."

Once, when I was too sleepy to respond, he flung himself onto the bed on top of me, landing on his hands and knees so that his considerable bulk would not squash me. "Daddy!" I screamed, and we both laughed and laughed.

At eleven or twelve, when I went through Confirmation ceremonies at Daddy's church, I did so with great reluctance. A few days later, Daddy called me into his study, shut the door, and asked me what was bothering me. I said I only got confirmed because I was the minister's daughter and thought I had to.

"But I don't believe in all that stuff," I blurted out.

"Dearheart," he said, "getting confirmed is *not* something you should do for somebody else. I want you to think for yourself!" And I was so relieved. I didn't have to pretend anymore.

There was a time I thought my daddy could do anything—that if he were president, he would promptly cure the ills of this topsy-turvy world. But three happenings somewhat changed my mind: the day he heated tar on the stove for a roof-patching job, and it exploded; the time he took little Phillips tree cutting with him and dropped a tree on him; and the incident involving the skunk that was raiding our garbage can.

The hot tar jettisoned onto the freshly painted kitchen ceiling, walls, and dish cupboards, causing Mom and Dad many tedious days of scrubbing it off.

Out cutting down some saplings with his axe one summer day, Daddy cautioned five-year-old Phillips to stay back out of the way but noticed he'd gone missing after the felling of one tree. "Phillips!" he called out again and again, becoming more and more alarmed.

Finally, a high, thin, frightened little voice came wafting on the wind, "Tree fell on me!"

Trapped under the leafy branches, Phillips had been reluctant to answer at first, knowing he was supposed to have stayed back near Daddy. But he wasn't hurt, and his daddy rescued him.

As for that skunk—well, early one evening, we heard the blast of Daddy's shotgun (actually, the caretaker Mr. Finney's shotgun, which Daddy had borrowed to send a groundhog in his big vegetable garden to kingdom come). Then came his shout, "Hot dog, I got him!" He had been lying in wait for whatever was getting into our garbage can by the back door to the kitchen, saw the skunk, and shot it. When he took us outside to see the dead skunk, it was gone!

The poor critter had crawled under the house to die, but guess what it did before expiring? We lived with that awful smell for the rest of the summer. Daddy had to crawl under the house to retrieve the body and then bury it.

### The Trouble with Kissing

Although they never said as much, my folks raised me to believe I would grow up to do something grand in the world. All in all, they were dandy parents . . . except for the fact that they never enlightened me on sex. When I started bleeding copiously one day at fourteen and suffered horrible cramps, I thought I was at death's

door! But Pauline matter-of-factly let me know that it was just a
coming-of-age thing for all girls and that now I could get pregnant.

This was in no way reassuring!

Having once felt my brother's little feet kicking my mother's
rounded belly, I knew where babies came from but didn't realize
how, exactly, they got there. I knew for sure that boys were involved
in the process. And I knew pregnancy could ruin a girl's life,
disgrace her family, cause her to marry a boy she didn't love, have a
baby out of wedlock, or leave town mysteriously for a few weeks or
months to solve the problem in some drastic way.

I knew that kissing could lead to more serious things as passion
took over and that boys could not always be trusted. And I wasn't
taking any chances, thank you! So it was that I went on to earn my
reputation in Ashfield as the Little Puritan up on the Hill.

### Pearl Harbor, 1941

Europe was a remote place to me in August of 1939 when war
broke out. I knew it was a terrible thing, but happening very far
away, not at all real to this thirteen-year-old girl in her safe and
sheltered life.

World War I was a distant bit of history. I first heard about it in
relationship to my own family when Daddy informed us that he was
an army private on a troopship going over to fight in that war when
the Germans heard he was coming and surrendered. We giggled and
said, "Oh, Daddy, that's not true!"

But when he gathered the family together that December day in
1941, there in the living room of our house in Bay Ridge, to tell us
about the Japanese attack at Pearl Harbor, anxiety and fear gripped
me. Daddy's younger brother Harry, Aunt Minnie, and my little
cousins Janet and Wayne lived in Pearl Harbor where Harry taught
high school.

Beloved curly-red-haired Uncle Harry, who was so much
fun, who made that huge colorful box kite and flew it with us one
summer in Ashfield, and to whom every piece of homemade pie
he ate was "the best pie I ever tasted!" Aunt Minnie, with her short

curly black hair and animated face—so excitable, so talkative, and, like Harry and all "the Jones boys," so full of good stories.

At Pearl Harbor that day, a bomb landed in their front yard. "It was a dud," Daddy told us. "And it didn't go off. They are safe and coming back home soon, but before this war is over, almost every family will have lost somebody they love . . . we must all love each other very much, and be brave and know that this can happen!"

# 4

# JULY DAYS WITH PIERRE, 1943

*From My Diary*

*After school let out, the family headed for Ashfield. I didn't even stick around for my high school graduation ceremony. Shortly after that, I went to Lake Winnipesaukee for a week, the New Hampshire summer camp for Presbyterian youth. I had a wonderful time, met some great kids, but really missed Robin.*

### June 26, Saturday

I'm at Winni in Cabin I. Talked with Dr. Sidon last night at supper and gave him Robin's regards. He said, "I certainly did like that boy; there was something so refreshing and original about him."

"Likewise with me and for the same reason," I answered . . .

I've met and become quite friendly with Mary Jane Govers from Darien, Conn. She told me she's the girl Robin used to go around with before he met me! Amazing as it may seem, we're crazy about each other and have been palling around . . .

There's one very likely-looking prospect named Bill Hagerman. I shall do my best to get to know him . . . He's a 6-footer, bronzy tan, good-looking.

*Bill was also from Darien. He and Mary Jane and I ended up spending most of our time together. Years and years later, I still remember both of them so clearly.*

### Monday, July 12, Ashfield

Right now I'm wearing a brown and white plaid shirt that is very big for me and has quite a story behind it. Every time I look at it or take a deep smell, burying my head in the material, I think of Pierre and the times he wore it when I was with him.

He left on the 10:30 train last night and I doubt if I shall see him again for a very long time. If all proceeds as scheduled, he'll leave for an Officer's Training Camp in Georgia on the fifteenth.

Maybe I'd better start from the beginning:

Last Tuesday afternoon, July 5 at about 5 o'clock I was in the middle of making cookies. I looked a positive wreck—my uncombed hair was tied back with a huge red ribbon, I didn't have any lipstick on, I wore a short red smock over a pair of shorts, so it looked like I didn't have anything on under the smock—and I was barefoot.

The dogs commenced to bark furiously and I dashed out the door to shut them up, a big spoon in one hand and a measuring cup in the other. There was Pierre, looking breathtakingly handsome—his hair all mussed and curly, shirt tail out over his blue jeans, a beard and mustache (well, practically) . . . We made a hurried date to go boating the next day and then he left, in mortal terror that Pop would come around the corner and, spying him as he was, forbid my ever seeing him again!

We set 3:30 as the time, him thinking I'd meet him at the lake (of all the crazy things!) and me taking it for granted that he would come up to the house first.

He finally arrived at 4:15 the next day. He'd gone down to the lake first and waited for me. But I acted very sweet and just let it ride. We went for a walk in the woods down below the

pond . . . Then we sat on some moss and talked—about poetry,
and books, and people, and fraternities at Andover. We got into a
terrific argument about Hamlet. He thought Hamlet a very strong
and admirable character, and I think just the opposite. We both
backed our viewpoints up by facts from the play. It's amazing
that we could both find ample facts for opposite viewpoints.
When it ended, we both felt the same as we had in the beginning,
only more so!

From Hamlet we delved into the subject of suicide and began
another heated argument. I insisted it was cowardly; he insisted it
wasn't.

We decided to go boating the next day for sure.

On Wednesday, July 6 we went swimming and then hired a
rowboat. Rowed over to one end of the lake and tied it to a big old
tree growing right up out of the water in a secluded nook . . . He
wore this plaid shirt—no buttons down the front, the sleeves rolled
up and the shirt tail definitely out.

Got tired of seeing him smoke, grabbed his almost-full package
of cigarettes, threw it overboard and followed it by his box of
matches. He almost threw me in the lake after his cigarettes, and I
was quite afraid of what he would do for awhile there.

I ended up sopping wet anyway. He held me with one arm—I
couldn't get away, using all my strength, teeth and fingernails—and
drenched me with cold water with the other hand.

That was enough for awhile, but I soon began to feel devilish
again. He was lying down looking quite comfortable and I was
sitting at the end of the boat next to where he'd stuck his feet. I
suddenly rocked the boat way over so that the water came pouring
over the side right at him and the boat almost turned a somersault.
He got a look in his eyes that made me wish I was home again, or at
least on dry land.

I hastily promised to be goodness and purity personified and
went ahead with every intention of carrying out that sacred oath.
But, gee whiz, he took the box of mints away, put them in his
pocket (the right-hand one in this shirt) and wouldn't let me have

any. It was all his fault! He pulled me down next to him on the bottom of the boat. I finally saw my chance, grabbed the box of candy and popped the two remaining pieces in my mouth. He got his arm around my shoulders and grabbed my arm—but, ha, ha, he was too late.

"Whee," I laughed merrily, "this candy is perfectly wonderful!"

He didn't say a thing, but also he didn't remove his arm from around my shoulders. I wiggled my shoulders and tried to sit up, but he held me down.

Finally I said sweetly, "Pierre, I'm not at all comfortable," and after waiting a minute took his arm away . . .

The boat was awfully uncomfortable, so I said, "If you were a gentleman, you'd take off your shirt and let me use it as a pillow." So he did. He looks much nicer without his shirt anyway. All his beautiful muscles, those wide shoulders and nice tan—sigh!

About ten minutes afterwards I got mad and tore his shirt—about 14 inches up one seam. He looked rather surprised when he suddenly heard that awful tearing sound. I learned how it feels to be choked. Ugh. What an afternoon.

"Why you little Jezebel," he said between his teeth.

On Thursday, July 7, looking for a little adventure after going swimming, then getting some sandwiches at Mike's Place and listening to the juke box until it was starting to get dark outside, we rode our bikes over to the Belding Place. It was at the edge of the village, up on a hill behind lots of trees. Once it was a fancy hotel kind of a place with lots of rooms. After that it had been rented out for some years and right now nobody had lived there for awhile. Bucky Brown's family were the last ones there and they suddenly left under mysterious circumstances a year or two ago. Ah, here was a mystery for us!

Pierre had a flashlight and we pried open a narrow basement window on the back of the house and squeezed through. We explored all the rooms, mostly empty, so many rooms, so many bathrooms! When we got to the kitchen, it was eerie! There on the counter was an open peanut butter jar and an open jar of jelly, the

remains of a dried-up piece of bread with moldy stuff on it and
some mouse poop. A few kitchen cupboard doors were open and
there were dirty dishes in the sink and what was left of a loaf of
bread. It looked like someone had left in a big hurry! Maybe to
escape the police?

About then I started feeling guilty—after all, we were breaking
the law! What if we got caught? "Let's get out of here," I said, and
Pierre started laughing.

It was good to be out in the fresh air again!

On Friday, July 8 I rode down to Pierre's place in South Ashfield
because he wanted so much for me to see his cabin. I tied Nonnie
and we went up through the woods to his cabin. It's really wonderful
and I could hardly believe he'd built it. We looked through his
yearbook and I came to one picture and exclaimed without even
glancing at the name, "That boy looks simply marvelous!"

"Does he?" Pierre laughed.

I looked at the name—Pierre Birel Rosette-Cournand. I
hadn't recognized him! I'm so used to seeing him as he is up
here—laughing, reckless, sloppy. I'm left quite unnerved after I look
at him sometimes. In the picture he had his hair combed and was
frowning slightly, his eyes very dark and thoughtful.

He showed me his beautiful rifle and promised to teach me how
to shoot sometime.

His cabin is way off in the woods, secluded from the rest of the
family, and he loves it. He says that every night he builds a roaring
fire and reads for about four hours, or just sits and thinks. He
certainly does know and take in an awful lot. I feel terribly young
and ignorant when I'm with him, once in awhile. We like to talk
seriously together, but I always get a little shy, and in such cases
don't always say what I want to.

Once I mentioned Dr. Cournand, his father, and he said quickly,
"He's not my father! He's my step-father." He told me he was born in
South Africa, that his father was an artist and died when he was still
a baby. His mother married Dr. Cournand some years later in France
and now he had three little sisters.

On Saturday, July 9 . . . Another misunderstanding and my reckless mountain boy went down to the lake at 3:30, instead of coming up to the house. I waited till 5:00 and then got so mad that I had to do something, so I started down after the mail on my bike. Just as I zoomed out of the driveway, there he was on his bike. I swerved and plummeted right on past him. He came down after me, cut me off and we both stopped down at the watering tank.

I wouldn't even say a civil word to him at first. But then he said, "I'm leaving tomorrow, so shed a tear or two and be nice to me!"

We ended up way back in the Ashfield cemetery underneath a few big trees, beside a huge tombstone. It was beautiful and the grass was green and sweet smelling.

We talked about nothing for a while, then I decided to show him how good I was at out-staring people. So we tried to out-stare each other. I suddenly said quietly, "No, I can't," and buried my face in the grass. Those eyes of his! Oh, brother!.

"Come on, try it again," he said. And before I could protest, he put a hand on each side of my head and lifted my face so I had to look at him.

I tried it again and then I just couldn't stand it anymore. I closed my eyes and said, almost sobbing, "No, please, it makes me feel strange inside!"

I will not try to out-stare him again.

At 6:00 I jumped up and said I had to get home for dinner. He wouldn't let me go and took hold of my bike so I couldn't get on it. I said, very coolly, "All right, have your fun, I can walk home."

I started to walk, he started after me. I walked a little faster, so did he. I ran and he caught me, took hold of my arms, propelled me back to the tombstone and sat me very gently on the grass. I got up on pretense of looking at his bike and suddenly started to let the air out of his tires. I don't know what the heck gets into me when I'm with him, but it certainly brings out the devil in me.

I didn't get very far in my new occupation.

Finally, at 7:15 he looked at his watch and jumped up. "Oh, no, I'm supposed to make a long distance phone call to New York at 7:00!"

I couldn't help laughing and saying that's what he got for making me stay. We waited five minutes and then he said, "Come, it's the time to depart, Jezebel."

Me: "Oh, no, I like it here. It's so restful," and I wouldn't get up.

He tried to pull me up, but I can be awfully stubborn and *heavy* when I want to. "All right, you asked for it!" and he picked me up with such ease that I almost fainted. After all, 120 lbs is 120 lbs . . . I yelled at him, called him names, beat on his chest, pulled his hair and kicked my feet. He carried me to the bikes and let me down a bit roughly . . .

He said good-bye and asked me to write to him. Also, that he'd leave me some of his shirts, since I liked them so much . . .

All might have ended than and there. But I couldn't sleep that night. I tossed and turned and dreamt about him . . . I lay there in the dark and couldn't bear the thought of his leaving . . .

Oh, no, I thought, I just can't be going off the deep end about him. I woke up in the morning determined to find out. I shall never forget what happened that Sunday morning . . .

I rode down to his place on Nonnie, this time uninvited and unexpected. I felt confused when I saw him, so just said lightly, "I thought I'd save you the trouble of sending me those shirts."

He'd stuck a tan shirt on hurriedly. He looked a bit tousled and sleepy and hadn't shaved.

"No!" I said, suddenly deciding that I ought to leave, but quick! "I can't stay. I've got to go home and go to church!"

He took hold of Nonnie's bridle and said very quietly, "No, you don't. Get off."

We tied Nonnie to a tree and then cut through the woods to his cabin. I didn't want to go up the path and I wanted to see if he could find his way through the woods. Once or twice I thought we were lost for sure, but he finally got us there. I think he knows his woods by heart and took a roundabout way on purpose!

I was hot and tired. He looked maddeningly cool and refreshed. I sat down outside the cabin and didn't want to go in for awhile.

He held the door open and said, "Come on in Jezebel, with your long red nails and mischievous smile." (He has quite a French accent, and I wouldn't want him any different.) I've been wearing my nails just as long as possible again and put on my brightest red polish because I know he hates it. It's fun, but even I finally couldn't stand it any longer and cut them this morning.

He took my watch away from me and put it in his pocket. His was on the table by his bunk. We talked a long while, and it wasn't all in fun, either.

He said he usually gets along much better with boys than girls. I knew that anyway—he's a man's man, which makes me feel all the nicer that he likes me.

He let me read an 8-page letter that he'd written to a friend of his, the son of Morse, the writer. It was quite intimate and personal and I felt honored that he wanted me to read it.

He showed me a billfold that the Captain of the Normandy gave him. He once traveled across the ocean with him.

He drew me the plans of the house he's going to build after the war. Up on a hill with a beautiful view. A huge room takes up half the floor space and reaches up two stories for the ceiling. There's a huge fireplace and mantle at one side.

He inherits a lot of money when he's 21, less than two years. He's promised to take me on a trip around the world.

I said, "Oh, how wonderful! With a chaperon, of course?"

"Oh, no," he answered. "I hate chaperons. I hope you don't really believe they're necessary."

Then he started to tell me how wonderful I'd be in the Victorian age, with my profile especially. And he tried to get me to pile my hair up on the top of my head so he could see the effect. He said, "That blue shirt is just the color of your eyes . . . You'd look perfect in a hoop skirt and a tiny 18-inch waist."

"Twenty-three inches is small enough for me," I said coldly. "I hate you! You tell me how wonderful I'd be in the Victorian age, but nothing about now!"

I grabbed his pen and wrote S.W.A.K. on the envelope containing the letter to his friend. He almost killed me.

"Give me my watch, please," I said, putting out my hand. "I'm going home right now."

"Oh, no you're not," he answered and didn't give me the watch.

I walked over to the little table by the bunk, grabbed his watch and ran out the door of the cabin, closing it behind me.

I'm a very fast runner, and I'd gotten a head start. I reached the place where the path goes into the woods and there he suddenly stood, with his arms out, blocking the way. He wasn't smiling, and had a funny look in his eyes.

I decided to light out in the other direction. Too late! He caught hold of me and started to half-carry me back towards the cabin. My arms were pinned behind me and I couldn't move them. I kicked him in the shins just as hard as I could when we were almost to the cabin. It caught him off balance and I kicked again and tried to pull away.

He fell down and pulled me with him. I ended up in a half-sitting position, but leaning way back against his arm, and he had me so that I couldn't move.

"Let me go," I gasped, "You can have your old watch, just let me up!"

He smiled wickedly—"Oh, no! You don't think I went to all this trouble for nothing, do you?"

I started to say something, but his mouth came down on mine hard, and the words stuck in my throat. Oh, brother, what a kiss! I couldn't do a thing and everything inside me went all helter skelter and my heart was pounding. Then my bewildered eyes viewed the trees and sky again and I looked at him, and gasped, "Oh, you, you . . . you could at least have shaved!"

He still had his arms around me and I could see that he wasn't ready to take them away yet. Just in time I jerked my head around and pressed my mouth against my shoulder. He laughed when I did that and kissed me on the neck under my hair. It sent shivers up and down my spine.

He let me go and looked at me. And I brought my arm around with all my strength to slap him across the face. Just before it reached his cheek, he caught hold of my wrist. He got my other wrist with his right hand and laughed.

"When you lead a rustic life like I've been doing, you can't help being a little crude at times. Here's your watch."

I just turned and ran all the way down the pathway. We came to Nonnie and saddled him up. It was after 12. Pierre was charming from then up to the moment I left. He tied his shirt onto the saddle.

When I got home I washed it out. I never saw such a dirty shirt! I soaked it in hot water for two hours and it shrank some. Then I scrubbed until my hands ached and finally got it fairly clean. I can still smell Pierre in it, and it's such a nice masculine smell. I had to sew brown buttons on down the front and sew up the rip.

I've been writing for three hours, so I'll have to give up and go to bed. But I just had to put all this down. I'm still not sure if I've gone off the deep end. What happened was exciting and unexpected . . . and wonderful! I like him a lot, of course, as I've written so much.

We talked 1/2 hour about religion. He ended up by saying, "Some people need religion. I don't. That's all."

### Thursday, July 15

Tuesday the phone rang and Mom called me. I wondered who it could be. It was Pierre! As soon as he said my name, I knew it was him and my heart jumped up into my mouth.

"Oh, Pierre, where are you?"

He laughed and said, "Why, New York . . . No, I'm right down here in South Ashfield and I'm coming up. O.K.?"

It sounded so funny for him to say O.K.

He came up and we went down to the lake. He told me that when he got to New York Sunday evening, he and the other fellows had rooms in a hotel, and the next morning they had breakfast with General Giraud! He sat at Giraud's table and talked to him!

Well, Monday morning and afternoon he had two long interviews with officials; then they said he wouldn't need to take the exams that were to be given Monday, Tuesday and Wednesday, which means they think he's wonderful, too.

I wore his shirt over my gray skirt just for the heck of it. When we got down to the lake we talked to Mr. Edwards for awhile. Then we sat on the bench and he told me about what he did in New York, and about talking to Giraud.

"You should see the uniforms we're going to have," he said. "A red cap with a bill, and big brass buttons down the front of our uniform."

I bet he'll look just grand. But not as good as he looks in just his jeans and an old shirt, or no shirt at all, with his hair all mussed up and needing to be cut if it gets much longer. We hired a boat and went rowing. We went way over to the other end of the lake, and it was a beautiful sunny afternoon.

We kidded around and talked a whole lot. He said they're going to be sent over to Africa to train native troops after the officers training. It's all like a big adventure to him, and he doesn't seem to be afraid of what might happen. Not that anything ever could happen to him . . .

After awhile he lay down in the boat and said for me to, too, but I sat up on the seat with my back to him.

Suddenly he grabbed me by the shoulders and pulled me over backwards. The skirt of my bathing suit flipped way back so that he could see my legs as far up as they go, and I struggled like anything.

"Look out," he said. "You'll tip the boat over!" He had one arm around my shoulder and with the other hand he held both of mine. I couldn't do anything but stay there. I felt so embarrassed and shy, and he didn't say anything.

I was right next to his hot bare skin. We'd gotten to being so natural together and I had broken through that quiet steady reserve of his a long time ago, but this was strange and terribly disturbing. It was also wonderful . . .

Pretty soon, because he wouldn't let me up, I put my head down on his shoulder and relaxed. It was so nice there. And I suddenly thought about him going away and I wanted to bawl.

Then I felt him loosen his hold on me, and I tried to get up. I don't know why—maybe because I'm so used to trying to keep any guy from touching me or putting his arm around me that it was just force of habit.

Well, he kept me down and swore between his teeth. We just lay like that for awhile and talked a little.

We talked about what we're going to do after the war, and I was so happy that I figure in his plans for the future. July 12, 1945, we have a date to go rowing again. And the war will be all over. I wonder what it will be like when he comes back. I wonder if he would ever ask me to marry him . . . I never thought about getting married before! I'd be so scared, and someone like Pierre would be so passionate. I'd be so scared . . .

It's so exciting and different to be with him. I can just look at him and my heart almost jumps out of place . . . Anyway, after awhile, he suddenly leaned over me and looked at me real seriously and I knew he was going to kiss me. I put the palm of my hand over my mouth and looked at him through the spaces between my fingers.

He pulled my hand away roughly and just looked at me.

"O.K." he said. "If you don't want me to kiss you, I won't. Don't worry."

And I felt so awful, because I *wanted* him to kiss me, hard and long like he did up in the woods, and I just couldn't admit it to him.

Then he leaned back again and didn't say anything. And when I tried to get up again he didn't let me.

We talked some more. He's going to get a horse after the war and we'll go riding together. It would be so wonderful to ride together all the time. Off on those old Indian trails and logging roads sometimes, and by the streams. We could take our lunch and ride way out in the country.

Pretty soon he leaned over me and the look in his eyes almost scared me—they were so dark and his jaw was clamped tight, and he was so handsome—his hair all mussy and that smooth tan and all of him so hard and muscular and lithe. And I wanted to put my arms up around his neck and cry because he was going. But that look in his eyes scared me.

"You don't want me to kiss you?" he said real softly.

"No," I said. I wanted to say yes, but I was afraid to. Honest, I wanted to tell him the truth, but I couldn't.

And he didn't kiss me. He let me up, and we didn't say anything for a long time. And I knew I'd gone off the deep end, and we only had few hours left. I forgot all about supper. We rowed to the far end of the lake, and he sang for me. He said the things he sang were from Gilbert and Sullivan operas. He sang because he loved to sing, and I've never heard anyone sing like that. His eyes were so dark again, and he sang in his deep voice and when he hit any real low notes, he pulled his chin in. He sang something in a kind of English accent, and it ended up with "and now I am the ruler of the Queen's Navy!"

I asked him how long the officers training would be, and he said about three months. That means his furlough would come around the first week in November, when I'm at Penn State.

When we started back from the lake the stores were closed. "Oh," he said, "I forgot all about this check I must have cashed!"

"That's O.K.," I said. "I forgot to go home for supper." We rode our bikes over to see Elmer at his apartment over the store and he cashed the check.

I told Pierre Bob Pichette was home on leave, and we stopped in at Pichette's. Mrs. Pichette said he was over at Kenneth Darling's, so we went over there and hammered on the door. Pretty soon Bob and Kenneth emerged. Gee, Bob looks wonderful. Lean and tan, with a crew cut, and even better looking than usual. Well, he and Pierre started talking away, and about ten minutes later Plink arrived on Nonnie to say Pop was mad as Hell because I hadn't gotten home for dinner, and that I'd better go and explain. So I jumped on Nonnie and cantered up the field by Nye's and then up the dirt road to the house. I tied Nonnie out at the barn and ran around to the front porch where Mom and Dad were.

He was awfully mad, and it seemed so unreasonable. He said I couldn't go anywhere else that night, and I almost cried.

"Oh, Daddy," I said, "this is the last night I may ever see Pierre. Please, please don't make me stay in. Weren't you ever young once?"

He finally said I could stay out till 9 o'clock. So I rode back down to Darlings and turned Nonnie over to Plink again . . .

We all ate supper at Pichette's, Pierre and Bob and I. Mrs. Pichette fixed chicken sandwiches, and I sat across from Pierre. Neither one of us could eat much.

Then we drove up to the Williams place. It was not yet dark, and Betty, Inis and D.O. were sitting out on the swing. She was so surprised to see me with Pierre. When we left, D.O. was with us and it was starting to get dark.

Bob drove over all the dirt roads and we ended up down in S. Ashfield at Pierre's. He went in to get a package of cigarettes. One of his little sisters saw me and went tearing into the house babbling something in French. Pierre came back laughing and we asked him what she's said.

"The young woman is wearing Pierre's shirt! The young lady is wearing Pierre's shirt!" We all laughed.

Earlier that day at the lake, Pierre put his hands at my waist and pulled the fullness of the shirt back. "What a bust," he said. "I mean waist." Gee, I could feel the color coming into my cheeks.

Well, to get back to Tuesday night. "Look," said Pierre, "let's go up to my cabin. We can build a big fire and roast marshmallows."

"Oh," squealed D.O., "that would be wonderful!"

"I can't," I said. "I have to be in by 9," and I felt like such a damn fool. It would have been wonderful there in the cabin with Pierre, sitting on the bunk or bench, watching the fire, and everything all dark and cool outside.

Bob just turned around and looked at me. Pierre said, "Come on up anyway." He drew some smoke into his mouth and crushed the cigarette against the running board. Then he looked right square at me. I wanted to say yes, but I was so afraid of what Daddy would say when I got home.

"No, I can't," I said miserably . . .

So we went back. When we got home I begged Daddy to let me go up to Williams and said we'd be right back. We took D.O. home and stayed about 10 minutes talking to her mother. Pierre and I went back and got in the car. We watched Bob kiss D.O. goodnight in the doorway. Bob came back to the car grinning and wiping the lipstick off. He looked so cute. "I'm making up for all the loving I missed while I was gone," he said.

The three of us sat in the front seat, and it was a tight fit. My heart started jumping out of place again. I was so close to Pierre. He put his arm up over the back of the seat, and I leaned up against him and put my head against his shoulder . . . I could feel the muscles in his arm tense and relax and then get tense again, but he didn't put his arm down around my shoulder. Because of Bob, I guess. That same quiet reserve coming back.

I just closed my eyes and wished we'd never get home. Have a flat tire or anything, as long as I could stay with him. I could hear him and Bob talking, as if they were far off. I have gone off the deep end and I never wanted him to go away . . .

When we got back to the house, there were Mom and Dad sitting on the back porch. I introduced them to Pierre, and we all talked for awhile. Pierre started to smoke, and his face looked real grim when the match flared up. I kept praying that Mom and Dad would go in the house. But they didn't. I tried to get up the courage to say, "Pierre, come help me water Nonnie." But that was so obvious. I wanted so much for him to kiss me, and Daddy and Mom wouldn't leave. I will never forgive them for that. Finally, Daddy practically said, "Bedtime, Little Girl," and Pierre and Bob said goodnight. They got in the car, and Pierre said, "Remember, te quiero," and he raised his hand in a kind of salute and tried to smile. But he couldn't.

The car drove away, and the tears were running down my cheeks. I went up to bed and cried and cried. Because I hadn't had the courage to be honest with him, and I knew I might never see him again. I couldn't bear to think of him overseas someplace, dirty and hungry and in danger.

I know I'm the only girl he has ever bothered with . . . "Te quiero" means I love you in Spanish . . . I wonder what will happen when he comes back. Nothing could happen to him, could it? Nothing happens to people like that, does it?

Yesterday morning, Wednesday, Plink and I rode down to his place in South Ashfield because she wanted to see his cabin. I thought he had gone, and yet somehow hoped he hadn't. He was still there! He'd just shaved and had a tan shirt on, tucked into his bluejeans.

And Pierre rode Nonnie. Yes, he honestly did! When we first got there, he said, "Hey, let me ride your horse."

"Do you think you could?" I said, sort of scared, because I didn't think he would be able to and was afraid something might happen.

Well, he did ride him. I know of so many people, good riders, who couldn't handle Nonnie, and from what Pierre said, he hadn't ridden since three years ago when he lived on a ranch out west.

When he got on, Nonnie just stood there a minute, testing him, and then started to act up. I wanted to yell, "Pierre, please get off!"

He had a cigarette in his mouth, looked very calm and had the feel of Nonnie from the minute he got on him. He put him into a slow canter and kept him down, and he certainly looked good on that horse. I went along with him on Winnie. He galloped him some and left me in the dust.

When I got back to the house on Winnie, one of Pierre's little sisters was running around screaming, "Oh, Pierre gallope, Pierre gallope!" She said something to him in French and he said very sternly, "Niche, niche!"

He had Nonnie standing still and a middle-aged, rather heavy woman was taking a picture of him. I hope it turns out.

Then he led us up to his cabin, walking ahead of us through the woods. Plink took one look at his build and almost collapsed. He had his thumbs hooked in his front pockets, and you could see how broad his shoulders were and how his body tapered down to the narrow waist and hips.

We showed Plink the cabin, and when we started back she ran ahead. I started to run, too, and Plink looked back just as Pierre grabbed my arm and said, "You don't have to hurry."

On the right-hand side of the path was a big tree with a ladder up the side of it and the remains of a tree house on the huge branches. I looked at it, and Pierre said, "Let's go up."

He was way up in the tree before I could say Jack Robinson. I started up the ladder and was about 6 feet off the ground when a rung broke. Pierre was standing on a branch above me with his legs far apart, not holding onto anything. When the rung broke and I started to fall, he grabbed both my wrists, and just balancing there, he pulled me up onto the branch beside him . . . "That's a long ways to the ground, Julia," he said, and then laughed. He hardly ever calls me by name, unless it's Jezebel.

I recovered after about 10 minutes, and we sat up in the tree house talking.

Over and over in my mind I kept saying, "Pierre, will you kiss me good-bye?" and I wanted to say it aloud. I knew it was up to me, that he wouldn't try to kiss me again unless he knew I wanted him to. He kept looking at me. It was maddening. "I wish I could tell what you were thinking," he said.

Well, I didn't have the nerve. So we left the tree house, and that's all there was to it. He climbed down first, and I jumped and he caught hold of me, and I kept my hands up on his shoulders. He looked directly into my eyes, like the day at the graveyard, as if it was a challenge. And I took my hands away.

We didn't say anything else at all. Except good-bye when Plink and I left on the horses.

I wonder if he will write to me very soon, and if his letters will be as reserved and non-committal as they were before.

I just read over some of the rest of my diary, and all that about Artie and the others seems so childish and silly.

### Thursday, July 22

The last night of Bob's furlough, Plink and I went down to the Pichette's to say good-bye. We all talked out on the porch for a long time. He said he'd gained 15 pounds, but he really looks 15 pounds lighter. He told us about a couple of his friends that were killed while being trained. It must have been so terrible. It's too bad Bob couldn't get to see Harold before he went overseas. They wanted so much to keep together.

### Wednesday, July 28

Just got a letter from Pierre. It was reserved and non-committal, as usual. But he signed it "Pierre," instead of the way he used to, "Your friend, Pierre."

He told me something about the training, and it was a long letter. He started out, "I have at last started on the great adventure, armed with razor, tooth brush and numerous packages of Chesterfields," and ended up by telling me the way he spent his last few hours in

Ashfield, "drinking cheap whisky, dropping a tear or two on my books, records and writings . . . and thinking of the bright new world I might return to with its colossal lakes."

I hope someday we'll have more than letters. "Lakes" was the only thing that meant "you and me together."

I wrote a long, long letter to him tonight, but will wait a few days to mail it.

*That's the last entry in my diary. Pierre and I wrote to each other all summer.*

See chapter 47, "A Brief History Lesson," to learn more about General Charles de Gaulle's Free French Army and the Nazi-occupied France Pierre would soon be experiencing.

# 5

# A Bolt of Lightning

## *And the Return of a Sailor*

One Saturday night in August, only a few weeks after Pierre left for Fort Benning, lightning struck. It hit at the base of the house, traveled along the plumbing, and exploded in my face as I was washing dishes.

I was so shook up, I almost didn't go to the square dance that night. But then I decided I should, that I might meet someone who would take my mind off Pierre. Which is exactly what happened.

Al Doughty, one of Ashfield's summer people, and two of his army buddies turned up at the town hall that night. They were in the Signal Corps, stationed at Westfield, and one of Al's friends danced with me and brought me home.

Art Smith was a tall lean and fit six foot three, twenty-two years old, and very good-looking. He thought that I was "a little country girl," he told me later, and that this would be a nice weekend flirtation. But after that, they came back every weekend they could wrangle a pass.

We hung out at the Doughtys' cabin in the woods near the high school, ate ice cream, listened to the jukebox at Mike's place, swam in the lake, and turned up at the Saturday night square dances. Once, we went roller-skating in Greenfield, which was great fun.

Anne Smith, whose family spent a month with us every summer, dated Al's buddy Jack. And Pauline went out with Al a few times. (But then she met Malcolm, the love of her life.)

One weekend, I found a lively date for Al. It was Elf, whose nickname suited her. She was the granddaughter of Mater and Pater Smith, friends of my folks. She turned out to be what we called in those days "fast," which meant letting a boy kiss you on the first date.

(Some years later, Elf would gain notoriety as a contestant in a popular television quiz show, *The $64,000 Question.*)

We tore around in Al's battered convertible. Art and I always ended up tucked snugly into the little rumble seat. He said he planned to open a radio repair shop after the war in his hometown of Malden, Massachusetts, close to Boston. And he asked me to marry him.

When it dawned on me that he was actually serious, I told him I was far too young to even *think* about getting hitched.

Art had grown up in a big family, the beloved little brother in a gaggle of sisters. Very aware of how young and inexperienced I was, he treated me with a touch of gentle chivalry. He had a sunny outlook on life and a gift for clowning. It was impossible not to like him!

One evening, when we were parked by the upper reservoir in the moonlight, after some careful persuasion on his part, I even kissed him. Being with Art was always fun. It could also turn exciting, but he kept his passion for me under tight control.

A week before I left for Penn State, Art came to see me in Brooklyn on a three-day pass. We visited friends of his, a policeman and his wife, in Manhattan.

As a joke (Art's idea!), we pretended we were married. This was fun for a while but turned embarrassing when they invited us to spend the night, and the wife asked me if we were practicing birth control. Aghast, I mumbled, "Oh yes, of course!" . . . and no, we really couldn't spend the night.

I was so put out with Art, who grinned all the way back to Bay Ridge on the subway. Otherwise, we had our usual happy time together. I hated to see him go, but it was nothing like the heart-wrenching parting with Pierre.

## Home from the Sea

Home on leave late that summer, Artie Gould had turned up unexpectedly one afternoon. He was wearing jeans and a plaid shirt, and I almost didn't recognize him! I had just come in from a long ride on Nonnie and was getting ready to unsaddle him.

"Hey, let me ride your horse," Artie said, stroking Nonnie's neck.

"Well," I countered, "I don't think that's a good idea. He can be a very difficult . . . nobody but me or my sister rides him."

"Oh, come on!" he said. "I'm a farm boy, and I can ride your horse!"

So against my better judgment, but remembering that Pierre has ridden him with ease a few weeks earlier, I let him.

Nonnie stood quietly while Artie adjusted the stirrups. But as soon as he swung up into the saddle, the horse took off and gathered speed, with Artie yelling "Whoa!" and hauling back on the reins. At the end of our driveway, Nonnie made an abrupt turn to the right and clattered at full speed down the narrow rocky lane.

I took off after them at a run. If Nonnie didn't slow down before he stopped abruptly at the gate at the end of the lane, Artie could fly off right over his head. Or what if he crashed into the gate or jumped it and galloped off into the pasture beyond?

Out of breath and sweating, I finally caught up with them. They were standing in front of the heavy wooden gate, Artie on the ground with the reins in his hand. They were both a little wild-eyed.

"I'm not getting back on that crazy horse," he said. He was pretty ruffled, not at all the carefree, laughing sailor who had fearlessly ridden the Cyclone roller coaster with me screaming at his side one day at Coney Island.

We started back up the lane with Nonnie walking calmly along beside us. Trying to come up with something positive, I said, "Well, that was pretty good, Artie—you stayed with him all the way!"

Silence.

Back at the barn, Artie helped me unsaddle Nonnie, water him, turn him into his stall, and give him some hay. We visited for a while, and then he left. I was never to see or hear from him again.

Years later, Pauline told me that Artie came home from the war in one piece. In his retirement years, according to his brother Edgar, he worked off and on for a cruise ship company. His assignment was to dance and socialize with the women guests. A perfect job for him! I bet he loved it.

Pauline at 18.

### Pauline Meets Malcolm

While my romance with Art Smith was blossoming, Pauline had met Malcolm Clark, a twenty-four-year-old Apple Valley farmer who shared her love of horses. He and his best friend and neighbor Ralph Townsley ran the Saturday night dances at the town hall that year, and Malcolm was the square dance caller.

He courted Pauline in a horse-drawn surrey, wanted her to marry him and not go off to college. But she'd been accepted at the University of Indiana, and Daddy was expecting her to go.

Daddy's brother, our uncle Russell, taught in the medical school there; and she would be living with his family, which included his wife, Juliet, and their adopted baby, Joe. Although Pauline was pretty sure Malcolm was the man for her, she wanted to give this whole stupendous matter more time and consideration.

"I should go for at least one year," she reasoned. "Or I'll never know what I missed!" So she and I both went off to college that fall. With his sisters suddenly absent, Phillips's family life in the city from now on would be lonely.

# 6

# OFF TO COLLEGE

It was October 1943. Now seventeen and on a train rumbling through the Pennsylvania countryside, I had begun my own great adventure. The landscape that grabbed my attention hour after hour was mostly farmland, flaming with autumn colors. The train would take me as far as Lewistown. From there, the trip to State College in the wide Nittany Valley would have to be made by car or bus over six (or was it seven?) mountains.

My assigned roommate Doris and her parents met my train in the gathering darkness and put me up for the night at their farm. The next morning, after a big breakfast, her folks drove us over the mountains to State College. They helped us unpack and settle in at Wylie Dorm, the house in town we'd be sharing with thirteen other freshmen girls and a "dorm mother." The real dormitories up on campus were full!

I arrived with all my stuff in Daddy's ancient stand-up wardrobe trunk. Vertically hinged, it had drawers on one side and hangers on the other. My clothes consisted mainly of two cardigan sweaters, a few blouses and skirts, jeans, a dressy two-piece blue-plaid outfit, ski pants and jacket, a tweed coat, kneesocks, a few pairs of silk stockings, a warm hat and gloves, a few head scarves, saddle shoes, boots, and a pair of high heels.

Fortunately, four of my friends and I could all fit into more or less the same size. So we were always borrowing one another's clothes!

## A Strange New World

We had entered a strange new world, teeming with life and unexpected revelations. Doris and I had few interests in common, but we liked each other, and she cheerfully accepted the mounting chaos in which I lived as the semester progressed.

That very first week, in a meeting for freshman girls with a woman doctor, I learned "the facts of life." Shocked, mortified at my own ignorance, I sat there with my mouth open and crept out of the auditorium afterward in a daze! My friends thought I was very funny. And I was suddenly homesick.

It was a campus awash with marines, sailors, army engineers, and air force cadets. Their barracks were all around us. These darling young men marched past us in formation every day on their way to campus.

Armed with my new and explicit knowledge about the dangers they posed, I formed my strategy. I would not drink, I would carefully observe curfew, I would develop a sixth sense about which men were reliable and which were not. As a result, the dates I trusted often became my friends. Those who were sexually aggressive, I quickly dumped. I avoided like the plague dating students with cars.

## My Favorite Professor

Dr. Eddie Nichols was my favorite teacher. He taught creative writing and made fun of those first few pieces I wrote about horses. But he also believed I showed quite a bit of talent as a writer. I loved his class.

He soon invited me out to his place in the country, picked me up, and took me out there about one Sunday afternoon a month, then deposited me back at Wylie Dorm that evening. I treasured my friendship with him and his wife Champ throughout my four years at Penn State and signed up for every class he taught.

Besides creative writing, I took courses in history, rural sociology, music appreciation, French, typing, and an economics course I dropped after only three class sessions because I was so hopelessly confused!

Except for an A in Eddie Nichols's class, my grades that first
semester were mediocre. Disappointed in me, Daddy laid down the
law: unless my grades improved dramatically, he was not willing
to continue to fund my college education. I buckled down and did
much better the rest of my freshman year.

But those first few months at Penn State were a heady time,
and I dated like mad . . . forget the homework! One young sailor
nicknamed me Blue Jay because of my eyes and my penchant for
wearing blue. Soon, everyone was calling me Jay, a name that stuck
with me ever after.

**Phil and Johnny**

Phil Jones, a marine from Upper Darby, Pennsylvania, and
Johnny Turney, an air force cadet from Philadelphia, became my
very special friends.

Phil was a good-looking fellow with wide cheekbones, dark
eyebrows, brown eyes, and dark-brown hair. He was thoughtful,
shy, sweet natured, and companionable. We went to movies and
dances, had some great hikes in the country on Saturday and Sunday
afternoons.

Once, he invited his sister down for a big dance. He fixed me up
with another marine, and we attended as a foursome.

Phil had played the oboe in his high school band, was a premed student
in college before enlisting. The marines' slogan was "First in battle,"
but I simply could not imagine Phil in battle or ever killing anybody.

Johnny was more romantically inclined, but smart enough not to
insist on intimacy. Fair skinned and blue eyed, he had dense blond
hair, a wonderful grin, and a happy outlook on life. He smoked
a lot—too much. I remember watching his handsome face light
up as he cupped his hands and held a match to his cigarette in the
darkness. Since childhood, he had been determined to learn to fly
airplanes someday. He would remain dear to me for many years.

**Mary Glen**

Only a block from Wylie, on our way to campus, my friend Mary
Glen worked part-time in her grandparents' doughnut shop. I seldom

had much spending money, so I only bought one doughnut at a time, the chocolate-covered ones being my favorite. Between those doughnuts and the sweet rolls we had for breakfast every morning, I gained a good ten pounds that year.

I first met Mary in typing class. We were the only students who hadn't taken typing in high school, so we were at the bottom of the class and gave each other sympathy. We were soon going hiking together.

Mary was a slim dark-haired beauty, her gentle nature reflected in her face. She was on my same wavelength in so many of life's important matters. I admired her serene spirit and backbone of steel and never wanted to lose her. She made me think of what my mother might have been like as a young woman.

A general major in art, music, and literature, she was two years ahead of me in school and already engaged to Joe Gale, a very tall long-legged fellow who played on the varsity baseball team. She had met him her sophomore year when he accidentally knocked her books from her hand in philosophy class, then walked her home to apologize.

## The Purity Corner Girls

College life was intense and full of earnest discussions back at Wylie Dorm, where five of us had formed the Purity Corner Gang. All but me were Pennsylvania gals: Jean McCreary, Betty Herring, Norma Lou Stephens, and Carolyn Lerch.

Norma Lou was from a farm family just a few hours away. I spent Thanksgiving vacation with her that year, horseback riding, eating her mother's great cooking, going into town to a movie one night, and flirting with her brother. The horses leapt from their stalls like wild broncos out of a rodeo chute and were a challenge to tack up, mount, and keep from running away with us as we dashed through the countryside on dirt roads.

Norma Lou's folks delivered us back to Wylie Dorm with a box full of fried chicken and chocolate chip cookies for our Purity Corner chums. Every time they brought her home from a weekend, we could count on another such feast.

Carolyn was founder and leader of Purity Corner. She had arrived at Penn State in a drab ankle-length skirt, black stockings, and high-button shoes, her reddish brown hair pulled back severely into a bun. A victim of ulcerative colitis and homeschooled through high school on an isolated farm, she had finally recovered her health enough to go away to college.

Within weeks, she had perky new clothes, a short haircut, had mastered using a light touch with makeup. We watched this transformation in awe and loved her dearly for her inquisitive mind, her affectionate nature, her fresh outlook on life, her quick wit, and her exuberant sense of fun and adventure.

Then along came Miles Cagle, a good-looking tall ASTP engineer. Carolyn, who'd never ever had a boyfriend, was suddenly and blissfully in love. She entertained us with stories of their times together and with a tuneful little ditty that went, "There's miles and miles of miles, but there's no miles like *my* Miles!"

When we heard persistent rumors that some of the engineers were married, the Purity Corner Gang went into action. We visited the ASTP office on campus. While a few of us flirted with the two soldiers on duty, Carolyn slipped into the room where files were kept and looked up names of engineers dating our friends.

Alas, Miles was married, as were several others. All were subjected to tongue lashings from their coed sweethearts and sent on their way. Outraged but undaunted, Carolyn added a few hilarious verses to her Miles ditty and soon acquired another boyfriend.

## Wylie Dorm Dropouts

Pat was a likable good-time gal in our dorm. One night, she didn't make it home before the doors were locked. Soon, we heard a commotion and whispering outside as her date and one of his buddies boosted her up the fire escape. We pulled her through the window and put her in the shower to sober up. A few months later, she discovered she was pregnant and left school.

By Christmas, we had lost two more Wylie Dorm girls, one to homesickness and the other to devastating rejection by the sorority to which her mother had belonged. Sororities never interested me.

Once, Pierre and I had a long conversation about sororities and fraternities, which he didn't like either.

## Pierre's Furlough

At night, I would often lie awake and wonder what was happening to Pierre. He had written to me in mid-October, saying that he'd bought a motorcycle, would graduate from officers training school in November, and planned to come spend his furlough with me.

Sometimes you do something you firmly believe is the right and unselfish thing to do and then regret it for the rest of your life . . . I told him not to come, that he should spend his furlough with his family in New York City. I thought, secretly hoped, he would come anyhow. But I did not hear from him again until he was overseas. Now years later, I realize he probably didn't plan to spend his *whole* furlough with me, but just a few days of it!

It was so hard to keep feeling close to him. My diary of our time together was tucked in the back of a drawer in my room at Ashfield. His letters became infrequent and gave me nothing to go on . . . but I kept writing to him and wondered if my letters were getting through.

## Robin Makes a Big Hit

Robin visited me on furlough that fall. We had a good time, and my friends were all crazy about him. I took a picture of two of them peeking around from behind him on the steps of Old Main. Soon, he was overseas, in the thick of the war and writing to me on a regular basis.

He served as a tail gunner on a bomber that flew missions over Germany and Austria. He told me that when they returned to their base from a mission, they'd check to see if all the other planes had made it back.

Too often, there'd be at least one plane and its whole crew lost. He sent me a picture of his own crew sitting exhausted and forlorn on a long bench beside a building at the airfield . . . waiting. I had a hard time recognizing him.

Art came to see me that fall too before being sent to Camp Crowder for further training. My friends sighed and carried on over him too. After that, he wrote often from Missouri, telling me how much he loved me, enclosing snapshots of him and his friends clowning around outside the barracks.

## Sad News from Malcolm

Back home in Apple Valley, Malcolm was taking care of Nonnie for Pauline and me. One day, in January, a letter came from him saying that Nonnie had injured himself in the pasture so severely that he'd had to be put down. Running from dogs, he had crashed wildly through a fence.

I was devastated. I wrote about my loss to Robin, who sent me a blistering reply. He was appalled at my making such a fuss over a mere horse when his friends were dying all around him. After that, I'm sure he never felt quite the same about his "dear little Miss Jones."

*Robin (aka Franklin Ward Bush) survived the war and came back home to Darien, Connecticut. We did exchange a few letters, but I realized he was deeply changed from the exuberant, joyous, lovable and optimistic teenager I had known and we soon lost track of each other. I was never to hear his voice or see him again.*

## A Letter from Pierre

At the end of March, I received a V-mail from Pierre. I cried and cried. I was so happy. As a lieutenant and commando in the paratroops, his life had evidently grown very difficult. He said that when the road was rough and rocky, it was good to have friends to hold on to. He ended with, "Eat an ice cream cone for me, Pierre."

I wrote him a long airmail letter right away. Then no word from him again, but I kept writing . . . and wondering. I hated using those dinky V-mails, but it was supposed to be the best way to write to servicemen overseas.

\*     \*     \*

In the spring of the year, a letter from Daddy said he planned a trip out to Missouri to see Grandpa and Grandma Jones at the end of the semester and asked if I would like to go with him. He thought maybe Art could get a weekend pass while we were there. Yes! Yes!

# 7

# RENDEZVOUS IN MISSOURI

Six months earlier, during Christmas break, my sister had a rendezvous with her sweetheart too at my grandparents' farm outside Holliday, Missouri. At a family gathering there, Malcolm met most of my uncles and their families. I'll bet he felt right at home on this farm that held so many good childhood memories for me.

I recall one time when the deeply rutted dirt road to the farm had turned to thick gooey mud after a few days of rain. Grandpa met us in the rain at the Moberly train station, and we made it almost to the farm before his car got stuck hubcap deep in mud. Daddy, wearing high rubber boots kept in the car for just such an emergency, gathered us up one by one and carried us to the house.

It was here at the farm that Pauline and I acquired our lifelong love of horses, thanks to Frances and Bess, Grandpa's gentle team. After working all day, they always seemed to have plenty of energy left for these two little girls, who rode them first around and around the barnyard and, later, out onto the dirt road at the end of the arrow-straight farm lane.

A railroad track ran along next to the road, and we always waved to the passengers as the trains roared by. They came through twice a day. The one at night shook the house, rattled the windows, and I was sure it would crash right through the middle of the house.

Once, when I was ten or twelve, I galloped along next to the train on Bess one day but was quickly outdistanced. That made me realize

what a stupendous feat it was for those movie cowboys to keep up
with the train, then grab hold and swing on board from their horses.

Grandpa had once taught in a one-room school where the slim
and lovely young Verdilla Stalcup was a student and stole his heart.
They were married right after she graduated. Grandma, who had
grown up on a farm, was thrilled at the prospect of escaping farm
life and going to live in town.

Alas, without consulting her, Grandpa quit teaching right away
and bought the farm. Grandma would bring six boys and one girl
into the world, lose the oldest boy and the only girl to death in their
late teens, and be a hardworking farmwife, adored by her children
and many grandchildren, for the rest of her life. By the time I
knew her, she had become a large woman who told wonderful
stories, encouraged us in the taming of the wild kittens on the
place, and dazzled us with her crispy fried chicken, luscious pies,
and cakes.

If a pie didn't turn out just right, she'd bring it in from the kitchen
to the dining room table, saying as she came, "Aw, I fell down on the
pie!" At first, I cried out in alarm, thinking she really *did* fall down on it.

Out in the barnyard, we watched in horror as our lovable
grandma wrung a chicken's neck; and the poor thing ran around
"like a chicken with its head off," one of Grandma's favorite
expressions. Witnessing this bloody deed one day, little Phillips
backed away and fell into a low watering trough.

Now here I was with Daddy, very, very early on Sunday
morning, June 25, 1944, at the Moberly, Missouri, station, waiting as
a passenger train chugged and rattled slowly to a stop, spewing steam.

At first, in the dim light on the platform, I didn't recognize the
soldier who jumped down off the train. His short-cropped hair was
bleached almost blond from the sun, and a deep tan made his eyes
look different. He came toward us at a run, caught hold of me, and
kissed me right in front of Daddy!

When we got back to the farm, Art and I went for a walk in
the semidarkness. Just after we passed through the gate out of the

barnyard, he put his arm around me, and I snuggled in against him. I'd forgotten how tall he was.

We talked and talked, soon dissolving the last traces of awkwardness between us. Then we sat on the ground at the edge of the pathway, and he pulled me onto his lap. He kissed me, and I kissed him back. By the time the sun started coming up, I told him that I loved him.

As the sun burned brighter, my hair caught his attention. Examining a length of it in his hand, he said, "You girls didn't by chance get a hold of some red hair rinse, did you?"

"Daddy's hair was kinda red when he was younger," I said hopefully.

"Wash it out, sweetheart," he said gently. "There's not going to be anything false about my Julie!"

We had only fifteen hours together. After a big country breakfast with the family, we took a blanket way out to the far end of the farm, by the Catalpa Grove, and spread it under the trees.

We lay down and did a lot of planning and daydreaming . . . and some smooching too. It was 101 in the shade, and there were lots of bugs around, but it was still wonderful. (The next day, I was covered with hundreds of horrible itchy chigger bites!)

When we were walking back, Art showed me very carefully how to go over a high fence. I pretended to listen attentively, then scrambled over it in the twinkling of an eye. He just stood looking at me, then started laughing.

"Heck, I've been climbing fences all my life," I said with a big grin. "It's practically second nature!"

Then in the middle of one of the happiest days I'd known, I thought of Pierre. I could almost see him standing there in his jeans and brown-and-white plaid shirt, open down the front. I could almost touch his tousled dark hair; he seemed so real.

I could feel those eyes watching me quietly . . . And I thought, *Oh, Pierre, after all this time, I can't forget you. I still remember everything about you . . . What will happen when you come back?*

It's not that I didn't love Art, because I did. It's just that I knew there was no one else in the whole world like Pierre.

I tried to tell Art about Pierre, but I couldn't do it.

# 8

## SUMMER 1944 IN ASHFIELD

Back in Ashfield, I missed Art, I missed Nonnie, and I
wondered what was happening to Pierre so far away in France.
Pauline was home from the University of Indiana, reunited with
Malcolm, and had no wish to go back to college. I had wanted to
get a job that would earn me spending money for my next year at
college, but Daddy said no.

Malcolm supplied Pauline with one of his horses, Ginger, a
spirited black Thoroughbred mare. My friend Gordon Nadeau,
sixteen, an Apple Valley farm boy, loaned me his little mare Shoo
Fly for the summer. When possible, he borrowed a horse from Pete
Bundy to go riding with me. Pete, the son of a family friend, worked
summers as a hired man at the Clark farm for several years.

Gordon was a self-taught pianist who could listen to a piece
of classical music a few times and then play it. He was really
good! One day, when Bernard Herman, conductor of the New York
Philharmonic, and his wife were our houseguests, I hatched a plan.

After Gordon and I came in from riding, I lured him into the
house with food, then invited him to play the old upright piano in
our dining room. While he pounded the keys, lost in the music, I
slipped into the living room and asked the great man to assess
Gordon's talent.

Impressed with this untutored youngster, Mr. Herman
encouraged him to apply for a scholarship and consider a career in

music. Gordon felt he couldn't do that but played for himself and his friends for the rest of his life.

He had a Down's syndrome sister, Jean, a few years younger than he was, plus an older brother, Alfred. Someone talked May and Charlie Nadeau into institutionalizing their daughter when she was about twelve. But when Charlie and his sons went to visit her, they found that she was very unhappy.

According to Martha Townsley, an Apple Valley neighbor, "Charlie couldn't stand it. He checked her out that very day and brought her home. And Jean grew up happily right there on the farm."

Russell Williams, a neighbor boy close by, remembers Jean walking down the road past his house each day to the mailboxes to fetch the mail. She also walked down the valley road to Ruth Clark's to get eggs. A strong, sturdy girl, she had a homemade stick horse she rode all over the valley for years and years.

The Apple Valley community took care of its own. The Nadeau house burned to the ground on Thanksgiving Day in 1954. (Gordon and Alfred had moved on by then.) After the fire, neighbors had a "working bee" cleanup and saved scorched trees for building lumber. Men in the valley built a new house for the family by spring.

Gordon's piano was saved from the fire and ended up in Preston Townsley's upstairs apartment at the Townsley Farm. Preston's daughter Shirley took lessons with it.

As for Jean, she outlived both of her parents. After her mother, May, died, Jean and her father moved to Mohawk Manor, a rest home on Water Street in Shelburne Falls. When Charlie died, Jean soon became a resident of Anchorage Nursing Home overlooking the Mohawk Trail between Shelburne Falls and Greenfield. She died in 1993 at the age of sixty-three and is buried near her folks in the Buckland Cemetery.

### Caught in a Cold Rain

Malcolm joined Pauline and me on some of our horseback rides that summer of '44 as did his best friend, Ralph Townsley. One chilly afternoon, the day we met Malcolm's mother, Ruth, for the first time, the four of us got caught in a hellacious rainstorm.

Ralph galloped on home along the valley road while Pauline, Malcolm and I thundered up into the Clark's dooryard, put our horses up, then went dripping and sloshing into the house, up the back stairs, and into the warm kitchen.

Ruth Clark and her sons lived in the second-floor apartment of the old three-story farmhouse. Grandma Clark lived downstairs.

Malcolm handed us a couple of his big plaid wool shirts to change into, and his mother hung up our wet things to dry on a rack in front of their wood-burning cookstove.

Pauline was mortified because she'd just had a perm, and her sopping wet curls smelled awful, but we giggled and pranced about in these shirts that came down to our knees. Malcolm told us later that he was shocked by our behavior, and I'm sure this first encounter with "the Jones girls" she'd been hearing about was distressing for his mother.

Malcolm came up to our place one night in August to ask Daddy for Pauline's hand in marriage and to lay before him his prospects as a future son-in-law. Daddy ushered him up the front stairs to his study and closed the door. Pauline, my best friend, Anne, and I stood outside on the ground under that upstairs window, straining our ears, but caught only a muted rumbling of voices.

Daddy, who considered Malcolm a diamond in the rough, gave his consent; and Malcolm emerged from his ordeal after about forty minutes with an elated look on his expressive face.

## My "Other Brother"

I had became so fond of Malcolm that when Pauline agonized earlier in the summer about whether to marry him, I stamped my foot and exclaimed, "If you don't marry him, I will!"

As time went by, I came to think of Malcolm as "my other brother," and the Clark farm in Apple Valley drew me like a magnet. It became my home place to return to after Daddy died in 1965, and Mom moved to an apartment in Northampton.

Pauline and Malcolm's wedding took place on September 1 at the Congregational Church in Ashfield, just two weeks before her twentieth birthday. The newlyweds took two horses and a foal with them on their honeymoon in Vermont. They left Malcolm's mare, Ginger, with me.

Most of Ashfield's able-bodied town boys, along with Harold and Bob Pichette, had been drafted by then. But most farm boys, including Malcolm, received deferments. Malcolm's brother, Richard, joined the merchant marines for a few years but was now home again on this third-generation farm.

After the honeymoon, my sister was soon embroiled in learning how to cope with her mother-in-law's expectations.

Ruth and her own mother-in-law had become widows in quick succession, leaving them with Ruth's three children—Malcolm, eleven; Richard, thirteen; and Barbara, sixteen. It was Ruth's hard work, frugality, and perseverance that had enabled the family to survive and hang on to the farm despite failing apple crops two years in a row and other catastrophes.

She worked as a census taker one year; and among other things, she took in washing, ours included. Malcolm remembered delivering the clean, ironed clothes to our place every few weeks before Pauline and I were old enough to be entrusted with laundry chores.

Now Ruth set about teaching Malcolm's young wife her duties, the same way Grandma Clark had once taken her in hand: laundry on Mondays, pie baking on Tuesdays, etc.

Pauline—who was nonconfrontational, a good cook, and hard worker—was nevertheless unwilling to slip into the role prescribed for her. When Malcolm asked her to accompany him somewhere, which was often, she dropped everything; and off they went—to butcher a neighbor's hog, trim a horse's hooves, make a run to the feed store in Shelburne Falls, deliver a calf Malcolm had sold to its new owner . . . whatever.

With our own mother's considerable behind-the-scenes help, Pauline was able to work things out amicably with Ruth and achieved a large degree of independence. This was the life Pauline had always wanted. A few years earlier, she had declared, "I'm going to marry a rancher or a farmer and never have to go back to the city again!"

## An Accident in the Orchard

While she and Malcolm were on their honeymoon, I had an accident on Ginger up in Hawley on a glorious September morning. I was cantering her through the Don Howes Orchard, ducking under tree limbs as I went. Miscalculating, I was whacked on the left side of my head by one stout limb.

Knocked unconscious for I know not how long, I came to, stretched my length in the grass under the tree, with Ginger tugging on my shirt. Blood dribbled down from my aching head, and the pain in my neck was fierce.

I would have expected this strong-willed, spirited Thoroughbred to toss her head and gallop off. But she stayed with me. Nickering softly, she kept nudging me until I staggered to my feet. She stood like a statue while I mounted her, then carried me gently about seven miles home. She refrained from her usual leaping about and shying as we went over a "scary" bridge in the upper valley.

Although in a great deal of pain for about a week, I never fessed up to my parents about my accident. Phillips was on hand to unsaddle Ginger that afternoon and help me take care of her for the next week. I told him I'd fallen down the steps to the hayloft.

"Don't tell Mom and Dad," I said and swore him to secrecy.

That very evening, Daddy had a treat in store for us. He took us all to Shelburne Falls for supper and to see *Scudda Hoo! Scudda Hey!*, a movie about two mules. For me, the whole outing proved a painful nightmare, and those mules were mostly a blur!

Fortunately, my neck injury gradually improved and didn't cramp my style too much when I departed for another rendezvous with Art later that month.

# 9

# A Week in Malden

*When Art's furlough came through in September 1944, he invited me down to Malden, near Boston, to meet his family and friends. The following account is excerpted from a long letter I wrote to Anne Smith.*

Dear Anne: I just got back from Malden Saturday night. Art met my Friday afternoon train [a week earlier] and kissed me in front of the army, navy and two conductors . . . He took me home, introduced me to his parents, and we tore off in two cars with three other couples to the Sheraton Hotel for dinner and went to the Totem Pole afterwards. I wore my blue two-piece dress and the three-inch heels Plink gave me . . . My, he's tall. My, he's goodlooking. My, I love him.

The Totem Pole was wonderful. Art and I danced mostly on their small dance floor behind the seats and we jitterbugged all the fast ones . . . I kept looking in the mirrors along the side of the dance floor to be sure I wasn't dreaming . . .

Sad to say, his friend Hollis brought along a bottle of whisky and everyone had some but Art and me. The nicest part was when we got home and sat on the couch in the living room, and talked mostly, until Art lost his patience . . .

Every day was beautiful, sunny and windy. And every minute of every day I loved him more. Malden is a beautiful place. It really is, and their neighborhood is especially nice . . .

Art's room was on the first floor and mine was on the second floor just above his. Almost every morning I went in and woke him up. He was so cute when he was asleep, and he snored. His hair had grown out and I think it's as nice as Malcolm's, and it's curly. It really is curly. My goodness it's nice. And his beard in the morning—Ouch!

He wore an old plaid shirt and flannel trousers most of the time . . . and it made me almost forget about the war . . .

He's so cute with his sisters. Two of them aren't married and live at home. Betty is 24 and is beautiful . . . she looks a lot like Art. She's crazy about music and knows more about it than anyone I know. Art says she's broken about 15 hearts, but is still waiting. Bunny is 27 and very tall, with reddish-brown hair and freckles. She's cute. She's in love with Windy, a handsome young Lieutenant in the Air Corps . . . I'm crazy about both of his sisters . . .

His parents are wonderful. His mom says "slick" and "gee" and swell" all the time and has a way of making people feel at home right away. His father's very intelligent and knows even more than Daddy does about current events. He listens to "The Lone Ranger" and Inner Sanctum" and a dozen others without fail, and it's awfully funny. Everyone kids him about it. He cans grape juice, mixes "butter" for Mrs. Smith and helps with the dishes and gets a kick out of it. He has a cute sense of humor and is just plain lovable. When I left, he put his arm around me, kissed me on the cheek, and said, "I hate to see you go, Julie. You're like one of the family." I thought I would bawl . . .

All day Sunday we were on the Charles River in Hollis's cabin cruiser, pulling a motor boat along behind . . . Hollis is in the Merchant Marines and is one of Art's best pals. He supplied the car all week and Art supplied the gas. The three of us went practically everywhere together. They all call him "the Admiral" and when he gets going we're all in hysterics. He's 23 and had a girl named Barbara up for the weekend.

At noon we anchored and two other boats jammed with people joined us! The whole escapade was in honor of Art and me. Again, drinks were mixed and I was amazed. Art and I didn't have any, of course, but everyone else did. I don't like that.

While Holly, Barbara, Art and I went for a jaunt in the motor boat, the rest of the gang piled ashore, started a fire and got dinner.

They waited on us hand and foot. I got to feeling rambunctious and almost drove Art crazy. Finally he jumped up and came after me with blood in his eye. I screamed bloody murder and ran for my life. All those people watching, and I'll be darned if he didn't chase me until he caught me, sling me over his shoulder like a sack of grain, carry me back and dump me on the ground. There was applause. Art sat down, ate another hot dog, two pieces of cake and a piece of apple pie. And I didn't let out another peep.

Lots of his pals were home on furlough and kept dropping in. In fact, people were always dropping in—I think the Smith house is practically home to about 250 people. Part of the time there were so many people between me and Art that I thought I'd go crazy. So every once in a while I would quietly disappear and end up in Art's room. Soon he'd show up . . . Well, pretty soon we'd join the rest again, feeling refreshed.

He is the sweetest, gentlest, dearest lug in the world . . . Then Tuesday night I got cramps when I was with Art. All of a sudden. They're the worst I've ever had. I cried and cried . . . Wednesday and Thursday I lost every meal I ate . . . Art was so sweet to me, so thoughtful . . .

Art left Friday afternoon and I stayed til Saturday noon . . . I started to cry at the station when Art left, then managed to stop. Then after supper that night I met his mother in the hallway, she put her arms around me and we cried and cried. Then I went into Art's room and lay down on his bed and started off again. Mrs. Smith came in to console me, and she started again. Bunny came in to console us. Then Mr. Smith arrived and said, "What is this, anyway: A Quaker meeting?" That cured us . . .

Oh, Anne, Art came up to my room Friday morning and woke me up by kissing me. I had my hair up [my homemade curlers were strips of white cloth], all except the top knot, and I was so mad I

thought I'd die. He just laughed and said I looked cute. Oh. well, he
had to find out sometime, I 'spose . . .

I guess he'll go overseas pretty quick. I'm scared . . .

Love, Julie

*    *    *

This letter resurfaced after sixty-two years of being tucked away
and forgotten. It brought that whole week with Art rushing back
to me. One of the pieces we danced to that night at the Totem Pole
became our special song:

> Long ago and far away I had a dream one day, and
> now that dream is here beside me. Long the skies were
> overcast, but now, you're here at last. You're here at last.
> Chills run up and down my spine, Aladdin's lamp is
> mine . . .

Reminiscing, I am eighteen again, head over heels in love with
this dear young man who loved me fiercely. I am suddenly full
of sadness and regret at the way I ended our romance about eight
months later. A wonderful big whole second family was waiting for
me there in Malden. If I had married Art when he returned from the
war, I might have had a happier, far-easier life. Why had I felt so
impelled to give him up?

# 10

# BACK TO PENN STATE

## *Adventures with Phil and Johnny*

Now a sophomore, I moved into a big two-story dorm on campus. Dottie Tillet, the flighty girl I had reluctantly agreed to room with, got married and didn't return to college. The stranger I was paired with turned out to be a lesbian. She had no friends of her own, so she hung out with me and mine. But she was easy to live with, and things were okay. We looked after her.

Our dorm did not have its own dining room. So we ate in the big separate campus dining hall nearby where we flirted with the football players when they congregated at special tables to be served much heartier fare and bigger helpings than the rest of us.

I took a full and eclectic load of subjects that included Greek history, rural sociology, French, animal husbandry, creative writing, typing, trigonometry, and more. Trigonometry was a mystery to me although I labored at it valiantly. If it hadn't been for my distressed teacher, on the verge of retirement, I'd not have made it through.

He tutored me after class, then sat beside me and coaxed me through the final exam after the rest of the students had handed in their blue books and left. I'll never forget that dear man.

To earn spending money, I hired out as a babysitter in the evenings, doing lots of my studying after the kids were in bed. I started out earning twenty-five cents an hour, but when the parents discovered I just naturally did their dishes too, they often raised me to thirty-five or forty cents.

When I accumulated enough to buy some clothes, they were almost always blue and on sale, for I had little sense of style. My underwear became raggedy; my bra straps were held on with safety pins.

That fall, both Phil Jones, now a marine lieutenant, and Johnny Turney, an air force pilot, traveled to Penn State on furlough to see me before being shipped overseas. My adventures with both of them are deeply etched in my memory!

## Phil's Short Weekend Pass

Phil was stationed in or just outside Harrisburg and came on a weekend pass. But transportation was such that he didn't get to State College via train and bus until after curfew Saturday night. I was in our dorm lounge to greet him first thing in the morning when the doors were unlocked. But we had very little time together because he needed to catch a bus back late that same morning!

Walking down to the Corner Room bus station with him, I had a great idea. "Why don't I just go with you? We can be together on the bus and then on the train, and I'll hightail it back again before curfew."

"Really?" He asked. "Really?" and paid for my two round-trip tickets. The bus journey over the mountains to Lewistown was wonderful. We watched the scenery and talked and talked, then rattled happily along on the train to Harrisburg. Once there, we had time to go out for lunch before I caught my train back.

After the waitress brought the check, Phil looked through his billfold and then, his face flushing red, asked me if I had any money. I gave him all I had. Put with his, it added up to enough to pay for the meal, plus a small tip.

We'd had such a good time. But I was never to see him again. We wrote often to each other; then he disappeared into the maw of the war in the Pacific where the marines took heavy casualties. I never knew what happened to him.

On the train heading back to Penn State that afternoon, I was so tired, I slept right through my station! The conductor wrote me a pass to return to Lewistown, and I waited, chilled and weary for the next train. Arriving finally at the almost-deserted, freezing-cold station in the middle of the night, I was exhausted and miserable.

A woman who had just seen a friend off noted my plight, and I told her what had happened. She took me home with her, fixed me a midnight snack, put me up for the night in her cozy house, fed me breakfast the next morning, and took me to catch my bus.

She had been so good to me. When I said thank you and goodbye to her at the station, I was too embarrassed to admit that somehow, I had lost my return bus ticket and had no money! When the bus driver came down the aisle to collect tickets, I told him my sad story and said I'd pay him as soon as I could borrow some money from my roommate back on campus.

"Don't worry about it," he said gruffly and passed on by. (Let me see, now . . . Was it Blanche in *A Streetcar Named Desire* who said she had always relied on the kindness of strangers?)

Back at my dorm on campus, I found that my friends had kept quiet about my overnight absence. I'd never been missed by the powers that be. When I appeared at the bus station later that day with the money I owed the bus driver, he wouldn't take it. "I've already turned in my tickets for that run," he explained.

### Snowbound with Johnny

When Johnny earned his wings that winter, he mailed them to me with a note saying he'd be down to see me on furlough in a few weeks. He drove his car from Philadelphia, arriving on a snowy, windy Friday.

We drove far out into the country that afternoon and parked in a farmer's field at the end of a long dirt road. We talked and talked, oblivious to the snow piling up around us. It grew dark; we were suddenly hungry, and Johnny revved up the motor. He flicked the headlights on and hit the gas pedal, only to discover that we were stuck tight in the drifting snow.

Abandoning our car, we struggled hand in hand toward the farmhouse where the porch light had just come on. We laughed and called out to each other through the wind and snow. "I bet they've been watching us!" Johnny said. And I yelled back at him, "I hope dinner's ready—I'm starving!"

The farmer and his wife, an older couple, opened the door as we came up on the porch; and they greeted us warmly. They spread our shoes and socks to dry out over a heat register, then fed us a big delicious dinner.

We sat around talking afterward, and they wanted to know all about Johnny's air force experience. He told them how he'd wanted to learn to fly ever since he was a little boy, and I showed them the wings he'd just earned. I told them about my family back home, about my love for horses, and about my ambition to be a writer.

I also called my dorm to explain what had happened. Then I handed the phone to the farmer, who said that he and his wife would look after us, that he couldn't extricate our car or get the road plowed before morning. They put us up for the night; and at first light, he towed Johnny's car in from the field with his tractor, then plowed the long farm lane out to the main road. After a big breakfast of sausage and eggs, coffee, and hot buttered biscuits with jam, they sent us on our way.

What fun it had all been. Johnny grinned like a Cheshire cat all the way back to campus. I hugged him when we said goodbye late Sunday afternoon. I felt the tears growing cold on my cheeks as I waved his car out of sight and asked the universe to keep him safe from harm.

### The Coal Miner's Son

This was also the year I met Jim Matthews in the dining hall and started dating him. From Grindstone, Pennsylvania, he was the son of a coal miner, the oldest of nine children, and was attending Penn State on a football scholarship. He was the first person in his extended family ever to go to college.

I'd never met anyone who spoke such atrocious English! Laughing about it, he told me, "My English teacher didn't speak good English." But he was eager to learn. So I started coaching him, especially on the past tenses of verbs—"knew" instead of "knowed," "threw" instead of "throwed," etc. He was a quick learner and years later became the principal of a big high school, having worked his way up from his entry job as football coach.

## Shocking News

I remember that balmy April day in 1945 when the bell at Old Main kept pealing and I leaned out my second-floor dorm window to find out why. Someone shouted up to me, "President Roosevelt is dead!"

The word spread quickly around campus as we called out the news to one another. A few months into his fourth term of office, it seemed he had *always* been president, and I was terribly shocked and sad. With the war still raging in Europe and the Pacific, what would happen to our country without him?

Robin, left, was tail gunner on a bomber. Johnny Turney earned his pilot's wings in 1944.

# 11

# STOPPING BY THE POST OFFICE, 1945

Although I kept writing to Pierre, I did not hear from him again after that letter in May of my freshman year at Penn State. I knew that the Allied forces under Dwight Eisenhower had invaded Normandy on the northern coast of France in June of 1944, starting the liberation of France from the Germans.

French and American troops triumphantly entered Paris on the twenty-fifth of August, and General Charles de Gaulle was installed as the premier of France the following day. Where was Pierre all this time? Why hadn't I heard from him?

I tried to convince myself that he was all right. Not until March of 1945 during my spring vacation from college did I finally have news of him. I was staying with Pauline and Malcolm in Apple Valley. One of my first days there, I stopped by the Ashfield Post Office to buy some picture postcards.

Lydia Pichette, Harold and Bob's mother, worked for the post office then. I told her I hadn't had a letter from Pierre for a long, long time.

"Why, Julia," she said, "Pierre is dead! He was killed in the war."

I stumbled down the post office steps, sick with shock and disbelief. The rest of my vacation was a nightmare. I was too numb and sick at heart to seek further information. I didn't even ask Mrs. Pichette about her sons!

Back at college the following week, I received an airmail letter from France, written by one of Pierre's superior officers. He had taken note of my undelivered letters to Pierre and had finally written, in French, to tell me of his death.

I could understand it well enough to learn that his men loved him and would follow him anywhere and that he was very courageous. On his last mission, he and his paratroop unit had been dropped to assist a group of French soldiers in breaking through the German division that surrounded them. He was killed on September 15, 1944, covering the retreat of his men.

When I asked my *formidable* French teacher to read the letter to me, he translated it word for word, glancing at me with compassion. I remember sitting there in his office, listening intently and unable to hold back the tears.

I made a copy of the letter and mailed it to Pierre's mother in New York City. She sent me a note of thanks, along with a close-up picture of Pierre, wearing his billed officer's hat. She enclosed an invitation to his memorial service in Manhattan on March 27, 1945, at the Unitarian Church of All Souls.

I wrote to Phillips Academy, requesting a copy of Pierre's graduation picture, the one I had seen and liked in his yearbook. I did so yearn for a good picture. The one his mother had sent me did not look like the rough-and-tumble boy I remembered. The school wrote back that they needed the written permission of a member of Pierre's family before they could comply with my request. But I didn't really know his family.

Remembering how much Norm Walker had thought of Pierre, I sent him a letter of sympathy. He wrote back, scoffing at the possibility that Pierre and I had grown so close.

But to this day, I believe Pierre did love the feisty, yearning teenage girl with whom he spent so many hours before embarking on his "great adventure."

Years later, I would come into possession of three letters I had written to him. They were on him when he died, perhaps the only ones he received after his last letter to me in May of 1944.

**My Visit to Pierre's Family**

One day, about six months after that wrenching news at the Ashfield Post Office, I summoned my courage and rode down to the Cournands' place.

Back then, Bird Hill Road began at Williamsburg Road—near the settlement of South Ashfield with its own combination post office and general store—and looped on over a few miles to catch Williamsburg Road again.

Pauline and I had often cantered along that narrow sparsely settled dirt road with trees on both sides. We started at the beginning, cantered up the hill and past the old Camp Ashfield for boys, completed the loop to Williamsburg Road, then turned around and rode back, branching off onto that short stretch of dirt road to the Thorp Place ("Lost Farm"). There, we picked up the wood road that cut on over to Briar Hill Road, turned off that onto Steady Lane, and completed the circle back into the village of Ashfield.

It was late afternoon when I visited Pierre's family. I had not been there since the time Pauline and I rode down on Pierre's last day home, and he took us up to his cabin.

I introduced myself to his parents, "I'm Julia Jones . . . Pierre was my friend." They were very kind to me and invited me to stay for supper.

I'm sure they recognized the girl who had once come riding onto their place and disappeared into the forest with their son, the girl who had sent them a copy of her letter from France.

We ate by the light of a kerosene lamp. Pierre's sisters were there, very quiet and looking at me with big eyes. I was uncomfortable, reticent, and on the edge of tears. I said very little when I had wanted to tell them so much and ask so many questions. I had especially wanted to ask them for a letter to Phillips Academy, giving permission for them to send me Pierre's graduation photo.

Mrs. Cournand was a small sad dark-haired woman. Dr. Cournand was distinguished looking, strong, and gentle. When it was time for me to leave, it had grown very dark outside. He escorted me and my horse out to the road by the light of his kerosene lantern.

"How will you find your way home?" he asked with great concern. And I said, "Oh, the horse knows the way!" I was riding Judy, Malcolm's skillful gymkhana mare. Somehow, she maneuvered the pitch-black night on Bird Hill Road, then on down to the highway, and carried me safely back up the mountain along the shoulder of the highway, and at last through a dark stretch of wood road and orchard to home.

On another evening many years later, I would sit at that same table in that same house with Pierre's youngest sister, Claire, who had become my close friend. By the light of a kerosene lamp and fortified by a bottle of wine, I would read her the diary of my time with Pierre. Only two years old when he left for war, she had never known her brother.

This was to be the first time in all those years that I shared my diary with anyone. It was in September 2003.

# 12

# ROLL OF HONOR

*The following is excerpted from a circa 1944-45 Honor Roll published by Phillips Academy, Andover, Massachusetts, honoring former students and alumni killed in World War 11.*

*Aspirant* **Pierre B. R. Cournand, '43**

Pierre Birel Rosset-Cournand, '43, son of Dr. and Mrs. Andre Cournand of New York City, was at Phillips a member of the Glee Club, the swimming team, Philo, the 8-in-1 Octet, and F.L.D. He was admitted to Harvard, but out of a desire to help the country of his birth chose to join the French Army. He received officers' training at Fort Benning, Ga., where he was made an *aspirant* in November 1943. He then volunteered to become a commando parachutist, and in Brittany shortly after D-Day he accomplished two important missions, in which he was wounded. After leave in England for convalescence he returned to France. In the Belfort Gap area he performed his last mission, in which paratroopers were dropped to a group of French soldiers to help them break through the German panzer division surrounding them. He was killed on September 15, 1944.

He was the recipient of many citations for his leadership and fearlessness. His parents have received his recommendations for the Crois de Guerre, the award of the Legion d'Honneur, the Crois de la Liberation, and the British Military Cross.

# 13

# A LIFE WITHOUT PIERRE

*I dreamed about Pierre for years. Always a variation of the same dream: I heard that he had not been killed after all and that he had come back. I searched for him at his cabin, in the woods, and on the dirt roads around South Ashfield. But I couldn't find him. Nor could I understand why he had not come looking for me up in the village.*

Back at college in the spring of 1945, I knew I must go on with my life . . . a life without Pierre. A life, rather, without the possibility of his return. Without the possibility of that trip around the world together, the possibility of a deeper, more honest connection.

He would go to Harvard. I would finish up at Penn State, perhaps go on to graduate school. We would have our summers together at Ashfield. I would get to know his family . . .

It might have been a whole new life. But since it was not to be, I had to accept this first staggering loss of someone dear to me. I had to adjust to a world that could be cruel as well as sweet, full of tragedy and uncertainty.

I had to rid myself of romantic illusions and prepare for an independent, self-sufficient life. I had to grow up! I had to know I could support myself and do it before getting married or committing to a love relationship. And I would only settle for a man with those qualities I treasured in Pierre.

Over the next five years, I would need to keep telling myself, "I can do this!" for I was still achingly young, and I was coming into my own sexually.

I wrote to Art, who was now overseas. I told him about Pierre and about my new resolve to become strong and independent. I told him I had a lot of growing up to do before marrying him or anyone else and that he needed to forget me.

He wrote back, sympathizing with me about Pierre but ardently protesting my decision. He kept writing, sent me a lovely carved jewelry box from India that I still have, and finally gave up.

After the war, he took a job working for an oil company. He came to Ashfield several times with Al, looking for me, but I was gone from home then. In a final letter, he wrote that he had started dating his friend Holly's sister, whom he had known all his life.

In the years to follow, Pierre became for me the pattern of a man against whom I measured all others. Time and again, the young men I cared about, even loved, fell short of the mark I'd set . . . all but one, the man I married eight long years after that rainy night I first connected with Pierre at D.O. Williams's party on Snake Rock Farm.

# 14

## SUMMER'S END

### *Phillips Rebels*

Summer's end, 1945, was also a critical time in my brother's life.

My parents were waiting up for me when I arrived home very late the night before our departure for Brooklyn, from which I would leave in a few weeks later for my junior year at Penn State.

I had attended the Saturday night square dance that evening with Merton Batchelder. Afterward, we'd ended up at his farm in South Ashfield where we proceeded to eat ice cream from his big chest freezer. He wolfed down a whole quart! And I thought, *He's going to be a very big man someday!* A tall robust blond, ruddy-faced fellow, he was in his midtwenties, perhaps older.

When he pulled around to the house on our circular driveway, I noticed that the living room light was on. I said good night quickly and started to open my car door. But I found it inoperative. On purpose, I believed.

"Merton, you need to get out of the car and open this stuck door for me," I said, then added, laughing, "like a true gentleman."

He sat silent for a few minutes, looking straight out the windshield, then sighed heavily, got out, and opened the door for me.

I hurried in the front door and into the living room where my parents told me Phillips had announced that he couldn't go back to the city.

"Please go up and reason with him," Daddy said.

Climbing the stairs to his room in the old servants' quarters, I found Phillips still awake. "I can't go back. I can't go back," he told me in anguish.

"He can't go back!" I reported to my parents.

The next morning, Daddy was missing from the breakfast table. Phillips and I couldn't eat, and Mother was visibly upset as we awaited Daddy's return. Pretty soon, he drove up and stomped purposefully into the breakfast room.

"It's all arranged," he announced. "Phillips is going to live with Pauline and Malcolm in Apple Valley. So get your things together, m'boy, and I'll take you down there!"

"Really?" Phillips said, stunned. "Really?"

It was September 1945. Malcolm and Pauline had been married for a year, living in the second-floor apartment of the old farmhouse. To make room for the newlyweds, Malcolm's mother, Ruth, had moved downstairs to share living quarters with Grandma Clark.

Richard's bedroom was on the third floor, and Phillips's room was at the bottom of the stairs on the second floor. Richard passed by it every morning.

At home, Phillips had always been a late starter. We'd have to keep waking him up, at least two or three times. But at the Clark farm, he staggered out of bed every day before the crack of dawn. Roused by Richard's one loud knock on his door, he was out doing chores before breakfast. And blissfully happy with his new life.

In the summers, he came back to the Place and worked on nearby farms. He would graduate from Sanderson Academy up in the village in 1947 and marry his high school sweetheart, Ereda Lilly, five years later.

As for Merton, the next time I saw him was years later when Pauline, Malcolm, and I had dinner at the successful little restaurant he had opened in Conway. Delighted to see us, he came to our table, visited with us, told us our dinners were on the house. The food was delicious, the helpings generous.

By then, he had been married for many years to Eleanor, whom I remembered as a thin dark-haired, dark-eyed, work-worn farmwife. She loved to dance, bringing her three or four energetic little boys with her every week to the Saturday night square dances. She and her husband had a small dairy farm next to the main highway in South Ashfield. By and by, she divorced him, a scandalous thing to do back then, and married Merton. And yes, Merton did become a *big* man.

# 15

# MY LAST TWO YEARS OF COLLEGE

My friend Anne Smith had already started her term at Hood College in Maryland that fall of 1945 and was dating naval cadets at nearby Annapolis. Before I left for Penn State, her folks took me with them to visit her. We had reservations at a hotel that Friday night, and as we checked in, Uncle Dudley said, "Julia, your Penn State football team is staying here and playing Navy tomorrow!"

Delighted, I left a message for Jim Matthews at the front desk before going up to my room. After waiting in vain, I gave up and crawled in bed. Soon, there was a knock on the door and Jim's voice saying, "Jay, wake up and let me in!"

I jumped out of bed, opened the door, and he gave me a bear hug. It was so wonderful to suddenly be with him again. I told him about my summer and about Phillips, and then he was gone. Team members had a strict curfew.

Anne and I tuned into the game the next day long enough to hear that Jim was injured in a pileup and carried from the field! Back at Penn State a week or two later, he told me he was hospitalized for twenty-four hours but was basically okay. "Those Navy guys play dirty," he said, laughing. "They had it in for me that day!"

\*   \*   \*

I became a far more serious student those last two years of college. I signed up for a wide assortment of classes: short story writing, more animal husbandry courses, botany, archeology, anthropology, English literature, the economics of labor, and shorthand. And ah yes, physics, which almost did me in.

Out tight little Purity Corner Gang dissolved when the other members started a Tri-Delta sorority on campus, and I wasn't interested. But we were still friends, and after graduation, we kept a round-robin letter going for several years. Alas, someone broke the chain, and we lost touch.

When I finally reconnected with Carolyn some years later and we made plans to get together, it was too late. She was married and had two children, but before I had a chance to visit her, a sad letter from her mother informed me that Carolyn had died of cancer.

## My Roommates

My junior year roommate was Helen Drennan—serious student, serious golfer, and still in love with Bill, her high school sweetheart. We grew fond of each other, and she was a good influence on me with her neat and organized ways. I made a huge effort and succeeded, keeping my usual chaos under control.

I went golfing with Helen a few times, but I was an inept student. Try as I might, I was never able to hit that elusive little white ball but enjoyed walking around the course with her.

Helen graduated a year ahead of me, went back home, and married Bill. My next roommate was Pam Whitfield, a darling girl with big brown eyes and curly brown hair. She was petite, artistic, impetuous . . . and messy! When she went out on a date, she tried on piles of clothes before deciding what to wear, then departed in a whirlwind without putting anything away. I loved her dearly.

After graduation, pursuing a career in art, she met by chance on the streets of New York City a red-haired sailor she had dated her freshman year. He was stationed at the Brooklyn Navy Yard. She and Red married within months. When I visited them about four years later in Chicago, they had a little redheaded boy that looked like him and a tiny curly-haired girl that looked just like Pam.

## Typist and Soda Jerk

Daddy paid my tuition and dorm expenses, and the rest was up to me. To earn spending money, I babysat and had a part-time job on campus typing letters for Dr. Cannon, who had a small instrument company in addition to his teaching position. He paid me $1 per hour (big bucks then!). Plus several nights a week, I was a soda jerk and sandwich maker at a drugstore in town.

Also, I bartered my services at the local riding stable: in return for trying out and assessing the new horses and taking others to be shod, I could ride the horse of my choice whenever I pleased. What a deal! My favorite was a lively little strawberry roan named Dixie. About twice a week, I rode her out across the farmland of Nittany Valley.

All this left little time for anything but attending classes and keeping up with my homework assignments. But a girl has to have *some* social life!

## Jim and Bill

About one night a week my junior year, I went out with Jim. We attended campus dances. I loved both the jitterbugging and the slow numbers where Jim held me tight. Or we just took a long walk on campus and up through Nittany Woods and bought ice cream cones at the dairy store. Or we went to a movie. Sometimes we met at the library to study together, after which he would walk me the long way home to Atherton Hall.

One weekend, I took him out to meet Eddie and Champ Nichols. "We really liked Jim," Dr. Nichols told me later. "But if you marry him, what will you two talk about for the rest of your lives?"

My last year at Penn State, Jim was in the army, worked with mental patients at an army hospital outside Philadelphia, and came to see me whenever he could get a weekend pass. He kept asking, "Are you ever going to marry me, Jay?" And I would say, "I don't know, I just don't know!" I did love him, but . . .

I met tall lanky navy veteran Bill Ireland, "Irish," in archaeology class the first semester of my senior year. He and his best buddy and I formed a team to survey and examine a one-acre piece of land outside State College. It was both hard work and great fun out in the sun, and we all got an A on the joint term paper we handed in.

These two fellows taught me more about archaeology than the professor did! I was the only girl in the class.

Soon, I was dating Bill, who started getting serious. During spring break, he took me home to Bradford, Pennsylvania, to meet his folks. His mother disliked me intensely, which was very upsetting! But I didn't much care for her either.

I still have an eight-by-ten picture of Bill and me at the Beaux Arts Ball that spring. We had such a great time! He was a tall rough-and-tough sailor with a mustache and a long knife in his belt. And I was a geisha girl with slanted eyes and dressed in a beautiful kimono Daddy had given me.

## The Livestock Expo

That spring semester, I took an ag course in showmanship—once again, the only girl in the class. At the big livestock expo at the end of the semester, I showed a draft mare and won second place. I'm sure I would have taken first place if the jerk who won first place hadn't cheated. We were instructed not to bathe our horses because of the very cold weather, but this dude not only hosed down his mare but checked out of the campus library all the books on showmanship. The rest of us were disgusted with him.

It's a shame the judges couldn't have graded us on the way we returned our entries down that long steep road to the barn afterward on that bitter-cold windy day. Mine was the only horse that didn't break away and gallop free. As the other horses thundered past us, I kept a death grip on the lead shank, pulled my mare's neck around, and kept her moving in a tight circle around me as we sashayed home. This was *not* easy, but I was determined!

I also took riding lessons for the first time. A seasoned no-nonsense horseman from Germany was our instructor. He made fun of the way I rode and helped me correct my bad form. In one exercise toward the end of the course, he had us ride without stirrups and play tag. I was in my element! None of the other students could catch me, and when the instructor tried, he couldn't either. Finally, he had an appreciation for me as a tough, self-taught seat-of-the-pants rider! (And I was so sore for the next few days that I could hardly walk.)

## A Memorable Graduation

Having missed my high school graduation ceremony (not willing to wait around for a week after school let out, I'd gone on to Ashfield), I was looking forward to this one. It was indeed memorable! Our caps and gowns never arrived. So at the last minute, we had to go through the clothes we'd packed, find something that would do, iron it, put it on, and race for the auditorium. Arriving sweaty and winded, the class of 1947 was a motley, disheveled crew.

Mom and Dad had arrived by car the day before to meet my friends and help me pack. For graduation, they gave me a big suitcase, which came in handy. (Anne's folks gave her a car for graduation!) Then we headed for Brooklyn and on to Ashfield a day or two later.

After an idyllic week of loafing and going horseback riding with Pauline on dirt roads and old logging trails, I started looking for a job.

# 16

## PHILADELPHIA INTERLUDE
## AND SAGAMORE SUMMER

Coming home from my junior year at Penn State, I took the train as far as Philadelphia so as to visit old friends Mary and Joe Gale, as well as Johnny Turney, now an air force veteran.

Joe had signed on with the New York Yankees after graduating from Penn State in '44. Fans for opposing teams loved yelling "Bird legs!" at him, for at six feet five, he was one long skinny piece of perpetual motion. He was a natural athlete but found he didn't care for the life of a pro baseball player. One year was enough!

He married Mary right after her graduation in '45 and used his Yankees' bonus toward law school at the University of Pennsylvania. They rented a one-room apartment in Philly, so restricted a space that when they pulled their Murphy bed down from the wall, there were only about twenty inches left between it and the couch I slept on. Very cozy, that night!

Next morning, I caught the trolley with Mary, and we walked the few blocks from the trolley to where she worked as a librarian at the Franklin Institute. Married life and her job suited her, she told me happily as we visited along the way in this bustling, noisy city.

Johnny picked me up there at the library. It was his birthday—his twenty-third, I think. He looked great in civvies, and his thick shock of blond hair had grown out long enough for me to muss up. He still had that lovely grin albeit his teeth were stained from nicotine.

We spent the day together, walking and talking, getting caught up on each other. I hadn't seen him since his furlough in the fall of 1944 when we got stuck in the snow in a farmer's field outside State College and had to spend the night. He was reluctant to tell me about any of his war experiences . . . didn't want to, so I didn't pry. He had sent me one picture of himself, up close and grinning, in the open cockpit of a small plane during training. But I don't know what kind of planes he flew in action or what he did. So we talked of other things.

I met his mom and dad for the first time that evening, and they welcomed me warmly. I stayed for his birthday dinner and overnight.

Late that evening, he walked me up the stairs to the second floor, put his arms tightly around me just outside his bedroom—mine for the night—and insisted on a lingering happy birthday kiss. I still remember it!

Next morning, he awakened me with a kiss on the cheek although I was just pretending to be asleep. After breakfast, he and his best friend drove me to my family's home in Brooklyn and stayed for the day.

**Sagamore Summer**

After a brief vacation in Ashfield, and with Daddy's blessing, I signed on as a waitress at Camp Sagamore, an informal summer resort in Pennsylvania. I was soon unpacking my bag in a rustic cabin deep in the Pocono Mountains. My first full-time job!

Each small cabin was outfitted with bunk beds, housed six girls or guys, with bathroom facilities nearby. There was an 11:00 p.m. curfew and a gruff, lovable night watchman who made the rounds with his flashlight. Lights off at 11:30 p.m., and the big camp bell on a post by the dining hall clanged us awake at 6:00 a.m.

Man, oh man, waitressing here was hard work!

I served three meals a day, collected the most tips ever recorded my first day on the job, and earned the camp name of Tips. We pooled all our tips, and nobody got rich that summer! I cleared only $50, but it was enough to buy a blue suit on sale and a fringed leather jacket that I wore for years.

Each waitress had charge of one long wooden table that seated twelve people. We stacked our heavy dinner plates and big serving bowls of food on both sides of a long wooden rack, hoisted the rack a few inches off the floor, and hotfooted it into the dining room to hand it all out to the guests from one end of the table.

First time I tried to lift that full rack, I couldn't budge it. So I had to unload it halfway and make two trips. After about a week, I could handle it fully loaded and keep up with the rest of the waitresses.

What a racket we all made after each meal as we ferociously shook the tableware clean in big metal dishpans full of boiling-hot soapy water!

In addition to waiting tables, I was a member of the kick chorus line in the evenings, worked part-time for Tex and Spurs (Joyce and Walt) at their riding concession, cleaned out stalls, taught the basics of riding to the guests, tacked up and groomed horses, and led the sunrise and moonlight rides when the weather and the moon cooperated.

Two afternoons a week, I worked in the bakeshop. Following the kick-chorus routine, I worked in the canteen for Beef and Stew on evenings I didn't lead a moonlight ride. Most days, I also went swimming.

I soon got to know Tom-Tom (Bill Renz), the drummer in the band, and settled into hanging out mostly with him for the rest of the summer. He too worked part-time at the riding stable, was seventeen, going into his senior year of high school in Plainfield, New Jersey.

On evenings off, we often teamed up with Walt and Joyce, who were in their late twenties. Tall and gauntly handsome, Walt was a wounded and psychologically scarred war veteran, moody and often irrational. They were having a hard time keeping their marriage together. They owned a good bunch of horses, my favorite being Buddy, a lively roman-nosed strawberry roan as homely as his name.

The sunrise ride was great fun. On our way back to the barn, we tied our horses outside a popular restaurant and bar where we were served a big country breakfast. (I was *always* hungry that summer.) Afterward, often with Joyce's or Walt's help, I unsaddled and put up the horses, then raced to my cabin to clean up, change clothes, and serve breakfast.

One night, Bill and I settled into the hayloft with Joyce to comfort her and keep her company. She was having some alarming difficulty with Walt and had vowed not to sleep with him that night. I awoke in the wee hours with a headache and stiff neck. Bill was asleep, his arms wrapped around me, and Joyce had deserted us.

"Bill, wake up!" This was embarrassing! We climbed down out of the hayloft and tried to sneak back to our cabins in the dark without being seen. Caught in the beam of the watchman's flashlight, we stopped in our tracks and explained our predicament to him. "You kids, I don't know how you do it!" he said and didn't report us.

When the bell clanged next morning, I burrowed back under the covers with a moan. But my cabinmates dragged me from my bunk, teased me about the hay caught in my long hair, gave me an aspirin, and gently bullied me into pulling myself together for the day's work.

Long on work and play, short on sleep, I was forever lamenting, "Why am I always so tired? I don't understand!" I gained twenty pounds that glorious summer, mostly muscle. A photo of me in the chorus line shows a very fit and sturdy girl!

One disastrous week, most of the camp came down with the runs. Some days, the dining hall was almost empty. Suddenly, a guest or one of us would get a wild expression on our face, clutch our stomach, and race across the dining hall and out the door.

A spirit of camaraderie prevailed among the guys and gals working there. "All for one and one for all" was the creed by which we lived. We had great bonfires and songfests, belting out "The Best Things in Life Are Free" and other favorites of the time.

Ah, memories . . . Johnny came to visit me at Sagamore, still my great friend who wanted to be my love. "Before I went away to war," he told me, "I thought you were perfect. When I came back, I discovered that you weren't, but you're still the best I've ever known!"

He planned to enroll at Swarthmore in the fall, and I would be heading back for my last year at Penn State.

# 17

## My Job at UMass

Finding a job after graduating from Penn State was easy. Right away, I landed a job as secretary for Dr. Arthur Musgrave, director of publications at the University of Massachusetts in Amherst, about forty miles from Ashfield.

For my interview with Dr. Musgrave, I wore a white dress, white high heels, and white gloves. When I had a flat tire on the way to Amherst, I removed my gloves, donned work gloves and a shirt Daddy had left in his car, and managed to change the tire without getting dirty.

After I finished and was oh so carefully putting my white gloves back on, a man stopped to help me. "You're too late, but thanks!" I said.

This job meant I could spend my weekends in Ashfield. Pauline and Malcolm were building their new house, down the mountain a ways from the old farmhouse, nearer the brook and with a great view of Apple Valley.

I filled a lot of nail holes with wood putty, did all sorts of odds and ends chores to help them. Pauline and I would work hard all morning on the house, then take off on the horses most afternoons for a long ride.

In Amherst, I rented a room on Lincoln Avenue with the Amos Averys, a Smith College faculty family with five children. Dr. Avery taught horticulture. He also repaired and collected clocks—wound up, displayed, ticking, and bonging the hour all day, all night, all over the house.

Every morning, I waited in line for the bathroom with the kids, walked to work and back in all kinds of weather—the campus was less than two miles away at the end of tree-shaded Lincoln Avenue. I often baked brownies or a fruit pie for dinner and helped wash dishes. I loved the Averys, their dog and cats included, and felt like part of the family.

I couldn't have been hired for my job without shorthand and typing, but I used my shorthand only once. Dr. Musgrave edited that letter so many times that I had to keep retyping it for him. Finally, I said, "Why don't you type your own letters? When you get it just the way you want it, I'll type the final copy for you."

So that's what he did, leaving me free to work on other things, such as redo his whole filing system and write news and feature articles. The college editor position was dormant that year, so I filled in as best I could.

I spent my summer weekends at the Place with my folks and in Apple Valley, catching a ride to UMass and back with Ashfield resident Walt Whitney, who worked at a bank in Amherst. That fall, Phillips was a freshman at UMass and now owned Daddy's 1931 Chrysler. So once classes started, I caught a ride to Apple Valley and back with him most weekends.

Industrious and in the money as usual, Phillips made apple cider from "drops" on those fall weekends at the farm, took gallon jugs of it back to his dorm on Monday mornings, and sold them to fellow students. He also picked up and delivered on campus for a laundry and dry cleaning service.

I had one romance at UMass after my boss introduced me to Warren Anderson, a curly-black-haired, ruggedly handsome, personable young man who was student body president and captain of the football team.

A great guy to spend time and go places with, Warren finally gave up on me when he found me unavailable for sexual intimacy. I had really liked him!

Jim came to see me in Amherst on furlough, met Phillips, then my parents in Ashfield, and Pauline and Malcolm in Apple Valley. I wasn't sure what they'd think of him, but Mom told me, "There's something awfully sweet about Jim!" Everybody warmed up to him, and he was pleased to experience Ashfield at last and get to know my family.

Over the next year at UMass, I saved $300, so my old friend Gordon and I started looking for a horse for me on the weekends. But I soon decided on another use for that money. I would go back to college and prepare for a career in magazine work.

By then, the college editor position had been put back in the budget and was offered to me with a good salary. I turned it down, saying, "Been there, done that!" or words to that effect, borrowed another $300 from Phillips to put with my own savings, and quit my job.

"Ms. Jones, I don't know what I'll do without you," Dr. Musgrave said. "I lie awake and think about that."

Next stop: summer school at Penn State. After that, I was enrolled for the fall semester at the University of Minnesota, which had a grand journalism school. The University of Missouri would also have been a good choice, but I had relatives in Minneapolis, and that affected my decision.

# 18

# MY POSTGRADUATE STUDIES

I don't recall what classes I signed up for at Penn State. My main purpose for going back was to make a decision about Jim Matthews. Out of the army now, he was also attending summer school there. After a few achingly sweet weeks together I set him free at last—one of the hardest things I have ever done. I loved him so much, and he had hung in there with me for so long . . . but I knew we were not right for each other.

Jim married beautiful dark-haired phys ed major Prim within a year, and they started a family. Upon graduation, he accepted a job coaching football and basketball at a high school in Easton, Pennsylvania, where he later taught math and history. He eventually became principal!

We kept in touch through Christmas cards. When my daughter Lisa, two of her small children, and I visited him years later in Easton on a return road trip from Ashfield, he and Prim were retired, still living in the house where they'd raised their children. They spent winters in Florida and played a lot of golf.

Jim and Prim and I reminisced about our college days, looked through one of their thick photo albums, and Lisa took a picture of Jim and me. We agreed that if we'd met on the street, we wouldn't have recognized each other.

**On the Way to Minnesota**

Soon after summer school, I hopped a train to Minneapolis and the University of Minnesota, with a stopover in Chicago en route.

My uncle Dave had offered me $100 to come help Isabel with Davey, their brand-new baby. So I rode the gritty El Train to the Oak Park station, then lugged my suitcase along endless blocks to Dave and Isabel's house. Dave and my little cousins—Liz, Ellen, and Sally—were delighted to see me, but Isabel was not!

This had been Dave's idea, not hers. She didn't want me near her darling little boy. Admiring him from a distance, I hung out with the girls, was as helpful as possible with housework and dishes, enjoyed my time with Dave, and departed with a crisp $100 bill tucked in my billfold. (I didn't keep my money in a bank in those days, just hid it in a drawer and paid cash for everything.)

As my train rattled westward, I contemplated the fact that Isabel didn't like me. This traced back to my unwitting theft of her husband on their honeymoon.

Uncle Dave married when I was about fifteen and brought his new bride to Ashfield. Eager to meet her, we were impressed by her smart haircut, stylish clothes, eye makeup, and rosy cheeks. Starting off on the right foot, I hugged her and said, "Oh, Isabel, you're so pretty!"

But then Dave proceeded to spend most of his daylight hours with me at our old pursuits—horseback riding, swimming, playing tennis and ping-pong. Isabel was relegated to mealtimes and the evening hours. She was hurt and outraged. Who could blame her for holding it against me?

**Finding a Job near Campus**

For those first few weeks in Minneapolis, I lived on the outskirts of the city with the family of Daddy's youngest brother, Joe. I dearly loved Uncle Joe and lovely slender, auburn-haired Aunt Leah. I remember our long talks and those mouthwatering cinnamon rolls she often baked for our breakfast. And I thoroughly enjoyed getting to know my young cousins Jimmy and Mike.

Joe was foreman at the Maico Hearing Aid plant in Minneapolis. Sometimes he strummed his old ukulele for us in the evenings and sang tunes like "Little Brown Jug" that I remembered him playing when he was eighteen or nineteen at Grandpa's farm in Missouri.

But I could not tarry. Classes started soon, and I needed to find a place near campus where I could earn my keep. I landed such a job with the Alfred Nier family, not too far from the St. Paul campus where Dr. Nier taught physics. In return for my room and board, I did housework and babysitting, occasionally baked a cake or pie. I quickly took a liking to their kids—two-year-old Keith and six-year-old Janet. In the winter, we built fat snowmen and had snowball fights. I pulled Keith on his sled and took Janet ice-skating.

Dr. Nier, brilliant and sweet natured, was one of the scientists who helped develop the atom bomb. Unbelievable! His wife had not gone beyond high school, and to me, they seemed a mismatched couple.

Annoyed with me, Mrs. Nier once complained that I seemed much more interested in my studies than in cleaning her house!

"Well, of course," I said, "but I try to do a good job for you."

(In the early 1970s, she wrote to tell me that Dr. Nier had left her to marry his longtime secretary "who's much older than he is!" But at the change of the seasons, he always came back to do the home-maintenance chores he had taken care of all the years of their marriage.)

## My Studies at the University

Every weekday, I walked to the St. Paul campus and back to save bus fare. It was bitter cold that winter, and the wind coming off the river stung my face like a swarm of winged needles. I took three semesters' worth of courses in magazine writing and editing, drawing, layout and design, and photography. I loved it all, especially photography and layout and design.

The sports picture assignment in photography class is the one I remember most. Using a large-format Speed Graphic, I slipped and slid out onto the ice during ice hockey practice on campus and snapped just one picture. It was a great action shot, showing the goalie just missing the puck.

Once, on a weekend jaunt with a few other college kids, I snapped a bunch of duck-hunting pictures. My favorite shot would, I know, have been the one of a bunch of horses running pell-mell across the pasture. Alas, I was so sleepy when I processed the film Monday morn that I mixed my chemicals wrong. As I looked at the negatives and glimpsed the horses, the scene turned black before my eyes.

## The Course I Almost Flunked

In the final project for one of my favorite courses, I created the pasteup dummy of a house organ for the employees of a make-believe company that ran a factory. I wrote the headlines for news stories and features, roughed in photographs, designed the newsletter logo and title. I purely loved doing it!

But in the midst of this project, I became deathly sick (as usual) with my monthly period, which caused me to turn in my assignment a few days late. My professor handed it back to me almost immediately with an F scrawled across the front in red ink. "I don't accept late homework," he said haughtily.

I lost my cool, felt my face flushing. I shoved my folder back across his desk, saying angrily, "I worked hard on this, and I don't care if you flunk me or not as long as you tell me what you think of it! I really *was* down-and-out sick and couldn't work on it for a few days."

Taken aback, he agreed to look at it. When I stopped by his office a few days later to retrieve it, he had changed the F to an A+ and given me an A in the course. He even smiled at me and said, "You did a superlative job, Ms. Jones!"

## Spring Break in Aspen

I met Jack McTarnaghan in the ski club on campus. Tall and lean, with craggy good looks and longish curly brown hair, Jack was part of a group of ten students, two carloads of us, who drove out to Aspen, Colorado, for a glorious ski vacation during spring break. I did the whole ten days for $80. This included gas, room, meals, and ski lift tickets. Daddy sent me $50 to help make this vacation possible, the only time I ever asked him for money.

We had reserved two rooms—one for the guys, one for the gals, two and three to a bed—in the Gray House at the foot of the ski lift. They served us a hearty family-style breakfast, and then off we went to the ski lift. At noon, we ate chili and lots of crackers at the Red Onion, then back to the mountain! We ate our suppers at the Gray House too. But on the last night, we splurged and went out to dinner at the Blue Deer restaurant. Jack treated me to that meal.

One of the fellows in our group broke his leg on the first run down the beginner's slope. His leg in a cast, he spent the rest of the vacation with other skiing casualties reading, swapping stories, eating, and waiting for the rest of us to come in from the slopes at the end of the day, eat supper with him, and tell him about our adventures.

I too was a rank beginner. The only skiing I'd done before joining the ski club was on the hill beyond our big front porch at Ashfield, with most of my time spent climbing up the slope.

That first arduous day at Aspen, it took me all morning and afternoon to make one run down the mountain. Jack steered me to the ski shop afterward to have steel edges and new bindings put on my skis. What a difference that made!

Under Jack's instruction, I became a far better skier. He was twenty-eight, a returning vet who'd been on the U.S. Army's ski team, competed with other Allied teams all over Europe for four years, and was trained in mountain search and rescue. He was a law student. I liked him a lot and started dating him when we got back.

On the return trip to St. Paul, I suffered my dastardly monthly period. Half out of my mind with pain, I broke my right hand when I banged it down hard on the back of the car's front seat. I endured the rest of the journey, checked into the hospital when we got to St. Paul, and emerged a few hours later with a cast up to my elbow. My ski buddies were anxiously waiting and autographed it for me.

This meant I couldn't keep working for the Niers, so I settled in with my aunt Margaret and cousin Steve for the last six weeks of the semester. They had just moved there, and Margaret was now head of family services for the Family & Children's Service of Minneapolis.

Steve was twelve and rode his bike everywhere when he wasn't taking it apart and working on it. Endlessly impressed with me, he was good for my ego. "Julia is indefatigable," he told his mother one day.

I set about learning to use my left hand for practically everything, determined to be useful and earn my keep in this two-bedroom apartment where I felt so welcome. I caught a bus to the St. Paul campus every day, and Jack usually gave me a lift home.

**Easter Sunday**

Jack still lived with his parents and now wanted them to meet me, so we made plans to rendezvous with them at their church's sunrise service on Easter Sunday. We were invited to their house afterward for breakfast.

Margaret and Steve were away that weekend. Jack came over Saturday night, and we stayed up so late talking and listening to classical music that he refused to go home. So he spent the rest of the night on the living room couch. Next morning, we slept late and missed the sunrise service, but we made it to his parents' fine house in a substantial old Minneapolis neighborhood for breakfast.

This was embarrassing! I told them that their son had slept on the couch at my aunt's place, but I didn't tell them Margaret wasn't home. They were in their sixties or older, and his dad was a retired lawyer. They were very cordial and were interested in me, my family background, and the courses I was taking. And breakfast, always my favorite meal, was delicious.

\*    \*    \*

After finishing my coursework, I landed a do-everything kind of a position on *Horse World*, a sixty-four-page monthly show horse magazine in Des Moines, Iowa. The publisher found me a place to live at a large regal, gloomy boarding house called Mrs. Doty's

Tearoom. I moved into my long narrow room on the third floor with the help of Jack, who drove me and all my stuff down from St. Paul.

Finally, I had finished my schooling and landed the job I wanted—on a horse magazine, even! A new and exciting chapter of my life began to unfold.

# 19

# Breakfast at Mrs. Doty's and My Dream Job

On my first morning of work at *Horse World* magazine, I went down to the dining room for breakfast in the basement at Mrs. Doty's. There sat the handsome curly-haired, brown-eyed young man I would marry fifteen months later. Wearing an army shirt and jeans, Bob Hensley was tall and lean, with dark hair and a ready smile . . . well-nigh irresistible from that first moment.

"You must be Julia," he said as I sat down at the table. There were only the two of us. "Well . . . yes," I answered as my heart skipped a beat, "but call me Jay."

He introduced himself; we ate breakfast, then rode downtown together on the bus, for he worked at *Horse World* too! That evening, he climbed the stairs to my room, knocked on the door, and called out, "Jay, would you like to go to Lafferty's for a beer?"

"Yes!" I said, opening the door. I hated beer and had no idea what or where Lafferty's was, but that sure didn't stop me.

Lafferty's was the "disreputable"—the austere Mrs. Doty's word—beer joint next door to her tearoom. I nursed one beer all evening, munched peanuts and pretzels. (After that first time together, Bob was fond of calling me One-beer Jones). We sat across from each other in a secluded booth and talked and talked and talked late into the night.

I learned that he was from Milwaukee, loved horses, had experience showing the American saddlebreds his father trained, was a pilot of small planes, and a competitive fencer. He loved classical music and the theater and had an inquiring mind and an adventuresome spirit. He had attended the University of Wisconsin, then moved to Des Moines and landed a job on *Horse World* magazine, hoping to qualify for the Veterinary School at Iowa State College in Ames as an Iowa resident.

He had mulled his independent way into a progressive and liberal turn of mind despite a conservative, restrictive, and moralistic Catholic upbringing. His parents were afraid he had Communist tendencies when they learned he had joined the American Civil Liberties Union.

He was twenty-three, an air force veteran who had not seen active duty. "They taught me to type instead of to fly," he told me ruefully. "That was a considerable disappointment, but the typing has come in handy." After his discharge, he had hitchhiked down to an airfield in Wisconsin for flying lessons every weekend until he earned his pilot's license.

Bob and I rode the same bus to and from work every day, ate breakfast and dinner at Mrs. Doty's. Sometimes we had lunch together.

Jack came to see me the Saturday following my first week of work. We were sitting on Mrs. Doty's porch that late afternoon when Bob came along the sidewalk, vaulted over the low fence, and came up the walk. He looked at Jack and me sideways, nodded curtly to me as he went in the front door.

"Who was that?" Jack wanted to know.

"Oh, that's Bob Hensley."

"Does he live here?" he asked, pursuing the subject.

"Yes . . . He works at *Horse World* too," I volunteered.

## Getting Fired!

At *Horse World*, I quickly discovered this was the job I was born for, and I threw myself into it heart and soul. I worked fifty to sixty hours a week, bringing work home with me most evenings and weekends. Out of my $40 weekly paycheck, I spent $10 for room and board, leaving $30 for all my other expenses. It was enough.

After my first three weeks, most of which time he had been out of town, the publisher, Russell Lundy, called me into his office and fired me.

Shaken to the core of my being, I insisted that "I was born for this job!" and flat out refused to leave. I told him I'd work for free until the current issue went to press, after which I would depart without a fight if he still wasn't satisfied with my work.

When that time came, Mr. Lundy called me into his office and handed me my paycheck. He said this was the best issue they'd ever put out; and it was because of my ideas, layouts, and writing.

A few weeks later, he called me into his office again and said, "What shall we do about Loycene?"

"Why do we have to do anything?" I asked. "She's such a competent managing editor." He said he'd come to realize she was behind the firing of everyone he'd hired in the past few years.

Well, I talked him into not doing anything. Loycene had been with the magazine since its beginnings five years earlier and had precipitated my firing—convinced, she told Mr. Lundy, that I couldn't do the work required of me. I liked Loycene and hoped to work things out; but a few months later, she quit of her own accord, and I absorbed her job.

Things had by then become rather complicated in my personal life, what with Jack appearing every weekend. Finally, I broke off with Jack and settled down to dating Bob. He was sexually experienced; but he accepted, if somewhat angrily, the limits I set.

Then Mr. Lundy fired Bob, who had written a lively "Wake Up, Wisconsin!" article that incensed some of that state's show horse owners and trainers. Needing a scapegoat, Mr. Lundy claimed that Bob had slipped the feature into the magazine in his absence. Besides, circumspect as Bob and I had tried to be, our boss had discerned a romance in progress.

Bob moved to Ames, worked on a campus construction crew that summer, and was accepted for the fall semester at Iowa State College as a second year prevet student.

## Remembering Larry

That late summer and early fall, busy with school matters and his construction job, Bob didn't hitchhike to Des Moines for almost two months. In the meantime, I met and started dating a young man whose name I forget, but Larry comes to mind.

Through a woman friend in my building at work, I had met his mother, a typesetter for a local printing company. She asked my friend and me over for dinner the following Sunday.

Just before we arrived, I learned that our hostess had been quite taken with me and wanted her bachelor son to meet me! Things were a bit awkward at dinner, but this was a nice guy, and he soon put me at ease. A fine-looking tall blond man of solid build, he was in his late twenties, worked for a big company in town. He was their "time-and-motion man," he explained, figuring out the most efficient work habits to engrain in employees.

Larry called me the next evening, and I started going out with him. This fellow was really grown up, the most mature young man with whom I'd ever had a close encounter. We'd gone out five or six times, and he was becoming romantic. But when I rebuffed his advances, he gently backed off.

He knew I loved horses, and he had good friends who lived on a farm outside town and owned some riding horses. So he made arrangements for us to go out there for breakfast one Sunday and spend the day. I was pretty excited!

But Saturday, I received a postcard from Bob saying he was hitchhiking down for the weekend to see me. I had no way of reaching him to tell him I had other plans. I didn't want to disappoint Larry; also, I really wanted to meet his friends and ride their horses. What to do?

I was so mad at Bob for taking me for granted, for being so inconsiderate. Larry had said on our date Friday night, "Get a good night's sleep tomorrow—Sunday's going to be a big day!"

Would I lose Bob if I told him I had been keeping company with Larry and had made an all-day date with him for Sunday? I would surely lose Larry if I spoiled at the last minute the plans he'd made with his friends. I really, really did like him and had wanted to explore this relationship further.

I agonized for hours, then finally called Larry and simply told him the truth. There was a long silence on the other end of the phone, and I was close to tears. Then he said softly, "All right, Jay . . . goodbye."

The disappointment, sadness, and carefully controlled anger in his voice haunt me still. To this day, I wonder what would have happened if I'd chosen to keep my date with him for that Sunday long ago.

## My Landlady Evicts Me

Late that fall, Mrs. Doty evicted me. She finally realized a romance had been going on between me and Bob before he moved away. "If you're not out of here in two weeks," she said imperiously, "I'll have the bailiff put your things out on the curb!" I was, in her eyes, a fallen woman.

She had already rented my room to two career girls. But when I met them on my own moving day and told them why I'd been evicted, they backed off and didn't rent the room after all.

Looking for another pad, I found the Colgans, a mellow couple in their late sixties. They did more than rent me a room; they adopted me.

Now Bob often hitchhiked the thirty miles to Des Moines on the weekends to see me. The Colgans happily fed him dinner and breakfast, vacated the living room for us in the evenings, and put him up for the night, all without charge. They treated us both like family. This became for Bob and me our home away from home.

One afternoon, we pooled our resources and went to see *The Wizard of Oz* in downtown Des Moines. We loved it. But then we didn't have enough money left for bus fare. So we walked the three or four miles back home to the Colgans.

## A Marriage Proposal

That December, Bob asked me to marry him. I said I needed time to think about it. "Hell, take all the time you want," he said. "We can't get married until I'm accepted in vet school."

But when he took me home to Milwaukee with him at Christmastime to meet his friends and family, he presented me with a diamond engagement ring. And I said yes.

His mother, Cecelia, was the village and school nurse in their community of Greendale, a suburb of Milwaukee. A devout Catholic, she had prayed for her "fallen-away" son to marry within the faith and thus be brought back into the fold. But despite her disappointment that this was not to be, she was always good to me.

Her attitude about Bob and his sister Mary, one year younger, seemed to be that they were crosses God had given her to bear. By her own description, they had both been selfish, stubborn, devious, and assertive kids, often at odds with each other.

She had met Bob's father during World War II when she was his nurse in the hospital where he was recovering from his wounds. Bill Hensley was a bitter man who had lost his job during the Great Depression and remained unemployed for many years. Now he had a job training American saddlebred show horses.

Through all of Bob's growing-up years, his mother was the breadwinner for the family. He seemed to have no happy memories from his childhood, except for one summer in his teens when he had bought a sailboat in secret and spent blissful weekends on it. (Many years later, in his midsixties, he would own another boat and sail it to France and back!)

Although he and his father shared a love of horses, Bob told me they'd never been close. I grew to love his dad but did not like the surly way he treated his wife.

We set our wedding date that spring after Bob was accepted for the fall semester of the four-year School of Veterinary Medicine. He worked on a construction crew that summer until I quit my job at *Horse World*, and we flew East together the last week in August.

Mom and Dad had come out to Des Moines that winter for a visit and to meet Bob. They heartily approved of him. Back home, Phillips and Malcolm were laying bets as to whether I would actually marry this one. The bums!

Actually, I did return my diamond ring to Bob in midwinter after an inexcusably rude remark he had made to me in a restaurant earlier that same evening. Watching me eat soup, he had said disdainfully, "Didn't your mother ever teach you good manners?" It seems I wasn't using my spoon correctly as I dipped it into the soup.

I had always thought of good manners as including consideration for other people's feelings. Stinging from his public rebuke, I decided I didn't want to marry someone capable of such conduct.

We were sitting on a bench on the Calgons' front porch, dimly lit by a streetlight, when I gave the ring back to him that same evening. Shaken and wordless, with tears in his eyes, he took my hand and slowly slipped the ring back on to my finger. I was deeply touched, and I kept the ring.

## My Job Responsibilities

Meanwhile, I was immersed in the magazine. Mrs. Lundy, Liz, was editor; and I was associate editor. She was a capable writer and editor but only came to the office for deadline week, leaving everything to me the rest of the month.

I wrote feature stories, covered horse shows, laid out the magazine, designed the ads, read galley proofs, pasted up the sixty-four-page dummy every month, and worked with the printer. Sometimes the Lundys and I drove at breakneck speed down to Fulton, Missouri, to the Ovid Bell Press for the final okay of the magazine.

I remember spreading pages out on my big double bed at the Colgans' to work on at night and on weekends. In the wee hours of morning, I would stack it all back together as I cleared the bed off so that I could get a few hours' sleep.

My favorite assignment was covering the National Arabian Horse Show in Cheyenne, Wyoming. I stayed with *Arabian Horse News* editor, Anna Best Yoder, at her ranch. One night, we sat up in the barn, waiting for a mare to foal. When we ran to the house to bring back a thermos of hot coffee, this savvy mare slipped her foal into the world without us.

The horse show itself was great fun. I snapped lots of pictures, took copious notes for my write-up, and presented the ribbons for a class the magazine sponsored.

Before I left to marry Bob, the Lundys offered to triple my salary and supply me with a car if I would stay on. But I had no wish to travel those icy roads of winter and declined the offer.

It would have been lovely if they had paid me what I was worth to them all along! But the experience had been invaluable. *Someday, I told myself, I would edit and publish my own magazine.* I could imagine nothing finer.

# 20

# An Ashfield Wedding

Starry-eyed, Bob and I promised to love, honor and cherish (not "obey," thank you!) on September 2, 1950. It was a mild and sunny Saturday afternoon at the little Congregational Church on Main Street. A group of Bob's friends flew in from Milwaukee for the wedding, but Bob's parents and his sister Mary did not come. Bob said he thought they didn't have the plane fare, but I wondered if they stayed away because I wasn't Catholic.

Pauline was my Maid of Honor. My childhood friend Anne Smith—now Mrs. Harlow Falevsky after a dazzling wedding in a hotel in New York City a few years earlier—was my bridesmaid. (Her folks gave them a house on Staten Island as a wedding present and Ski went to work for her father at the David Smith Steel Company.)

Anne told me in later years that the only fault she ever found with her parents, my beloved "Aunt" Emma and "Uncle" Dudley, was that "they solved all my problems and made my life too easy.")

Anne Alevizon arrived by bus Thursday evening from Rutland, Vermont, where, with a master's degree from Columbia, she now held down a job as Bookmobile librarian. Bob and 1 met her bus in Greenfield, where Daddy's car surprised us with a flat tire. As we watched Bob change it, Anne remarked, "My, Julia, he is so patient!"

**Dinner at the Whale Inn**

The wedding party and special friends met the night before the wedding day at the Whale Inn for a festive dinner. The Whale Inn in Goshen was one of our favorite places over the years for family gatherings. It was run by two large older women, who, in the early years, always wrote down and served our individual dinner orders themselves.

Standing solemn and intense, with hands behind their backs, they committed each person's choices to memory and never made a mistake. When he was little, my brother called them both "Mrs. Whale." And while we waited in the outer room to be called in to be seated, their two great big dogs lay happily nearby to keep us company.

Early on the morning of my wedding day, I washed my hair and wound it still damp into curlers made of strips of cloth. I remember Anne Alevizon shouting out my bedroom window, "Ten cents for a look at the bride!"

In prep for my wedding, I had paid $20 for a calf-length white dress, adding some sheer white fabric over the bodice to make it more modest and to match my veil. I wore three-inch heels with it, and Hey, I looked great!

Our mediocre photographer caught it all in black-and-white pictures that have, at least, not faded. My favorite is the one of Daddy and me before the wedding. We had just come out our front door and stepped down off the porch.

Ashfield summer resident Emerson Conselman, well-known baritone from New York City, sang at our wedding. The words to one sentimental and lofty song Bob had selected were, "Because God made you mine . . ." and so forth.

As the bride's gift to the groom, I gave Bob a set of gold rocking-horse cuff links he had admired in a jeweler's window in Des Moines a few months earlier. To my great disappointment, he didn't have a groom's gift for me.

Daddy and me on my wedding day.

Our front porch was the setting for our reception, with the wedding party seated around our ping-pong table. Afterwards, Bob and I escaped in Daddy's car, with handfuls of rocks rattling under the hubcaps. Our destination: a rustic log cabin in the woods less than 10 miles away, courtesy of Charlie Streeter, the local veterinarian who had doctored our horses through the years.

Pauline and Malcolm loaned us two good horses, Judy and her dam Ginger, and we explored the vicinity on horseback. We drove up to Windsor, Vermont on the first day of our honeymoon to attend the annual Arabian Horse Show, built a fire on the hearth in the evenings and planned our future together. All this was my idea of a perfect honeymoon, except for the fact that I was literally too uptight to make love on our wedding night.

After sleeping naked with my arms wrapped around my husband, who radiated male energy all night, everything happened just naturally very early the following morning—the most exciting, profound, wildly satisfying event of my whole life up to that point. Our lovemaking became the glue that would hold a tumultuous marriage together over the years to come.

Just after sunrise Pauline and Malcolm came thundering up to the cabin at a gallop, having unloaded and saddled their horses at the end of the long driveway. They expected to find us still abed. But we were already up and invited them in to eat a big country breakfast with us.

Neither Bob nor I knew much about building a fire. We ran out of newspapers right away. So it was that we turned up at the Place in Ashfield early Sunday morning to collect a supply of old newspapers. When Mom opened the door in surprise, I cried out with mock anguish, "Mother, I've come home!"

After the honeymoon we spent a few days in Brooklyn. One evening we stepped out to dinner in the City and attended a wonderful production of "Swan Lake" with Anne Falevsky and "Ski," her former naval officer husband. She told me that night that he didn't like her nickname for him. So after that we tried to remember to call him Harlow,

Then, trouble in Paradise! One night Bob had an asthma attack and I lay awake listening to his labored breathing, terrified that I might lose him. The following day, I kept an appointment with my family's dentist, Dr. Mouradian, to have a root canal performed on an infected front tooth.

"Nothing to it," quoth he. "It won't hurt." But the painkiller didn't take, it hurt like Hell, I cried, and Bob held my hand tightly through the whole ordeal.

After all of which, slightly subdued, we caught a plane back to Iowa.

## A Scary Prediction!

A few days before the wedding, I'd kept an appointment for a physical exam and instruction in birth control. The doctor was alarmed at the sight of my back and diagnosed scoliosis, a sideways curvature of the spine.

"It will gradually get worse and you'll be in a wheelchair by the time you're 40," he predicted.

"I will NOT!" I said to myself, and it didn't happen. I never told Bob what the doctor said. Through the years to come I rode horseback, swam, skied, fenced competitively, hiked, cut and split firewood, put in big vegetable gardens, practiced Yoga. Sometimes my back did hurt. I even went down flat for a few days at a time now and then, but for the most part I was okay.

I had written to Johnny Turney earlier that year, telling him about my engagement. He sent me a short letter of farewell in return, and wrote, "You sound happy." I would never hear from him again.

Gordon Nadeau had written to me that winter to say he'd completed a two-year apprenticeship and received his certification as an oculist, qualifying him to make eyeglasses from prescriptions. He was thinking about moving to Des Moines to set up his practice, said he needed my reaction and advice. I replied that I was engaged to be married, and wished him success.

## Anne Alevizon's News

Although she had a good time making fun of me, Anne was so inspired by my wedding that she eloped with her sweetheart Mitch (Wilfred Mitchell) on September 11. She had met him in January '49 in North Creek, New York at a Cobble Creek Lodge square dance while visiting her sister Rita.

A former suitor of Rita's, now her husband, owned and ran the lodge. A bombardier during the war, he was a German prisoner of war for several years. Afterward he craved a life of peace and quiet and fishing. He found all this in the Adirondacks. And when he discovered that Rita was widowed, he tracked her down. His persistence won out and they were married in 1948.

Anne's husband Mitch worked in a lumberyard, having recently finished a three-year stint as a U.S. Army paratrooper in Japan. A few years after their marriage, he and Anne moved to Orono, Maine, where Mitch attended the University of Maine—about a month after the G.I. Bill expired—and earned a degree in forestry.

Bob and I visited them through the years whenever possible—at Orono, after their first of four children was born, and one or two children later in West Virginia. Mitch was a research forester there, where they lived in a valley with several other forestry families.

We liked Mitch, a rather serious and attractive fellow with dark blond hair and hazel eyes, who could work alone and happy in the forest all day. He had a warm rapport with his kids. But Anne was basically a city girl and it did not seem like the best kind of life for her, although I don't recall her ever complaining about it. In fact, she would look back on these years as a happy interlude in her life.

Our wedding portrait.

# 21

# THE PAMMEL COURT YEARS

Back in Ames, Iowa, I found a job at the College Photo Lab, processing film, making little mug shot prints of all the newly registered students, and doing some copy work. After two or three months, I landed a staff position as feature writer and assistant home ec editor for the Cooperative Extension Service at this land grant college. It paid $3,000 a year. (Big money!)

We lived in a six-by-twenty-feet trailer—with a washhouse, toilets, and showers close by—in Pammel Court, the housing "village" for married students. We had adopted a tiny gray kitten named Jennifer, who ran up and down on top of us in bed in the early morning, pouncing on our feet when we wiggled our toes.

Our heat came from an oil burner by the door. I turned it off at night, afraid of fire. On many a freezing-cold morning, we argued about who should get up, close the window, and light the fire—usually me because Bob said I was the one who had turned off the stove and insisted upon fresh air at night.

We paid $20 per month rent and $40 for food. I could make a big delicious meat loaf with only one-fourth a pound of ground beef in it.

Between us, Bob and I owned a magazine rack, mine; a portable typewriter, his; and some useful wedding presents. These included a set of Revere Ware pots and pans, a pressure cooker, and an electric bake oven.

We got down to $5 before pocketing our first paychecks, then paid $5 for a bicycle without a basket—we were so unbelievably frugal! That was our family vehicle for the next four years. Bob went grocery shopping on it every weekend and seldom arrived home without breaking an egg or two on the way.

No longer was I troubled by my recurring dream about searching for Pierre along the dirt roads and deep woods of South Ashfield.

At first, to make extra money in the evenings and on weekends, I peddled Vanda Beauty Counselor Cosmetics door to door in Pammel Court. But I soon gave that up. Selling things was not for me!

I did, however, gain a new respect for cosmetics. I had never bothered with anything more than a touch of lipstick; but after my first Beauty Counselor training session, which included learning how to apply makeup to my own face, I noted that the men on the city bus I rode home couldn't take their eyes off me!

Every spring, we planted a small vegetable garden in a plot for students at the far edge of Pammel Court. I remember walking over there hand in hand after dark to inspect by flashlight the little seedlings breaking ground and trying to figure out what they were.

Bob worked a part-time job at the school's veterinary clinic, full-time in the summers. He also received a check every month from the GI Bill, a dandy post-World War II benefit program for veterans.

## A Visit to George Ford Morris

While on vacation back East in the summer of 1951, Bob and I visited artist George Ford Morris in Red Bank, New Jersey. We considered George Ford the best living horse artist and had made his acquaintance while we both worked at *Horse World* where we carried a feature story about him in one issue.

He and his wife greeted us warmly, and we spent the day with them. Hanging on the wall of his studio was a magnificent huge oil painting of two winged horses battling in the sky. He called it *Fighting Pegases* and told us he'd painted it to counter the criticism that he worked from photographs.

He said he liked to do much of his painting from the live subject, catching the spirit and personality of the horse, but also took photographs and found them helpful in finishing up the paintings in his studio.

That day, he asked me to pick out some prints I'd like to have. I chose a lithograph print of *The Plebian* (a Paris cart horse) that looked like a charcoal drawing. It was a front view in which the horse filled the doorway of a stable. George Ford also gave us prints of a team of draft horses, a herd of Arabians, and a sepia-toned show ring print of a class of harness ponies.

## Update on the Mitchells

We visited Anne Alevizon Mitchell and her husband in Orono, Maine, in the summer of 1952. Their firstborn, Stanley, was a baby; and Anne's sister was living with them in their student housing at the university. I wouldn't have recognized her!

Soon after Anne's marriage, she and her dynamic dark-haired beautiful sister Rita had a car accident on the way to see their mother. (Anne's father died in 1946, and her mother now lived alone in the house he had built outside Manchester, New Hampshire.) Their car overturned on a slippery Route 4 near Rutland, Vermont, and Rita was thrown out onto the road.

Seriously injured, she spent most of the next year in rehab. Unable to cope with all this, her husband of two years divorced her.

After rehab Rita lived with her mother and ran a small mail-order business from their home for almost a year until, according to Anne, "they drove each other nuts." Rita was a night owl, and her mother an early bird. She then lived with Anne and Mitch for a few years. Seriously crippled and confined to a wheelchair, she was still able to be helpful with the baby.

Rita would move to San Diego in the mid-1950s. It has a fine climate plus many programs and services for the handicapped, including designated first-floor apartments and buses with special equipment to accommodate wheelchairs. She liked it and made a life for herself there.

## A Narrow Escape!

The Korean War was heating up in the fall of 1951, and I talked Bob into resigning from the air force reserve unit he belonged to on campus. He had served his time, I argued, and now his commitment was to me and our life together. He finally agreed, and none too soon! A week later, his unit was called up and sent to Korea.

My best friend at work was Chuck Benn, our blond-curly-haired staff photographer, a bachelor in his late twenties. We went on many assignments together and collaborated on a handful of freelance articles for magazines. Bob was fond of Chuck too. He would set my suitcase outside the door and wave goodbye as we set off for one homemakers' club workshop or another.

## Our W0I-TV Appearances

Iowa State was one of the first colleges in the nation to start its own television station. Bob and I and our friend Imogene—a beautiful petite blonde—often ended up as "actors" in their short home ec features. We did laundry, went grocery shopping, bought home furnishings, etc. It was fun.

On many a Saturday night, Imogene, her husband Bill, Bob, and I ended up over at Holly and John Heer's house on Duff Street in Ames for supper. After eating, we moved on into the living room to watch wrestling on TV with them and their small children.

John was so enthralled by these outrageous macho wrestlers that we had more fun watching him than watching the show. He was a publications editor at Iowa State, and Holly worked as a typesetter for a local printing company.

## Over Backward!

During lunch break one day at work, I tried out another staff member's big heavy wooden swivel chair. Clowning to myself, playing the big executive, I swung around, leaned back, stretched out my legs, and plopped my feet onto the edge of the desk.

*Wham!* The chair crashed over backward with me. I landed hard, hitting my neck against the thick top of the chair back. I ended up in the hospital with x-ray technicians and doctors nodding their heads over me.

The verdict: acute muscle spasm with resultant displacement of an intervertebral disk. They gave me some sort of shot into the muscle, put me on painkillers, and sent me home with a traction apparatus I was instructed to use every four hours. Heat treatments every day were also prescribed.

I carried my right shoulder lower than my left for many months, appreciated the relief that traction gave me whenever I could "go hang myself." During this period, I kept going to work every day; and Bob did the laundry, ironing, and most of the trailer cleaning. This injury and the one I'd suffered riding Ginger in the apple orchard would plague me off and on for years to come.

## Our Prefab House

After two years of trailer life, we moved to a small prefab in Pammel Court. It had a bathroom and one bedroom. Living in the prefab right behind us were our best friends, Imogene and Bill Lauger. He was a landscape design student, and she worked as a secretary on campus where I saw her often.

We bought a spin-dry clothes washer and stashed it under a counter Bob built in the kitchen. When it went into the spin cycle, our whole house shook.

Enrolling in an adult ed evening class in town, I built a plywood desk, a dining table, and an end table with a file drawer in it. I learned how to retie springs in an extension homemakers' workshop. Then Bob and I rejuvenated an old $10 couch, and I made a red sailcloth and pillow-ticking slipcover for it.

We installed floor-to-ceiling bookshelves in the hallway, nailed up a piece of four-by-eight plywood as a partition between kitchen and living room, and covered it with wallpaper. I made curtains on my new portable Singer sewing machine, and we transformed the walls with a colorful array of paint.

I wrote an article about fixing up our little house on the cheap. Chuck took pictures to go with it, and we sold it for $300 to *Town Journal* magazine. We also collaborated on an article for *Country Gentleman*, which earned us $800.

## Snowbound with Chuck

In the dead of winter one year, Chuck and I were snowed in for a memorable week in Spencer, Iowa. We had great fun tramping the

snowy streets, window shopping, going to the movies, listening to
records in a music store—I bought Stravinsky's *The Firebird* Suite
there—trying out the few restaurants in town, and talking late into
the night.

Once, Chuck told a fellow staff member, "When I get married,
I want it to be someone just like Jay!" He got married about a year
after Bob and I left. Pretty soon, he and his wife produced a little
boy, who looked just like his daddy on the Christmas cards Chuck
sent us.

## Happy Years

Those first four years of our marriage were perhaps our happiest.
My job, my office mate Candy Hurley, my department chairman,
fellow staff members, and the home ec specialists I worked with
were grand people. I traveled all over the state to do feature stories
and interviews and learned so many new things.

Bob started a fencing club at Iowa State and taught me to fence.
It was a sport I loved and at which he excelled.

Bob was good at his studies, and his work at the clinic absorbed
him. We forged deep friendships with other couples in Pammel
Court; he loved my cooking, and the years passed swiftly. We lived
very frugally and piled up money in a savings account.

## Our First Baby

We had our first baby, a nine-pound two-and-a-half-ounce
boy, a month before Bob graduated. It was an easy pregnancy—no
morning sickness, no debilitating monthly periods, and despite my
huge appetite, I only gained fifteen pounds.

The doctor had told us it would be a small baby, but then Dougie
was a whole month late. He grew so fast during that bonus month
that I miscalculated how big my belly was and kept closing doors on
him.

It was a "precipitous delivery," which put the baby into an
incubator and necessitated a blood transfusion for me. Bob left
shortly afterward, catching a ride to Kentucky that very night with
classmate Ed Brannaman to check out a job possibility in Lexington.

Luckily, Mom had come to stay with us and was there for me while he was gone.

We soon bought a new Ford station wagon for $2,000 cash. Chuck went with us to help pick it out, for he was a savvy car buyer. Our own experience was limited to horses, bicycles, and airplanes. Chuck's parting gift to us was a priceless set of pictures he took at our house of little Dougie and his parents.

Bob's graduation exercises on a memorable sunny day included a special ceremony for the veterinary students' working wives. I proudly accepted my PHT degree—Putting Hubby Through.

About two days later, after packing all our worldly goods into our new vehicle and a U-Haul trailer, we set out for Lexington, Kentucky, with our baby and our cat. A job with Dr. Ed Thomas, a veterinarian specializing in horses, awaited Bob there. We were deeply connected and passionately in love. The future looked bright.

Horse Country, here we come!

Bob with Dougie at three weeks . . . and about five years
later in Kentucky with Doug, Jennifer and little Lisa

# 22

# THE UNRAVELING

Over the next eleven years, we had five more children—Jennifer, Lisa, Joel, Scotty, and Timmy. Although we were vigilant about birth control, these little darlings kept slippin' on through!

Bob proved to be a fine veterinarian and a good provider. He was, for the most part, a good father to our children when they were very little. One after another, we reached the goals we'd set. Yet this monogamous, highly charged marriage began to unravel. Years of counseling did not help, and it finally came completely apart in 1969. What went wrong?

Bob and I had seemed ideally suited to each other; yet Ernie Jordan, our marriage counselor, once told me, "Your very essences are in conflict!"

\*    \*    \*

We lived first in a duplex on Barberry Lane in Lexington where our elderly landlady was likely to turn up unexpectedly. Dressed all in black, she came wandering through the apartment one day, looked in on me as I lay soaking in the bathtub, and said, "You fixing to go out, honey?"

My pregnancy had been hard on my back, and I had to be very careful for many months. Bob got into the habit of rushing home at noon to fix lunch, change the baby's diapers, and play with him, giving me a chance to lie flat on my back. By the time Dougie could sit up, I had recovered enough to push him in his stroller for long walks in good weather on the lovely tree-lined streets.

Then our cat, Jennifer, was hit and killed by a car in front of our house. Our next-door neighbor wrapped her in a newspaper and brought her tearfully to me. I was heartsick. When Bob arrived home that evening, he cried, then carried her into the backyard and buried her.

("Why did you name me after a cat?" our daughter Jennifer asked me accusingly years later. "We didn't really," I said. "It's just that Jennifer was our favorite name for a little girl.")

## Phone Call from an Old Friend

One day, I had a call from Bill Chisolm, one of my favorite people from my growing-up years. He was in town and would be attending a concert that evening at University of Kentucky (UK). Mother had given him my phone number, and he said he'd love to see us.

Bob and I made arrangements to meet him at the concert. We sat in the balcony, and Bill was seated down on the main floor. After the performance, I started looking for him; and right away, there he was, waving up at me, a broad smile on his animated black face.

"You look so much like your mother," he explained a few minutes later as we hugged each other.

We brought him back to Barberry Lane for dessert and a great visit.

Bill was often a guest at our home in Bay Ridge, starting in the late 1930s. Once, when I was grumbling about having to mop our big kitchen floor, Bill came to my rescue. Squatting down, he dipped a scrub cloth into the bucket of hot, soapy water and then swished it energetically around on the floor. I quickly caught the spirit. Together, we mopped that floor sparkling clean in no time!

He was a gentle, soft-spoken, energetic man of average height, lithe and strong, with dark skin and wooly black hair. Well acquainted with New York City, he had spent many summers there earning the money that put him through college. Selling newspapers at night, he had slept on benches in Central Park in the daytime.

When I first met him, Bill was bursting with enthusiasm and full of plans for his school for Negro boys and girls living in poverty in his home community of Rock Hill, South Carolina.

Still a young man, he had constructed the first Durkee Training Institute building himself, with only an old man with a donkey cart to help him. He pried the rocks he used out of the hard ground with a pick and crowbar. Soon, other men joined him in his work. He recruited capable men and women to teach with him, inspired them with his dream.

His school was not meant to be a substitute for public school. At Durkee, the students took such classes as art, music, domestic science, interior decorating, and carpentry, in addition to learning a host of practical skills that would help them earn a living. The school also became a social center for young and old.

After whites burned it down in the late 1940s and Negroes working with Bill had rebuilt it stone by stone, grander than before, the school was renamed William Chisolm Institute.

Bill had a fine singing voice. He and his traveling choir of young people from Durkee came to New York one summer to sing in churches and other places to raise money for their school. Our own parish house was packed when they gave a presentation for our church.

In 1953, Bill published a slim volume of his poetry, *Splintered Darkness*. Mom was his editor and helped him get it published. I treasure the copy he sent me, even located another copy of it on the internet recently. It was a rare and precious find. These eighty-six deeply felt, sometimes joyous and sometimes desolate poems tell Bill's own story, his school's story, and the story of his people.

Bill was murdered by a white man some years later. No one was ever held accountable or punished for the death of this wonderful man.

## Our First House

After about a year on Barberry Lane, we bought for $16,000 a small three-bedroom redwood house on Cane Run Road on the northern outskirts of Lexington. It was a friendly neighborhood of young couples, most of them with small children.

We were barely settled and were in the process of choosing paint colors when we received a letter from George Ford Morris. He was coming to Lexington soon and would like to have a good visit with us during his stay. We hadn't seen him since our visit to his studio in Red Bank, New Jersey, about six years earlier.

Bob invited him to stay with us; then we scrambled to get the walls of one room painted and ready for him to occupy. We finished up and moved the furniture in just before Bob left for the airport to meet his plane about a week later.

George Ford set up his easel in his room and spent several hours a day painting. I remember sitting there quietly, watching him. Starting with a large fresh canvas, he held his brush at arm's length and first of all "drew" the whole outline of the horse. I was astounded, for that's not the way I would have expected him to proceed. He told me that as a small boy, he had cut out silhouettes of horses and dogs from a slice of bread, a piece of paper or cardboard, whatever he could find.

When a young local artist, Joe Petro, brought one of his finished paintings to the house for him to critique, George Ford set it up on his easel and explained the importance of focusing attention on the horse, not allowing the background to intrude. Joe had meticulously painted every leaf on every tree in the distance. Now the master selected a brush and smudged out all this detail with deft strokes. I held my breath. Dead silence in the room. A shocked look on Joe's face.

**Stallions in the Living Room**

George Ford stayed with us four or five days. During this time, he visited several big Thoroughbred farms where he studied and sketched various stallions, then took some photographs for reference purposes.

He was working on a whole book of stallions and had brought many of the finished paintings with him. One evening, he arranged ten or twelve of them along the perimeter of the living room for viewing. As I looked closely at each horse, it seemed as if he actually moved, twitched a muscle, caught my eye with his. It was an unforgettable experience.

I thought about his visit and his wondrous stallions many times as I made lined draperies for our picture window in the living room and curtains for the rest of the house.

George Ford soon sent us the deluxe edition of his wonderful large-format book, *Portraitures of Horses*. Published in 1952, it was hailed by pundits in the equine world as "the horse book of the century."

On the frontispiece of our copy is a drawing of Dougie in diapers, holding the lead shank to an appealing mare whose head dips down gently close to his.

## Our Christmas Baby

Jennifer had been born the year before on Christmas Day 1955. This little darling was so easy, so different from Dougie, who was always hungry, still in diapers, not sleeping through the night. I weaned him at six months because he never seemed to get enough milk. At nine months, he was far too adventuresome for his own good. I dressed him in red so I could spot him easily after he climbed the back fence and was on his way, toddling happily out across the fields.

Jennifer slept through the night within a few weeks, was rarely fussy, awoke each day with a smile, always got enough milk when I nursed her. She adored her big brother. When he sometimes snatched her toys away, her brown eyes would fill up with tears, and she would ask in anguish, "Why, Dougie, why?"

One day, they were both out in the backyard. She was in the bouncy chair, and I heard her crying. I ran out to find that Doug, trying to look innocent, had just poured a pail of water over her head.

## Next Came Lisa

Lisa was born only twenty months after Jennifer, on August 25, 1957. Another easy baby, this one had blonde hair, fair skin, and blue eyes. She became a bit tempestuous by the time she was two, and loved to wear frilly little dresses.

We turned the two-car garage into a playroom, with a fenced-off laundry area in one corner. I fastened short pipe legs to the top of a round oak table a neighbor gave us and covered it with several coats of bright red enamel paint. To go with it, I found four or five little chairs at secondhand stores and yard sales.

I took the kids, with Lisa in her stroller at first, for long walks on the farm across Russell Cave Pike from us where they grew acres of gladiolas for the florist shops. The owner let us have flowers that had fallen over and been left. We brought huge armfuls of them home to decorate the house.

Meanwhile, I scrubbed floors, washed windows, washed and ironed clothes, sewed dresses for my little girls, and never did catch up on the mending or on sleep. I was always doing dishes at midnight!

Pretty soon, I had a scary sick spell. At first, the doctor thought I might be suffering from a brain tumor, but he determined instead that I was simply sleep deprived. He put me on a "central nervous system relaxant," and I slept from twelve to fifteen hours a night for weeks before recovering my old vim and vigor.

### Gordon Stops By

My old friend Gordon dropped by one morning on a cross-country drive from Apple Valley back to Texas. A tour of duty with the marines had put at least twenty pounds of meat and muscle on him, transforming the skinny farm boy I remembered into a fine-looking young man.

Doug, Jennifer, and Lisa warmed up to him immediately. He stayed all day, wanted to be sure to meet Bob, and we reminisced about Apple Valley people and our gymkhana adventures. In addition to making eyeglasses, he now owned a small ranch, but I was disappointed to learn that he rounded up his cattle with a pickup truck. After a short visit with Bob in the early evening, he headed out.

### Joel Joins Our Bunch

He was born on September 11, 1959. He had big brown eyes, smiled a lot, and was bald as an eagle. By the time he was two years old, he would be transformed by soft blond curls that sprouted all over his head.

While Joel was still in his bassinet, Mom and Dad came to see us. After observing me in action, Daddy pronounced, "Julia, you have become a household drudge! You need to hire some help around here."

So I did.

## Henrietta to the Rescue

I survived the difficult years that followed because of Henrietta, that wonderful black woman who became my friend. A big woman, she was six feet tall, with a wide face, lively brown eyes, and a sunny disposition.

She started with one six-hour Saturday morning a month—her husband Elijah delivered her to my door before daylight in his old pickup truck. I worked right along with her until noon, then fixed our lunch. We sat down and ate it together at our kitchen table by the window—something that delighted her.

She'd been earning sixty cents an hour, but the minimum wage was $1. "Henrietta," I said, "don't you work for anybody for sixty cents an hour!"

One day, she received a phone call at my house. I heard her declare proudly, "No, ma'am! I works for a dollar an hour!" (My neighbors were not happy with me!)

She'd had little schooling, married her Elijah at thirteen, had their first baby, a stillborn little boy, when she was fourteen. Then came eight more children and later on, many grandchildren, all of whom she helped to raise.

"Miz Hensley," she told me once after we'd worked together all Saturday morning, "you is the hardest-working white woman I ever knowed!" I didn't tell her that I was always almost comatose for the rest of the day.

## My Afternoon Nap

My daily nap routine started when Joel was about two years old. When I put him down for his nap on the bottom bunk bed in the room he shared with Doug, he didn't want me to leave him. As a result, I would lie down next to him until he fell asleep, then gently slip away.

Upset by the fact that I was gone when he woke up, Joel started wrapping his arms around my neck, locking the fingers of both hands together into a double fist I could not escape. Even when he was sound asleep, his sweaty little arms held me fast. So I slept right along with him. My afternoon nap habit stuck, even after his need to keep me prisoner subsided.

## Flip and Tiddley Wink

One evening, when Joel was about two and a half, he and I set out to do the week's grocery shopping. On North Broadway, we saw a little dog get hit by a car. I made a U-turn, rescued him from where he lay in the middle of the street, and took him home for Bob to examine.

The diagnosis: no broken bones, no sign of internal injuries. He was evidently just in shock.

A small dog with short legs, he looked like a funky little Welsh corgi. Leaving him in Bob's care, I said, "Come on, Joel"; and we headed back out the door. "We gonna get another dog?" Joel asked, trotting eagerly along beside me.

When nobody claimed our patient, who made a quick recovery, we named him Flip. He was part of the family for the next fifteen or sixteen years.

As for Tiddley Wink, her adoption was not so successful. When Bob was asked to euthanize this puny little Thoroughbred foal along with her blind twin, he obtained permission to bring her home instead. She was only a few hours old when he carried her in the door. She had diarrhea all over the playroom floor that rainy night. After which she took over our fenced-in backyard and was the neighborhood wonder for the next four or five months.

She was so cute, at first. I bottle-fed her, kept a close eye on the kids as they tried to make friends with her. But she proved to be an untrustworthy little maverick, and soon, the kids weren't allowed in the yard with her. Bob finally found a farm nearby that would board her.

One day, when Tiddley was not much more than a yearling, Bob took Doug with him to go feed her. When they arrived back home,

Doug, close to tears, told me his dad had put him up on Tiddley's back. She immediately dumped him and kicked him, leaving a big bruise on his thigh. Doug was eight or nine.

Furious, I asked Bob what had possessed him to do such a thing. "I wanted to see what she'd do," he said.

"Then why the hell didn't you get on her yourself?" I yelled.

We moved Tiddley to the Tolemans' farm a few miles away. Ed and Laura were fellow Unitarians, and their son David soon became Doug's best friend.

Bob spent some serious time training Tiddley over the next year and started riding her. One early evening, he said she was ready for me to try out. She did fine at a walk and trot, but when I put her carefully into a canter, she bucked me off. Unhurt but miffed, I yelled, "I thought you had her ready to ride!" At which point, Bob said she'd bucked him off too—every time he rode her.

## A Forced Landing in Pewee Valley

Bob co-owned a little Cessna single-engine plane. We had some exciting, often harrowing adventures in it, including a very bumpy forced landing crosswise of rows of potatoes on the grounds of the women's state prison in Peewee Valley, Kentucky. The weather had suddenly turned bad and closed in on us on our way to a class reunion at Iowa State. We hitchhiked into Louisville, still wearing our grubbies, which brought disapproving looks our way at the airport, and caught a commercial flight.

When we landed in Des Moines in the middle of the night, the luggage we had checked was nowhere to be seen on that moving belt. We filed a missing baggage report and then contacted our old friend Ben Chaiken, who dragged himself out of bed, picked up us at the airport, and put us up for the night. He drove us to Ames the next morning. Our luggage caught up with us there a few hours later, thank goodness, since we'd both packed our favorite duds.

Upon our return, Bob's classmate Ed Brannaman, now a practicing veterinarian in Danville, Kentucky, met our plane and drove us to a spot on the highway near where our Cessna languished in the potato field. He and I watched Bob take off, narrowly missing the power lines. Then Ed drove me to the Lexington airport where we met Bob and retrieved our own car in the parking lot.

We'd been gone five or six days. I had switched Joel to a bottle for a few days and left him with our friend Nita while Henrietta and Howard looked after the rest of the bunch. Howard Aldous was a fledgling veterinarian from Canada who was apprenticing with Bob for about six months. He ate his breakfast and dinner with us every day, spent his evenings with us, and became our friend. The children loved him.

While we were gone, he stayed at the house, with Henrietta arriving early every morning to send him off on his rounds after a hearty breakfast. She stayed on until he got home where she had dinner waiting for him and the kids.

Howard was six feet five, and these two made an interesting pair. Jennifer wrote a story for English class that year about a family with a mother named Henrietta and a father named Howard.

## Our New House and Scotty

Scotty joined our family on July 5, 1963. Tenderhearted, energetic, shy, and easy to please, he would become the beloved little brother of the crowd. He was blond, fair-skinned, and blue-eyed, with a sprinkling of freckles across his nose and cheeks.

This was also the year we bought land in neighboring Jessamine County and began to build a spacious rustic Frank Lloyd Wright kind of a house on the side of a hill. It had a long back deck overlooking the East Hickman Creek.

Henrietta helped us move. All day long, she organized things and packed box after box, just barely keeping us ahead of the movers.

"Miz Hensley," she said after seeing our new place, "what you want to be out here in the bushes for?" She believed it was best to live in a community the way she did, with family and neighbors nearby to help you through the hard times.

But we were building a community of sorts ourselves, having bought acreage with the John and Theresa Griffin family and John Scruggs, a bachelor landscape architect. We each had our own building site, with two additional sites marked off for future buyers, and we shared five or six acres of pasture.

### I Wanted to Run Away

The summer and fall of 1964 proved a marathon for me of supervising the building of our house, looking after the kids, and getting ready to move. We had lucked onto a savvy local builder with a very sunny disposition. J. T. Collins worked from architect drawings that I had altered to make all the rooms bigger. One of the first things he did was construct a plywood replica of the house to see how it would all fit together.

When school opened, we still lived in Lexington, and I had to deposit Doug at the end of our Jessamine County driveway every day to catch the bus by 6:00 a.m. The overcrowded schools had gone into double sessions, with grades five through nine on the early shift. We took the girls, two little boys, and baby with us each morning. Once in a great while, Bob made that early run with Doug so that the rest of us could sleep a little later.

Soon, suffering from pleurisy, struggling to keep going, I became so overwhelmed that I wanted to run away. Here was our dream house waiting for us, and I had reached the point where I felt I would give anything and everything just to be free! But I couldn't leave my children, and how could I support them and look after them by myself?

### Daddy's Visit and Departure

I wrote an anguished letter to my parents, and Daddy flew out to Kentucky right away to spend a few weeks with us. Retired by then from the Union Church in Bay Ridge, he and Mom had made that rarest of transitions from summer people to permanent Ashfield residents in 1956. For several years, he then served as part-time minister for Unitarian churches in Amherst and Bernardston. It was the first time in his life anyone ever called him "conservative."

Daddy and I moved that last load of belongings to our new house one day in late November. As was his habit of the years, he spread everything out next to the car, stood back, and studied the situation.

Then he packed it all into my little Renault—a very tight fit. He looked startled when I told him we had to stop at the supermarket for the week's groceries. Somehow, he crammed them into the car too, tucking our Thanksgiving turkey in front of the driver's seat, behind my legs.

Daddy stayed on to spend Christmas with us. His considerable help and companionship made things better. I got more sleep. My health improved. I realized that our new house was a purely wonderful creation.

"I can do this!" I decided.

Henrietta started coming more often. She was with me a scant month later in January of 1965 when Mom called with the devastating news of Daddy's death. The cause: circulatory failure due to a bowel blockage only finally diagnosed upon autopsy.

Mom and Dad had been with us for the weekend a few days earlier, stopping over on the first leg of Daddy's annual speaking tour across the country. But he was not well. At my uncle Ellery's in Cincinnati, he had seen a doctor, who missed the diagnosis and put him on some inappropriate medication.

Nevertheless, Daddy spoke that Sunday at our Unitarian Fellowship, and we spent the afternoon at Rena and Johnnie Niles's home on Boone Creek outside Lexington. (Rena and John Jacob, folk singer and author, were friends we had made when Bob became Rena's vet for Boone, her hunter jumper.)

John Jacob and Daddy hit it off immediately. What a joy it had been sitting in that sunken living room, a fire on the hearth, and listening to these two literate, eloquent men discussing their favorite poets.

That night, all night, I sat on the floor by Daddy's bed, listening to him sleeping, terrified that he was slipping away from us. The next morning, we put him and Mom on a plane to Chicago where my uncle Dave was a physician.

I remember dashing up the portable steps to the open door of the plane and running down the aisle of the cabin to find Daddy, to say goodbye one more time. He looked up, and the last thing he ever said to me was, "Julia, you are my only worry . . . but Bob is such a great guy!"

My favorite picture of Daddy.

My brother, Phillips, flew out to Chicago to be with Mom for those first few days after Daddy's death. Then they boarded a train to Lexington, bringing Daddy's ashes with them. He had recently told Mother he wanted to be cremated and have his ashes spread in some beautiful place.

A crop duster friend with a small plane scattered Daddy's ashes over the Kentucky hills for us. And I was grateful to Mom for the way she explained cremation to my children in their first experience with death. "It's almost like magic the way Granddaddy was turned into ashes after he died," she told them. "Then the wind carried his ashes all over the mountains so that he would be a part of the whole world forever."

She found this poem in Daddy's billfold. We think he probably wrote it:

> I hold that when a person dies,
> his soul returns again to earth
> arrayed in some new flesh disguise.
> Another mother gives him birth.
> With sturdier stride and mightier brain,
> the old soul takes the road again.

This gave me some comfort. I loved the idea of the old soul taking the road again.

But Daddy had seemed indestructible. I thought he would always be there for me. It took me a long time, many hours and weeks of walking the night, before I pulled myself together; and life went on. I miss him still.

### A Very Full Life

So we settled into our fabulous new house and our new life. We bought two good saddle horses and a pony named Dandy for the kids. On days that Henrietta came, I worked with her all morning, rode my horse in the afternoon, then drove Henrietta home.

Shanghai, a big rambunctious sixteen-hand palomino gelding, was my horse. Our neighbor John Griffin had attended a horse sale and brought him home. He said a little boy had led him into the sales ring where he seemed perfectly gentle. But when John saddled and mounted him the next day, he was quite a different horse and promptly ran away with him. He had obviously been tranquilized for the sale.

John led him, with the saddle still on, down to me, told me his sad story, and said, "Would you like to try him?" Yes yes yes!

Shanghai gave me a great ride, breathing a little fire along the way. I called my horse-loving friend Nita Schwartz in Lexington. She drove over to our place right away and tried him out. "Wow, that's a horse and a half!" she declared, and together, we bought him from John for $125 each. When she came out to ride with me, I rode Bob's horse, Rocket.

Rocket was a Kentucky mountain horse, a buckskin gelding raised by Sam Tuttle near Natural Bridge. Sam had him under saddle as a two-year-old and brought him to Natural Bridge with a few other horses one weekend to rent to some members of our riding club. The young woman that rented Rocket couldn't handle this green-broke youngster; so Bob, who had rented a calmer horse, swapped with her.

He liked Rocket so much that I went to see Sam Tuttle the following week, bought Rocket for some ridiculous price—$125 is what I remember—and gave him to Bob for Christmas. It was a wonderful surprise.

Within a few years, we added a lively little filly, Misty, and Boone, the tall bay gelding Rena Niles gave us. Boone was no longer up to the chase but made a good extra horse for us. Joel learned to ride on him, would stand on our stone wall in front of the house to get him saddled and bridled; then off they would go.

### Along Came Timmy

Timmy was born on August 18, 1966, shortly before my fortieth birthday. He was an exuberant, outgoing, irrepressible little fellow from the very beginning.

Within a year or two, the other kids started calling him the Destroyer because of his penchant for getting into their stuff while they were at school. But when tragedy struck our family a few years later, little Timmy would be my salvation.

Our five kids in 1963: Doug, Jennifer with Scotty, Lisa
and Joel. Now, we thought, our family was complete!

And then along came
Timmy in 1966. Here
he is by the pasture
fence, holding our pony
Dandy's lead shank.

## A TV Set for Henrietta

One year, despite my objections, Bob decided to replace our old black-and-white TV with a larger set. "What you plan to do with your old TV, Miz Hensley?" Henrietta asked.

"Would you like to have it, Henrietta?"

"Yes, ma'am!"

"But you don't have electricity!"

"We work it out," she said happily.

They ran an electric cable from the next house in their community on Columbus Lane off Roister Road south of Lexington, and that TV served them well for years! Myself, I never could figure out how anybody had time for television.

But one program I did watch was *Playhouse 90* on Sunday evenings. When the kids were little they loved to watch *Captain Kangaroo* and, later, *Mickey Mouse Club*.

## Partners

By the time we moved to Jessamine County, Bob had launched his own veterinary practice. I kept the books, answered the phone, contacted Bob on his car radio, transcribed his hard-to-read handwritten diagnosis and treatment account of each farm visit, did the detailed monthly billing, and gathered together all the information needed for our tax accountant.

I put in about eighty hours a month on the business. I didn't receive a paycheck—which, for tax purposes and otherwise, was a big mistake!—but I felt that Bob and I were definitely partners, that it was "our" business.

Bob wasn't home very much. He worked a seven-day week in his busiest season and was gone many evenings to altruistic save-the-world kinds of meetings. The raising of the children was left mostly to me, but we clashed again and again on disciplinary matters.

To our mutual dismay, we had discovered that we held vastly different ideas about rearing children. Sometimes I felt like a lioness defending her cubs. I do not doubt that he loved us; but he was a critical, demanding husband and father, difficult to please. This was hard on the kids, particularly Doug, and my own vibrant self-image began to erode.

Bob had a lot of anger in him, probably stored up in his childhood years. Fortunately, he usually kept it under tight control.

## Doug on the Run

One day, twelve-year-old Doug came bursting in the outside door to the kitchen. He raced across the slate floor and out onto the deck, leaving the sliding glass door open behind him. Over the deck railing he went in a flash and down the tree. A few minutes later, he burst into the kitchen again.

"Doug, what on earth!" I said as he sped by. He flung a grin back over his shoulder and said, "I'm practicing my escape route." Then out onto the deck, over the railing, and down the tree he went. He'd had an angry confrontation with his dad the day before and was taking no chances.

Joel, on the other hand, adored his father, was stubbornly determined to please him. When he was slow to learn to read in first and second grade, his father worked with him impatiently, trying to hammer the words into him. And Joel tried so hard!

But Bob was pleased by the ease with which he learned to ride a horse. Unlike reading, riding and working with horses just came naturally to Joel.

## School Days in Jessamine County

I was proud of my children's behavior on this first year of integrated schools in Jessamine County. When a girl next to Jennifer on the bus held her nose and said, "Phew! This used to be the niggers' bus," Jennifer retorted, "I don't smell anything. If you don't like this bus, why don't you get off?"

And when out on the playground, one of Lisa's new friends said, "Let's call that nigger girl names!" Lisa said, "No, that would be mean!" Instead, she befriended the little girl.

Joel was the family comedian. On his first day of school, he left to catch the bus, clutching his notebook, pencil, and lunch box. He was so excited! When he arrived home, I wanted to hear all about his day.

He looked up at me with mournful eyes. "I never found my room!"

I wrapped my arms around him. "Oh, Joel, my poor darling!" Then he broke into a gleeful smile, looked up at me, and said, "Naw, just kidding!"

## Doug's Schooling

Alarmed by Doug's and Bob's increasing antagonism for each other, I decided it would be best for Doug to go away to school. He and I visited several schools in the northeast and settled on the Barlow School, a small progressive prep school in Amenia, New York.

From grades seven through nine, we had sent him to the Lexington School, an academically tough private school that managed to challenge him. He particularly loved his French class; and his teacher, Jennifer Cook, became my close friend.

During that period, I bought him a $15 guitar. After his first lesson, his teacher said Doug had experimented with playing pieces in different keys. "I've never had a beginning student do that," he said.

Steve Brines, a friend of mine, played bluegrass music on his banjo and invited Doug and me over to his apartment in Lexington one evening. Doug watched intently as he played; then Steve handed him his banjo to try out. The next day, Steve told me reluctantly, "I'll never be as good a musician as your son is right now!"

In the fall of 1969, Doug enrolled at Barlow. He had small classes and good teachers. He found kindred spirits there. I'd sent him off with all-new clothes from a great sale at Ben Snyder's in Lexington, but he arrived home for Christmas in hippie clothes donated by schoolmates. He was letting his straight dark brown hair grow long, and next time we saw him, he looked like an Indian. A happy one.

## Good Times and Bad

Although I loved being a mother, my days and nights were exhausting. Plagued by sinusitis and painful bouts of strep throat, I was chronically short of sleep and deathly sick for a week every month—in severe pain and emotionally fragile. I do not imagine that I was easy to live with at such times.

Even so, there are good memories from those years together. Bob and I shared many happy times—including a few exciting skin- and scuba-diving vacations in Bimini, flying down to the Bahamas in his small airplane to a landing strip on one of the islands.

There were also those grand trail-riding weekends in Kentucky's beautiful, often-rugged back country with our Elkhorn Saddle Club.

We both fenced competitively, especially Bob, who won many championships in foil, épée, and saber. As for me, I actually won the women's tristate foil championship one year for Kentucky, Ohio, and West Virginia!

I never will forget the fencing meet in which, spurred on by Bob, I competed only six weeks after Jennifer was born and won second place. For the next three days, I was in such unbelievable pain that I just stayed in bed.

We were active in our Unitarian Fellowship, went out dancing, often had people over for dinner or brunch, went to parties at friends' homes, and attended art shows, concerts, and plays. On many of those latter occasions, I was so exhausted, I barely made it through the evening.

One of my survival tactics was to slip away to a darkened, out-of-the-way bedroom and sleep until Bob found me when it was time to leave.

Nita once said, "I don't know how you do it all!" To which I replied, "I just muddle through!"

## A Citizens' Campaign

Daddy's visit had only served to delay the inevitable. Over the next few years, Bob and I grew distant; I'm not sure why. In late summer and fall of 1968, I became deeply involved in a citizens' campaign to prevent a sewage plant from being built across the road from us. This caused me to be away from home a great deal. I started meeting new people in our neighborhood and in the county at large. It was a heady experience.

The space between Bob and me widened. Our once-active sex life that had remained so strong through the years was now all but dormant. One evening, I finally said, "We need to do something about this marriage, Bob. Other men are starting to look good to me!"

He reacted with anger, refusing to talk about it. We were still doggedly attending marriage counseling sessions in Lexington; but I realized it was probably too late, for both of us, to pull it all back together.

One day, Jennifer came upon me in the kitchen as I stared out the window into our woods. "Mom, do you love Dad?" she asked.

"Why do you ask?" I wanted to know.

"Because you are so unhappy!"

And I confessed to her—this sensitive, beautiful thirteen-year-old daughter so dear to my heart—that our marriage had run into some serious trouble of late and that we were trying to work things out.

## Howard to the Rescue

In turmoil, I called our old friend Howard Aldous up in Canada. He and Donna now lived in Ontario, where Howard was head veterinarian for the National Stud Farm. I told him what was happening and, almost in tears, asked, "Can you come?"

After making the necessary arrangements, he must have left almost immediately, driving practically nonstop. He arrived at our house the next day, about a four-hundred-mile road trip.

He went out of town with Bob to a veterinary meeting for a few days, got reacquainted with the children, and rode my Shanghai, a horse big and spirited enough to suit him. He stayed with us for about a week and calmed the troubled waters.

Despite Howard's time with us in the winter of 1968-69, divorce still loomed on the horizon. I realized I would soon be on my own again, this time with six children to look after.

I decided to undergo a hysterectomy, solving one of my major health problems. This surgery in June of 1969 proved less painful and traumatic than one of my monthly periods, now banished forever. I rebounded quickly, became more energetic, and felt great!

We started formal divorce proceedings that December, and the holidays were soon upon us. We tried to act as if our family life was not falling apart around us, but Christmas 1969 wasn't much fun. I had by then started a full-time job at the University of Kentucky (UK) as a writer and publications editor.

## Remembering Kathy

Kathy Cook was a stylish, attractive young woman from New York City, a graduate of the Juilliard School of Music. How she landed in Lexington, I do not know; but one day, I bought a tube of mascara from her at Embry's, an upscale women's clothing store on Main Street where she worked at the cosmetic counter.

We struck up a conversation, and she fascinated me. A few weeks later, I stopped by to say hello to her and was told in icy tones that she no longer worked there. Disturbed, I proceeded to the personnel department to see if they could give me any information about her. "She's in jail," they told me haughtily.

Next stop, the Fayette County Jail. Upon my insistence, one of the staff escorted me to Kathy's dimly lit jail cell, and I talked to her through the bars. It was a horrible place!

"Kathy, what are you *doing* here?" I asked.

She told me she had designed and carried out the decorating of a suite of offices for a "friend," picking out the paint, wallpaper, lighting fixtures, curtains, furniture—everything. After depositing his substantial check for her work, she set about paying her pile of bills. His check bounced, as did all of hers. Her creditors descended on her, and she ended up in jail.

I asked her if she'd ever been in jail before, and she said no.

Promising to find someone to help her, I contacted a local American Civil Liberties Union attorney Bob and I knew. He interviewed Kathy the next day, then had her released to my custody while he worked on her case.

Evidently, she had refused to sleep with her "friend," and he had retaliated by stopping payment on his check. Within a few months, a new hearing was held, and all charges were dropped.

Kathy lived with us for about three months in that winter and spring of 1970. I'd had to let Henrietta go, so Kathy had come along at just the right time! She was a tremendous help with the kids, who loved her, and with the housework.

I'd never met anyone like Kathy. She was such a bright spirit. She had a whole different slant on being an independent woman and on working, living, and loving. She became a good friend to Jennifer, and they worked on some big art projects together.

And she took Scotty, who was just a few months short of seven years old, to the opening day of the races at Keeneland. He arrived back home with shining eyes and told us all about his exciting day.

## Losing Scotty

Early one evening soon after that, on April 7, Scotty was struck and killed by an out-of-control motorcycle on our country road.

I wasn't home at the time, having gone reluctantly to a dinner meeting at UK. Before I left, I noticed that Bob and Joel were saddling two of the horses. I remember saying to Jennifer and Lisa, "Look after our little boys while I'm gone."

I had a terrible sense of foreboding at the dinner and tried to call our number several times. The line was busy. When I finally got home, there were a few extra cars parked along our driveway. I walked in the kitchen door to find that Jim Russell and Blanche Bushong from my job at UK were already there, as were John and Theresa Griffin, our neighbors.

Three-year-old Timmy looked up at me with frightened eyes. And Bob said bluntly, "Scott was killed on the road tonight."

"My Scott, mine?" I asked.

"Yes," Theresa said gently, "your Scott." She has lost her own little boy, Rodney, just a toddler, a few years earlier when he was electrocuted by their faulty TV set.

I stumbled out the door, got back into my car, and drove to Nicholasville. I had to see Scotty! He was not at the first funeral home where I stopped. At the second funeral home, he was indeed there; but they wouldn't let me see him, probably afraid of having a hysterical mother on their hands. I drove on home where I asked Bob why he had left Scotty by the side of the road all alone.

"I don't care to discuss it," he said. And he never did.

In the middle of the night, I called Jack W., one of my new and trusted friends in Jessamine County, waking him up to tell him what had happened. "Oh hell!" he said, his voice breaking up with emotion.

In the darkness of early morning, Lisa, Joel, and Jennifer, with Timmy by the hand, came downstairs and crawled into the big queen-size bed with me. We clung to one another and cried for Scotty. (After that, I often woke up in the morning to find all four children in bed with me.)

After breakfast the next day, still numb from shock, I drove into the Nicholasville Elementary School and visited Scotty's first-grade room. There was his empty desk. I can see it still. That and the anxious faces of his classmates.

His teacher gathered up all Scotty's papers and belongings for me in the suddenly silent room, and I talked to the children for a few minutes.

"He was a very happy little boy," I said, and I told them about a letter he had just sent to his brother Doug. "I like my home, and I like my school," he had written in large carefully formed letters on lined paper.

I thanked them for their part in making this such a wonderful first year of school for Scotty.

Before driving home, I stopped by Jack's office for a few minutes. He already knew about my visit to the elementary school. Even our current e-mail system is no match for the word-of-mouth news network in a small town.

The next day, Joel came into the kitchen with Scotty's dented metal canteen. He'd found it down by the bridge. Wordless and heartbroken, we held each other close.

Years later, Lisa told me they had also found Scotty's little green gum boots at the accident site and kept them for a long, long time after we'd moved away following the divorce.

When the first shock and disbelief faded, I spent a weekend with Doug at the Barlow School in Amenia, New York, and made a brief visit to Mom, Pauline, and Malcolm in Ashfield.

Doug and I spent much of our time together walking the hilly trails in the woods around Barlow. He knew them all well from many hours of exploration. We were given a room with twin beds at the school and lay there talking each night until we finally fell asleep. We were a comfort to each other.

It was my children—who still needed me, especially Timmy—who enabled me to drag myself out of that quicksand of grief and go on.

Kathy returned to New York City shortly after Scotty's death. We wrote back and forth for perhaps two years. Then came her last letter saying she was married. "Marriage is a strange new country for me," she wrote. "But I am trying my best to learn how to live in it!"

## Our Marriage Was Over

Bob was now sleeping in the lower bunk bed in Doug's room, all alone. One night, I crawled into bed with him; he put his arms around me, and I asked in tears, "Oh, Bob, is it really over?"

"Yes, dear," he answered gently.

At one point in our long drawn-out divorce, I realized that Bob seemed to believe everything belonged to him, to parcel out to the rest of us as he saw fit. I reminded him that half of all our possessions, by law, were mine.

"Only because you're married to me," he retorted, discounting my role as full partner in our marriage.

By the time the divorce was final in August, I had borrowed some money and taken out a mortgage on a small run-down farm near Wilmore.

For a brief interlude while going through the divorce, Bob and I were almost friends again. When we went for a companionable walk one day, I asked him why he had married me. "Because you were the best thing that ever came down the road for me," he said.

Ah, well . . . So be it. The marriage I had wanted, expected, to last forever was over.

Timmy wasn't quite sure what was happening to our family, but he was a brave little boy. At one point, when he witnessed Bob and me arguing, he grabbed my hand tightly, shouting, "And it's all your fault too, Dad!"

But it wasn't, of course. Bob and I were both culpable. We simply had not been blessed with the insights—and in my case, the physical and emotional stamina—to make this once-promising marriage work.

By the summer of 1970, my financial situation was dire. Shortly after Christmas, Bob had closed out, withdrawn and kept all the money from our joint savings and checking accounts. "You can take care of all the household bills for a while," he said, "and see what it feels like!"

Paying these expenses depleted my new checking account every month. Our divorce would be final in a few weeks, and I was practically broke.

When I applied to a Nicholasville bank for a loan to make a down payment on the farm I wanted to buy, I was turned down point-blank. The loan officer explained that a divorced woman with children was psychologically fragile, among other things, and was simply not considered a good risk.

"May I please see your supervisor," I said with admirable self-control. Then mad as a hornet, I lit into the head of the loan department, accusing him of gender discrimination, meanness of spirit, shortsightedness, and Lord only knows what else. There on the open floor of the bank, heads turned and conversation stopped. I got my loan!

Early one morning a few weeks later, our doorbell rang on Ashgrove Pike. I opened the door to greet a bewildered serviceman, who said, "I thought this house would be empty. I was hired by Dr. Hensley to fumigate it!"

"But we're still living here," I said, stunned, standing there in my bathrobe with the kids starting to stack up behind me in the hallway. He apologized for waking us up, for being there at all, and left.

We began laughing because of the shocked look on his face, and the kids ran around the house in mock distress, screeching and holding their noses. But I was really angry with Bob for doing this.

A few days later, we started moving out.

# 23

# ENCOUNTER ON I-75 AND CITIZEN JAY

My years with Bob had shredded my positive self-image. I strove to regain it and go on. Two things helped me in this endeavor during the last year and a half of my fractured marriage—an encounter one morning on Interstate 75 and my intense involvement with a Jessamine County citizens' group.

### Encounter on I-75
*The following is Excerpted from a November 25, 1969, letter to Pauline and Malcolm:*

> I took off bright and early for Cincinnati to visit Margaret [Mom's younger sister, very dear to me and fatally ill with leukemia]. Bob had flown up to Chicago [piloting the small plane he co-owned with several other people] yesterday morning for an art exhibit . . . His car was home again when I left . . .
>
> About 9 a.m. I stopped to help a man who had been sitting there with a dead car since 4 a.m. He was so funny. I couldn't get him started with my jumper cable. He said, "Well, thanks for stopping anyhow. Nobody else even stopped!" I said, "Oh, I'm not going to leave you sitting here. I'll tow you into a service station."

He looked at me almost in disbelief. "You have a tow chain? Lady, will you marry me?"

I towed him about eight miles to the next exit and then to a service station. Once there he wanted me to have breakfast with him, but I said I was due in Cincinnati for breakfast. He was about 45, an outgoing, plain-spoken man from Alabama, driving a late model Ford. He tried to persuade me to spend the morning with him.

Then he said, "Are you married?" "Yes," I said. "Any children?" "Yes, I have six children."

"Oh, Hell," he said. "Lady, I never met anyone like you. I would trade my car and everything I have for you!" Oh, he was funny. Then he pulled out his billfold and I said, "Put that away, I don't want your money. Whenever I've had car trouble, someone has stopped and helped me."

"I can see why they'd stop and help you," he said, "but I'd been sitting there for five hours!" He stuck the $5 bill in my pocket and wouldn't let me return it.

*Reminiscing about this incident, I wonder what would have happened if I'd called Margaret to change our breakfast plan to lunch and had instead spent the morning with this appealing man. And what if I'd told him, "Yes, I'm married, but I'm in the midst of a divorce right now"? We might have seen each other again, become friends, or something more. Ah, the road not taken . . . But I was not yet that liberated a woman.*

### The Planning and Zoning Battle

In 1969, Fayette County to the north of us appropriated through eminent domain the farm across Ashgrove Pike from us where they planned to build a sewage plant. A neighbor, Joyce Trebolo, and I started a citizens' group to protest their action and advocate setting up a planning and zoning board for Jessamine County.

During our well-organized campaign, we circulated petitions against the sewage plant and collected thousands of signatures. I also wrote numerous articles for the local radio station and weekly newspaper, the *Jessamine Journal*. Within a few months, fiscal court adopted planning and zoning, but it was too late to stop the sewage plant. (Placed on the back of the farm, it was well constructed and well run and did not eventually "ruin the neighborhood" as feared!)

My articles for the paper included in-depth weekly coverage of fiscal court meetings, which stirred up citizens to the point that they flooded the courtroom every week and spilled out into the hallway.

The county attorney complained to the *Journal's* editor about my verbatim quotes of things he said during fiscal court. "Did she misquote you?" the editor asked. "No, I just didn't expect to see it in the newspaper!" he answered. The editor, pleased with my articles, had seen a big increase in circulation.

One day, I turned on my car radio and was startled to hear my own voice in a lengthy interview with a reporter from the *Lexington Herald-Leader*! This whole battle was an empowering experience for me. I was out in the world again, doing something significant for my community.

In this whole endeavor, we worked closely with the politically savvy president of the Chamber of Commerce. Jack W. was a charismatic six-footer who carried a gun, had earned his way through high school as a bootlegger, and once tossed a man through a plate glass window. Over the next two years he became a friend I could count on. He helped me with decisions about the children and steered me though the horrors and dangers of a bitter, traumatic divorce.

### Aunt Margaret and My Cousin Steve

My beloved aunt Margaret died in the winter of 1970. Following the funeral service, her son, Steve, my tall blond, blue-eyed bachelor cousin, and I stayed over in her apartment, talking late into the night, lying on the living room carpet and listening to Simon and Garfunkel records.

I've known and loved Steve since he was born when I was ten. He and Margaret lived in Manhattan, and we saw them often when he was a baby and then a little boy. She would let him stay with us for weeks at a time in Ashfield. He loved to follow Phillips around, calling him Phoops.

Steve was an exceptionally bright and observant kid. Once, when he was only five or six, he eluded his babysitter, caught the bus and then the subway to Bay Ridge from Manhattan, got off at the Eighty-ninth Street station, walked to Eighty-second Street, and turned up in high spirits at our front door.

When he was twelve, I stayed with him and his mother for six weeks in Minneapolis. Now retired, Steve lives near Harvard Square in Cambridge where he was for many years a vice president of Abt Associates, a big sociological research company. We became close friends in our grown-up years and spend time together when we can.

Whenever I hear "The Sounds of Silence," I relive our sad, companionable, mellow evening together at Margaret's place almost forty years ago.

# 24

# ON MY OWN AGAIN

*. . . And Reconnecting with Pierre*

*There follows a copy of the annual letter I mailed out that first Christmas on the Jessamine Creek. Read between the lines for the heartache and the trauma of this brutal transition in our lives. Through the years, I had written annual family letters with a very positive spin to them. Few people had guessed that our marriage was in trouble.*

**Our 1970 Christmas Letter**

Rt. 1, Frankfort Ford Pike
Wilmore, Kentucky 40390

Christmas 1970 finds the Hensleys settling into a different way of Life. Bob and I were divorced this past summer. In August, the children and I bought and moved into the white frame farmhouse pictured here [a pen-and-ink drawing by my friend Joe Martin, staff artist at UK]. The big kitchen was once a log house, with five rooms and a side porch added on later. It is in a lovely setting about 20 miles south of Lexington, back at the end of a 7/10-mile rocky lane, tucked into a crook of the Jessamine Creek, a cliff curving around to further isolate our 22 acres. We lived for months without the conveniences, learned to appreciate a crackling coal fire in the

grate, water carried from the well and heated in a big kettle on the stove. Now we have central heating, plumbing, good wiring, a great kitchen, two bathrooms. Out back is a little weathered building we insulated, tin-roofed, and fixed into a cozy three rooms—one for Joel, 11, one for Doug, 16, when he is visiting from his Dad's or from the Barlow School in New York; and a shop for fixing things and working with clay. Ahead of us is the repairing and redecorating of a long-neglected house. Joel is developing into a skillful handyman. Jennifer, 15, and Lisa, 13, are creative and enthusiastic.

Timmy, 4, dark-haired, dark-eyed, exuberant, has made the transition most easily. Scott, 6-1/2, was killed on April 10, struck down by a motorcycle on our country road. He was a warm, loving, blond, blue-eyed, happy little boy. We miss him.

I have, since last December 15 been working full time for the University of Kentucky as Home Economics Extension editor. Before that I worked briefly part-time for the *Jessamine Journal*, our county's weekly paper, a job that got me happily back into the professional world after a 15-year absence.

We hope 1970 has been good to you and yours. Write to us. Better still, stop by our new Kentucky home. Our telephone number is 606-859-4043.

—*Jay, Doug, Jennifer, Lisa, Joel, and Timmy*

## Moving Day

The kids had looked at the farm with me before I bought it. They fell in love with the long rocky, tree-shaded lane, the old stone walls, the green fields and woods, the creek, and the cliff that rose up behind it. They were somewhat leery of the old run-down house with its primitive privy. Even so, they started looking forward to our move as the beginning of a wonderful new adventure in their lives.

"I think we can fix up the house and be happy here," Jennifer said bravely. Leaving our beautiful new dream house on the Ashgrove Pike would still be devastating for them all . . . except Timmy, just barely four and not quite sure what was happening.

So we packed up boxes and rented a U-Haul van. On the day we moved, my old friend Henrietta was on hand, as well as Doug and his best friend, David Toleman, who were indispensable in toting furniture and all the other big stuff. On every trip back and forth to the farm, we included Tim's bouncy horse, which he rode to his heart's content while the action swirled about him.

By the time we unloaded the last vanful, the kids had hit upon a fitting finale. One by one, again and again, they climbed out of an upstairs front window and jumped enthusiastically from the porch roof onto a "safety net" held aloft by the rest of us.

We used a strong padded packing blanket from the van. The last one to jump on the first round, after watching the others intently from below, was Timmy. He ran into the house, up the stairs, climbed out the window, and sprang from the roof with a triumphant yell.

The next day, Henrietta came back. I remember her unpacking boxes and putting dishes into the kitchen cupboards, shaking her head and mumbling to herself about the outrage of it all.

## Living Poor

At first, wrenched from their comfortable middle-class life and grieving for their little brother, the children had trouble coping. We were living like the poor folk they'd read about! And I lay awake in the night with a lacerated heart and shattered dreams, wondering how I could possibly cope with it all.

But I had a job to go to every day, and the kids soon started school, with day care for Timmy. And we had work to do to make our new digs more livable.

Returning from work one late afternoon in September, I was met by Jennifer and Lisa, just bursting with what they had to show me. "Wait," they said, "we have to do something first." A few minutes later, they ushered me through the front door into the living room.

They had transformed it with colorful Indian bedspreads, which covered the couch, cardboard boxes, and big floor cushions. Illuminated by candlelight, the room had become an Arabian nights dreamscape.

## Reconnecting with Pierre

Sometime during our first year on the farm, I rediscovered the diary of my time with Pierre. Reading it clear through one evening, sitting close to the fire on the living room hearth after the kids were in bed, I was sixteen again—caught up in the excitement, yearning, and heartache of my first love.

Closing the diary at last, I gazed into the dying embers and thought about how far I had come on my life journey, how much I had accomplished. I was now forty-four, still strong and healthy . . .

Remembering how I had put my past behind me after Pierre's death and gone on with my life, I resolved anew to become an independent, self-sufficient woman and make my own way in the world.

I stepped out onto the front porch that moonlit night, marveled at the sound and fury of our fast-running creek. The horse in the yard raised his head expectantly and stood watching me. I spread out my arms and shouted, "The world is mine!"

Over the next eleven years, my most prized possessions would be a good trail horse, a pickup truck, a wood-burning stove, a sharp axe, a tough pair of work boots, and a jackknife. I bought a chain saw and learned, with fear and trembling, how to use it. (Within a few years, Joel became skilled with chain saws, and I gratefully gave up that particular chore.)

## Doug Moves On

Bob had custody of Doug, and that was okay with Doug, who said, "We can't take everything away from him!" But his father soon kicked him out for infraction of the rules, and he came on out to the farm, sleeping on the living room couch whenever he stayed overnight.

When Bob informed Doug that he didn't have the tuition money to send him back to Barlow, I asked the school to reserve a place for him anyhow. "He'll let me go," Doug predicted, "because he doesn't want me around!" At the eleventh hour, Bob did send him back to Barlow where he was a junior. Visiting us at the farm during Christmas vacation, Doug walked the night playing a borrowed flute.

Instead of returning for his senior year (the headmaster having asked him not to return!), Doug worked as a groom at several racetracks in Kentucky and River Downs in Cincinnati where he unknowingly fathered a daughter he would not meet for more than thirty years. He lived in a tack room, played his five-string banjo, loved the horses in his charge.

It was also in Cincinnati that he bought an Indian sitar. This would lead directly to his introduction to Persian music a few years later at the University of Oregon in Eugene.

Thus, Doug became a "West Coast person" and missed out on most of our adventures living on the creek.

## Down on the Farm

My other kids all learned to work up firewood, haul water, tend a woodstove, make do with secondhand clothes, and live for a while in a house with the upstairs ceilings coming down, no running water, a roof that leaked, uninsulated walls, and the numbing cold on a winter's day before a fire on the living room grate and in the stove in the kitchen warmed up those two rooms.

The soaring price of gas forced us to limit drastically the use our new gas furnace. For our main source of heat, we bought first a secondhand coal stove and then a wood-burning stove. After that, we could always get warm in the kitchen around the stove.

On weekends, we were busy fixing up the house. We did a lot of painting and repairing. Joel, Jennifer, and Lisa all proved to be hard workers. Even then, Joel could fix just about anything. As for Timmy, he rode his bouncy horse and helped out with gusto when we found "important" jobs for him to do.

I hired a local man, George Brumfield, to do some remodeling, install plumbing, and add two bathrooms. He enclosed the back porch and turned two-thirds of it into a laundry room. Then he tackled the little backyard house I called the Outback. It consisted mostly of a tobacco stripping room with a root cellar below. He put in a trap door down to the root cellar, flooring over the stone stairway that had dominated what now became a usable adjacent room.

Within a few years, we would have the walls of the main house filled with blown-in insulation. It made a big difference!

I wrote an in-depth article about insulating and fixing up the house and sold it to *Home Energy Digest & Wood Burning Quarterly* magazine.

## Our Honky-tonk Piano

When we moved an old upright piano into the house—a substitute Bob provided for the baby grand we were leaving behind—it plunged through the floor just inside the front door. Termites! We had that section of floor replaced and the house treated for termites and powderpost beetles.

The kids used the piano as a launchpad for leaping enthusiastically onto the couch. I banished it to the Outback where they banged on their honky-tonk keyboard to their hearts' content until it was completely trashed and ended up in the town dump.

## One Dark Night . . .

One night, when Timmy was at his dad's (he usually slept with me that first year), I was awakened by a loud tearing sound and something big and solid falling on me. At first, I thought there'd been an earthquake, that I was being buried in the rubble of my house.

A large heavy section of the plaster ceiling over my bed had torn loose and crashed down on me. I grabbed some blankets and spent the rest of the night on the living room couch, then heard another section of ceiling crash down a little while later. That inspired us to redo my bedroom ceiling and the water-damaged ones in the two upstairs bedrooms as well.

But the roof still leaked for many more years. On rainy days, we got out every bucket, saucepan, and big bowl we owned to catch the drips.

## Joel Leaves Us

That following spring, I was out in the front yard with Joel one day. He looked back at the house and said, "I'm not living in this dump anymore! Why won't you let me live with Dad?"

"Joel, we keep no prisoners here," I said. "When school lets out, you can go to live with your dad. If that works for you, we'll change the custody arrangements."

"Really?" he said in amazement. "Really?"

He packed up and moved to his dad's that summer, leaving a hole in our lives. He explained that his stepmother, Jan, the young woman Bob married a few weeks after our divorce, had told him his father cried at night for his children.

When Jan took her own life about five months after Joel went to live with them, he stayed on with his father, determined to try to make him happy, not wanting him to be all alone. On weekends, he enjoyed going on calls with his dad to the racetrack and bluegrass horse farms. But he was left all alone on many school nights when Bob ate a quick dinner, changed his clothes, and went off to one meeting or another in Lexington.

That early winter, lonely for his brothers and sisters, Joel came back to us. "Dad doesn't have happiness in him," he said.

My old friend Anne Alevizon Mitchell and I lost track of each other for a few years during this period. When we reconnected, I found that she too was now on her own with her four children. Living in Plattsburgh, New York, on Lake Champlain, she had found a well-paying job as librarian at the State University of New York (SUNY). She and Mitch separated after twenty-one years together. He was faithful with the monthly child-support checks and stayed involved in his children's lives.

# 25

# EARLY YEARS ON THE CREEK

Somehow, my kids and I survived the tumultuous free love, drug-soaked hippie-era '70s. The winters were hard on us—the plumbing froze, and we were sometimes snowed in for a month or more. But before too long we had our woodstove in the kitchen and a big stack of firewood to keep us warm—or at the very least, from freezing to death!

We had shelter, friends, books, music, a vegetable garden we ate out of all year long, a red raspberry patch, and fresh eggs from our own chickens. We never went hungry. We became mostly vegetarian to save money, ate lots of brown rice, lentils, and soybeans.

The proprietor of a fruit stand on Harrodsburg Road near the river saved his imperfect fruits and vegetables for us. From these freebies, I made batches of applesauce, lots of peach pies, and peach jam.

That first winter on the Jessamine Creek, I was up early every morning to lay a wood fire on the coal grate in the living room. Once it had warmed the room somewhat, I called to the children, who carried their clothes sleepily into the living room—reminiscent of my own childhood when, on cold mornings at Ashfield, we donned our clothes by the warmth of the fire Daddy had kindled in the dining room fireplace.

Now I often fixed breakfast over the wood fire in our living room—hot chocolate, scrambled eggs or hot cereal, toast, and fruit. Our first year on the creek, we bought a Warm Morning coal-burning stove for $15 at Mount Sterling Court Day. But it cowed us with scary explosions in the firebox and put a greasy black film on the white kitchen walls.

We quickly replaced it with a brand-new wood-burning stove. Now the dressing-by-the-fire routine on cold mornings took place around our wonderful Fisher Mama Bear stove.

In those frozen-plumbing winters, I did our laundry at the Laundromat in nearby Nicholasville. While the clothes were sloshing clean and tumble drying, I took a sponge bath and washed my hair in the bathroom there. I dropped the kids off at their dad's house once a week for their showers and shampoos. And sometimes I took a sponge bath at work after hours.

On the way home from UK every day, I filled two five-gallon jugs with water at one of the local gas stations. For the first few years, we bared our bottoms in the outhouse and learned to appreciate warming up again around the living room hearth or the stove in the kitchen after being *really* cold.

I was *so* frugal with water. Rinse water from dishwashing was reused for washing dishes from the next meal; the soapy water went into a mop bucket for floors and, lastly, to flush the toilet (after we got one!).

The women's lib movement in the '60s and '70s got short shrift from me although I was aware of it and particularly admired one of its leaders, Robin Morgan. Doug told a friend, "My mother is a liberated woman. She just doesn't talk about it."

No, I didn't. I was too busy surviving! But I had, for sure, become sexually emancipated and somehow managed to have three serious love affairs during the '70s. Mostly, however, I was raising my kids and engrossed in a challenging job.

**Money Matters**

Money was a worrisome thing. Even though I was very frugal, there was never enough. My meager paycheck and inadequate child support almost always ran out before the end of the month. It was scary.

Our first year on the creek, we were dependent on gas for our furnace as well as for our cooking stove and water heater. One winter day, when Joel was home alone, the gas man came to our remote farm to cut off service because our bill was way overdue. Joel looked up at him with big eyes and said pitifully, "But then we'll be cold!" And the serviceman didn't have the heart to do it.

A few times, I resorted to the ploy of mailing an unsigned check. The utility company would send it back to me for signing, and that would give me a few more days to come up with payment. Also, a good friend often helped us out by cashing a check for me, then holding it until I could cover it.

## Baby Chicks in the Kitchen

When we started raising chickens, the weather was so cold that I had to bring all those peeping yellow chicks into the kitchen. Putting them in a big cardboard box near the woodstove, I changed the newspaper bedding two or three times a day. To no avail! That chicken shit stank to high heaven and drove us out of the room.

I fixed meals in a big hurry; we ate in the living room until the weather warmed and finally got those little stinkers out of the house. I never did manage to develop any real affection for chickens although I became mighty proud of one of our roosters, a gorgeous colorful fellow we named Chanticleer.

## Tim's Room

The first year, to feel safe in our new surroundings, Tim slept with me in my downstairs bedroom next to the living room. The second year, he slept on a lounge chair next to my bed. After that, we moved the lounge chair back into the living room for him, and I kept my door open at night.

When he was twelve and still sleeping in the living room, Lisa started teasing him. She bet him a dollar he wouldn't be sleeping in his own upstairs room before he was thirteen. So the night before he turned thirteen, he made up the bed in his room and moved in. But Lisa didn't pay up.

A few months later, he caught a ride to town with her; and she charged him a dollar, saying, "Now we're even!" Thirty years later, when Tim recounted this story to the rest of us, Lisa, who had clean forgotten about her behavior at the time, handed him a dollar bill.

### Linda Adopts Us

Linda Kanzinger came in the front door one evening with Doug in the fall of '71. As she walked through the house and into the kitchen, she said, "Oh, this is such a human place!" Soup simmered on the woodstove; and my homemade bread, still warm, was turned out onto a cutting board.

She was a beautiful full-bodied young woman with long honey blonde hair, lively brown eyes, and glowing young skin. She loved our scene and felt a deep kinship with our family.

At that time, she and Doug were living together at his dad's house and playing music together. They had met through mutual friends during a concert at UK. Free-spirited, quick-witted, and imaginatively dressed in colorful offbeat clothes, she would have been hard to resist!

Doug was working then as a groom at Keeneland Racetrack. When he took a job a few months later at the River Downs Racetrack outside Cincinnati, Linda stayed on at his dad's for another few months, after which she was back and forth between there and our farm.

One day, in March, she stuffed her belongings into a backpack; and Bob drove her to catch a ride with friends to Denver. She stayed overnight with an old friend of mine there and with a Barlow classmate of Doug's in Boulder, her next stop. Her final destination was Eugene, Oregon, where she attended the spring and summer semesters at the University of Oregon (U. of O.). She was a sophomore, having gone to UK her freshman year.

Before returning for the fall term, she came back via Greyhound bus for a visit. One day, she and I drove to Cincinnati to see Doug at River Downs.

Intrigued by what Linda told him about Eugene and the university's music curricula, Doug applied there too. He included letters of recommendation from a few of his Barlow teachers, was speedily accepted despite his lack of a high school diploma, and headed West in his '64 Volkswagen van.

It was September 1972. Unlike Joel, Doug had almost no experience with cars, so I sent him off with a paperback copy of *How to Keep Your Volkswagen Alive*. The semester had already started, and he enrolled a few weeks late. Robert Trotter, dean of the music department, soon took a particular interest in him.

Linda came back to Kentucky and lived at the farm with us off and on in the 1970s. In good weather, I would often come home from my job at UK and find her sitting under a tree, working diligently, paints and fabrics spread all around her. A gifted artisan, she created beautiful crocheted scarves and blankets, as well as colorful clothes from scissored free-box offerings and her own painted fabrics.

Over the years, she became many things to me—daughter, sister, fellow writer, close friend, and confidant. Intellectually far keener than I, she has at times also been a mentor.

**The School Situation at Home**

After the divorce, Jennifer and Lisa continued school in Jessamine County and were members of the marching band. Lisa played flute and piccolo while Jen played clarinet. (Doug too had once played clarinet there in the marching band.) And at home, Joel played his drums.

The first year at the farm, I dropped Timmy off at nursery school in Lexington on the way to work every morning. As for Joel, he had attended Sayre private school in Lexington for the second, third, and fourth grades. After the divorce, he entered fifth grade at Wilmore public school. The following year, I enrolled Joel and a year later, Timmy at Innisfree, a State-approved open-classroom school in Lexington for children five through thirteen.

**Innisfree School**

Founded by a group of teachers and parents in the fall of 1971, Innisfree was patterned after the educational concept brought to life at Summerhill by A. S. Neill, whose book about the school I had read with consuming interest.

Our parent-teacher-student meetings were exciting, exhausting events. Everyone had a vote, kids included. Some involvement was required of every parent, a few of whom served as part-time teachers. Tuition was affordable. Prospective students and their parents were interviewed in depth before acceptance.

I designed brochures for the school and wrote articles about it for local newspapers and radio stations. We had twenty-eight students the second year and over forty by the end of the third year.

Here's a sampling of instruction offered, in addition to reading, writing, and arithmetic: Classical guitar, piano, candle making, tie-dyeing, group singing, cooking, gardening, biology and animal care, group and individual sports, square dancing, photography and filmmaking, contemporary politics, bicycle repair, beekeeping, trampoline, geology, astronomy, yoga, self-defense, social psychology, Appalachian culture, current events, Civil War history, religious and social movements, transactional analysis, personal ecology, and an introduction to Spanish and French.

Field trips included camping out in the Red River Gorge, bike hikes, visits to Mammoth Cave, planetariums, museums, art exhibits, the zoo, a pig farm, the Berea Craft Fair, Shakertown, Fort Harrod, and the Perryville battle site. The kids also experienced time at other unique schools, such as Lotts Creek Community School in the eastern Kentucky mountains.

Innisfree was a good place for my boys. When Joel was caught smoking pot, his schoolmates sentenced him to cleaning the basement. Joel refused and was expelled. About three days later, he told me, "I'm going back to school!"

"So how are you going to do that?" I asked.

"I guess I'm going to clean the basement!" he said.

We had many Innisfree potluck suppers at the farm and took turns hand cranking our freezer for great homemade ice cream. One evening, as we all sat in the living room, warmed by a fire on the grate, Joel snuggled up to me on the couch and asked, "Mom, do you sometimes feel rich?"

I did indeed.

But after four years, we couldn't keep the school going. That fall, we had bought supplies and hired two more teachers on the strength of a $10,000 grant the Kentucky Department of Education had promised us. When the grant was denied us at the last minute by a new administrator, we had to close down and declare bankruptcy.

Tim went on to fourth grade in Jessamine County, well ahead of his classmates in reading, but he never loved public school half as much as Innisfree.

**Lewis-Wadham**

Uncle Dudley and Aunt Emma Smith, parents of my friend Anne, sent me a check for $4,000 so that I could enroll Joel at Lewis-Wadham, an open-classroom school in New York State. Joel and I had visited the school first and met one of the teachers. After enrolling, however, Joel discovered to his great disappointment that this appealing teacher had not returned for fall semester.

His enthusiasm for the school deflated, he drove the school van at night on icy winter roads, didn't go to most of his classes, slept part of the day. One night, he was apprehended by the state police and returned to the school. None of this was ever reported to me by the school authorities!

Shortly thereafter, he left Lewis-Wadham and took a bus back to Kentucky, through with a school whose only merit he could recognize was facilitating his nightly drives. He was fifteen years old. To this day, he is a superlative driver.

**Trouble with the Law**

Joel was soon working in a bicycle shop in Lexington and earned enough money to buy a very good bicycle. After that, he became my long-haired wild child—lovable, funny, adventuresome, maddening. He experimented with some drugs and was in and out of trouble with the law.

He told the most amazing stories so convincingly that one juvenile court judge said, "Nobody could make up something like that!" and dismissed the charges.

Once, he drove his dad's Jaguar without permission, and Bob had him arrested. Joel rode around for hours with the sheriff (a friend of mine), had a wonderful time, and was released to my custody at the end of the day. The judge conferred with us in his chambers, gave both Joel and Bob a talking-to, and dismissed the charges.

In Lexington one night, Joel was picked up with some marijuana. The two young police officers who searched him confiscated the pot, talked to him about the dangers of smoking pot, then let him go.

Another time, friends in Lexington told me Joel had obtained keys to one of their cars and was driving it at night. "What should we do?" they asked. "Call the police!" I said, at my wits end, for he had been driving my car at night too.

So Joel and I ended up in the chambers of a stern-looking woman judge. After studying Joel with his long hair, soulful brown eyes, and anxious, attentive face, she admonished him to behave himself, go home, and mind his mother. "Yes, Your Honor," Joel said respectfully.

Over my objections, she dismissed the charges. Nobody, it seemed, wanted to shunt this youngster into the State's juvenile detention system. Years later, cognizant of what happens to appealing young boys in our jails, I was to be grateful for this.

Doug and Tim also had their run-ins with the law. I began to think this was a rite of passage in those times, especially for boys.

Joel acquired his first car at sixteen, trading his bicycle for it. Soon after that, he used my little Chevy pickup truck for keeping us in firewood. Short on cash, he once sold our woodpile right off the front porch, then scrambled to replace it.

## Lisa's Adventures

Bob paid Lisa's tuition at Barlow her last two years of high school. There, she was befriended by Peter DuFault, her history

Joel, my lovable wild child.

teacher. He and his wife, Ruth, had a farm nearby where Lisa spent
many happy weekends.

That Christmas, I gave her a violin, evidently a pretty good one.
She took lessons, played it in the school orchestra, and learned to
play country fiddle from Peter DuFault. When Barlow offered a
dulcimer-making class, she and Jennifer signed up for it. (Jen was
attending Barlow for one semester to earn credits for completing
high school.) After making their own dulcimers, they learned how to
play them.

Following her graduation in '75, Lisa came back home
to Kentucky. She bought a pickup truck and became her own
independent, self-sufficient woman.

She had a special rapport with horses and hired on as a hot
walker and exercise rider at a local training track. Then she worked
the Keeneland horse sales, also held jobs for one year each as a
groom at Hurricane Stud horse farm in Fayette County and resident
horseman at Clifton broodmare farm in Scott County.

In between, she waitressed for a few months at Alfalfa, an
organic foods restaurant in Lexington. But she much preferred
outdoor jobs. One summer, she worked at Pepperhill Farm, the day
camp Tim attended. In charge of one group of campers, as well as
the horseback-riding program, she said this was her hardest job
ever. But the kids all loved her, and she was chosen Counselor of
the Year.

I was official photographer in exchange for Tim's tuition that
summer and gave Lisa a photo album of her Pepperhill experience
for a Christmas present. As for Tim, after attending Pepperhill for
three or four summers as a camper, he went back and worked as a
counselor for another few years.

## Jennifer Quits School

When she was sixteen, after her junior year of high school, Jen
ran off to join a group of back-to-the-land hippies in the hills of Lee
County where she lived for the next five years. They cleared land,
raised big gardens, worked and played music together, fell in and

out of love, lived an exhilarating, challenging subsistence life full of hardship and joy.

They cooked and heated with wood, canned their garden produce on a wood-burning cookstove, and raised hogs, chickens, and a milk cow. They also became well acquainted with old-timer Edgel McQueen, an endearing master storyteller who taught them "the old ways."

On many a weekend, Tim and I tossed our sleeping bags into the car and drove the eighty miles to hang out with Jennifer and her friends. We either parked at the Yellowrock stone quarry, walked a half mile along the railroad tracks, and hollered across the river until someone came by boat to fetch us; or we parked at a place on the other side of the river and walked three miles in on a rugged and hilly dirt road, then down a steep mountain trail.

On one of our visits when Tim was six or seven, he was to spend the night up the mountain from us with neighbors in their log cabin. But after dark, we heard his voice and another calling to us. We went out on the porch and yelled, "Are you all right, Tim?"

"No!" he wailed.

Jennifer's fella, Lee, went out with a flashlight and brought the boys back with him. Tim was sopping wet and shivering. I pulled off his wet clothes, wrapped him in a big towel, held him on my lap, and rocked him 'til he fell asleep.

Tim and another boy, a few years older than he, had been out exploring when darkness came upon them. Not able to determine how to find their way back to the neighbor's, they decided to go down the mountain to Jen and Lee's place. They could see the light from their cabin below, to the left. But on their way down, Tim walked off a cliff, fell almost twenty feet, and landed on his butt on some leaf-covered ground. "Tim, don't move!" his companion called out and groped his way down the steep rocky trail to him. The boys made their way down the rest of the mountain in the dark.

They reached the knee-deep, ice-cold creek they knew flowed by Jen's cabin, waded into it, and followed it downstream in the pitch-black moonless night. When they saw the lights of the house above them, they started yelling.

Once they were safely inside, Lee blew on a very loud cow horn, using a prearranged signal that let the neighbors up the mountain know all was well.

I took Tim back to Lexington the next morning and had him checked over by a doctor at the Hunter Foundation where I paid $15 per month for family medical coverage, including dentistry. He was fine. Miraculously, he had suffered no permanent damage.

Another time in Lee County, Tim was out on the porch fashioning a pistol out of wood, using a sharp hatchet to do so. He wanted the pistol to replace a pellet gun the adults had decided needed to be put away. In the process, he buried the hatchet deep into the meaty part of his left thumb. He came rushing into the house, bloody and frightened, making himself not cry.

I cleaned out the wound with alcohol, pulled the edges of the gash together with tape, and wrapped his thumb and hand in sterile gauze. After that, I had him drink a glass of wine. He slept peacefully all night, and by morning, his thumb was no longer painful. A few days later, his dad unwrapped the hand and found that his thumb was healing just fine.

## A Backwoods Wedding

Joel gave us a scare too on the occasion of a wedding between two of Jennifer's friends in Lee County. It happened in a steep-sided mountain hollow near an abandoned one-room schoolhouse. Spring flowers were in bloom. It was a lovely ceremony and joyous celebration with a feast prepared for afterward and the wine flowing freely.

Keeping a close eye on Timmy, I lost track of Joel until he came plummeting out of a tree, landing nearby with a thud. Full of wine, he was feeling no pain, but he had injured his left arm. A few of the men took a door off the schoolhouse and carefully toted Joel up the mountain on it. Then they transferred him to the back of a four-wheel drive pickup truck, wrapped a blanket around him, and held the door as level as possible as they drove three miles out the narrow up-and-down mountain road to where my Travelall was parked.

I had left Timmy in Jennifer's care and followed the makeshift ambulance into the hospital in Richmond. By then, it was night and cold. Bearded, long-haired, muddy booted, colorfully dressed, and smelling of marijuana, three of our party burst into the emergency room, with me and the two men carrying Joel in on the schoolhouse door bringing up the rear.

A nurse called out, "We have an injured little girl here," and led the way down a corridor. Joel turned his head and shouted, "I'm a boy!" The guys went on home after Lee called his folks, who lived just outside Richmond, and made arrangements for me to stay with them. He drew me a map showing how to get to their house.

X-rays soon determined that Joel had dislocated his left elbow and knocked a chip off the bone. Surgery to remove the bone chip was scheduled for the next morning. I found my way to Lee's parents' house and spent the night after relating the day's adventures to them and calling Bob. Early next morning, Lee's mom, Nancy, fed me a big breakfast; and I returned to the hospital.

Bob was already there in the waiting room, having visited Joel first. As soon as the doctor appeared to tell us the surgery was over and that Joel was doing fine, Bob left. Joel didn't cry through the whole ordeal—not until I was sitting by his bed later that morning, and he said, "The food here is terrible," choking back tears.

There was bright moonlight that night as I walked the mountain road back through the forest, then carefully made my way down the steep rocky trail to Jennifer and Lee's place. Joel was going to be okay. All was well with my world.

Three weeks later, as soon as his arm was out of the cast, Joel began a series of strengthening and stretching exercises. By the time school was out, he had a job mucking out stalls and mowing at a neighboring farm and riding school.

### Marijuana Bust!

One morning, when I'd spent the night at Peg Payne's house in Lexington, we opened her Sunday paper to a front-page feature story about a big marijuana bust. A dozen metro and state police had boarded two boats on the Kentucky River and set out on an all-day hunt through the backwoods of Lee County. They found a few odd plots of marijuana and arrested a handful of growers.

One of them was Lee, who was growing pot within his rows of corn. He was arrested, and the crop destroyed. An attorney secured his release shortly with a $500 fine and no jail time to serve.

This was nevertheless a frightening event for Jennifer, who had anticipated Lee's perhaps spending a year in jail, leaving her on her own with their new baby.

I'm no fan of marijuana, but the police have wasted huge amounts of taxpayers' money through the years trying to stamp out a weed that has grown in this part of the country for many years. Meanwhile, alcohol, which has caused untold trouble in the world, is bought and sold legally.

During her years in Lee County, Jennifer and several of her friends experimented at length with weaving baskets from the inner bark of the black willow trees that grow abundantly along the Kentucky River. When she returned to civilization in the fall of 1977, she had little Ezra with her, plus her self-taught basketry skills. She landed a job waitressing in Lexington over the winter, then worked at Shaker Village between Lexington and Harrodsburg for two years demonstrating hand weaving, spinning, and basket making.

Meanwhile, she had begun her romance with Eddie Heller, also a former member of the Lee County community. In 1978, they moved in with us while they built a small frame house on the farm. Their plan was to save enough money to buy land of their own in a few years and build a more permanent house.

They ended up liking the farm and the family situation there so much that they bought twelve acres from me for $18,000, the going rate for such land at the time. Their down payment and monthly checks allowed me, at last, to pay off my own mortgage within a few years.

"Jennifer, Eddie, and I are getting married!" three-year-old Ezra announced one day in the fall of 1979. The ceremony, followed by a potluck reception with a heart-shaped wedding carrot cake made by Lisa, was held outdoors on the farm. Afterward, we lit off a huge bonfire, sang songs, and watched an incredible sunset.

## My New Son-in-law

Eddie would make all the difference in our lives on the farm. Of average height, with shaggy blond hair, keen blue eyes, and a football player's build, he had the true pioneer spirit and the skills to go with it. His day job was as a tile contractor, and he was amazingly good at his craft. The rest of the time, he was an enthusiastic gardener, raised chickens, was an all-'round farmer and jack-of-all-trades. He could cut and work up a load of firewood, build a house, run a fence line, butcher a hog.

In Lee County, Eddie had built his own one-room log house with a fireplace and chimney at its center and a sleeping loft. He and other men in the community had felled the trees with a crosscut saw and hauled them to the building site with a mule. As he laid up his walls, he had notched the ends of the logs to fit into each other.

After leaving the Lee County community and marrying Jennifer, Eddie returned to lead a work party to dismantle the cabin in preparation for rebuilding it to form the core of his and Jennifer's new house in Jessamine County. He claimed he knew every one of those notched logs by heart and where it would need to be placed during the rebuilding process. But I took many close-up color slides of those logs as the cabin was being dismantled, just in case!

## Update on Doug

Meanwhile, Doug attended the University of Oregon in 1972-73 where he and Linda both worked part-time at the the Book and Tea Shop (co-owned by the mother of a Barlow schoolmate) in Eugene. In the summer of '73, he left the U. of O. for a three-year interlude in Salt Lake City where he studied the Persian language at the University of Utah.

The draw to Salt Lake City was his former Persian music teacher, Gholam-Hossein Janati'Ata'I (a.k.a. Bob), now living there with a sister and brother who were twins, Firooz and Firoozeh.

While home for a few months' visit after his first summer in Salt Lake City, Doug met Cathy Allen when he did some mechanical work on her parents' Volkswagen at their home in Lexington. Heading West again, he missed her so much that he called her from

a restaurant in Indiana and invited her to join him. She caught the
next plane to St. Louis where he picked her up at the airport.

They lived together in Salt Lake City where Cathy worked for a
while as a masseuse and then started nursing school. On weekends,
Doug played drums in a night club with the belly dancing ensemble
led by his former Persian teacher, Bob: santour, two drums (Doug
and Firooz), double bass, and oud. His day job was as a Volkswagen
mechanic, a trade he'd learned right out of the book I'd given
him, *How to Keep Your Volkswagen Alive*. His specialty became
rebuilding engines.

Having had his fill of grease and brake fluid, not to mention
skinned knuckles, Doug returned to Eugene to take up serious
study of the classical guitar with his former U. of O. teacher, Dave
Case.

By then, he and Cathy had gone their separate ways although she
was in Eugene long enough to persuade him to move into the perfect
little house, which he was reluctant to do because of the $130 rent.
He was very happy there for the next three years.

When I visited him in that house, I slept on a pad on the floor,
waking up each morning to watch his two kittens scamper by at eye
level, jumping on each other and tumbling about. Doug had a bike
and borrowed one for me, and we rode all over Eugene and along
bike trails in a grand park at the edge of town.

When Doug's '64 Volkswagen bus finally died, he abandoned it
at the farm, replacing it with a '61 model. We lived for years with
that disreputable old bus smack in the middle of our yard. Joel
finally got rid of it for me, but I felt pangs of remorse and nostalgia
as I watched it being towed out the lane.

## My Yoga Teacher

Early in the 1970s, Lisa and I signed up for weekly yoga lessons
at the Lexington Unitarian Fellowship to which I belonged. There,
we met Chuck Coleman, an excellent teacher and nice guy, who
became my friend.

He was a quiet, rather serious fellow in his early thirties. The
name Chuck didn't suit him, so I called him Charles. He told us he'd

been overweight and unhealthy until he took a yoga class and started learning about eating right.

Now fit and healthy, he was attending UK, majoring in foods and nutrition, driving a school bus, teaching yoga, and waiting tables at Alfalfa, the natural foods restaurant close to the campus. His main vehicle was a bicycle, but he also had an old pickup truck.

One evening, after class, he told us about a Jessamine-County farm he had wanted to buy. "But someone else beat me to it," he said. "They bought it the second day it was on the market."

"That's *my* farm!" I said after he described it in loving detail.

A few evenings later, he drove out to see us and fell in love with the place all over again, leaky roof and all. We were using our picnic table to eat on, but I showed him the old oak pedestal table I hoped to refinish and repair someday for a proper dining table. Offering to remove the several coats of red enamel paint and to refinish the tabletop for me, he drove off with it in the back of his truck.

We did some fun things together. One early morning, Timmy, Charles, and I met friends of Charles for a picnic breakfast near Cumberland Gap, then climbed up the rugged mountain trail all day to visit the restored nineteenth century Hensley Settlement at the top, spend the night in sleeping bags on the floor of a log cabin nearby, then slip and slide back down the mountain the next day.

It was an exhausting outing. Timmy, seven, survived it best and in great spirits. We ate supper in the cabin by the light of a blazing fire that night, then sat around, talking. The fire burned down, and the cold air crept in. Timmy climbed into my sleeping bag with me during the night to keep warm.

On another occasion, Charles and I spent a blissful day on a guided tour of Lilley Cornett Woods in southeast Letcher County. These 550 acres encompass the first and largest preserved remnant of old-growth forest in eastern Kentucky. It remains much the same as when Daniel Boone saw it for the first time. Besides huge six-hundred-year-old trees, there were many birds, wildflowers, and flowering plants to see. Once, we caught sight of a white-tailed deer.

We also had a grand visit with Wendell Berry, author, teacher, farmer, and advocate of the self-sufficient rural lifestyle. Contrary to Charles's assurances to me, the Berrys were not expecting us at their farmhouse in Henry County that day! Nevertheless, they graciously invited us in.

Among other things, Mr. Berry showed us his composting toilet and described how it worked. Before we departed, his wife, Tanya, served us fresh-baked bread and sliced apples as we sat at the little kitchen table by a window looking out over the rolling farmland.

Within a year or two, Charles graduated from UK and rented a farm in Estill County near where my friend Cookie White and her children lived. Whenever I went to see Cookie, I stopped by Charles's place for a visit too. He heated the small frame house with a woodstove, took care of a few acres of land, and planted a large vegetable garden. Exuberantly into a self-sufficient lifestyle, he ate heartily of his homegrown foods and canned much of it for the winter months.

Once, I spent the night with him there where he cooked us a great vegetarian supper and a delicious breakfast the next morning, featuring his own chickens' eggs. At bedtime, he gave me his narrow bed and crawled into his sleeping bag on the floor nearby, and we talked until we fell asleep.

On another occasion in 1973, Charles and I drove my Travelall to Ohio to pick up a load of organic apples for the Good Foods Co-op to which we belonged. We had car trouble, couldn't get it fixed 'til morning, and the local motels were full. As a result, we spent an uncomfortable night in the front seat of my car—talking, singing, telling stories, and trying in vain to get some shut-eye.

Late one fall, I helped Charles work up a pile of firewood and load it into his pickup truck. As we sat in his truck relaxing, he suddenly asked, "Have you ever thought about having more children?"

"Charles," I answered, "I'm older than you think, and I can't have any more children!" A pregnant silence ensued.

Shortly thereafter, he took a job as nutritionist in the WIC Program for low-income families in eastern Kentucky, commuting from Estill County. Soon, he met and married a young WIC nurse, moved closer to his job, and I lost track of him. I did stop by for breakfast one morning when she was spending the weekend with him at his farm in Estill County. I liked this shy, pretty country girl.

As for my oak tabletop, I spied it in Charles's corncrib one day and retrieved it. After removing two coats of red enamel paint, he'd run out of time to work on it. Lisa soon refinished it for me. I had the pedestal base repaired and two leaves made for it. That was about thirty-five years ago. Teamed with eight ladder-back chairs I bought for $9 each, it has been my dining table ever since.

## The Three Musketeers

Peg Payne and Vicki Johnston became two of my best friends in the mid-1970s.

I first met Vicki when she was thirteen and joined the fencing club Bob had started in Lexington. She babysat for us when Doug was still in diapers, and she and I practiced fencing on the strip inlaid in the playroom floor of our redwood house on Cane Run Road. Tall, athletic, long-legged, and determined, she was great to practice with and a challenging competitor in fencing meets.

Vicki's family moved to Casper, Wyoming, when Vicki was sixteen; and I didn't see her again 'til she moved back almost twenty years later, divorced and with a ten-year-old daughter, Fayette. Vicki had married Jiten, a brilliant young student from India whom she met at the University of Wyoming. After only a few months, she left him. She was pregnant and lived with her folks in Cheyenne, where her father was superintendent of schools, until about a year after Fayette was born.

She went on to earn her college degree in art and art education, then taught in schools around the state. The most memorable of these was an unplumbed two-room, two-teacher ranch school in Alvada. There, she was responsible for grades four through eight.

Peg and I met one Sunday morning in 1973 at the Lexington Unitarian Fellowship. We both wore our hair pulled back into one long thick braid. There was that instant feeling of rapport, and we have been friends ever since.

She grew up in Stamford, Connecticut, where she had a horse of her own to care for and ride. Recently divorced, with two children to raise, Tom and Laura, Peg was on the testing and counseling staff at UK. We often met for a quick lunch on campus and found that we had similar views of the world.

We both belonged to the Sierra Club and went on several of their overnight backpacking trips. I bought a lightweight waterproof tent, and these outings were great fun, but also very strenuous and sweaty. Carrying a pack was too hard on my back! I much preferred riding my horse long hours into a campsite.

We now had two extra riding horses on the farm. Misty was the feisty little filly Lisa and Joel rode sometimes, and Courbette was the good-natured, easy-gaited gelding we boarded for a friend of Joel's in exchange for his use. Peg liked him and came out to the farm to ride with me, sometimes bringing the kids with her. Her red-haired Tom and my Tim became friends in their early teens.

By this time, Vicki had come back to Lexington, found a job teaching art in the Fayette County School System, and looked me up. She too was a horse lover. She liked to ride Misty. I introduced her to Peg, and "the rest is history!" The three of us became the best of friends and were soon calling ourselves the Three Musketeers, riding our horses all over Jessamine County.

## Jeff, Our Chimney Sweep

In 1977, I answered a local chimney service ad and met Jeff Gitlin. A fledgling sweep, he was also part owner then of Alfalfa restaurant. Before that, he'd worked as a waiter at the Fig Tree in Lexington. He was soon made president of the state chimney sweep guild. I was straightaway accorded an honorary membership, attended their meetings, and developed a series of guild-sponsored wood-heat safety articles for Kentucky newspapers and radio stations.

We held a variety of potluck workshops to educate sweeps in such things as different types of chimney-lining techniques. My own kitchen flue was the beneficiary of one of these sessions. I took pictures and wrote up many of our workshops for the news media.

Jeff was a strong, tough, slim, long-legged young man with shaggy supercurly dark brown hair, wire-rim glasses, and a trick back, which, like my own, gave him considerable trouble now and then.

He soon developed the habit of giving me an abrupt kiss, full on the mouth, whenever he came out to the farm. This never failed to startle me and set me to wondering . . . Our friendship deepened through the years that followed, and I think I was always halfway in love with Jeff. But he was such a young fella, about twenty-seven, when we first met; and I was already into my fifties.

## One December Day

The following is excerpted from a letter I wrote on December 28, 1976, to my old high school chum Anne Alevizon Mitchell:

> Right now Timmy, 10, and I are in our kitchen, warmed by a woodburning stove. Tim is floating a model boat he just put together in the sink and singing, "Where are the simple joys of maidenhood . . ." The floor is strewn with Nicana, a two-year-old German Shepherd, and Flip, 16-year-old something-or-other, and two cats are draped on the rocking chair by the stove. The rest of the house is FREEZING COLD.
>
> My new horse, Apache, a four-year-old Appaloosa, is munching hay in the barn, along with his Appaloosa pony sidekick Comanche. (We went Indian several years ago.) There are several inches of snow on the ground and the wind is howling in the chimney.

## Snowbound

Fierce snowstorms hit Kentucky in the winter of 1977-78. One day, Tim and I were socked in by snow drifted five feet deep in the lane. Joel, handy with chain saw and axe, had been gone since first light to get us a load of firewood, after which he spent the rest of the day using tow chain, shovel, and his native ingenuity to rescue stranded motorists. Toward dark, he headed home with a pocketful of money and a load of firewood, but he couldn't get back in the lane.

We lost power for just a few days, ran out of propane for water heating, cooking, and our backup furnace. The stack of firewood on our front porch dwindled to nothing.

The year before, Lisa and I had cut a storm-downed sycamore tree on the back of the farm into rounds with a crosscut saw. And there it lay. This is not one of your great firewoods; but hey, it was pretty well seasoned by then, and it does burn. So I spent a few hours a day splitting those rounds into firewood, stuffing it into feed sacks and, with Tim's help, dragging it all to the house. I cooked on my Fisher stove, and we had lots of soup-and-cracker meals.

Tim ice-skated on the frozen creek; we built snowmen, had some hellacious snowball fights, operated by candlelight and flashlight, went to bed early. When the electricity came back on, we listened to music, watched a few good TV shows, and read lots of books. Tim made and painted a village of cardboard buildings to go with the train set his dad had given him for Christmas and which was set up at his dad's house.

I couldn't get to work at UK, and Tim's school was shut down too. After three weeks, I paid someone to plow our lane. Joel popped in with a load of firewood, and the propane truck arrived and filled our tank. I drove my car out to the end of the lane, shoveled out a space, and parked it there. Then a big snowstorm closed us in again.

It took a stir-crazy Joel a week, working from sunrise to sunset, to shovel himself and his pickup truck out the lane. I hiked out the lane to my car every morning and went back to work. With school still closed, Tim went to his dad's, toting a bagful of railroad village to show him.

## Brandy and His Mules

It's impossible to include everything from those early years on the creek. But I cannot leave out our elderly farm neighbor Peyton Brandenburg, a tall angular strong man who worked his land with a team of white mules. Brandy could be cantankerous, but when he discovered that Joel had cut down one of his trees, he forgave him and let him keep the firewood he'd harvested.

"I just love having you children down here on the creek," Brandy told me.

When I bought hay from him one year, he tried to steal a kiss in the hayloft. "It's been a long time," he said, "since I chased a pretty girl around in the hay!"

One of Brandy's farm gates opened onto our lane. When a gravel truck crashed though our bridge at the entrance to the lane, Brandy wasn't satisfied with the replacement bridge the gravel company built. He painstakingly reinforced it himself with metal rods run through concrete piers, utilizing expertise from his many years as county road commissioner.

When he retired, sold his farm, and moved to town, we missed him.

## Henrietta, Goodbye . . .

I could no longer afford to have Henrietta come, but my girls were a big help around the place. Joel could run a chain saw, wield an axe, and fix just about anything. Tim carried in firewood, ran the vacuum cleaner, and did various chores.

Henrietta and I kept up on each other's lives by phone. "Miz Hensley, you just like one of my own family," she told me.

After she suffered a stroke in 1976, Tim and I went to see her. With her family all around, she sat in a wheelchair, had shed many pounds, and looked years younger. Her face lit up when she saw us. Unable to speak yet, she held tightly on to my hand, and I felt so very sad.

When she died at sixty-four of uterine cancer in 1982, her daughter Catherine called me. She said, "You've been Mama's old friend for so long. I wanted to be sure you knew she's passed."

I attended Henrietta's funeral service at the Baptist church in their community. It was overflowing with friends and family and neighbors.

At the Greenwood Cemetery (now called Cove Haven) in Lexington, a fine-looking young man came up to me with a big smile and hugged me.

"You remember me, Miz Hensley? I'm Benny," he said. Henrietta's son, grown up and with children of his own! I hadn't seen him since he was nine.

Henrietta never would let me snap her picture. "No, Miz Hensley, I looks like a hawg!" she'd say, backing away and covering her face.

"You do not," I told her vehemently, but to no avail. So I have only one five-by-seven-inch water-stained photo that Catherine gave me of Henrietta dressed for church, looking a bit self-conscious, wearing a curly black hat, a string of white beads, a sleeveless plaid cotton dress, and white gloves. But I have pictures of her in my mind that will last forever.

Whenever possible, I borrowed a horse trailer, loaded up my horse, and went trail riding with my Elkhorn Saddle Club in Kentucky's wilderness areas and Tennessee's Big South Fork Country in the Cumberland Mountains. Sometimes we camped out. This was my great escape from the everyday demands of my life, and it kept me sane!

# 26

# RETURN TO APPLE VALLEY

In the 1970s, the kids and I managed a trip back to Apple Valley about every two years. Our favorite time to go was in July when blueberries, peaches, and red raspberries were all ripe for the picking.

Pauline raised and trained Tennessee walking horses, and we went riding together almost every day. Lisa, in particular, shared my love of Apple Valley and horses. In the late '70s and early '80s, the two of us often traveled there to pick Clark apples in the fall of the year. We earned money for four weeks, had a great visit, and loved our road trips there and back.

The kids and I usually made a three-day odyssey of it. Heading out in our station wagon, we stopped over that first night for dinner, bed-and-breakfast with my uncle Dave and Aunt Isabel in Morgantown, West Virginia, where Dave taught gross anatomy at the state university's medical school.

Dave and I would roll out of our beds at the crack of dawn the next morning for a vigorous, heart-pounding hike up and down the long hills of their subdivision. After breakfast, it was on to my old college friend Mary Gale's in northern Pennsylvania. Mary always sent us off after breakfast the following day with a hefty picnic lunch.

On the last leg of our journey, we usually stopped for an hour or two with Lisa's old friends, her Barlow teacher Peter DuFault and his wife Ruth at their farm outside Hillsdale, New York. Lisa brought along her violin so that she and Peter could play country fiddle together, just like old times.

On our first visit to Mary and Joe, they were living in an apartment in Kingston where Joe had a thriving law practice and took on many pro bono cases.

We hadn't seen each other since my Philadelphia visit more than twenty-five years earlier although we'd kept in close touch. Mary was much as I remembered her. But Joe, no longer the lean young athlete, had morphed into a mountain of a man. Compelled to quit smoking, he had munched on cashew nuts instead, ate heartily, and just kept on expanding.

He was deeply involved in Republican Party politics, loved to attend and bet on the horse races, was a city person and a night owl. In contrast, Mary was a gardener, a bird-watcher, and an artist—early to bed and early to rise. She taught art at a local private school. Their married daughter now lived in California, and their son attended law school.

The next time we visited them, they had built at Mary's quiet insistence a lovely house outside Dallas, their land including a wide expanse of woods and overlooking a reservoir. Our friendship grew stronger through the years, and Mary came out to visit us at the farm in the 1980s. After Joe died, Tim and Lisa both stopped to see Mary on their solo road trips across the country.

## Pauline and Malcolm

The year Pauline and Malcolm married, the Clark farm bought its first tractor. Nowadays, the farm is fully mechanized and has kept on growing and prospering under hard work and good management.

To her great dismay, Pauline soon discovered that she had severe environmental and food allergies. Among other things, this meant she could not ride her horse up through the orchards during spraying season. When they built and moved into their new house, Malcolm cut down the old orchard behind it to give Pauline respite from her symptoms. Once the stumps were pulled, he plowed a section of land for their big vegetable garden.

Their farm in the valley became my home place after Daddy died in 1965. Mom soon sold the Place on South Street and moved to Northampton. She spent time with old friends there, enjoyed life in her own apartment, was close to Phillips and Ereda in nearby Amherst and just a short drive from Ashfield.

Whenever we returned to Apple Valley, we picked up Mom and brought her out to the farm for a long visit. First from her apartment in Northampton, then from her retirement home there, and, many years later, from Rockridge, a lovely retirement and nursing home overlooking the Mohawk Trail and not far from Apple Valley.

Sometimes she said vehemently, "I should be with my family!" Yet whenever I returned her to Rockridge after a visit in Apple Valley, she was relieved to be back there.

The last time I went to collect Mom at Rockridge, she was sitting out on the front porch. Amazed to see me, she thought we were meeting by chance at the same hotel. As I talked to her, she looked puzzled, finally asking, "Julia, do I *live* here?" I told her gently that she did. "Let's go up and look at your room," I said. "Then we can pack a few things to take to Pauline and Malcolm's farm in Apple Valley." She slowly slipped back into reality, and we were soon on our way.

Mom died in her ninety-second year, following a series of small strokes. As per instructions in her living will, her caretakers made her comfortable and let her go peacefully over the next few days. Her grandson Dana paid loving tribute to her during a memorial service at the Congregational Church in Ashfield.

**New Generation Coming On**

As soon as they were old enough, the Clark boys—Aaron, Brian, and Dana—were paid for the farm chores they did every day and started saving money for college. They all loved the farm, finding it a wonderful place to be growing up.

Aaron, the oldest, was severely injured in an accident when he was twenty-two. The three brothers were earning money for college by painting the electrical towers that march across the landscape. Aaron was knocked to the ground from very high up when hit by an electrical current turned on by mistake. His brothers saw him fall and ran to him, thinking he was going to die before he reached the hospital.

Paralyzed from midchest down, he went through months of rehab, then came back to the farm. "What do you plan to do now?" his folks asked matter-of-factly. He learned carpentry and partnered a kitchen cabinet business in the valley with a friend for several years. His daughter, Heather, was born while he was in rehab. He and his wife, Jackie, went on to have a son, Eli, a few years later through artificial insemination.

A hefty insurance settlement from the accident enabled Aaron and Jackie to build a grand handicap-access house on the farm. It includes a ramp and the gun shop Aaron owns and operates for hunters in the area, many of whom he has known all his life. He goes deer hunting himself on his ATV in the fall of the year.

Malcolm's brother, Richard, married late, had no children, and died before his time. But his vision and determination resulted in the building of an apple storage facility on the farm and the marketing of their own crop. In his will, he left his share of the farm to his three nephews—Aaron, Brian, and Dana.

Over the years, Aaron learned to run most of the equipment on the farm and became a skillful computer-savvy business manager. He and his two brothers now own and operate Clark Brothers Orchards. The dairy herd was phased out when Malcolm retired.

In 2006, Malcolm's sister, Barbara Graves, self-published *Tales of Apple Valley*, a nostalgic little book about the valley and its people. Her stories are interspersed with poems written by Ralph Townsley. In those early years, families in the upper and lower valley "were farmers with small dairy herds and some apples." Their children attended the one-room school on the edge of the Clark farm, down next to the Apple Valley Road.

Now only two of the original family farms remain—the Townsleys and the Clarks. New homes and new residents with varied professions and trades, including artisans of national reputation, give a different atmosphere to the valley. But the old logging roads we rode through the forest, the surrounding hills that change colors with the seasons, and the brook that winds its way along the valley floor beside the road are still just as I remember them.

### Early Memories of Ashfield

Still full of nostalgia from my early years in Ashfield, reminiscing about a few happenings in particular is a whole lot of fun: Midget breaking loose from her cart and leaving it behind, with Pauline and me in it; the terrible mistake I made during a game of croquet on our front lawn; the time Chummy Hall and I were skinny-dipping and had some unexpected guests; my friendship with Ralphie Pease, who had a big crush on my sister; our serious bad manners as Pauline and I clip-clopped our horses past two churches on Sunday mornings; stealing peaches from Ms. Wylie; the time a couple of teenage summer residents on the run had an uncomfortable encounter with Malcolm, and Sugar on Snow Day in Ashfield.

When we bought our pony, Midget, a little black cart that could seat two or three small children was part of the package, along with a harness for her. Forest Hill Riding School was printed prominently in white letters on one side of the cart. Daddy painted over some of the letters, leaving For Riding, which we thought was *so* clever! Pauline always harnessed Midget up—never letting me do it because, she told me, "You're not smart enough!"

One day, she harnessed Midget and hitched her to the cart, and we hopped in to go for an outing through the village. About halfway down our hill, Midget broke free of the shafts and ran off without us.

We screamed bloody murder and held on as we bounced and bumped on down the hill, then past the Days' and Gilberts' houses. After that, the cart swerved to the left and came to rest on a strip of grass by the sidewalk in front of the impressive yellow Curtis house, which was set way back from the street. (George William Curtis was a longtime editor at *Harper's Monthly* magazine and spent his summers in Ashfield.)

Midget, munching grass nearby, raised her head to gaze at us. We looked about furtively, hoping nobody had witnessed this embarrassing event!

Pauline's friend Chummy Hall often stayed at Mizentop, her Grandmother Hall's grand old summer home across South Street from us. There, she kept her own horse, Babs, went riding with us, and taught us the rudiments of horsemanship. All I ever saw her wear was jeans and a white cotton shirt with the shirttail hanging out.

Plagued by eager young men, she often sought refuge at our house. She called one of them Frogface behind his back and made fun of him to us.

So the stage is set for my croquet story. Chummy was playing croquet with our family one afternoon on our front lawn when "he" appeared, and we invited him to join us. He was a friendly, well-mannered, nice-enough-looking young fellow. As we played and I finished my turn, I shouted, "It's your turn, Frogface!" and we all froze. He glanced accusingly at Chummy, and after a few uncomfortable moments, the game continued.

Another time, Chummy and I were skinny-dipping in our pond when three of her bothersome young men appeared on the shore. We kept stirring up the mud, just keeping our heads above water, and visited gaily back and forth with them until they *finally* left. Once they were out of sight, we couldn't stop laughing.

Skinny, red-haired, and awkward, Ralph Pease thought my sister was wonderful and often walked up to our place from the Pease home on Scrap Alley in the village. Pauline spurned him, even when he cleaned out stalls for us, but I liked him. He was a sweet guy, and I did my best to plead his case. Once, he gave me a box of Valentine chocolates, certain that Pauline wouldn't accept it. This way, he reasoned, she'd at least get to enjoy some of it.

On trips back to Ashfield, I was always glad to see Ralph. He became a good carpenter and married Lucille Curry, and they raised a smart, beautiful daughter of whom they were both inordinately proud.

It took Pauline and me a while to realize what a faux pas it was to ride our horses noisily past the open-door Episcopal and Congregational churches late on Sunday mornings during their services. Daddy must have rebuked us because we stopped doing it. Instead, we detoured through the Curtis place's expanse of fields and orchard, which brought us out at the bottom of Norton Hill Road near Elmer's Store, bypassing both churches.

Jean Wylie, who retired to Ashfield after years of housemothering Smith College students in their residence on campus that she managed, lived across the road from the exit to our circular driveway. Her charming white cottage was surrounded by flowers. Open her little wooden gate in the stone wall, and you could walk along the flower-lined path through the front yard to her door.

She had some tempting fruit trees in her backyard. One night, Pauline and I sneaked over by flashlight and filled a sack with delicious, juicy peaches.

A few days later, Ms. Wylie—white haired, dignified, and gracious—invited us over for hot tea, homemade cookies, and bowls of fresh sliced peaches. Her parrot was in its cage nearby; and her friendly cocker spaniel, Penny, was curled up on the floor, watching. As always, Ms. Wylie was just lovely to us. But we knew she knew, and we never swiped her peaches again.

The last time I saw Ms. Wylie was many years later when I visited her at the Ashfield House on Main Street near the old post office (now a pizza place). Georgianna Gorman had by then turned her Ashfield House—first a hotel and then divided into rental units—into a retirement and nursing home. Its long front porch is loaded with chairs, making it a wonderful spot for sitting and watching and interacting with village people as they walk by. It has become a lovely final home for many of Ashfield's elderly residents.

After she died, it came to light that Ms. Wylie carried on a long correspondence with Adlai E. Stevenson, the Democratic candidate for president in 1952 and 1956, who lost both elections to Dwight D.

Eisenhower. Ms. Wylie evidently instructed her attorney to see to it that all the letters from her old friend were destroyed following her death.

Ashfield summer people did not necessarily distinguish themselves with good behavior! One night at our place, after Pauline and Malcolm had joined us for dinner, a car roared up the hill; and we heard the sound of breaking glass. The car sped past and disappeared down our narrow lane beyond. We all hurried out to the road and shone our flashlights onto a lot of broken glass.

Since the lane came to a dead end, the car soon reemerged, its headlights revealing the shards of glass ahead . . . and Malcolm standing in the road, waiting for them. Two anxious teenagers got out, and Malcolm clamped each one by the shoulder with his big farmer's hands.

We recognized one of them as Hammie Smith, whose family owned a renovated farmhouse beyond the Emmet-Hall place in South Ashfield. Malcolm, concluding they'd been drinking, asked for an explanation of the broken glass.

It seems the two of them had been on the run from "the law" they believed to be in hot pursuit. They had tossed glass gallon jugs out of the car window "to slow them down."

Malcolm sent us to fetch brooms, dustpans, and buckets. Then he supervised the culprits by flashlight as they cleaned up every last piece of glass. It took a long time.

Sugar on Snow Day was a popular annual event in Ashfield. It happened around the Fourth of July, pulling whole families from the village, farms and nearby towns to the ground floor of the Ashfield Town Hall.

We lined up at a window, surrendered our large round metal dishes to smiling local men who handed them back to us packed with snow from a truck parked outside. Then we took our places at the long wooden tables stocked with pitchers of maple syrup, forks, napkins and bowls of pickles and crackers.

This was not your usual maple syrup. It had been boiled down to a consistency thick enough not to dissolve into the snow. We poured little puddles of syrup onto the snow, lifted each chewy treat that resulted with a fork, tugged it off the fork with our teeth, ate it with crackers and pickles to cut the sweetness.

Some first-timers, including me, got into trouble when we swirled lines of syrup around on the snow, then discovered that it came up onto the fork en masse, impossible to eat without making a big sticky mess.

Snow in July? My sister-in-law Ereda's father, Donald Lilly, was in charge of Sugar on Snow Day while she was growing up. She remembers the huge pile of snow her brothers and father accumulated at their farm up in Watson in late winter, then covered over with tarps and sawdust to keep it from melting.

Ashfield resident Ann Lilly recalls a time when the snow was kept in a more convenient location in the old ice house behind the Ashfield House in the village. Blocks of ice were cut from the Big Pond in winter and covered with sawdust to keep it and the snow cold. Ann can still remember "the smell of the wet sawdust as we all waited impatiently for our sugar on snow".

Back at the town hall our sweet feasting, all we could eat for twenty-five or fifty cents was followed by a square dance. We climbed the wide and well-worn wooden steps to the second floor as the band was warming up on the stage at the far end of the long polished maple dance floor.

We chose our partners, formed our squares and waited for the caller to begin. After three vigorous squares came a polka or jitterbug number, followed by a slow dance or two. Then there was another threesome of squares, and on and on. We were always ready for the intermission that allowed us to cool off and troop downstairs to the basement for cold drinks, snacks or hot coffee.

### The Pichette Boys

The Pichette brothers also figured prominently in my memories of Ashfield. Although I never saw Harold again after he went off to war, I did see Bob when he was home on furlough in July of 1943.

Inquiring about them up in the village, I learned that they both survived the war and came back home to Ashfield. Harold married Viola Rivard, and Bob married her sister Jeanne from one of the few other Catholic families in the area.

Always the best of friends, the brothers went into business together running a garage between the Sandy house and the Ashfield Historical Society, just across and down Main Street from the two-story white frame house on the corner where they grew up.

Their father, Louie, had operated a garage at the same location for a number of years; and his sons worked with him in their teens.

At this writing, Harold and their sister Mona, who went to school with Malcolm, are still living. But Bob had a mysterious ailment that began plaguing him while he was still in the service. Finally, diagnosed as multiple sclerosis, it caused his death in his early forties. Harold received a medical discharge. Sadly, Neil, the oldest of his three sons, died in the Vietnam War when he was twenty-three.

I remember the two brothers as drop-dead good-looking. Harold, the older of the two, had wavy blond hair, blue eyes, a ready smile, and an outgoing personality. Bob had dark brown hair, brown eyes, and was a bit more reticent.

For several summers, a week or two before the Fourth of July, the Pichette boys set up a stand on Main Street across from the Congregational Church and sold firecrackers, making a bundle of money for the American Legion. I had fun hanging out at the booth with them for an hour or two in the afternoons.

Once, the summer Pauline and Harold were sweethearts, her hair caught fire from a firecracker's sparks; and Harold sprang into action, snuffing it out with a few claps of his hands.

By the time I connected with Pierre at D.O.'s party, he and Bob were already friends from picking apples together in the orchards of Apple Valley. The last time I saw Bob was the night Pierre and I sought him out when he was home on furlough. We had supper at his house, then piled into his car, picked up D.O. at Snake Rock Farm, and headed for the Cournands' place in South Ashfield.

When I was about thirteen, I had a big crush on Bob.

I would take my dog, Skipper, for a walk in the early evenings. Down the hill we sallied toward the watering trough where South Street joins Main Street. Within sight of the Pichette house, I'd start whistling for Skipper and calling his name until *finally* Bob came out his back door and said hi. We talked until almost dark. Then reluctantly, I called Skipper to me, and we went on home.

One afternoon, Bob knocked on our front door with a rifle slung over his shoulder and asked me if I'd like to go squirrel hunting with him. "Yes!" I said, oblivious as to what that might entail. Off we went down the rocky lane together, then headed off towards the fields and woods below our pond.

Suddenly, Bob raised his rifle and shot a dear little striped chipmunk as it poked its head inquisitively out of the stone wall along the lane.

Horrified, I screamed at Bob and attacked him with both fists, tears streaming down my face. "How could you *do* such a thing?" I raged, then turned and ran. After all these years, I still remember the dumbfounded look on his face.

Daddy, Pauline and me bringing in our 1935
hay crop. That's me on top of the hay.

# 27

# MY JOB AT UK, 1969-78

## *And a Few Romances*

According to Jim, he stood gazing out his office window that October day in 1969, watched me get out of my car, and fell in love with me as I walked across the parking lot.

A few minutes later, I was ushered into his office for a job interview. This young chairman of UK's Department of Public Information for the College of Agriculture and Cooperative Extension Service was only thirty-seven. Tall and lanky, with a thick mop of black hair and keen brown eyes in an angular face, Jim Russell stepped forward to shake my hand.

I was applying for an information specialist position. My duties would include responsibility for all the home economics publications, as well as writing articles and special features for Kentucky newspapers and radio stations, plus weekly columns for county home ec agents to adapt as their own.

Jim showed me a stack of current publications, offered me the job at a salary of $9,000, promised me a raise within months, and took me around to meet other members of the department. Noting that there was only one artist on the staff, involved with agricultural and 4-H publications, I turned the job down.

"This is a mediocre bunch of publications you've shown me," I said. "They need rewriting, better layouts, and good illustrations to make them come alive. Without a full-time artist for home ec, it won't happen."

Startled by my refusal, Jim let me go; but a month later, he called me back in. After adding a new position to his staff, he had found an artist he wanted me to meet. I liked Dorothea, was delighted with her drawings, and he hired us both.

In the meantime, Ed Easterly had offered me the editorship of the *Jessamine Journal*, our county's weekly newspaper. Although I was tempted by his job offer, the UK position was much more up my alley, and it paid better. Nine thousand dollars is not much money, but it sounded good to me back then!

After the divorce, I went hippie with my kids, wore headbands, sandals, and colorful, offbeat clothes to work, kept odd hours, put in lots of overtime. The administration tolerated me because Jim backed me without question.

Almost immediately, seeing the need, he had hired a full-time editorial assistant for me. Joanna was a lovable young woman and good editor who managed to keep both me and my files reasonably well organized over the next few years until she resigned, reluctantly, to go do missionary work in Africa with her husband.

Many of the articles I wrote about woodstove safety and the alternative lifestyle were picked up and used all over the country. I was asked to speak at professional meetings. The home ec publications improved dramatically, were often reprinted by other states.

It was a challenging, exhausting, heady time . . . and I loved it.

The following year, Jim resigned, hired on as farm editor of the Louisville *Courier-Journal*, soon came back courting. With a mustache and hair grown shaggy long, he now looked like a Mississippi riverboat gambler.

Sometimes I took the day or afternoon off to travel around the state with Jim, who was on the prowl for stories and pictures. Once, he jumped out of the car to photograph a black farmer working his mule and followed that up with an interview. The photo and feature story appeared in the paper next day. Jim gave me an eleven-by-fourteen-inch matted and framed print of that farmer and his mule, my favorite of all his pictures.

Another day, just after sunrise, I met him at Keeneland to watch the early-morning workouts and eat a hearty breakfast in the Keeneland Kitchen with the jockeys and grooms. A few days later, he sent me a grand eight-by-ten-inch photo of one horse's morning run on the mist-shrouded track.

Jim would often arrive at the farm in late afternoon with a portable typewriter, a six-pack, and cigarettes. He would pound out an article or two at the kitchen table, call them in to the newspaper, then eat supper, spend the night, and leave for Louisville early the next morning.

Several times, he went on camping trips to the Red River Gorge with the kids and me. He had the endearing habit of crawling out of his sleeping bag in the cold, damp morning, kindling a fire and putting the coffeepot on to perk. My kids liked him. We felt like family and had a lot of fun together. Jim and I never ran out of things to talk about.

He gave me some great records—*Camelot, Credence Clearwater Revival*, various symphonies. To this day, when I listen to *Camelot*, I am suddenly with Jim again and close to tears when Lancelot sings:

> If ever I would leave you, it wouldn't be in
> summer—seeing you in summer I never would go . . .
> It couldn't be in autumn . . . I've seen how you sparkle
> when fall nips the air, I know you in autumn and I must
> be there . . . Or on a wintry evening when you catch the
> fire's glow . . . Oh no not in springtime, summer, winter or
> fall—no never could I leave you at all!

"That's how I feel about ever leaving you," Jim told me. He urged me to sell the farm, move closer to Louisville, and live with him. "There are other farms on other creeks," he said.

I truly loved Jim, but I couldn't do it. I couldn't throw my lot in with him. He smoked too much, drank too much, didn't eat right, drove himself too hard. He had a cynical, fatalistic streak in his nature. And I couldn't bear the thought of watching close-up as he self-destructed. The perfect way to die, he told me once, would be as a war correspondent killed in action.

So we parted in tears one evening when the creek was running full. Unwilling to break our ties completely, we kept in touch. Within a few years, he married the smart, sexy, pretty daughter of a tenant farmer. They had at least one child together, and he told me at lunch one day that they were happy. "Well, happy enough," he added with a crooked grin. "It's not good to be too happy."

His ambition was to be a columnist, and he reached that goal in 1979. The Monday morning after his first column appeared, my phone rang with the news from a former coworker at UK that he had died of a heart attack. He was only forty-seven.

## Along Came Bletch

When I met Bletch, an information specialist and publications editor for West Virginia University, this man seemed totally right for me. He and his family had even summered at Ashfield! He'd gone swimming at the Big Pond, hung out at Mike's place, attended square dances in the town hall, picked wild blueberries in the dew-soaked early mornings. Our paths had never crossed because he was five years younger and ran with a different crowd.

He was so skillful with Magic Markers that he could whip up on short notice a whole slide set of sketches and text that taught the basics of any subject needed. One day, he gave me his only copy of a Magic Marker book he created for young children on *The Inside and Outside of People*. I've used it with Tim, my grandchildren, and now my great-grandchildren.

When I needed to produce on short notice a slide show for our associate extension director to take to Washington DC, one phone call to Bletch got me started in the right direction. I had never put together a slide set. It was a big success, describing our nutrition-education program for low-income families and using many of my own color slides, with Lisa's country fiddle music in the background.

Bletch was multitalented, intellectual, resourceful, funny, down-to-earth. He was divorced, had a son "just like me" who lived with his ex-wife. Twice, he came to see me at the farm; we got together at professional meetings, and I spent time with him when I visited my uncle Dave in Morgantown, West Virginia. All systems were go, and we decided this love was meant to be.

He tried to land a job in Kentucky so that we could live together at my farm and see how that worked for us. But no luck. When he finally found a position to his liking out in Tucson, Arizona, he wanted me and Tim to go there with him.

Bletch and I had seemed so right for each other. But I could not do it. The pull of my kids, my farm, and my hard-won independence proved too strong.

## My Riverboat Captain

Jack and I were from different worlds. "I never knew anyone like you," he said early in our acquaintance. I'd never known anyone like him either. This relationship would become a journey of discovery.

It bothered me that he carried a gun. "I never shot anyone with it," he told me. "But it has saved my life three times."

He'd grown up rough and wild, yet he had cultivated good manners. He was profane and steeped in the Southern vernacular. Bulky and wide shouldered, he was six feet four and moved with the quickness and grace of a cat.

He attended college for two years on a football scholarship, partied a lot, and dropped out. Politically savvy, he was an indispensable ally in our Marble Creek Citizens' battle to secure planning and zoning legislation for Jessamine County through fiscal court that year.

When I met Jack in the fall of '69 at a community development dinner meeting, our affinity for each other was immediate. About four months after my divorce the following year, he became my sometime lover. Despite a reputation for occasional violence, he was the tenderest, gentlest man I ever knew.

He met all my kids, including Scotty, and once told me, "Jay, you're raising your boys too gentle. It's a hard world they'll have to face out there, and they'll need to be tough." But my three surviving sons have persevered and made good lives for themselves. Jack would have been particularly proud of Tim, who became a world-class fencer . . . this little boy he had loved and hoped to raise as his own.

One day, when Timmy and I stopped by Jack's office, he gave him a cap gun and two rolls of caps. When Tim refused to shoot off the caps, Jack said, "What are you, a little girl?" That made Tim mad. He grabbed my hand tightly and whispered, "Let's leave, Mom!"

"Yes, let's," I said, and we did. Tim wasn't into guns, and I had never bought him any toy guns to play with. But he really liked Jack and was very upset by this turn of events. Back at the farm, with a determined look on his face, he marched down to the creek and shot off both rolls of caps in rapid succession. I never saw that cap gun again.

In the early winter following my divorce, my mother visited me. She was distressed by the "deprived" way the kids and I lived, but she appreciated the beauty of our surroundings there on the creek. She was proud of the independence I had achieved, and she wanted to meet Jack.

We arrived at his office one evening in darkness and a drenching rain. He came outside, slid into the backseat of my car to meet my mother, and visit with us, his thick iron gray hair wet from the rain, his fine, strong face dimly illuminated by the dome light.

"Does he remind you of Daddy?" Mom asked me later. I hadn't thought about it, but in some ways, he did—his charisma, his earthiness, his warmth and ready laugh, the sense he gave you of being quickly in charge of a situation.

Before long, Jack dissolved his business partnership and moved to New Orleans, having decided to leave his unhappy marriage and become a riverboat captain on the Mississippi. During World War II, he had been a navy frogman. He still had nightmares about some of his war experiences, but he had a love for rivers and the sea and a yearning for a more adventuresome life.

We wrote to each other, but I was not to see him again until one snowy winter's night more than a year later. I awoke to hear a car crunch the gravel of my driveway. Somehow, I knew it was Jack and went to the front door in my nightgown. Standing there in the dark, looking through the glass panels, I watched him get out of his car and walk toward the house in the moonlight.

He stepped lightly up onto the porch and rapped on the storm door, then realized that I was standing there, opened both doors, and enveloped me in his arms. "Ah told you Ah'd come back when Ah got my captain's papers," he said in an accent even more Southern than before. "Oh, but Ah've missed you!"

Six-year-old Tim was asleep on his lounge chair in the living room, dimly lit by the moonlight. Jack stood gazing at him for a long time. "Don't wake him up," he whispered.

Before that night was over, Jack told me what it was like on the Mississippi, bringing barges up to Louisville and other ports. He loved all of it, getting his crew together, including always a good cook, making ready to leave, securing the barges, all the chores and responsibilities involved, watching the river . . . Sometimes he had to bail a few crew members out of jail. They made runs of two and three weeks; then it was back to New Orleans for a week or so. He wanted me and Tim to move down to New Orleans to be with him.

He had planned to meet with his attorney the following day and sign the final papers for his divorce. But toward morning, sensing my turmoil, he said, "You're never going to marry me, are you, Jay?"

I was quiet for a few long minutes, then said, "No, I'm not."

It wasn't the kind of life that appealed to me; my family was here in Kentucky, and much as I loved Jack, I knew deep in my bones that he wasn't the right man for me. Also, I didn't want him raising Tim.

When we parted in the early dawn, we knew our time together was over; and we stood a long, long while with our arms around each other. I can still remember the sensation of being completely engulfed by his bulky warmth.

## Leaving UK

After Jim resigned, our staff suffered for almost a year under an incompetent acting chairman. Finally, the administration hired a grand new fellow, Dr. Milt Morris. He accorded me the same trust and freedom that Jim had, and the next four years at work went smoothly.

Years later, at an American Association of College Editors (AACE) meeting, Milt told me he had been instructed when hired to "get rid of Jay"; but once he became familiar with my work, he had refused to do so. The administration, he said, considered me a troublemaker and didn't approve of my lifestyle.

When Milt resigned and accepted a similar position at the University of Florida in 1978, a new control freak chairman precipitated my resignation. Don Springer expected me to be at my desk by 8:00 a.m., take an hour off for lunch, then leave at 5:00 p.m. But that wasn't my style. I kept odd hours, often took work home with me, put in scads of overtime, earned high job evaluations.

He considered me insubordinate, which I guess I was. I protested illegal hirings. I refused to attend frivolous "compulsory" ag college meetings that had no bearing on my own work. I was allergic to cigarette smoke; and when I attended a staff meeting in Dr. Springer's smoke-filled office one day, I excused myself and left, saying, "I just can't handle this smoke!"

When he instructed me to do away with my couch, I refused, saying, "This is *my* office, and I need this couch!" It was essential for my afternoon nap. Other staff members complied and rid their offices of personal furniture.

Dr. Springer also told all of us our desks should be completely cleared off at the end of each day, but this was beyond my capabilities.

One year, he forbade me to accept an invitation to report on some phase of my work at a national AACE meeting, saying that I should "give someone else a chance."

I complied with his request and prepared the presentation for another staff member to deliver. Then I took some vacation time and attended the AACE meeting at my own expense. Once the meeting chair knew I was coming, she asked me to report on another one of my projects, which I did. When my friends at AACE heard what had happened, they paid for some of my meals and filled my gas tank for the drive back to Kentucky.

Fellow staff member Blanche Bushong had known and liked Dr. Springer before he came to UK. Early in his chairmanship, he asked her advice on what to do about me. Telling me about their meeting, Blanche said she suggested he leave me alone and told him, "Jay is the most talented member of our staff, present company included!" (Thanks a lot, Blanche!)

For two years, this new guy and I valiantly hung in there with each other. Until he called me into his office one day in the summer of '78 and told me he was tired of trying to keep a maverick in the corral.

"Mavericks aren't *supposed* to be in the corral!" I quipped. One thing led to another, and he asked me to resign. Which I did.

At the time, I thought Dr. Springer unreasonable. But I realize now that a department chairman shouldn't have to put up with a staff member he considers a thorn in his side.

So I was on my own again.

When I told Tim I'd been forced to quit and would have to find a new job, he looked shocked. A little while later, he came back into the kitchen, patted me on the back, and said, "That's okay, Mom, I have confidence in you!" He was twelve years old.

# 28

## A RIDER IN THE WILDERNESS

One September Sunday, a few weeks after my resignation from UK, I headed for the Cataloochee Ranch in the Great Smoky Mountains of North Carolina. Monday morning, on this ranch above Maggie Valley, I tied on my bedroll and swung into the saddle for a stunningly beautiful rugged seven days on horseback with a weathered trail boss and about ten other strangers.

These Trail Riders of the Wilderness outings were sponsored by the U.S. Forestry Service, and 'twas just the break I needed after a punishing summer. I helped pay for my adventure by snapping three or four rolls of color film with my Pentax K1000 and selling the resulting prints to my companions on the trail.

We rode all day through the forest, met the chuck wagon and cook in late afternoon at a predesignated site in the mountains, took care of our horses, set up our tents, ate, then gathered 'round the campfire. We got better acquainted, told stories, and enjoyed the guitar playing and singing of one young trail rider from New Jersey before collapsing for the night.

The tent mate allotted me was Joan Romaine, seventy-two, who raised sheep and ponies in the Shenandoah Valley near White Post, Virginia. Each morning, we ate a hearty breakfast, took down our tents, packed our gear, saddled up, and did it all over again. About half the time it rained, sometimes a real gulley washer accompanied by thunder and lightning. Out came our yellow rain slickers, and we went right on.

My horse was jarringly rough gaited, even at a walk, but otherwise dandy. I could wrap his reins around the saddle horn and be off taking pictures to my heart's content from various vantage points along the trail. He just plodded contentedly along with the rest of the horses. I doubt that he missed me.

One man sat his horse like a gunnysack of potatoes. By the end of the first day on the trail, he was a wreck. They transported him back to Cataloochee that night in a prone position.

Each evening thereafter, he came in with the chuck wagon to rejoin his wife, eat with us, and enjoy vicariously our day's adventure.

"I was so sure I could do this," he told us, still hurting. "After all, my horse would just be walking most of the time!"

But even an experienced rider like me could feel the pain after a day in the saddle on a rough-gaited horse. So after unsaddling him, rubbing him down, and giving him hay and water, I would go running along the trail for about thirty minutes to work out the kinks.

One day, we rode a section of the Appalachian Trail where hundreds of trees sheared off by recent storms were strewn like giant pickup sticks before us. We spent a grueling twelve hours in and out of the saddle as we worked our way through this mess, and it was a sorry bunch that straggled into camp that night.

We ate fresh-caught groundhog for dinner one evening, and it was pretty good. As we sat around the campfire afterward, the lively refrain for one song was, "Groundhog, better go deep. I'm gonna git you 'fore you sleep!" taught to us by our chuck wagon cook.

One night, there was a black bear in camp. As I gazed out the front of our tent, I saw her coming right toward us. I closed the flap and pulled out my jackknife. We held our breath. At the last minute, we heard her veer off to the right. All that sleepless night, Joan and I listened to her growling, but we realized the next day that it had actually been one of the men snoring in a tent nearby.

We poked our heads out at first light and saw that the bear's two cubs were up a nearby tree with her. Soon, all three climbed down and trundled off.

"What did you plan to do with your jackknife?" Joan asked me. "Defend yourself?" I replied, "Oh no, I was going to cut an escape hatch for us out the back of the tent." Then we dissolved into laughter.

Back at Cataloochee Ranch the following Sunday night, we mingled with the locals in a lively country dance. One brawny long-legged backwoodsy fellow latched on to me, kept allowing as how I was "the spittin' image of Loretta Lynn," and taught me to clog. His boots stamped out the lively steps for me to mimic. The foot-tapping old fiddler kept a-playin', and it was all such fun, I never wanted the music to stop.

That night, I fell asleep the minute my head hit the pillow. Come morning, I longed to saddle up and have at it for another blissful week in the wilderness, another Sunday night dance, and another clogging lesson.

But it was time to go home and start looking for a job. I picked up a young hitchhiker from Canada along the way, and he was mighty good company.

"It's people like you who keep me on the road," he said.

This was his second odyssey of hitching rides across the United States. He would work until he had enough money for a trip, then hit the road again. The first time, he had taken a northern route. We sent each other postcards for several years, and then I lost track of him.

# 29

# MY FREELANCE CAREER

Back in Kentucky, when I couldn't find another job to my liking, I became a freelance writer and photographer. My friend Dr. Sam Quick, the human development specialist at UK with whom I had collaborated on many publications, wrote a glowing detailed three-page letter of recommendation for me. But it was so over-the-top that I could not use it. Any prospective employer reading it would expect a miracle worker and would only get me.

So . . . I decided that if I was even half as incredible a writer and editor as Sam claimed, I ought to go to work for myself! Luck was with me. I sold my first article, on woodstove safety, to *Home Energy Digest & Wood Burning Quarterly* magazine. Editor Carey Bohn added my name to the masthead, and I supplied him with a feature story just about every issue.

Meanwhile, I filled orders for pictures from my wilderness ride companions. My tent mate liked the pictures so much that she hired me to take pictures for the wedding of a niece at her farm that same fall.

Joan Romaine paid all my expenses, including plane fare, film, and the resulting prints. The newlyweds bought copies of all the pictures I took and ordered eight-by-ten-inch enlargements of some of them. I cleared $500 and had the bonus of staying on at Joan's for a few days' vacation.

I had pictured her as someone who went out to feed her ponies and sheep early each day, but she was instead the mistress of a big estate in the Shenandoah Valley outside Washington DC with houses on it where her employees lived. I stayed with her in her lovely antebellum mansion, ate my meals with her, lingered for a few lazy days following the wedding, rode her horses, and had a thoroughly good time.

## Egon and Lilly

When I placed an ad in the *Jessamine Journal* a few months later for "a creative darkroom technician," Egon Kornicer was the only applicant. He was man in his late sixties or early seventies, of average height and strong build, with glasses and thinning hair. He spoke fluent English with a heavy accent. Photography was his passionate hobby.

He'd been an official high in the government of Croatia when Hitler's army invaded Poland. With his wife, Lilly, he had fled the country with what belongings they could carry and very little money.

Lilly told me that before immigrating to America, they lived in a house crowded with other refugees where she cooked for everyone, and Egon repaired appliances and small engines to bring in survival money.

By the time I met them, Egon, a professional engineer, had patents on a number of industrial-application products he had developed and marketed in the United States. This brought in enough money for him and Lilly to buy a nice house in Nicholasville and live comfortably.

Working in his fully equipped darkroom, Egon developed my black-and-white film and was delighted with the challenge some of my negatives offered. He was very skillful as he could make a dandy print from a really bad negative. Unwilling to be obliged to report taxable income from his services, he just charged me for the paper and chemicals he used.

Very serious about his work, he was also a lot of fun; and I was often by his side in the darkroom, showing him just what I wanted. He and Lilly loved me like a daughter, and I became tremendously fond of both of them.

Lilly said I reminded them of their own daughter, Vessna, who was living in Connecticut and raising their grandson, Onie. But

Egon disapproved of Vessna's divorce, lifestyle, ideas, and hippie clothes. "They don't get along, and he is always yelling at her," Lilly told me sadly.

I stopped by to meet Vessna once when she and Onie were visiting. As I came across the yard, I could hear her and Egon hollering at each other. Lilly answered the door in great distress. I liked Vessna, finding in her a kindred spirit. Lisa and I even went to see her once at her wildly messy house in Connecticut.

No more than five feet tall, Lilly was a determined, energetic, forceful little woman dedicated to taking care of Egon. She told me once that if she got sick and knew she was going to die, she would *eliminate* Egon first "because he couldn't live without me!"

I was shocked! But I did not doubt her ability to do so.

## A Rare Breed of Horse

In addition to my *Home Energy Digest* features, I sold articles to other alternative-energy magazines, horse magazines, *Mother Earth News* (*TMEN*), and a few Sunday newspaper supplements.

A short feature I wrote for *TMEN* about a rare breed of horse, the American Bashkir curly, triggered a flood of inquiries, six thousand of them, to the ABC Registry. I had written the article after seeing my first curly out at the horse park north of Lexington and interviewing the head horseman there.

People bought up all the curlies for sale that year and put in orders for foals yet unborn. I became a celebrity of sorts among curly breeders. At one annual meeting and horse show I attended in Ely, the registry awarded me a big trophy for publicizing the breed and "saving it from extinction."

Other freelance pursuits included taking pictures, designing brochures, and writing articles for a day camp in Lexington that Tim attended, as well as for Lotts Creek Community School down near Hazard.

My best in-depth article and pictures about the Lotts Creek school and its founder, Alice Slone, appeared in the *Cleveland Plain Dealer*'s Sunday supplement, giving widespread publicity to this quality school for Appalachian children. Most Lotts Creek students go on to college, have successful professional careers, and often return to serve their own communities.

I looked forward to my visits to the school and time with Aunt Alice, who became very dear to me. Her niece Alice Whitaker was one of the parent/teacher founders of Innisfree School. We took our Innisfree kids on a field trip down to Lotts Creek one weekend where I first met Aunt Alice.

One of my favorite projects for the school was the publicity brochure I wrote and laid out, using my own black-and-white pictures. They reprinted it year after year.

## Woodburning Basics

In 1979, I wrote and self-published a brochure, *Jay Hensley's Woodburning Basics,* had one thousand printed, put them in my backpack, and went to a trade show in Minneapolis. They let me in free on a press pass, then said later, teasing me, "We ought to charge Jay for being a walking booth!"

There I met, briefly, Eva Horton, exclusive U.S. importer for Jøtul stoves, as well as founder, early president, and a current director of the National Chimney Sweep Guild. She had contracted for two booths, carpeted and elegantly furnished to show off her stoves.

A few years earlier, with her gracious permission by phone, I had based my first how-to-do-it flue-cleaning articles on instructions she had written. She had learned how to clean chimneys herself during a two-week apprenticeship—climbing ladders and scrambling on roofs as she worked alongside professional chimney sweeps in Norway, her native country.

I remember being in awe of her—artist, sculptor, entrepreneur, "stove queen," independent woman. To my everlasting amazement, she was destined to become one of my dearest friends after we met again six years later.

As for *Woodburning Basics,* I sold all my brochures at the Minneapolis show, mostly to chimney sweeps. I also took an order for five thousand copies from Woodcutters Manufacturing, a woodstove company in Washington state. They included a copy of my brochure with every stove they sold. Whenever they placed a new order for five thousand copies, I would have ten thousand printed and sell the rest to sweeps in bundles of one hundred.

Although I never made any real money with *Woodburning Basics*, it helped spread my name around the wood-heat industry. I followed it with *Jay Hensley's Coalburning Basics*, which was equally good but never received as widespread use.

One of my favorite pieces of copy appeared on the last leaf of my *Coalburning Basics* brochure. I was trying to think of some memorable way to wind it all up when, sitting on my living room couch, I reached randomly into a bookcase close by and pulled out a volume of short stories by Franz Kafka. In it, I quickly found the inspiration I needed. Here then is the copy that resulted:

### Bucket Rider

Coal can indeed be your comfort through the long winter. But before you buy your stove or furnace, make sure you can keep your coal bin full of its proper fuel. Locate a reliable dealer and lay in a good supply. Otherwise, you may feel eerily akin to Austrian novelist Franz Kafka's bucket rider in his short story of the same name:

His coal was all used up, "his stove breathing out cold," and he was in danger of freezing to death in his frigid rooms. Mounting his empty coal scuttle, using its handle for the simplest of bridles, he rode it "at a regular canter" through the hard-frozen streets of that 19th century town. Hovering at last above the vaulted cellar of the coal dealers shop, he begged for coal "in a voice burned hollow by the frost."

Alas, he was wafted away by the flapping apron of the coal dealer's wife, ascended into the region of the ice mountains, and was lost forever.

Stay warm. May your coal bucket never take you on a wild ride into the night.

## Jobs for UK

I also did at least one big job a year under contract to the University of Kentucky—slide sets, brochures, and a few substantial editing projects, all of which paid very well. Dr. Sam Quick, one of my biggest fans, was instrumental in sending most of these plums my way.

## Kentucky Horse Farm Girl

Of all the feature stories I wrote, my favorite was "Kentucky Horse Farm Girl" about Lisa. In 1980, I spent a sunny autumn day with her at Stanley Petter's Hurricane Stud off the Georgetown Road a few miles north of Lexington. I took lots of pictures. That night back at the farm, she crawled in bed with me, and I turned on my tape recorder. I interviewed her until she fell asleep.

I sold the feature story that resulted to *Horse Lover* magazine. They ran it verbatim in the fall of 1981 with a whole slew of my photographs. I added a sidebar they requested about Lisa's advice to other young people who might want to work on a horse farm—a tough job, with few days off, just the thing for a hardworking, horse-loving outdoor gal like Lisa.

When she worked the Keeneland Sales one fall, I sold another feature story about her to the *Chronicle of the Horse*.

## The Boston Energy Show

In the fall of 1980, I visited my cousin Steve in Cambridge and attended the Boston Energy Show. There I saw my first masonry heater, laid up dry at the trade show by the Boston schoolteacher who had designed it.

When I went back to visit Mr. Fitzgerald at his home a few days later, he showed me two other heaters he had built and coached me on the whys and wherefores of this age-old way to winter warmth. The more I learned about these amazing enclosed fireplaces, the more intrigued I became.

Based on an ancient technology and used for centuries in Europe, they are energy efficient, clean burning, environmentally friendly, safe, and beautiful. One short-duration fire a day can keep your house warm, except in bitter-cold weather when it takes two fires.

A long convoluted flue path gives the flue gases time to soak into the masonry mass, which starts to radiate this stored heat into the house a few hours later. The steady warmth it supplies hour after hour is often likened to sunshine.

I had intended to write an article about Mr. Fitzgerald and his heaters from my extensive notes and photographs. To my great disappointment, someone beat me to it that winter with a long article in *Mother Earth News*. But I did take home a set of his plans, and Eddie laid up a masonry heater in the basement of the log house he and Jennifer were building on the farm.

I would go on to write many articles about masonry heaters, join the Masonry Heater Association of North America as an associate member, attend and write up all their annual meetings. Someday, I promised myself, I would have a custom-built masonry heater at the center of my own house. (This would come to pass twenty-one years later in Berea, Kentucky.)

### New Orleans Trade Show

Carter Keithly, director of the Wood Heating Alliance (WHA), read my magazine feature "Woodburning Stoves, an Uninsurable Risk?" and picked up the phone. He invited me to put together and moderate a panel discussion on the subject for their upcoming 1981 trade show. This big international expo was to take place in New Orleans that spring. They would pick up the tab for my plane fare, meals, and hotel expenses for one day and one night.

The panel discussion was a big success and generated much interest. I handed out several hundred copies of *Woodburning Basics*, met so many good people, made great industry contacts, had a fine time, and stayed on three or four days extra to attend the trade show and seminars.

Two of the people I met were Bill Paynton and his wife, Val, from Attleboro Falls, Massachusetts, where they owned a company that designed and manufactured top-of-the-line chimney caps. I was destined to meet them and spend time with them again and again around the USA. They were such good company, and wherever they went, they knew the best restaurants in town. The first of countless gourmet meals they treated me to was in New Orleans.

Nick, my new love back in Kentucky, had an acquaintance named Tom who worked as an aide in a mental hospital in New Orleans. He rented a one-bedroom flat on the edge of the French Quarter. So by prior arrangement, I unpacked my bags at his place after my one free day and night at that elegant hotel.

We liked each other, shared grocery expenses and cooking chores, went to the Mardi Gras together one night, and I had a great New Orleans adventure.

Tom was a fun guy to hang out with, but he was down on his luck at the time. He possessed only two bath towels, one set of bedsheets, two pillows, and two pillow slips. Whoever arrived home first got to sleep in the bed. When we'd spent the evening together, we made a last-minute race for the front door—and the loser got the living room couch.

*   *   *

Ah, travel, meeting people, learning new things, seeing my articles and pictures in print . . . I knew I'd never get rich at it, but this was the life for me!

# 30

# THE TROUBLE WITH MY CARS AND TRUCK

Not surprisingly, my son Joel figures prominently in these four-wheeled adventures.

A pickup truck was on my list of necessities in the early 1970s. For my trail-riding weekends, I had been borrowing a one-horse trailer from JT, who built our house on Ashgrove Pike. This was unhandy. I had to drive eight miles to collect the trailer, hitch it to my Travelall by myself, then clean it out, hose it down, and return it afterward. I usually finished up in the dark when I was dead tired and returned it the next morning—early. The rides were often on a Sunday or for the whole weekend, and I had to be at work at UK by 8:00 a.m. Monday.

I also used my Travelall for hauling hay and firewood. What I really needed was a truck. If I had it fitted with a rack, I could even jump my horse up into it for trail rides and forget about those borrowed horse trailer chores.

So I saved up my money and found a 1967 six-cylinder, sidestep green Chevy pickup truck—absolutely fell in love with it—at a local dealership. It cost $700. Since I was going to be out of town for a week on my job, I asked the dealer to hold it for me, telling him I'd come get it when I returned.

When I got back, I discovered that Joel had talked the dealer into letting him pick it up "for my mother" and had been driving it for almost a week. It seems that he too had been lusting after a pickup truck.

Anyhow, this was *my* truck! I had a custom-fit rack built for it. Backing it up to a hilly place, I would jump Apache into it and take off for a trail ride. However, I didn't like the way the truck handled with that high center of gravity. I felt it wasn't safe, that I was putting my beloved Appaloosa at risk.

One early morn, I took chain saw in hand and ventured forth to cut a load of firewood from culled trees at a friend's farm. It was an arduous task. After writing articles about how you should *never* go into the woods alone to cut firewood, I was doing it myself. This made me a little nervous! By the time I threw all the wood I'd cut into my truck, brought it home, unloaded it, and stacked it in the shed, I was plumb wore out.

And when you're hot and sweaty, loading and hauling bales of hay isn't that much fun either. (Being an independent, self-sufficient woman is a drag sometimes.)

Joel to the rescue. "Mom, just let me get the hay and firewood."

Within a few months, I signed the truck over to Joel. He and that little workhorse of a truck were made for each other.

Shortly thereafter, I found a good deal on a horse trailer, one high enough to clear the rocks in my lane, and bought it. When my Travelall finally gave out, I found a good deal on a full-size 1984 Ford pickup truck to pull my trailer.

## The $3,000 Check

Next comes the tale of the $3,000 check. My cousin Steve spent a few years in Germany in the '70s setting up and running a European subsidiary in Heidelberg for his company, Abt Associates. Before leaving the United States, he had gone on a fast track to learn German. I admired him tremendously for being able to function so well in another language.

Through the years, he was in the habit of sending me a check every Christmas, usually $100, "to buy something special for yourself!" One early spring day in 1981, I received mail from the Commerzbank in Bonn, West Germany. Enclosed, without explanation, was a check made out to me for $3,000, drawn on Steve's account. I was astounded.

At the time, I was driving a 1973 Subaru station wagon whose front end was stabilized with an actual two-by-eight oak timber from the barn. Joel had cut it to fit with a chain saw and jammed it in place under the hood to keep the front tires from splaying outward.

"Don't go over any bad bumps, Mom," he had cautioned.

Our long rocky farm lane was a series of jarring bumps I negotiated from that time on at about five miles per hour.

Joel had supplied me with this station wagon after totaling my late-model Subaru coupe with most of its payments still to be made. He was not insured to drive it; so he had spent his whole bank account, $700, on a replacement.

He transferred my good engine from the wrecked Subaru into the station wagon he bought, and I drove it for a few years. Then it broke down and needed serious attention. Dr. Joel to the rescue with his custom-fit two-by-eight, jammed in place under the hood. I drove that station wagon—very carefully—for another anxious year or two.

So now with a great sense of relief, I used my $3,000 from Steve to pay cash for a red Datsun B-210 hatchback, circa 1977. Then I called Steve, who was scheduled to be back in the United States by then. As soon as I heard his voice, I said, "Oh, Steve, thank you! Nobody has ever done anything like this for me!"

"What are you talking about?" he asked.

"The $3,000 you sent me," I said, my heart thumping fast and my face growing hot.

"Oh my god, so that's what happened!" he said.

Before he left Germany, he had arranged for his bank in Germany to transfer $3,000 to his checking account in Cambridge because he would have bills to pay right away. The check had gone missing. Commerzbank had just put a tracer on it

(Steve told me later that a new bank employee, unaccustomed to handling such transfers, had looked up Steve's last check to the United States, found my name on it, and sent this new check to me too.)

"Oh, Steve," I confessed, mortified, "I already spent the money. I bought a car! But I'll take it back right away."

"Wait," he said, "tell me about your car."

So I told him about needing to replace my station wagon, which was held together with a two-by-eight, and about the dandy little red Datsun I'd bought.

"Keep the car," he said. "I'll make that an interest-free loan, and you can take as long as you need to pay it back."

My four-year-old grandson, Ezra, came bopping down to my house the next morning and said, "Mama Jay, I like your new little sports car!"

It took me about five years to pay Steve back at the rate of $50 or $60 per month. As for that station wagon, I ended up giving it to Joel, who drove it for years without mishap.

After some years, my "little sports car" needed $400 or more of repairs, including a new clutch. My mechanic advised me not to put any more money into it. Since I could not even get it into gear, I sold it to Joel for $200. He started the motor, let it warm up for a good long while, then babied the clutch into gear, and sped off. Soon, he replaced the clutch disk, which cost him $15 and an hour's work, and drove that little car for years.

When it came to cars, Joel was pure genius.

# 31

## SLEEPING SCARED

### *Fire in My Life*

Our first summer place was a few miles outside the village of
Ashfield, at the top of Bug Hill Road off Cape Street. We called it
Landaff. After our one idyllic summer there, it burned to the ground
the following spring. I remember gazing sadly at the charred ruins
a few months later. The stone front porch and pillars were still
standing, and behind them, devastation.

Revisit Landaff with me as it was before being destroyed by
fire. Walk through its grand stone entrance off the narrow dirt road.
Tread the long tree-lined driveway with me until we finally glimpse
the side and back of the shingled two-story house ahead on the left.
Walk around to stand on the big front lawn with me; gaze over a
low stone wall at the view beyond of mountain after mountain after
mountain on to the horizon.

Now let's walk up the steps onto the spacious stone porch
and through the front double door. It opens into an entryway with
stairways on left and right. A center area beyond rises two stories
high, ringed at second-floor level with a railed balcony, off which
open at least six large high-ceilinged bedrooms.

My own room had a canopied double bed, accessible by
climbing two portable wooden steps although I also found it
possible to race across the room and take a flying leap onto it. 'Twas

a lovely bed for snuggling into and dreaming the night away. I must have been six going on seven that summer.

When Phillips went missing one day, we finally spied him trudging happily up the driveway, singing a little song. "Look!" he said, holding out the handful of envelopes he had pulled from our stone-cradled mailbox at the entrance. And he gave them up proudly to his mama.

"But I think what I brought back was the outgoing mail," my brother confessed to me with a laugh years later.

### Mater and Pater

Phillips thinks my folks probably found Landaff through Mater and Pater Smith, friends with a large hidden-away summer estate on the left off Cape Street, past the DAR forest, almost to Goshen.

I remember Mater's rather regal erect figure. She was a dear soul and a lover of children. Pater was distinguished looking, bearded, the less outgoing of the two . . . but my memory is hazy there. At get-togethers, we played with their grandchildren—Elf, her brother, Henny-Penny, and others.

We took part in all kinds of games and competitions. I was the perennial stand-on-my-head-the-longest champion and won most of the foot races. We also exerted ourselves in diabolical contests the grown-ups decreed, such as the three-legged gunnysack race. Teams of two thrust one adjacent leg into the same gunnysack, then held the sack up for dear life as we thumped along awkwardly to the finish line and back.

Phil and I both remember running free over the tree-covered hilly estate and playing to our hearts' content in the little cabin along a stream. Great memories. Good food, messy heat-split hot dogs on buns with relish and mustard, and sticky, crusty marshmallows, all roasted on long sticks over the fire.

### The Ovitt Family

I've often wondered if there were two Bug Hill roads. Daddy took us up and down the shorter steeper one from Cape Street. It had lots of bumps, which he emphasized on the way down by hitting the brakes at the right moment while we all screamed in delight.

The Ovitt family's little run-down farm across from our Landaff gate was in the V formed by the short bumpy road and a longer more gradual route that may have been the official Bug Hill Road, if it didn't have another name altogether.

Pauline and I played with the Ovitt children, who were numerous. I remember Ralph and Shirley in particular, the older children. We took turns swinging out bravely on a long rope attached to a high barn timber, then let go and hurtled down with a whoop into the hay below.

I remember going into the woodstove-heated kitchen of the house afterward, where dear, friendly dark-haired Mrs. Ovitt was nursing the new baby. Small brothers and sisters gathered around adoringly.

The Ovitts were poor folk, and that made us sad. We liked them, and we had a lot of fun with them. Mom and Dad never did tell us which children from which families we were allowed to play with and did not restrict our friendships.

## Our 1938 House Fire

After Landaff burned down, Daddy found us another Ashfield summer home, the Shattuck Place, on South Street overlooking the village. It too was visited by fire.

Awakening in the wee hours of that August morning in 1938, I heard a crackling sound and was aware of a flickering light in my room. I rolled over toward the window. Was Daddy out there with a flashlight, working on something? An early riser, he was always into one project or another.

I stuck my head out to call to him and saw that the laundry room roof below was fiercely burning! Waking up Anne, who was sleeping next to me, I said, "The house is on fire! Go wake up your family."

As I started for Pauline's room, I heard Anne's fourteen-year-old brother, David, in Phillips's tiny room next to us, screaming, "FIRE! FIRE! WE'LL ALL BE KILLED!"

"Oh, shut up, David!" I yelled over my shoulder as I sped past. I shook Pauline awake in the center room, then headed for the twin bedroom where I flung the door open and yelled, "Daddy, Daddy, wake up! The house is on fire!"

Daddy jumped out of bed, Mother tried groggily to wake up, and little Phillips sat up sleepily on the cot between Mom's and Dad's beds.

I remember Pauline and me emptying out her drawers onto the bedspread, then rolling it all up into a bundle, and pushing it down the front stairs. I remember Uncle Dave, who'd been sleeping upstairs in the ell, holding his hand and saying he'd burned it trying to open the red-hot metal latch of the door to the laundry room where our cat, Spud, and her five kittens were kept at night.

The fire had started in the "dead" ashes of their litter box. We found the charred bodies of Spud and all her kittens the next day, were comforted by being told the smoke did them in before the flames could have reached them.

I remember the fire engine coming, gruff shouting as the fire hose broke, Pauline running to let the horses out in case the barn caught fire. I remember Anne and me being sent down the hill to the Days' house to spend the rest of the night. As we left, we looked back to see Daddy perched on the ridge of the roof to the ell with a garden hose, directing a small stream of water onto the fire, while firefighters found a closer fire hydrant and were attaching a new hose to it.

I remember finally falling asleep at the Days' and dreading to get out of bed the next morning. But when Anne and I went outside and raised our eyes toward the Place, expecting to see charred ruins, like at Landaff, the house looked just same as always! The serious damage, which we couldn't see, was to the roof and upstairs of the ell, plus extensive water damage throughout the interior of the house.

I remember going into the breakfast room and starting to eat some candy. It tasted of charred wood; and I threw the whole box of chocolates, one piece at a time, out into the field beyond the barn.

I went upstairs to my room and picked a dollar bill off a charred shelf. At that slight touch, the shelf fell off the wall.

I remember being told that two people had carted our heavy piano right out the front door. And someone had carried the fish aquarium from the living room out onto the front lawn, slopping out all the fish on the way.

In the cool of the morning, Anne and I walked up to Mizentop, the Halls' grand summer place to which the rest of our family and guests had been evacuated. In one of the many bedrooms, I found Mom and Dad and my little brother all wide awake in one great big bed.

And I have slept scared ever since.

### Fire in Pammel Court

Years later, in 1951 at our trailer home in Pammel Court, I lit our pump-up bottled gas stove one Saturday afternoon. Suddenly, the newspapers I'd stored underneath erupted in flames! I grabbed a bucket, dashed out the door to a nearby spigot for water, and put the fire out. It took three bucketsful. Then I had a big mess to clean up and no time to fix dinner for company that night.

In one of the bathroom facilities for the court a little while later, I told what happened to a young woman who came in. "And we're supposed to be having company for dinner!" I lamented, almost in tears.

"Don't worry," she said. "Just tell me your trailer number." She arrived at my door soon afterward with a delicious hot casserole. It's what she had fixed for their own dinner, I'm sure. And that's how I met Imogene Lauger. She and her husband, Bill, were to become good friends.

### A Fire at the Ashfield Dump

The next significant fire in my life happened in early summer of 1965 at the Ashfield town dump. Pauline and Malcolm discovered that after Daddy died, Mom gathered together all his papers, sermons, letters, articles, and some of his books. Then she hired a boy from the village to take them to the dump and burn them!

We think she went a little crazy, and we never confronted her with her dastardly deed.

Mom was of liberal bent for those times. Although she stuck by Daddy through the years, we knew she felt that he often went too far in his progressive social and political pursuits.

Destroyed in that town dump fire was Daddy's unpublished book, *One Mortal Lad*, a novel about a Missouri farm boy's growing-up years. I was the only family member who had read it, and it was good! I suspect it was partly drawn from Daddy's own boyhood and coming-of-age sexual experiences, which may be what bothered Mother.

## Lisa to the Rescue

Two other fires in the making were aborted by the ever-vigilant Lisa!

When Joel was about three, she discovered him playing with matches in our Lexington, Kentucky, redwood house on Cane Run Road. He was hiding behind the lined draperies for our big picture window with a box of kitchen matches, gleefully lighting one match after another and blowing them out. Lisa was five years old.

Some years later, at our farm on the Jessamine Creek, Lisa was taking a load of folded laundry up the stairs to Tim's room one day. Smoke was seeping out from under his door!

She quickly unplugged the space heater that had tipped over onto a plastic bean-filled chair, which was smoldering. Tim had bounded out of his room in a hurry, knocking over his heater on the way. "But I knew it had a cutoff safety switch," he told us later, defensively. The switch was however broken.

\*   \*   \*

I believe that these experiences with fire, especially the night I awoke to flames outside my own bedroom window, set my feet on the path that eventually led me to publishing *SNEWS: The Chimney Sweep News*. My sole original objective with this magazine was to keep people from burning their houses down.

# 32

## MEETING CLAIRE

My twenty-six-year-old daughter, Lisa, and I did an eight-hundred-mile road trip to Apple Valley in late September of 1983 for our annual monthlong stay with Pauline and Malcolm. While there we earned money picking apples at Clark Orchards. I would pick all morning, then take the afternoon off to do other things—ride with Plink, snap pictures, take a nap, help with supper. Lisa worked diligently all day and was a much faster picker than I was.

We both loved walking up to the orchards each morning in the fresh cold air and looking out across the fall-color-tinged valley to the other side of the mountain. We carefully set the long narrow handmade wooden ladders in place under our side-by-side trees.

Malcolm's brother Richard had fashioned these ladders wide at the bottom, tapering to a blunt nose at the top, easy to maneuver up through the branches. We shouldered our canvas bags, climbed our ladders to the top of the tree, and commenced picking, working our way down the ladders, shouting back and forth to each other. At noon, we walked on down to Pauline and Malcolm's for dinner.

That year, over three or four evenings, I pasted up the camera-ready copy for the thirty-six-page November issue of my own magazine (more about this in the next chapter!). I worked on their dining table, sizing all my photos and marking where they and the ads needed to be placed.

Before I went to bed, I cleared the table for the next morning's breakfast. When I had completed the camera-ready pasteup, I mailed it, special delivery, to the printer in Wilmore, Kentucky.

One day, I picked "drops" for cider by myself in the orchard up behind the old farmhouse all morning, then walked on down to Pauline and Malcolm's house for dinner. Malcolm arrived shortly thereafter, saying, as he took his boots off, "I think Pierre's sister Claire is picking apples up behind the main house."

## Meeting Claire in the Orchard

I raced back up there with a pounding heart. The orchard seemed empty. I shouted, "Claire Cournand!" And a clear voice from the top of a tree close by answered, "Yes?"

"I'm Julia. I was Pierre's friend," I said, and down the tall narrow wooden ladder she came. Sturdy and petite, with short-cropped brown hair, and wearing a bulky sweater over work pants and boots, she set her heavy load of apples down, looked at me, and stood there expectantly.

I don't remember much about our brief conversation except that we were very glad to meet each other. She did say that she'd never known the brother whose death had been such a tragedy for her family. Only two when he went off to war, she had grown up under the shadow of his loss.

We agreed to get together soon. There was so much I wanted to share with her. Until Claire, there had never been anyone I felt I could talk to about Pierre.

When I asked Claire many years later about her first impression of me, she said, "I remember the lovely smile and the sweet musical voice. It was a wonderful moment." She also recounted her first fleeting impression of Malcolm that noontime.

She'd been loaned out to Clark Orchards for the day by Ed Pape, a neighboring apple grower. From her high perch among the heavily loaded branches that morning, she had seen me scrabbling on my hands and knees, picking drops under the trees nearby. Then she had watched me pass by her tree on my way out of the orchard at noon. A few minutes later, she saw Malcolm walking by down below.

Although she knew him by sight, she had never met him. "I thought it would be polite to introduce myself," she said, and down out of the tree she came.

"I'm Claire Cournand. I'm working in your orchard today," she told him. He glanced at her, grunted, and continued on his way. Somewhat surprised, she concluded that he was just one of those taciturn Yankees. In fact, he had connected with the name and hurried home to tell me.

## Revisiting Old Haunts

A few days later, Claire invited me for dinner and to spend the evening. The Cournand property in South Ashfield was hers now, and she thoroughly enjoyed the local people and summer residents she had long known. Although she normally moved back to Manhattan in the fall, she was living full-time at her summer home that year. In the dead of winter with its deep and drifting snow, this would become quite an adventure!

She was self-employed as a translator of books, mostly novels—French to English, English to French. However, after running out of translation work that early fall, she had signed on to pick apples to earn some money. Later on, she would work for Clark Orchards again, picking, then sorting and packaging apples in the assembly line down at "the storage."

Arriving at her place on Bird Hill Road, I closed my eyes for a few moments, and the past took hold of me. At first glance, the little two-story red frame house looked just the same, a first-floor addition at the back hidden from view. But the large open field Pierre had circled astride Nonnie that July afternoon in 1943 was now filled with tall mature trees.

Claire gave me a quick tour of the house with its four small bedrooms and large bathroom upstairs, the wonderful old wood/ gas cookstove in the kitchen, the wood-burning heating stove in the parlor . . . and could this be the same dining room table where I had joined the family for dinner on my last visit so many years ago?

There's also a small bathroom on the first floor, a back pantry, and screened-in front porch. I remembered it all. Little had changed since Pierre's time, except for the 1950s addition of the long "playroom" with a ping-pong table at one end and large fireplace at the other

Soon, I was asking Claire if she knew the way to Pierre's cabin . . . and if she would take me there. Flashing me a look of both surprise and concern, she hesitated, then nodded her head. I also asked her if she had a flashlight we could use in case we got lost.

"Lost?" she said, indignant. "We won't get lost—these are *my* woods!"

But I insisted on the flashlight, and we started off. It was late in the afternoon. The old path Pierre and I had trod was gone, but we found our way through deep woods to the cabin site.

All that remained of Pierre's skillful handiwork were the stone chimney and fireplace, a scattering of dank, rotted logs, and pieces of rusted metal roofing. Devastated, I fought back the tears. We stood there in silence for a very long time . . . then we got lost on the way back to Claire's house.

Night was descending, and it started to rain, a steady drizzle. I envisioned us sitting all night in the darkness with our backs against a tree, telling each other our life stories . . . and on the lookout for wild beasts. There were bears and wildcats in the forest.

We kept walking, shining the flashlight ahead of us, often going in circles, seeing the same trees and rock formations. We finally came to an old logging road. Claire stood in the middle of it, beamed her flashlight in both directions, then said decisively, "This way!"

We tramped along in the rain and finally came to a clearing. "It's the Thorp house," Claire said. We were soon knocking on the kitchen door of this old New England farmhouse.

## Lost Farm

An elderly couple greeted us warmly and served us hot tea by the wood-burning cookstove while we dried off. When Claire introduced me to Charlotte and Carl Thorp as "one of the Jones girls," they smiled. They remembered my sister and me cantering through their Lost Farm dooryard to access the old logging trail that cut on over to Briar Hill Road. I remembered them too smiling and waving to us as we dashed by.

Claire and I walked on back through the rain to her house where she fixed supper and opened a bottle of wine. We ate by the light of the fire that Claire kindled in her big fireplace. We talked and talked. It was a grand evening.

After that, whenever I went home, I spent time with Claire; and over the years that followed, we forged a close friendship. She told me a little about Pierre's early-childhood years after his father died and before his mother met and married André Frédéric Cournand, then a young doctor in Paris.

Born in Paris in 1895 and with a degree from the University of Paris, Dr. Cournand became an instructor at the College of Physicians and Surgeons at Columbia University in 1934. He had immigrated to this country with his family in 1930 when Pierre was six years old.

The Cournand family joined the ranks of Ashfield's summer people in 1941, the same year Dr. Cournand became an American citizen. In 1956, he shared the Nobel Prize in medicine and physiology with his colleagues Dickinson Richards and the German physician Werner Forssmann.

I consider Claire's friendship a gift from the universe. Here was the connection to Pierre's family that I had longed for, but it became much more than that. She has added a wonderful dimension to my life.

Well educated, straightforward, and with great personal warmth, she is literate, compassionate, and thoughtful. She is, when the need arises, outspoken and firm in her opinions and beliefs. She has been a peace activist on the streets of New York City. She has a unique perspective on people, history, and world events. She has lived and studied in France, speaks three languages, and is quietly at ease with people from all walks of life.

How Pierre would have treasured this sister of his if he had survived to get to know her through the years.

# 33

# OUR LIVES IN THE 1980S

*The Hensley-Nichols Years*

**Update on Claire**

Claire and I wrote to each other through these years. I had good visits with her whenever I went home and found her at Ashfield too. In one letter to me, Claire wrote, "I'm forever grateful for having met, through you, your sister's family and enjoy them thoroughly."

She had become well acquainted with Pauline's youngest son, Dana, who was running Clark Orchards now. Working for him off and on when she wasn't doing translations, she thinned apples, cut out suckers, and picked.

In 1985, Claire was still dividing her time between Ashfield and New York City, beginning to consider the possibility of selling her apartment on Madison Avenue and moving to Ashfield permanently. She told me, "When I'm in Ashfield, I can't imagine being anywhere else!"

Her father was to celebrate his ninetieth birthday in September that year, and the family from France would gather at Claire's in Manhattan for the occasion, so she was closing up the house and moving back to the city on Labor Day.

When Tim had a fencing competition scheduled in New York City two years later, I gave him Claire's phone number and address on Madison Avenue. She wrote me a letter about meeting him, which I excerpt here:

> It was wonderful to meet Tim, a well-grown, cheerful, handsome and positive lad if I ever saw one. We spent all afternoon together, and I also traipsed downtown to see him fence. I didn't bring him much luck . . . he kept having electrical problems, but was a wonderful sport.
>
> I kept thinking what a pity Hollywood doesn't make old-fashioned adventure movies like "The Prisoner of Zenda" any more. He would have been a perfect romantic hero with his curls and his gallant body.
>
> Anyway, thank you for sending him to me. We talked a lot about you and the family, and I can see now why you always smile when you talk about him.

Except for his long and very curly hair, Tim was the spittin' image of his dad at his age—the resemblance is uncanny. Of all my children, I've always thought Tim was the one Pierre would have liked best.

### A Visit with Dr. Cournand

In the mid-1980s, Claire took me with her to visit her father at his wife's spacious estate outside Great Barrington. Claire's mother had died unexpectedly when Claire was seventeen and attending Oxford University in England. This deep loss had been hard for her to bear.

A few years after his second wife Ruth's death, Dr. Cournand married Beatrice Bishop Berle. She had been widowed after a happy and eventful forty-year marriage to Adolf Berle, a brilliant member of Franklin Roosevelt's administration. She was a social worker and practicing physician in New York City for many years, an admired intellectual, and mother of three.

Her autobiography, *A Life in Two Worlds*, published in 1983, is well worth the read. She is also the author of *Eighty Puerto Rican Families*.

The Cournands and Berles had been friends for many years. Beatrice and Andre married in 1975 when he was eighty and she was seventy-three.

Beatrice greeted Claire and me graciously that sunny, breezy afternoon, then left us to sit with him at a small round table out on the terrace. Dr. Cournand was retired now and in failing health after a distinguished career as a physiologist, a pioneer in the clinical application of heart catheterization.

I reminded him of my visit so long ago when, after my dinner with the family, he escorted me and Malcolm's horse, Judy, through the darkness out to Bird Hill Road, lighting the way with his kerosene lantern. He remembered me and said brokenly, "Oh, my Pierre!" with tears in his eyes.

Dr. Cournand died in 1988, a few years after our visit. He was ninety-three. Following his memorial service at Columbia University, Claire became acquainted with Father Luis Dolan, the visionary Catholic priest who had given the blessing.

"Father Luis was my father's parting gift," she told me. Within months, she signed on to work with him in an endeavor to promote dialogue and better understanding between various ethnic and religious groups on four continents. It was a commitment that would completely absorb her over the next twelve and a half years.

### Meanwhile, Down on the Farm . . .

At the time I met Claire, I was still freelancing, living at my farm with Nick. I had known this very attractive tall white-haired laid-back guy slightly through our Unitarian Fellowship. We finally zeroed in on each other at the fellowship's 1980 Christmas dinner and were soon spending all our free time together.

Nick Nichols was forty-four when we started keeping company. He was a voracious reader and intellectually inclined. A gifted actor, he belonged to Junkyard Players, a local semiprofessional theater company. His day job was teaching courses in world history and Problems of Modern Man at Eastern

Kentucky University in Richmond, about a forty-five-minute commute from Lexington.

Divorced for about a year from his third wife, a talented young actress, Nick lived in Lexington with his nine-year-old stepson, Sean, and two daughters, Wendi, sixteen, and Stephani, three-and-a-half.

My son Doug had a friend, Mia, at Barlow who once told him she thought the ideal situation was "to live alone and have a lover down the road." That originally sounded good to me, but now I had that lover down the road, and he was much too far down the road for comfort.

One evening, three months after Nick and I got together, we were lying snug in bed at his house, having about a week earlier progressed to that stage in our relationship. Hating the idea of getting up, going home, and being apart again, I said, "Nick . . . come live with me and love me and be mine!"

There was a long startled silence. Then, "Okay."

Over the next two weeks, on evenings and weekends, Nick, with Stephani in tow, brought a few pieces of furniture and other miscellaneous belongings out to the farm, five or six large cardboard boxfuls at a time. Wendi moved in with her boyfriend, Michael, whom she married a few years later; and Sean went to live with his father.

One of the things I loved most about Nick was that he didn't expect me to be perfect. A few weeks after he moved in, I said, "Oh, Nick, I have some grievous faults!" He looked at me, laughed, and said fondly, "I know."

The rest of our menagerie in that spring of 1981 included Joel, twenty-two; Tim, fifteen; two horses; our feisty yellow tomcat named MacAttack; and Nick's mellow gray cat, Trampas. A few months later, Bridgette, the troubled daughter of a wealthy Lexington family, moved in with Joel. They lived in the little three-room house out back, heated first by a coal stove, then by a wood-burning stove.

That had been Joel's pad where he had played his drum set to his heart's content and hung out with his friends.

## Update on Lisa

Meanwhile, Lisa had signed on to work at Kettlespring Farm in Clark County, thirty miles away. Owner Pat Shely managed it, for the most part, with the help of her longtime partner Linda, a hired man, and Lisa.

Pat and Linda were both physical education teachers, and I had fenced Pat competitively years earlier. One time, I was seven months pregnant with Lisa, which Pat told me years later had made her very nervous.

Lisa lived at Kettlespring Farm in a small two-story rock house with an attached tiny log house moved from elsewhere on the farm that served as her kitchen. She planted flowers around the foundation, carried water, used an outhouse, bathed in the waters of Kettlespring in all but the coldest weather, worked hard, became close friends with Pat and Linda; and she was happy.

In 1981, she helped them build a new tobacco barn. Another member of the tobacco crew that year was Don Pasley, who currently serves as a popular and effective representative in the Kentucky legislature. He told local firefighter-farmer Tommy Rector, whose sister Theresa he was courting, about Lisa.

He described how this pretty blue-eyed girl with thick supercurly hair could hang tobacco all day in a barn she'd helped to build. Intrigued, Tommy signed on to work in tobacco at Kettlespring Farm the following fall of 1982. But alas, Lisa was not there. She was picking apples with me in Apple Valley.

They would not meet until the following spring when Lisa, eager to make Tommy's acquaintance after he called her on the phone, stopped by his rental house in town one rainy night when she had to make a run into Winchester with the old Chevy farm truck.

Tommy was a good-looking, muscular, personable, quick-witted fellow, so easy to like. But when he answered Lisa's knock on the door that night, he was smoking a cigarette. This was a habit she deplored.

Even so, their affinity for each other quickly blossomed. So much so that Lisa cancelled her plans to move to Apple Valley in two weeks and work for the Clark farm. A few years later, Tommy told me, "I didn't know what love was about before Lisa."

But she did move to Apple Valley the following November, about a month after she and I had picked apples there and met Claire. "If I don't go now," she said, "I may never do it." So she drove her pickup truck back to the valley she had loved ever since her early childhood.

She lived in a cottage on the Clark farm that had, in Malcolm's youth, been a one-room schoolhouse for children of the upper and lower Apple Valley. Learning to cope with frigid temperatures and snowstorms that left deep drifts, she loved working on the farm and spending time with Pauline and Malcolm.

She and Claire, only a few miles away in South Ashfield, became good friends. A young farmer in the valley, a widower with two small children, took far more than a passing interest in her.

But she missed Tommy too much to stay. So she came back home to Kentucky the following spring. She married Tommy Lee Rector in October 1984 in the Seventh-Day Adventist Church outside Winchester, which she had joined a year earlier.

### Jennifer and Eddie

By 1980, Jennifer, Eddie, and four-year-old Ezra were living in their little house on our Jessamine Creek farm and preparing to build a more permanent house on their twelve acres. By then, Jennifer had juried into the Kentucky Guild of Artists & Craftsmen, quit her job at Shakertown, and started basket weaving in earnest. She made her baskets in many sizes and shapes, displaying and selling them out of her booth at the craft fairs.

In addition to this, Jennifer began raising Romney/Corriedale sheep. She dyed, spun, and wove their wool into beautiful scarves on her big loom and sold the lambs for meat. Many a night, I received an SOS call from her and met her at their barn to help deliver a lamb or two by lantern light.

Jen and Eddie's barn down near the creek was the result of a weekend work party soon after they built their little house. Family and friends had pitched in to get the job done. We finished off each workday with a potluck supper and bonfire.

But they had located their barn on low ground a little too close to the creek. In the spring of '81, heavy rains caused flooding that trashed most of our fence line along the creek-side perimeter of the farm, uprooting fence posts, carrying away heavy metal gates, and inundating the barn.

Early the next morning, Eddie—waist deep in cold, churning water—chainsawed an escape hatch in the side of the barn so that he and Jennifer could lift out each waterlogged ewe and carry her to safety on higher ground.

Nick and Steph had moved in with me shortly thereafter. Nick went right to work with Joel and Eddie, digging postholes and building a new fence. He came in at the end of that first day exhausted, soaked with sweat, and grinning. "I've never worked so hard in my life, and I've never been so happy!"

The consummate actor had flung himself wholeheartedly into a new role, and he loved it. For a while.

### Nick Meets Egon and Lilly

I dropped by Egon and Lilly's house one day with Nick and Stephani in tow soon after they moved out to the farm. The Kornicers were impressed with Nick, liked him very much. Curly-haired, affectionate, bright-eyed little Steph immediately won their hearts too. They smiled happily, sighed with relief, obviously feeling that I was "safe" now that I had a man.

We stopped by their house often. Lilly brewed Turkish coffee for Egon and offered some to Nick and me one morning, but we couldn't drink it! It was extremely strong, bitter, and loaded with sugar.

Nick and I marveled at Egon's resourcefulness. When his lawn mower was beyond repair, he bought a new one. To get rid of the old one, he mowed the front yard about halfway with his new machine, then put it away, and placed the defunct mower out on the lawn at the end of the newly mown section. Thieves came in the night and stole it.

Egon continued to be my "creative darkroom technician" until about 1985 when he and Lilly retired and moved away. Nick and I visited them once in their retirement village in northern Tennessee. Their small condo held all they needed, including the darkroom Egon installed.

Five or six years later, Lilly left Egon quite suddenly before she could carry out her plan to do him in. He was bereft and inconsolable without her. His daughter, Vessna, soon came to fetch him, planning to take him home to live with her. But he died from a heart attack during their road trip East. It is just as well.

## The Gourmet Chef

My kids liked Nick. It didn't hurt that he baked four loaves of whole wheat bread at a time and started a family tradition with his hearty Christmas Eve pizzas. Just about the only thing I didn't like about Nick was his pot smoking, which I wouldn't allow in the house.

He was not only great fun to live with, he was a gourmet chef and did most of the cooking during our years together. His father had abandoned the family when Nick was seven. His mother was a teacher. She left the cooking chores to Nick from an early age, and he also took care of his little sister.

When I fixed breakfast for him our first morning together at the farm, he was astounded. Nobody had ever done that for him. So I usually just did breakfast, my favorite meal of the day. Except on Sunday. Nick's Sunday morn pancakes were the best! He beat the egg whites and folded them into the batter.

As a little boy, Nick had yearned for his father. As an adult, he tracked him down, met him briefly, and didn't like him. His mother was rather strange, and Nick didn't remember her ever hugging him. He eventually had a stepfather he liked, a taciturn man who often took Nick places with him.

He loved being part of my family, reveled in living on the farm, enjoyed tremendously his friendship with Eddie. One evening, as we sat together on the front porch swing, he said, "I'm going to die here!"

## Ezra and Steph

Ezra and Steph were growing up like brother and sister. They loved to run around catching fireflies in the front yard after dark, putting them in jars to make little lanterns, just as my other kids had once done.

Together, they raised a fair amount of havoc around the farm and in both households. One day, they disappeared altogether for hours. We clanged the loud schoolhouse bell by the back door many times, the signal for our family to gather for a meal. When they didn't come, I scoured the neighborhood on horseback.

Finally, just as we started to panic, they reappeared. A young couple had come walking onto our farm and blithely taken the kids along down the creek with them for an afternoon's adventure.

"We saw a waterfall and caught crawdads," Ezra reported happily.

And Steph, deathly afraid of snakes, reported seeing one wriggle out of a tree, plop into the water, and swim right past her leg.

Stubborn, very smart, needy, imaginative, and tempestuous, Stephani was not easy to raise. I felt as if she resisted everything I tried to teach her. But she was my kid, and I loved her.

## Junkyard Players

JYP and its core of talented actors were an important part of Nick's life, and he was in one play after another throughout the year. He was really a wonderful actor. When he was in *Night of the Iguana*, I clean forgot that the tottering old man up on the stage was actually Nick. The other actors were people I enjoyed getting to know, and we often had them out to the farm for potluck suppers.

Soon, I became the official JYP photographer. Pushing the film speed to the limit, I took color slides during dress rehearsals and live performances. At the cast party following the last night's performance, I usually had a slide show for them.

Stephani became a fine actress, starting out in an elementary school *Mary Poppins* play. Joining Junkyard Players (JYP) very early as a regular, she and Nick often went off to rehearsals together. She had roles in the following JYP productions: as Beads, the fairy, in *The Merry Wives of Windsor*; as another fairy in *A Midsummer*

*Night's Dream*; as a witch in *Macbeth*; and as Scout, one of the lead roles in *To Kill a Mockingbird*.

Her stunning portrayal of young Helen Keller in the Lexington Children's Theatre production of *The Miracle Worker* was so affecting that Nick sat next to me in the audience with tears running down his face.

She played the roles of Michael, one of Wendy's little brothers, and, later, of Wendy's daughter Jane in the UK Guignol Theatre's *Peter Pan*. She had to overcome her fear of heights in the scene where Peter and the children flew out the bedroom window into the night on their way to Never Land.

She was Tevye's daughter, Bielke, in the Asbury College seniors' *Fiddler on the Roof* and one of the children in the Kincaid Community Theatre's *Carousel* in Falmouth, Kentucky. She also played the role of Millie Owens—sister to Madge, one of the romantic leads—in the UK Guignol Theatre's production of *Picnic*.

Steph came through as a true professional in all these roles. She also appeared in many commercials for which she was well paid.

**Jen and Eddie's New House**

They picked their building site at a high point on the farm overlooking the creek. In the spring of 1981, they had torn down Eddie's log house in Lee County and trucked the logs to Jessamine County to form the nucleus of their new house. Several years passed before they started work on the structure.

Once the basement was excavated, Eddie laid up its concrete block walls, roughed in the plumbing and wiring, and they were ready to erect the log walls. Eddie had thought he knew every notched log by heart, but it had been too long, and he was having a little trouble!

"Here, look at these," I said as I handed him the pages of close-up color slides I'd taken the day the work party dismantled his house. With the help of a magnifying glass for studying the slides, he was able to identify each log.

Joel, Nick, and Tim all helped with the building project and soon had the logs in place, all but the very top layer. With Nick manning the tractor from the far side of the house, a strong rope tied from the tractor to the center of each log in turn, they pulled it up a track of two stout boards, then carefully set it in place.

One afternoon, Ez and Steph ran down to my house, screaming, "Come quick, Mama Jay! A log fell on Tim!"

Terrified, I raced up to building site with them.

These were square-hewn oak logs, each one very heavy. Joel and Tim at each end of one log had been jockeying it into place. Tim was perched near the top of a tall ladder reaching up from the basement floor, when his end of the log swung loose and came toward him. When this happened, Joel, at the corner of the house, lost control of his end too.

Quick-witted and lithe, Tim jumped off the ladder, landed on his feet, then fell back onto his butt. The log hurtled down; but just before it would have landed its full weight on him, it came to the end of its rope, stopped, and hung there, coming to rest lightly on his lap. Tim was unhurt, not even bruised.

Needless to say, the crew knocked off for the rest of the day.

After finishing the log core, they built two bedrooms upstairs and added a downstairs bedroom, sitting room, and bathroom at the rear of the house. They used windows and doors salvaged from houses torn down in Lexington. They finished it all off with a metal roof. Eddie had laid up a concrete-block chimney, and they installed their woodstove in the kitchen end of the front room.

The completed house stuck up so abruptly from the landscape that Eddie decided to add a wide two-story porch across the front. This softened the lines. Now it looked like the sturdy dwelling of a prosperous pioneer family.

With a whole lot of work still left to do, the family moved in. It was midsummer 1984. They celebrated Ezra's eighth birthday the end of August. Jennifer would be chinking logs, refinishing, and/or painting doors and windows for years to come.

Eddie and Joel had a few years earlier patched the roof to our farmhouse so that it no longer leaked. Now Eddie and Nick went to work on our plumbing, bringing the pipes inside the house and along the walls, protecting a run under the house with heat tapes. A few years later, Eddie built us a seven-thousand-gallon cistern in back of the house. After that, we had hot and cold running water all year long!

## Joel and Bridgette's News

One evening, in early 1983, Joel and Bridgette announced that they had a baby on the way. "I never would have dreamed I'd be getting married," Joel said in a mild case of shock as we all sat around the kitchen table, absorbing the news.

Shortly after that, they were married by a justice of the peace. We'd like to have had a family wedding, but Bridgette's grandmother Wenneker, matriarch of the family, had offered them $500 to go away and get married quietly.

After they moved to an apartment in Lexington, where their rent had been paid up for six months as a wedding present from Bridgette's father, their living quarters at the farm became my *SNEWS* house. Joel worked in construction, and his marriage soon turned into an emotional roller coaster.

## My Own Magazine

So just what was *SNEWS*?

In February of 1983, I put a second mortgage on the farm and, with Nick and Jeff Gitlin's encouragement, bought a twelve-page newsletter for chimney sweeps. Right away, I turned it into an independent magazine, *SNEWS: The Chimney Sweep News*. Finally, I had my own magazine! I would edit and publish it for the next sixteen years. Jeff became my technical advisor, and he proved invaluable.

At that time, Jeff was a member of the prestigious technical committee for the National Chimney Sweep Guild (NCSG). When he signed on with *SNEWS*, the powers that be at NCSG were not pleased, for they considered me an adversary.

(Although I encouraged all sweeps to join the guild, I also carried sweep-authored articles critical of various aspects and policies of the guild.)

Annoyed by NCSG's attitude, Jeff promptly resigned from their technical committee.

While I was putting together the first issue of the magazine, Nick came to the door of the *SNEWS* house, pressing a bloody handkerchief to his face. "I need to go the emergency room!" he said.

He had been cutting up some logs for firewood when the chain saw kicked back into his face, slicing an ugly deep gash from one side of his nose to his chin. I drove him to the local medical center in nearby Nicholasville and waited anxiously while the doctor stitched him up.

The next day, Nick moved painfully, bent over like an old man due to his body's sudden and intense reaction when the saw kicked back. The wound healed to a fine line, not marring his wonderful face.

I published ten issues of *SNEWS* a year, from twenty-four to forty-four pages, full of feature stories, photographs, technical information, industry news, a very popular centerfold comic strip based on a real sweep's experience, and advertising. Each issue had to be pasted up camera ready for the printer. To get it all together, I put in many sixteen- and eighteen-hour days. I loved it!

Working in the living room with piles of magazines and envelopes all around us, Tim helped me affix address labels, stuff envelopes, and mail out each issue. We broke even the first year, then started to make a little money. I kept the books, managed the subscription list, sold advertising, conducted lots of interviews, and encouraged sweeps to send in articles, which they did.

I attended my first sweep convention in St. Louis that spring, stayed at the local YMCA, and took a bus back and forth to the convention hotel every day. With my hair in two long braids, I manned my *SNEWS* booth, and sweeps greeted me warmly. The California sweeps even took me to dinner one evening and made me an honorary member of their state guild.

Every spring and early summer, I traveled around the country to cover conventions and set up my booth at trade shows. It was great fun getting to know sweeps and other wood-heat industry folks. I became a big fish in a small pond!

But *SNEWS* was proving to be a huge undertaking. It was as if I had adopted a cuddly little critter that had grown into a monster and swallowed me whole. Finding time for any personal life was daunting.

## Daddy Joel

Leslie Alexandria Hensley was born to Joel and Bridgette in June 1983 and became an important part of our lives. Joel adored her from the moment he laid eyes on her. He changed her diapers, gave her her bottle, and got up in the night with her. I remember her as a baby crawling through the grass down by the creek, her little head raised high in a floppy bonnet, looking all around her with joy.

One Christmas when she was two and a half, she sat on our living room floor with her opened presents spread around her. She gazed at them in wonder, looked up at us, and said, "These are for my whole life!"

A few years later, in not-so-happy times for her little family, she said, "I will love my daddy Joel forever and ever . . . even if he's in jail!"

Lisa and Tommy on their farm over in Clark County also started raising a family—first Josh, delivered during an ice storm after a perilous journey to a Lexington hospital, then Hannah, and, last of all, Elijah.

They grew up with a minimum of sibling scrapping and became one another's favorite playmates. They made up all sorts of adventures and chase scenes around the farm and eventually produced a series of very entertaining video sequences.

## Our Hog-raising Adventure

For one year, along with Jennifer and Eddie, we raised and butchered our own hogs. Nick jumped out of bed as excited as a little boy on the morning he and Eddie were scheduled to pick up those first weanling pigs. There was an ideal fenced-in area along the creek down below the barn. It had a low shed, which needed some work to make it serviceable again, and a semicircular rock-bordered watering hole built out into the creek to catch its flow. Hog Heaven we called it.

Eddie raised a crop of field corn in the bottoms to feed the hogs, and we all had a grand time harvesting it together.

Our first hog-butchering day that cold fall morning was another matter. I remember the stricken look on Nick's face after he killed our hog. He denied that it bothered him, but I knew better.

We all took part in the work that followed—pouring scalding water on each carcass, scraping off the hair (Tim was good at that), hanging them up on stout frames in the field behind the house, gutting and cutting them up—that part was Eddie's job because he knew exactly what he was doing. I documented it all with my Pentax K1000.

Nick mixed up our share of the ground sausage in the bathtub, seasoned it well, then took it into town to be stuffed into individual casings. Eddie salted down the hams, hung them in a tightly built shed, and smoke-cured them. This all turned out to be the best pork chops, bacon, sausage, and ham I ever ate. We stopped being vegetarians.

But hogs are intelligent, personable animals. Nick and I didn't have the heart to go on buying these cute little piglets and raising them to eat. Besides, our hog-butchering scene had been hard on my Appaloosa gelding, Apache, who'd found the pigs companionable. On hog-killing day, he disappeared to the back of the farm until the carnage was over. Did he think he would be next?

## Apache

Apache was my beloved trail horse for many great weekend adventures with my saddle club. I bought him in 1976 when he was a three-year-old and entrusted Shanghai, about twenty-three by then, to my horse-trader friend Ed Spaw. He found a home for him where he would be lightly ridden. Although Shanghai still breathed a little fire going down the road, long trail rides were too hard on him.

The day Ed delivered Apache, I rode him out our long farm lane bareback, then took his bridle off, and slapped him on the rump so that he could canter on home. Instead, he elected to walk along beside me the whole way back, like two old friends.

After working with him a while, I could race across the yard toward him and fling my arms around his neck. He would brace himself and stand rooted to the spot, awaiting the onslaught.

He had a great disposition. Once, when a friend came out with his family to pick wild blackberries, I cautioned his young children to stay away from Apache since I'd just bought him and wasn't sure of him yet. We forgot about the kids until we heard them squealing happily. They were gathered around Apache, poking him, patting him, pulling his mane and tail while he just stood there, enjoying the attention.

Another time, I watched while Jennifer's lambs cavorted around him. He stood there calmly, not running off. Finally, he reached his head around, grabbed one lamb's wooly coat with his teeth, and shook him. Was he just playing too?

## A Close Call

Apache and I had a terrifying mishap on a trail ride in a rugged wilderness area of Kentucky one day. The most frightening thing that ever happened to me.

As we made our way single file astride our horses along a narrow ledge, I looked down toward the cliff bottom far below and panicked. I shifted my weight and urged Apache to hug a little closer to the cliff. That evidently caused him to lose his balance, and he fell off the ledge.

It happened so fast! Suddenly, here I was left standing on the ledge without him as he scrambled to his feet on another ledge about four feet below me. I was leaning way over and still had the long reins in my hand. I called down to him, urging him by a tug on the reins to jump back up onto the ledge in front of me. He managed to do so, then picked his way carefully as he followed the horses in line ahead of us, with me walking along at his tail.

Afterward, the older couple behind us who had witnessed the accident explained what had happened. As Apache started to fall, I had swung out of the saddle, flipping the reins over his head as I did.

"We never saw anything like it!" they said. It was pure reflex action, I guess. Apache stayed calm. Just a wonderful little horse.

## Losing Apache

In 1986, he got into trouble on our lush spring grass while I was gone for two weeks, covering a sweep convention in Oakland, California, and with a side trip to Ely, Nevada. By the time I returned home, he had foundered, with no one realizing he was in trouble.

It proved too late to save him although I tried. I called the vet right away; then I worked with him myself for two weeks, spending anguished hours with him every day. I tied him to a branch overhanging the creek for a few days so that the cold running water would relieve the pain in his hooves, something that had helped cure another horse in the past. But when his cannon bone poked through the sole of one foot, I had to have him put down.

It broke my heart to lose him. He had been on this same pasture without incident ever since I'd bought him. But a horse's metabolism changes, and this was a sad lesson for me to learn.

After that, we turned half of my huge vegetable garden into a paddock, and Joel constructed a run-in shed for it. I took care to put up my horses there every night and part of each day in the spring, exposing them gradually, only a few hours at a time, to the fresh grass coming on.

## A Rare Old Breed

On the way out to Oakland, I had detoured to Ely, Nevada, for a few days, where I stayed with Sunny Martin, secretary of the American Bashkir Curly Registry.

One day, she took me to visit Benny Damele's ranch where curlies caught wild out on the range and easy to train were their cow ponies of choice. We arrived in time to watch Benny and his cowhands brand calves all morning. I took a picture of Benny on his curly gelding, Shoshone, and won first prize with it in a registry photo contest the following year.

Sunny was perhaps in her late sixties, a tall strong, sturdy, energetic woman with a permanent limp from an accident with her truck. Called Sunny because she was allergic to direct sunlight, she always wore a wide-brimmed cowboy hat.

She kept her little herd of curlies on her place, and one day, we rode two of them out across Tip-Toe Valley toward the foothills while she told me one amazing curly story after another. It was a hot day, but whenever the sun slipped behind the clouds, it suddenly turned *really* cold. Now I understood why cowboys always wear warm vests. Sunny had loaned me one of hers that day.

She told me that curlies are a rare old breed, traced to the Ural Mountains of Russia and once treasured by the fierce Mongolian horsemen. Foals arrive with a kinky, curly mane and tail and a wooly coat like a lamb's. They lose this curly coat (and sometimes their manes and tails too!) in the summertime.

They can survive unpampered in the bitterest cold weather, weather that would often kill another breed of horse left to fend for itself in the wild. They make good riding and endurance horses, seldom need to be shod, are unusually intelligent and friendly to people. They even seem to have a sense of humor.

Speculation is that they came across the early land bridge from Asia, then migrated southward over the years. They still pop up in the wild horse herds of our American West and are the cow pony of choice on many ranches.

## Mother's Gift

Along about this time, Mom died peacefully at Rockridge in her ninety-second year, leaving me an unexpected $3,000. That fall, with help from Nick, I was able to buy an American Bashkir curly weanling stud colt named Velvet's Red Riches (we called him Red), an Appaloosa mare in foal to a curly stallion and a nine-year-old sorrel curly gelding whose dam was a Missouri fox trotter. I called him KZ, for Sunshine Kyzyl, and he became my trail horse.

I think that Mom, knowing how much I loved horses, would have been pleased at how I spent that $3,000. She had died after a series of small strokes. Her living will made it possible for her to stay at Rockridge and be lovingly taken care of until she slipped away from this world. Pauline was with her a quite a bit those last few weeks, but she didn't call me until after her death.

I went home for her memorial service at the Congregational Church in Ashfield. Over the next few days, Pauline and I sorted through Mom's belongings. We did a lot of reminiscing about our childhood and old family friends whose pictures and letters Mom had saved.

We picked out things we each wanted to keep or thought our children would enjoy having—some earrings and necklaces, photographs, a few rugs and paintings, a jewelry box . . . It was hard to be really sad, for Mom had lived a long, full life and kept her wits about her until the end.

Back in Kentucky, I discovered that curlies didn't like to be kept in stalls. They much preferred the paddock and run-in shed. Each morning, with wheelbarrow and manure fork, I cleaned out the paddock, a far more enjoyable chore than mucking out smelly stalls!

One very cold winter morning after a heavy snowstorm the night before, I looked out at my curlies in the paddock. The snow was staying on their backs, not melted by the heat from their bodies because of an extra layer of insulating fat under the skin.

Nick liked to groom and take care of the horses, but I never could convince him to learn to ride, which was a big disappointment to me. I think he would have loved it on a good gentle horse if he hadn't been too timid to try.

Jessamine's Curly Mac, the first curly born in Kentucky, was foaled on my farm. Early one morning before daylight, I went out to the barn; and there was our brand-new foal, a little stud colt! Giving a little squeak, he tried to stick his head up over the bottom half of the stall door. His coat of thick tight curls was still sticky to the touch. I took a bunch of pictures of him the next morning, then wrote and sold a series of feature stories about him.

Except for my many articles about them, I never made any money with my curlies. Even so, I thoroughly enjoyed them. Red, whose daddy was a Bureau of Land Management stallion from a wild herd, grew up to be a superlative stallion who won many blue ribbons in competition and sired nothing but curly offspring, even from noncurly mares.

I first rode Red as a two-year-old and found him to be gentle, responsive, and sure-footed. But the way he moved was hard on my back. On the other hand, KZ, with his easy Missouri fox-trot, always gave me a wonderful ride.

## My Friend Neal

The year we bought our curlies was the same year I became acquainted with Neal, who was covering the sweep convention in Oakland for an alternative-energy magazine. A freelance writer and former sweep, he had already written a few articles for *SNEWS*, and we'd often talked on the phone.

The day we met in person in Oakland, he introduced himself, and we started talking. Soon, with a surprised look on his face, he said, "You're not at all what I expected. You're so lovable!"

We spent one magical evening together, wandering through the Berkeley campus and eating chocolate ice cream cones, beginning a friendship that was to endure for more than ten years.

If he hadn't been happily married, with four kids (two of his own and two stepchildren), it might possibly have turned into something more. But I find that friendship often lasts longer than romance, and I have no regrets.

Neal visited me at the farm several times—once alone, once with his family, and once for four or five days in 1994 when he was working on a chimney sweep article for the December '95 issue of *Smithsonian* magazine and went on calls with Jeff Gitlin. I visited him and his family twice in Albuquerque. In between, we saw each other at a few sweep conventions and kept up with each other by phone.

I finally had to break off our friendship. Neal protested, saying, "Don't do this, Jay—it would leave a hole in my life!"

We don't see each other anymore, and that has left a hole in my life too. Still, Neal calls me once in a great while. I recognize his voice the moment he says my name, and we talk about our lives and our writing. He currently holds down a full-time job as a science writer and works on a novel in his spare time.

## Tim Learns to Fence

When he was fourteen, Tim announced, "I'm going to learn to fence and go to college on a fencing scholarship!" He took fencing lessons from his dad and was soon winning fencing competitions in Kentucky and around the country.

At eighteen, he was admitted to the University of Illinois where he enrolled in the College of Agriculture. The first year, he was given a partial fencing scholarship; and for his sophomore year, he received a tuition waiver. In his last two years, he earned the equivalent of a full scholarship.

Tim competed on the varsity team all four years and served as its captain in his senior year. His dedicated fencing coach, Art Schanken, became for him a father figure.

Following his graduation in the summer of 1988, he landed a job through Nick as swordplay coach for actors in the Shakespeare in the Park performance of *Romeo and Juliet*. On the set, he met Tara Bellando, the dark-haired, dark-eyed beauty who played Juliet; and they became sweethearts.

Tara was a part-time weaver in her family's business, Churchill Weavers, in Berea. Tim started hanging out with her in Berea and began to make new friends there. He worked on a Madison County tobacco-harvesting crew that fall and did various odd jobs in the area.

## Computer Blues

In 1986, under Nick's prodding, I computerized the magazine. That whole process was a nightmare! Crawling in bed every night exhausted, I would close my eyes and find myself staring at a computer screen until sleep rescued me.

I felt like killing Nick and throwing the computer in the trash! Until I discovered the problem wasn't with me but with a flawed PageMaker desktop publishing software program, which I replaced.

Now I was able to generate my own camera-ready copy the easy way—no more laborious pasteups and cutting in corrections on my light table. I just flowed copy into my page layout on the computer screen, allowing spaces for pictures and ads, then put it all on a disk for the printer.

By then, Junkyard Players had gone belly-up. Nick had quit his teaching job at EKU and signed on as my *SNEWS* partner. Disappointed with the caliber of his students—freshmen and sophomores, many of whom dropped out before their junior year—he had also complained that I worked all the time. He wanted us to be together more.

At first, it was lovely having him to bounce my ideas off and to accompany me on road trips. He handled the whole business end of the magazine, carried the heavy stuff when we traveled, helped set up and run the *SNEWS* booth.

Everybody liked him. "Where did you find this darling man?" one sweeping woman asked me. The fact that we had been together since 1981 helped squelch rumors about Jeff and me.

But in the long run, our *SNEWS* partnership proved a mistake! Nick had lost the theater and teaching connections that gave balance to his life. He now became financially dependent on me. My meager income could not stretch far enough to cover a second salary. We were going under until he injected $4,000 of his own money into the magazine to keep us afloat.

He became increasingly discontent, started to call me Lady Bountiful and Earth Mother sarcastically.

Home for spring break from his senior year in college in 1988, Tim said, "Nick's not happy here. Why doesn't he leave?"

Why indeed? Nick and I had tried in vain to salvage our love relationship, and there was no use letting this drag on. I told Nick it was time for him to go. He was reluctant to leave the farm, yet he knew I was right.

We had been together since 1981, and for most of that time, he was my lover and my best friend. Great fun to live with, he accepted the ups and downs of life and love with good humor. He was forever reading books, then discussing them with me in vivid detail. We shared many companionable evenings on the front porch swing after dinner, watching the kids catch fireflies and listening to the creek, to the owl in the tree in the side yard, and the other night sounds.

But now our time together was almost over.

Parting from Nick was hard, but letting my Stephani go was downright traumatic. I kept her for the rest of the school year after Nick left in January of 1989, heading for Phoenix where he'd grown up and where the theater scene so dear to his heart was booming. ("Hey, diddle-dee-dee, it's the actor's life for me!")

Nick's mother was now in a nursing home there, and Nick moved into her small house, which would soon be legally his.

## Tim Comes Home

As my time with Nick was coming to an end in the summer of 1988, Tim graduated from college and told me, "I want to do what you do, Mom, and work on the magazine." So Nick left his computer with us and taught Tim the business end of *SNEWS* before he departed for Phoenix alone in early 1989. Tim also took a crash course in accounting.

Nick returned early that summer to be in the cast of *Carousel* up near Cincinnati, along with Steph, who played one of the children in some crowd scenes. Nick was the wise town doctor and the dear old angel hanging stars.

Before they both left for Phoenix soon after their last performance, I said, "Steph, you need to start thinking about the kind of person you want to be when you grow up."

"I want to be just like you, Mama Jay," she said, "only not work so hard!"

## Goodbye, Nick and Steph

The morning we packed up Nick's blue station wagon for the trip, Tim took a few pictures of the three of us. When the prints came back, we saw that Nick was crying. It was not an easy goodbye for any of us. I had a strange empty feeling as I watched their car disappear out the lane.

Nick enrolled Stephani in a school for the performing arts that fall, and she loved it. Her aunt Jan, Nick's sister, and her son Jason also lived in Phoenix; and I think life was good for Steph there. When Tim and I visited them a few years later, she was obviously very happy and had a great relationship with an attentive Hispanic boyfriend.

As my new *SNEWS* partner, Tim proved an excellent business manager, proofreader, advisor, photographer, and traveling companion. Everybody loved him. The magazine prospered. Life became easier. He and Jeff kept me out of trouble, for the most part.

Jeff came out to the farm one day shortly after Nick and Stephani's departure. "Don't let him come back!" he said vehemently.

"I won't," I assured him. I'd had no idea that Jeff didn't like Nick.

### Update on the Aldouses

In the mid-1970s, Howard and Donna moved to the coastal city of Vancouver where he went back to school. This time, he earned an MD degree at the university while working part-time as a veterinarian for a local riding school. He went on to establish a family practice he enjoyed tremendously in Kelowna, British Columbia.

There I visited them and their two teenage sons, Kent and Patrick, for a few days, circa 1980. By then, Howard owned part interest in his brother Pat's heli-ski business, which flew people into the mountains to ski in winter and hike in the off-season. They supplied small rustic cabins for their skiers and hikers.

For years afterward, I dreamed of visiting them again someday long enough to enjoy one of those heli-ski or heli-hike adventures myself. But alas, I never did. It would be more than twenty-five years before I saw the Aldouses again.

### Reconnecting with Linda

I reconnected with Linda Kanzinger when I visited Doug at the University of Oregon. She lived with us again at the farm now and then and moved to Wisconsin in 1981 where she met Erik Jonas. She brought Erik with her when she came to see me and meet Nick at the farm in 1983. I was on deadline at *SNEWS* at the time, and it was a very hectic visit!

She and Erik soon married, moved to Spokane, Washington, and later, to Portland, Oregon. They were together for eleven years.

Very much the confident, independent woman, Linda started the Alcott Press in 1986 and went on to self-publish four exceptional, well-illustrated one-of-a kind books: *The Complete Book of Fabric Painting*, one of the first volumes on this subject; *The Complete Book of Fabric Painting*, revised and expanded (with an extra 150 pages of material); *Fabric Painting Resources: 1001 Products and Resources for the Fabric Painter and Surface Designer*; and one on clothing styles for "big, beautiful, bodacious women," *Size-Positive Style: Clothing for the Plus and Supersize Woman*. All are available at http://www.amazon.com.

**Update on Peg Payne**

In 1982, my friend Peg married widower and fellow Unitarian Tim Taylor, a retired UK researcher/professor of grasslands ecology. Raised on a farm in one of Kentucky's poorest counties, Tim was drafted during World War II, fought in Europe, brought home a French war bride, Andre, and went to college on the GI Bill. After graduating from Berea College, he earned his PhD at UK.

As therapy of sorts following Andre's death, Tim dismantled his great-uncle Ross Taylor's two-story log cabin, complete with front porch, stone fireplace, and chimney. Log by log and stone by stone, he rebuilt it all on the home place farm in McCreary County where he was raised. Planning to retire there, he also began to renovate the eighty-four-acre farm's old worn-out pastures.

Peg and Tim's chocolate wedding cake was in the form of a one-room log cabin, with white icing for chinking. 'Twas delicious! They moved to Tim's *real* log house on Good Spring Farm five years later after adding a bathroom, kitchen, bedroom, and sunroom downstairs, plus a bathroom and office for Peg on the second floor. Peg transferred to a staff position at Somerset Community College nearby and soon made a name for herself there.

Black Baldy cows—a Hereford-Angus cross with mostly black bodies and white faces—now graze on the lush pastures of Good Spring Farm and produce a crop of calves every spring.

The crowing of roosters and barking of dogs greet the day, and Peg's chickens produce a plentiful supply of eggs. Wildflowers grow in abundance; and walking trails through the deep woods beckon you to visit a waterfall, fishing pond, and caves. Surrounded by the Daniel Boone National Forest, Peg and Tim's farm is a great place to visit, and our friendship continued full tilt.

Peg Payne Taylor, 1988

Curlies love to be groomed. Nick puts the finishing touch on our gentle young stallion Red. Comanche's Curly Mac, a sturdy three weeks old here, was foaled on our farm.

# 34

# BROKE-BACK AFTERNOON

**My November 1989 *SNEWS* Column**

If only . . . My doctor looked down at me. "It IS painful and it WILL get better," he said. He was talking about the three crushed lumbar vertebrae that were to keep me flat on my back for the next 11 days in the hospital, except for those brief intervals when I was able—with a back brace, much help and a lot of pain—to sit up, stand up and walk a few steps. It was October, 1989.

"We used to put broken back cases in a body cast," he said. "This brace changes all that." He took my hand gently and said, "You're lucky. You'll make a 100 percent recovery."

I thought about a lot of things. About North Carolina sweep Danny Yearly and the continuing misery he has been through with a far more serious back injury. About who would ride with my 13-year-old grandson Ezra now that I was laid up. About how much it hurt. About how strong and vital I'd been one moment in the Saturday afternoon sunshine, and how helpless the next. About the 40 people Tim and I had invited to a potluck supper at the farm. About the November issue of *SNEWS* abandoned at home . . .

I'm an excellent rider. I have a good, dependable horse. But he must have swished his tail onto the live electric fence as I leaned way out of the saddle to unhook it. He caught a terrific jolt of electricity and passed it on to me. I hit the ground and I couldn't get up.

I would miss my trail ride the next day. I would miss the wonderful three days of riding in the mountains of Tennessee with my riding club two weekends later. I would have to give up the November trip I had planned to New England. One moment's carelessness had spoiled it all . . .

I'm home now. I get discouraged and I need a lot of down time. But I'm getting pretty good at walking. I can sit down and work at my computer again, finally.

So, now you know why this November issue is so very late.—Jh

## Hurricane and Earthquake

That late September, Hurricane Hugo and the tornadoes it spawned had roared through the South. While I was in the hospital, an earthquake shook California. In San Francisco that October 17, my son Doug awoke from his nap as the city began to tremble and shake.

A bookcase crashed to the floor in the next room. A box holding his Persian music cassette tapes bounced over onto its side, spilling the contents. He grabbed his sitar and stood in a doorway, cradling the fragile instrument in his arms. He called to his cat, Alyosha. He wondered if the two-story building would collapse. He wondered if he would die.

Finally, the fearsome heaving of the earth subsided. The earthquake did little damage in Doug's neighborhood; but elsewhere in the city, walls fractured and fell, chimneys crumbled, buildings toppled onto people and cars, sidewalks heaved, water and gas lines broke, fires raged, and a section of concrete multilevel highway collapsed onto the rush hour traffic. I watched the rescue efforts on TV from my hospital bed and thought I saw an unconscious Doug on a stretcher being carried through the rubble from the collapsed highway. I put in a call to him and had some anxious moments before he returned my call the next day.

Back at the farm, Tim and I went ahead with our potluck gathering. Bolstered by painkillers, I sat in the lounge chair in the living room, warmed by the wood fire in our coal grate, and visited with our friends.

Somehow, I managed to produce another issue of *SNEWS* by the end of November. I called it my disaster issue. It was crammed with pictures and stories from the hurricane, tornadoes, and earthquake. Letters, photos, and phone calls from subscribers poured into the *SNEWS* office for months, telling other sweeps about fantastic experiences and heavy workloads generated by the severe weather and disasters that had engulfed so much of the country.

My back started to mend. I wore that awful, wonderful brace for six months and was riding my horse again by July, very carefully.

# 35

## WEST COAST DOUG

Out in California, Doug attended the San Francisco Conservatory of Music, working toward a degree in performance guitar. He had a part-time job in the conservatory library and managed with the additional help of student grants and loans, also played at lots of weddings, parties, nursing homes, etc., and taught some private students. Plus money from me when I could send it. His father paid for his very fine professional guitar.

After sharing a house a block away from the conservatory with some fellow music students for a few months, he "inherited" a place to live near Haight-Ashbury from a guitarist classmate. This was a room on the third floor of a gated row house across from the Golden Gate Park where he walked his dog, Kolya, every day. Sharing a bathroom and tiny kitchen with other tenants, he lived there for ten years until the building was sold, and the tenants all had to move out.

He wrote home often, long detailed letters about his life, his music, his loves. We always had a great time together when I visited him every few years. We haunted the used bookstores, ate in Asian restaurants, walked up and down those steep streets, spent time with his friends, attended musical events, and watched a good movie or two. My credit card got a vigorous workout!

It was always so hard to leave.

Once, when I visited him, he was out of underwear and socks; his jeans were worn so thin, you could see bare skin. At the

Laundromat, we washed the clothes that were salvageable. Then I replenished his supply of jeans, socks, and underwear.

He had his guitar, flute, Persian drums, Persian setâr, sheet music, records, record player, his dog, his cat, pictures on the wall, and books of all kinds. No matter that his clothes were turning to rags and he had barely enough to eat—he had his necessaries. By this time, he had replaced his '61 Volkswagen bus with a much newer VW bug, given to him for $100 by some musician friends.

One year, I planned my San Francisco visit to coincide with an AACE convention held on the University of California campus in Berkeley. This would give me a great opportunity to visit with colleagues from my Cooperative Extension Service years at UK. My old friend Mel Gagnon, a writer for the U. of California agriculture college, also arranged a backpacking outing for me and some friends in the Sierra Nevada mountains.

I'd met Mel in San Antonio in the early 1970s. He was divorced and had custody of his six children, so we had a lot to talk about whenever we got together! Through the years, we had become close friends. He was a big athletic red-haired six-feet-three teddy bear of a fellow, great fun to spend time with.

At the AACE convention, Mel was in charge of the table decorations and a huge display of California produce. Accommodations were in a residence hall, with the meetings and meals held there too. Mel created a bountiful harvest of donated melons, apricots, avocados, peaches, strawberries, rounds of cheese on big wooden blocks, grapes, dates, artichokes, dwarf sunflowers—you name it! When the convention ended, he filled my backpack with food and still had lots more to give away.

Heavily loaded, I staggered back to Doug's third-floor digs, and we ate extremely well for the rest of my two-week stay.

The backpacking trip was a blast. Mel was under the impression that I was a seasoned camper and backpacker, but I'd only been on a few Sierra Club outings in Kentucky. He filled the pack he provided for me with thirty-five pounds of stuff! I wasn't sure I'd survive the

long, hot, sweaty hike around Echo Lake and into Desolation Valley
of the Sierra Nevada wilderness area.

Our group included Mel's longtime companion Dorothy, several
friends of hers, and a friend of Mel's named Bill, a freelance outdoor
writer and orienteer. Bill and I really hit it off and ended up writing
to each other for several years.

"We marry the wrong people before we are half formed!" he told
me sadly one day. He had a wife who hated hiking and camping out.

We made camp in a beautiful forest of tall trees near the foot
of Mount Ralston and scouted the area before settling down to eat
a scrumptious dinner around our campfire—steak, baked potatoes,
sweet corn, salad, and wine. We were dead tired by the time we
crawled into our sleeping bags.

Waking up the next morning to gaze at the tall trees stretching
above us in the first rays of the sun was well worth the hard, sweaty
trek into the forest the day before.

After breakfast, we climbed Mount Ralston. It was a difficult
trek in the hot sun, up a treeless slope with loose shale underfoot. We
came to snowfields before we reached the top, and I foolishly skied
back down them on my hiking boots, my camera dangling from its
cord around my neck. We took pictures of ourselves at the summit,
elated and flexing our muscles. From there, we gazed across the
mountains to Lake Tahoe and decided to drive there the next day.

Back at our campsite, we changed into bathing suits and took
a "refreshing" dip in a little lake nearby. I jumped in and came up
screaming and screaming! It was ice cold from melted snow.

We departed the next morning, our backpacks lighter minus
the food we'd carried in. Two of Mel's sons met us partway with
more steaks and wine and joined us for a noontime feast. Mel had
backpacked with his kids and Dorothy for years and sure knew how
to plan things.

After that, we hiked out to our cars and drove on to Lake Tahoe
where we booked into a motel, showered, shampooed, and took naps.
Then feeling squeaky clean and refreshed, we sallied forth into town.
We wandered through one of the South Lake Tahoe casinos, which
stretched on for blocks.

There were hundreds of old people there playing the slot machines, one-armed bandits desperate for a landslide of money to spill into their hands. I hated the whole scene, could hardly wait to get out of there. We ended up that evening at a dinner show featuring Bob Newhart, who was right entertaining.

Next morning, we passed by a row of slot machines on our way into breakfast at a local restaurant. Mel handed me a fistful of dimes and said, "Go ahead, Jay, forget your scruples and *do* it!" I reluctantly started sliding in the dimes and immediately won $44, which I had to split with Mel.

Then it was back to San Francisco to hang out with Doug again and help him work his way through all that good food.

Soon after our backpacking adventure, Bill wrote that he had landed a job as editor of *California Horse Review,* a thick four-color magazine with lots of advertising. He asked me to do a series of articles on different horse breeds, and I got right to work! Here was a great opportunity to make some good money.

The first and only feature I sent him was a long one about the endangered American Bashkir curly breed of horse. The magazine ran it in full with a whole bunch of good photographs I'd sent. When the managing editor wouldn't let Bill pay me more than $100 for an article worth at least $500 or $600, Bill apologized profusely to me. He quit his job in anger and frustration.

After earning bachelor's and master's degrees in performance guitar, Doug became immersed in the music scene in the city, worked for a year as a proofreader for a law firm, and met Shauna there. They were soon living together at her place.

Doug was guest guitarist on occasion for the San Francisco Symphony Orchestra and other Bay Area orchestras and ensembles, and taught guitar for several semesters at Mills College in Oakland. In addition he arranged concerts for himself and other musicians, had programs printed and premiered works commissioned for him by composers he had contacted. Since then he has gone on to commission and premiere close to 50 works by nearly as many composers from various parts of the world.

Along with fellow musician John Casten and conductor Kent Nagano he also co-founded the ISKRA ensemble. According to Doug, iskra means "spark" in Russian, and it was the name of Lenin's pre-revolutionary newspaper in Switzerland.

Originally it was going to be a conducted ensemble, but soon after they established a three-concert series of contemporary Japanese music at the Asian Art Museum, sponsored by the Japanese consulate, Kent left for Europe for the chance of a lifetime. In Paris he conducted the world premiere of a new opera by Messiaen, one of the most important 20th century composers, and put on by the Paris Opera. Kent Nagano has been at the helm of world-class orchestras ever since.

And so, back in San Francisco, ISKRA was turned into a chamber music ensemble that most consistently included voice, flute, clarinet, violin/viola, cello, harp, and guitar. This was not the only instrumental group Doug did a lot of work for, but it lasted the longest because it was the most flexible. People could come and go, the group could break into smaller units now and then and still keep active. It basically ended when Doug left for Paris himself some years later.

Around 1987, he began to make contact with Persian musicians in the area, many of whom had left Iran after the revolution of 1979. He started taking Persian language courses at the University of California in Berkeley.

In 1989, Doug received a $10,000 Alfred Hertz Traveling Fellowship to study music in Iran. However, the state department refused him a visa because of the current situation with the kidnapping of U.S. embassy personnel. So when he heard that Dariush Tala'i, an Iranian târ and setâr master, was teaching at the Sorbonne, Doug used his grant money to go to Paris instead.

In the year before leaving for Paris, he traveled to San Jose every week for lessons with three Iranian masters, as well as rehearsals with two Persian music ensembles with which he performed.

Now in his thirties and living with Shauna, Doug had no interest in marriage. "I'm too much like Dad to ever be a good husband or good father," he once told me sadly.

# 36

# EVA HORTON AND ME

When I first met Eva at the Minneapolis Trade Show in the spring of 1979, she had already become a legend in her own time as the sole importer of Jøtul stoves in the United States and founder of the National Chimney Sweep Guild.

Seven years earlier, Eva had been a thirty-nine-year-old suburban housewife, art teacher, and mother of two in Portland, Maine. She hatched the idea of importing Jøtul stoves when friends admired her own family's beautiful and efficient Jøtul, the stove her parents had shipped to her. She consulted an attorney about sales contracts, then headed for her native country of Norway. There, she visited the Jøtul stove foundry and met with the company's board of directors.

She told them wood heat was coming into its own again, and the United States was a wide-open market for a top-quality stove. She requested a franchise to sell Jøtuls there. Stunned by her boldness and put off by her gender and her youth, the men nevertheless listened. Then they cautiously offered her a franchise for the city of Portland. She refused it. Six months later, she came back and gained the exclusive right to sell Jøtul stoves east of the Mississippi.

Once the import franchise was hers, she founded Kristia Associates, hired staff, began setting up and training a dealer network of people "who would run their businesses from the heart." Her first order for 250 Jøtuls arrived on Christmas Eve 1973.

When the *Christian Science Monitor* article headlined EVA HEATS AMERICA! and syndicated to sixty newspapers surfaced in 1974, demand for her Jøtuls exploded. She called Norway and ordered four thousand stoves and was soon awarded exclusive sales right for the whole country.

One of the first things Eva had done was redesign and rewrite the slick, impersonal Jøtul sales literature. Then she hired young Charlie Page to head up a team to produce Jøtul's first technical repair and maintenance manual. This project consumed one intense year.

"Eva was a born organizer," Charlie told me many years later when he ran his own company, Jump Start Marketing. "She was decisive, knew what she wanted, and no bullshit allowed. And she was the greatest marketer, with no formal training . . . She knew the captains of the ships that brought her stoves over from Norway, was usually at the dock to meet them. She even knew the names of the stevedores who unloaded the stoves."

Deina Duval was Eva's executive secretary that first year. "Of all the people I worked for or with in my life," she told me by phone, "Eva was one of the most honest. She played no games. She had no hidden agenda. She'd sit on the floor and help us do a big mailing . . .

"She was utterly authentic. She surrounded herself with good, capable people, mostly women, and paid them well . . . Nobody intimidated her because she was empowered by her own enthusiasm."

Eva, now divorced from her husband of twenty-three years, had thrown herself heart and soul into running her company. She ended up managing a multimillion-dollar business, learning how to do it as she went along. She was dyslexic, unable to balance her own checkbook, but she had the savvy to hire people who could do whatever she could not.

## The Chimney Sweep Guild
Alarmed by the rising incidence of fires linked to inadequate chimneys and/or the improper installation and use of woodstoves, Eva contacted the Worcester Brush Company for the names and

addresses of their chimney sweep customers. In January 1977, she called a meeting of sweeps, helped organize the Chimney Sweep Guild, and served as its executive director for the first three years.

Donating her own time and that of her skeptical staff, she planned and managed the annual meetings, started a newsletter for members, and underwrote most of the organization's considerable expenses. She shared her managerial and marketing skills with sweeps, even convinced them to share their own technical expertise with other guild members—not an easy accomplishment. She traveled the country touting the services of professional sweeps, members of the guild.

In the early 1980s, Eva abruptly pulled out of the stove-import business, selling her subsidiary back to the parent company, which she claimed had no heart. By then, one hundred thousand Jøtuls were warming up homes all across America.

Eva's sales contract with Jøtul included the sale of her Kristia Associates building, stipulated that all Kristia employees would be retained and that she herself would be retained as a well-paid consultant with all benefits for the next six years. She expected the company to be outraged by her terms and try to negotiate, but they signed the contract without a fight.

### Breakfast with Eva

I met Eva for the second time during the Northeast Regional All-Fuels Heating Expo in Sturbridge, Massachusetts, in the winter of 1985. She had been invited as special guest and speaker to reminisce about the early days of what was now known as the National Chimney Sweep Guild.

On the second morning of the expo, I ate an early breakfast with Eva and Toby, her charming new husband. We spent several hours locked in conversation while Tony slipped away unnoticed.

Eva had by then returned to her career as artist and sculptor, producing an impressive body of work. She had also just bought two Victorian houses in Portland on the uppermost tip of Maine, planning to remodel them for a bed-and-breakfast business. She would call it Victorian Terrace.

EVA HORTON AND ME

Eva was convinced that "we knew each other well in a former life, for what else could explain our extraordinary rapport?"

At Sturbridge, I urged her to do a sculpture to commemorate her years with the chimney sweeps. After giving the project much thought, she created a bronze bas-relief sculpture of an exuberant sweep on a rooftop, surrounded by chimneys and with a huge sun coming up behind him.

It was stunning. She had it reproduced, mounted it on a mahogany board, and offered it for sale to sweeps to be used as a wall hanging or award plaque. She sent me one, and over the years, I was awarded two more by chimney sweep guilds. I gave that first bas-relief to a delighted Jeff Gitlin.

Over the years, Eva and I got together whenever possible, wrote to each other, indulged in long telephone visits. She photocopied large sections of her personal journal for me, compiling the pages into a large scrapbook for me. We shared the most private aspects of our lives.

She told me how she grew up in the 1930s and '40s, a "war brat" in Nazi-occupied Norway where soldiers in gray-green uniforms were an everyday sight. They were friendly to this shy little girl, seeming to want her to like them. Afraid of them at first, she came to realize that many were just lonely, homesick boys of seventeen or eighteen. But she also recognized by the submachine gun often slung over their shoulders that they could be deadly.

The father she loved dearly was involved in the Resistance but told his family nothing. He was often away for days at a time, gone they knew not where.

"We learned a little about his Resistance work after the war," Eva told me. "I knew he'd had to be dishonest, to lie, to betray people who trusted him . . . for the sake of Norway and us. But I wasn't proud of his having been a spy. I didn't tell anyone. It tarnished those wonderful childhood memories of my times with him—fishing, hiking, camping out. 'How often did he lie to me too?' I wondered."

## Victorian Terrace

Eva's Victorian Terrace venture quickly became a huge success. Whenever I visited her there, I had my own luxurious and artistically decorated room on the second floor in one of those charming, elegant houses. Her office, kitchen, sitting room, and a deck looking out on the ocean were also on the second floor.

She and Toby, an alcoholic who hovered in the background of her life, shared an apartment on the third floor. Toby's main interest in life was sailing, something Eva tried to share with him because he insisted and because he loved playing captain on his small sailboat. But she didn't really enjoy it.

Her relationship with Toby mystified me. After observing them together during several visits, I finally asked, "Eva, why do you stay married to Toby?"

"Because I don't want to be alone," she said.

"That's not a good enough reason!" I told her.

Within a year, she kicked him out and reclaimed her life. That must have been sometime in the mid-1990s.

Eva and I had a grand rendezvous in Cambridge in 1998 after I'd covered the national guild's annual convention in Boston. She'd made reservations for us at the Hyatt Regency where we enjoyed a gourmet dinner in the hotel's revolving restaurant, then talked half the night up in our room.

At dinner, she gave me a combination copy of volumes 1, 2, and 3 of *God's Little Instruction Book*. I love this warm, wise, funny, fat little book, which she inscribed, "To Jay, my soul mate."

The following morning, my cousin Steve, who lived in Cambridge, met us at the hotel for a lingering two-hour breakfast. Afterward, as he drove me to Ashfield for a visit, he said of Eva, "She is a powerful woman!"

# 37

# OUR LIVES IN THE 1990S

Because of her work with Father Luis, Claire was often not at Ashfield when I was. Consequently, I visited her two or three times in Manhattan at the Cournand apartment on Madison Avenue, which her father had deeded to her. Once, I was with my friend Anne Smith Falevsky, whom I was staying with for a few days at her home on Staten Island.

In Manhattan earlier on the day we visited Claire, Anne and I had stood gazing up at the Twin Towers. They were so stark, reaching unbearably high in the air. I didn't like them! "How would people ever get out if one of those buildings caught on fire?" I asked. (Fire safety was something I emphasized in my magazine, and it was always on my mind!)

Claire's linguistic abilities, commitment, enthusiasm, and penchant for hard work made her uniquely qualified for her years with Father Luis. Funding was spotty, and they operated on a shoestring budget.

They mainly worked out of the small church office on the lower East Side of Manhattan, creating and overseeing projects for the Puerto Rican youth of the parish. But they also traveled to twenty-one countries in the course of their work. Claire helped Father Luis organize roundtable discussions, seminars, and conferences at the United Nations, as well as interreligious pilgrimages in the Soviet Union, Eastern and Western Europe, the Middle East, Latin America, India, Korea, and South Africa.

In South Africa, she was able to meet many of Pierre's cousins and visit the small mission church in Northern Transvaal where her mother had married Pierre's father seventy-seven years before.

When Father Luis died suddenly as they ate lunch together at his apartment one Sunday in October 2000, after he had celebrated two Spanish Masses, it meant the end of a deep friendship and a particularly rich and fulfilling period in Claire's life.

## Meanwhile, Down on the Farm . . .

These were intensely busy years for me too: Raising curly horses, spending every possible weekend on trail rides, continuing with my downsized vegetable garden that fed us all year, traveling in spring and summer to sweep conventions and trade shows, and always working on the magazine, which sometimes ran forty-four pages. Plus raising another little girl after only one year's respite from putting a kid on the school bus every morning!

Joel's daughter, Leslie, came to live with Tim and me in June of 1990 when she was almost seven. She was with us for more than two years while her divorced parents tried to put their lives back together. Her aunt Jennifer was close by there on the farm to help look after her, especially when Tim and I were on road trips for *SNEWS*.

In my editor's column, every issue, I periodically updated my subscribers on life at the farm. The following is excerpted from my July '90 column:

> The juggling act grows more difficult. I arrived home May 20th from the NCSG convention and a week's vacation to a family crisis that put the magazine on hold for five weeks. My granddaughter Leslie, just turned seven, is living with Tim and me now. She has become my first consideration.
>
> A game of croquet out in the side yard just before dark, a bedtime story ("Grasshopper on the Road"), a knock at my bedroom door and a small anxious voice ("Mama Jay, it's thundering! Can I sleep with you

tonight?") all bring back the joys and responsibilities of
the motherhood role I thought I had left behind . . .

A sweep friend called recently to say goodbye, not
expecting to survive upcoming major surgery. "Don't lose
your dream, Jay," he said. "Without our dreams, the world
is a crock of shit."

Finding me in tears, Leslie asked me why, then sat
next to me and sang me a song she had learned in day
camp, about friendship and loving someone "until the end
of time."

When she came to the farm, her daddy Joel drove up from
Florida and stayed for two months to help her make the transition.
They had many adventures together. He was the one who most often
read to her and tucked her in at night.

At first, we had to start her bedtime routine early because she
needed to gather up a whole slew of dolls scattered about the house
and yard. "You poor neglected little babies," she said, "isn't anybody
taking care of you?'

She would carry them tenderly into her room, tuck each one in
under a colorful washcloth, tell them stories, and sing to them.

## Tim's Ordeal

Tim gave us a bad scare that summer. In July, he was diagnosed
with an advanced case of testicular cancer. He endured two
operations and months of chemo, shed all his long curly hair, was
completely bald for months, and made a full recovery. Throughout
his ordeal, he missed only one fencing competition, winning most of
those in which he did participate.

But I was a basket case. It was his courage and optimism that
pulled us all through. "I think it was harder on Mom than it was on
me," he said.

Along about this same time, Tara and Tim's love relationship was
faltering. But when Tara found out that Tim had cancer, she stayed
with him during this traumatic period, often visiting him for hours in
the hospital.

Tim was devastated. "Losing Tara was worse than having cancer," he told me. But soon, he worked it all out in his mind.

"I thought we were meant to be together for the rest of our lives," he told me during a *SNEWS* road trip when a song on our car radio reminded him of Tara. "But now I realize we were meant to be together for two years."

## My Affinity for France

As far back as I can remember, France was a country I longed to visit. I started learning French in kindergarten at Shore Road Academy with Mrs. Merrill, beloved motherly Mrs. Merrill with her golden red hair coiled loosely up off her neck. We practiced words and sentences and sang "Frère Jacques" and other little songs. Oh, how I wanted to go to France and sing along with the children there and talk French to them!

I learned the Marseilles, "Alons enfants de la patris . . ." in the third or fourth grade, never forgetting the words or the tune. It was such a bloody song. Why did it grip me so strongly?

For so many years, I loved France from afar, wrote a term paper on Provence in high school, and dreamed of going there. I would live with a French family in a village in Provence, pick grapes at harvest time, and hold up my skirt to stamp the vat of grapes into juice, staining my legs purple . . . But I never did.

I took French through my sophomore year of high school at Shore Road Academy and won the top French award for the school the last year I was there. I read *Jean Val Jean* and wrote a book report on it, all in French.

When I met Pierre, I tried speaking to him in French. He could understand me just fine, but I lacked the skill to carry on a real conversation. "Someday," I told myself, "I'll go to France with Pierre and *really* learn to speak French." But I never did.

It would be my son Doug who lived out my dream for me many years later, walking the streets of Paris and meeting two of Pierre's sisters. Doug spoke both French and Farsi, but he told me that Farsi was the main language he needed during his stay in France because of the musicians with whom he studied.

At the University of Oregon, Doug had developed an interest in Persian music and learned to play the Persian drums. It was only the lack of good teachers in Eugene that kept him from pursuing this whole genre of music in more depth. Later, in the San Francisco Bay area, he discovered a number of expatriate musicians who had come to the States after the 1979 Iranian Revolution and with whom he studied santour, târ, setâr, and oud.

After receiving his Alfred Hertz Traveling Fellowship, he headed for Paris in the winter of 1990 to study under Dariush Tala'i, an Iranian târ and setâr master who was teaching at the Sorbonne.

Here, finally, was my opportunity to go to France! I saved my money and promised to join him there for a month in the summer. But alas, it was not to be. Leslie came to live with us, my money went to summer day camp for her, and Tim was diagnosed with cancer. I could not leave them.

When I told Claire about Doug's plans, she gave me the telephone number for her sister Muriel Jaeger, who lived in Paris. Doug contacted Muriel as soon as he arrived in Paris, and she invited him to a birthday party a few evenings later.

At the party, Doug met dancers, writers, thespians . . . and Claire! She had flown over from New York for a short visit. She and Doug soon spent a wonderful day together at the Louvre art museum in Paris.

Doug eventually settled into a little bedroom/kitchen suite in an old house in Meudon that belonged to Muriel's friend Guidette. The minimal kitchen had a bathtub in it, and he shared a community toilet. Meudon was on the outskirts of Paris on the train line that continued to Versailles.

He lived on fruit, cooked beets, bread, wine, and cheese and walked everywhere through the countryside and even into Paris. It was months before he took his first metro ride.

One night, Doug missed the last train from Paris. He walked along the railroad tracks all the way to Meudon. "I had my portable cassette player with me and worked on memorizing some of the pieces I was working on as I walked."

Doug had brought his setâr to France and gave his first performance in Paris at Muriel's house for a gathering of her friends. At the Sorbonne, he studied târ with Dariush Tala'i, setâr with Ghasemi, and ney with Hossein Omoumi—all masters of their instrument.

Keeping in touch with Muriel, he went to a couple of Persian instrument performances with her. She even hosted a performance at her house by Oumi.

When Doug's girlfriend, Shauna, flew to France to visit him for a few weeks, they drove through the eastern half of France, all the way down to the Mediterranean Sea and back again, exploring and photographing old castles along the way.

Doug had arrived in France in January and returned to San Francisco the following November with a beautiful sitar. He'd spent half his grant money on it.

## Friends of the Creek

Meanwhile, back in Kentucky, we heard that Nicholasville planned to place a sewage plant on the creek not far from us; and I joined a citizens' group, Friends of Jessamine Creek, determined to stop them. At meetings and potluck suppers, we came to know many of our neighbors living along the creek. There were only about twenty of us, but we worked hard to circulate petitions and educate citizens as to the necessity for a state-of-the-art plant at an acceptable location.

We hired a karst topography expert to make a presentation to fiscal court, and one farmer testified about losing his mule in a cavity that opened up in the ground as he was plowing. We attended city council meetings, making life uncomfortable for the mayor and other officials. I wrote articles for the newspaper, and we manned information booths at local fairs.

We could not be ignored, and we won our campaign. A state-of-the-art tertiary treatment plant was situated at a more suitable location, and the creek was monitored on a regular basis thereafter for water quality.

**Candy Kreigh**

In 1992, I met Candy Kreigh, who hauled her horse trailer down from Wisconsin in answer to my For Sale ad for Velvet's Red Riches, the six-year-old American Bashkir curly stallion I had raised from a weanling.

Red was a great horse. Candy loved everything about him and took him back to Wisconsin with her. However, when it came right down to it, I could not bear to sell him; so we made a lease arrangement: Candy would train him, show him, advertise him at stud, and breed him to her own Arabian mare. The first curly foal from this mating would be Candy's and the second, mine. No money exchanged hands.

Candy was a strapping, high-spirited woman in her thirties and a skillful horsewoman. She trained Red, winning many blue ribbons with him and a trophy for Best Curly Performance Horse East of the Mississippi.

Meanwhile, with several trips back and forth and meeting at a few curly horse shows, Candy and I became friends. She was a dynamo! She had gone to Cornell on a scholarship and then launched into a dual career. In addition to her demanding full-time job as a lab technician, she raised, trained, and showed horses and gave riding lessons to children.

Red's first get by Candy's mare was a handsome stud colt, First Riches; the second was a beautiful filly for me, Red's Curly Jessamine. Both had curly coats.

Candy had Richie gelded, and he became her daughter Keri's horse. She brought Red and my filly, Jess, back to the farm as soon as she was weaned.

Four or five years later, Candy bought Jess from me for $3,000. By then, I had sold Red to a young horsewoman from Ohio named Kristen Engasser. She showed him, bred mares to him, and wrote me a letter a few years later, thanking me for selling her "this wonderful horse."

**Memories of KZ**

Through the years, my horses were terribly important to me. None of them would ever replace Apache in my affections, but my curly trail-riding buddy KZ came close. Before I bought him, he had been used mainly as a parade horse, didn't know how to back up on signal, and wasn't very flexible. When I worked with him on backing, he didn't understand what I was asking of him until I gave him a carrot one day when he shifted weight to his back feet.

Then he got it, and his cooperation was a cinch as long as he won his carrot. Finally, I could easily back him clear across the yard, and he no longer required a carrot. I kept riding and working with him until he turned and stopped easily and could sustain a slow canter. Walking horse, Thoroughbred, quarter horse, you name it—he could keep up his comfortable fox-trot and outlast any of them. He always finished up the ride with high energy, ears alert and working like a mule's.

He was strong willed and the leader of our little herd of horses until Red matured and quietly asserted his dominance.

I think KZ had a sense of humor too. One night, I got home too late to put him up in the paddock. He usually came when I called him, so I hollered out to him in the bright moonlight. I looked out across the pasture and didn't see him anywhere. I called and called, then started getting worried. Suddenly, I felt a living, breathing presence nearby, then turned around; and there was KZ standing close behind me. I don't know how long he'd been there, but he followed me back to the paddock.

Unfortunately, KZ was not always respectful of me, sometimes didn't come at all when I called, which is a drag if you're trying to get ready to go on a trail ride. So when I heard about a weekend horse-training workshop by Dan Sumerel, I signed up for it.

After he shared his philosophy of conflict-free training with us, we each took our turn working in a round pen with a horse we'd never seen before. Controlling his actions by shaking a long stick with a plastic sack tied to the end of it, we made him canter around and around, changing direction on signal.

No matter how shy or frightened or uncooperative or wild the horse had been at the beginning, he would gradually learn to keep his attention riveted on us, then finally allow us to invade his space and come to us. When we turned and walked away, he followed right along with his head close to our shoulder.

At home, I worked with KZ in the same manner in our paddock, and it didn't take long to change his attitude. Now he always came when I called, faced me, never turned his back on me, or ran off.

I consider Dan Sumerel the best trainer I've ever been exposed to, but he evidently couldn't make it businesswise and faded from the scene after a few years. He describes his training methods in a delightful book, *Finding the Magic*—a history book, how-to book, philosophy book, and, most of all, *a love story.*

When Dan was first introduced to horses at forty, it was love at first sight. He became a keen observer of the horse/human relationship as he learned to ride and developed his own training methods.

His book is out of print now and a rare find on the Internet, but I did discover one recently and use it as a loaner copy for horse-loving friends. Dr. Kathy Jones, my equine veterinarian cousin out in Sacramento, loved it!

## Troubled Times

The spring of 1996 was a time of heartache and emotional trauma for our family. Jennifer and Eddie had separated by then. Battling alcoholism and shaken by the loss of Jennifer, Eddie took his own life. Our whole family had loved Eddie, and this was devastating for us all.

At the same time, Joel's life was going into a tailspin. He had settled into a good job in Florida and was finally getting his life under control when Bridgette sued him for nonsupport. After a court hearing in Lexington, he was sentenced to three years in jail.

Before Joel started serving his time, Bob and I paid for a psychiatric evaluation. He was found to have attention deficit disorder (ADD) and a learning disability, which shed light on a lot of the problems he'd had in life. The UK psychiatrist told him he was perfectly bright but that his mind worked differently from most people's.

"You could get your high school diploma if you wanted to. You could even go on to college," he told Joel. "It might just take you longer."

Joel was stunned, then elated, then determined to earn his GED as soon as possible. He was incarcerated in a wretched county jail three hours east of Lexington. It took me a whole day to go to see him and then drive home again. At the jail, it was eerie. One-way seeing glass and disembodied voices greeted me, and I was directed to a visitation room where Joel was seated on the other side of a glass enclosure, and we had to talk to each other by phone.

The first time I visited him, Joel was desolate. "Mom, I can't make it here," he said with bowed head, and my heart sank. But that evening, he called me at home. "Don't worry about me, Mom," he said cheerfully. "I've adjusted!"

Soon, he had a job working in the laundry and also signed up for the GED study course. Within three months, he earned his GED. The food was terrible, the ventilation system didn't work, and the cells were always full of stale cigarette smoke. Although the jail was within sight of beautiful mountains, the men were never allowed to go outdoors. Magazines, articles, and books I sent Joel were confiscated.

But he was a model prisoner, and I soon requested his transfer to our Jessamine County Jail, which was by comparison a decent, well-run facility.

"Forget it," Joel was told. "We never transfer prisoners. It's not going to happen!"

But it did. After about four months, Joel called me one day to say, "Mom, I'm out of here! Jessamine Country deputies are coming to pick me up today. But I have to tell the other prisoners that I'm being released, not transferred."

Someone in authority had taken a personal interest in Joel and arranged for the transfer.

So Joel settled into the Jessamine County Detention Center, and we were allowed contact visits with him every Saturday and Sunday. We could hug him, sit holding hands, have private conversations in their visitors' room. I could take books and magazines to him. It was a whole new ball game. His father and I went to see him every weekend; Tim, Jen, and Lisa came whenever they could.

While there, Joel worked in the kitchen and painstakingly spent one whole night writing a script for *Seinfeld*. It was unbelievably good, timed to the last minute to allow for commercials—a funny, funny segment true to all the characters. It was almost as good as watching it on TV. I could never have written it. Unfortunately, *Seinfeld* did not buy unsolicited scripts.

Within a year, Joel was paroled. The first day back at the farm, he solved a problem for me. He had built a sturdy toolshed for me several years earlier. Since then, a groundhog had burrowed up into it, mounding the dirt floor so that I couldn't close the door. Joel dug out about two inches of dirt, smoothed it off, and laid up a floor of heavy creek rock. Now the critter couldn't get back in.

After a few weeks of painting houses with a family friend, Joel landed a job with a gutter-installation crew. He was soon made their troubleshooter, returning to take care of any problems with the homeowner.

He also fixed everything that needed fixing around the farm and started laying in a supply of firewood for the winter. Weekends, his dad hired him to replace the long second-story wood deck on his house. Ezra helped for a day or two, but for the most part, Joel accomplished this challenging carpentry job alone.

After six months, Joel was allowed to return to Fort Pierce, Florida, where he married his girlfriend, Nancy; and they set about raising their little girl, Emy, together. She was about five years old. Joel had been sending money orders to Nancy almost weekly, helping make it possible for her to put a down payment on a house. Once Joel joined her and Emy there, he purchased his own home renovation and repair business and was soon hard at work.

Now and then, I would run into people who worked at the Jessamine County Detention Center. They would always smile when they saw me and ask how Joel was doing. And I could tell them he was doing just great!

"Jail was good for me," he told me. "I learned what I had to learn."

Meanwhile, his daughter Leslie, now called Allie, was being sent to private schools, in Chicago for three years and then in

Tennessee for one year, by her maternal grandparents. She spent her summers at camp and in Florida with her grandparents. These were hard years for Allie. She was well loved by her grandparents but given little access to the cherished Hensley side of her family. Once he was back in Florida, Joel did manage to see her now and then.

After her first year of high school in Tennessee, Allie returned to Lexington to try to live with her mother again and attend high school there. When she was sixteen, she called me one day and said, "Please help me, Mama Jay!"

Things were not going well at home with her mom. Allie was also into drugs, alcohol, and sex with her boyfriend, and her grades were slipping; she realized she was in deep trouble.

We called Social Services. Going into action immediately, they interviewed her at school and did not allow her to return home that day. She was put in Jennifer's temporary custody for a few days, then evaluated at Charter Ridge psychiatric facility in Lexington. Joel drove up from Florida, gained custody of her, and took her back to Fort Pierce with him.

There, he arranged for counseling and spent as much time as he could with her. She soon earned her GED and started community college.

## ADD and Me

After Joel was diagnosed with attention deficit disorder, I took the tests on my own and discovered that he doubtless inherited ADD from me!

Finally, I comprehended why I couldn't get my stuff organized or set up and keep a good filing system, why I was forever losing things, why my mind kept buzzing along and never gave me any peace, why I was so easily distracted until I finally managed to became completely absorbed in a project or a problem. And why I often felt as if I was just plain going crazy.

People meeting me for the first time were apt to find me so spacey that they couldn't comprehend how I managed to do the magazine. It wasn't easy! Especially if I was short on sleep or had skipped a meal.

Steve Schumacher, the healer I go to a few times a year in Louisville, suggested I start taking a 150 mg DMAE capsule once or twice a day. It really does help. I call it my brain descrambler.

## Update on Doug and Jennifer

In 1994, Doug was living in Seattle, working full-time at a plant and landscaping shop, and playing his music evenings and weekends. He met fellow musician Heather DeRome that late summer at a music festival, soon married her, and moved to her apartment in Victoria on Vancouver Island in British Columbia, Canada. He started the citizenship process and joined the teaching staff at the Victoria Conservatory of Music.

Wonderful Heather, with her long thick black hair, intelligent dark eyes, and lovely face. I'm so glad Doug found her, and I love her to pieces. She is bilingual and was delighted to discover that Doug also speaks French. Rowan was born August 9, 1995, and his little sister joined the family three years later. They named her Julia after me. And despite his earlier misgivings, Doug is both a good father and good husband.

On August 18, 1996, a few months after Eddie's death, Jennifer met Dave Zurick in Berea at Tim's thirtieth birthday party. In addition to being a geography professor at Eastern Kentucky University in Richmond, Dave is a world traveler and an award-winning author and photographer.

Jen's whole life changed dramatically when she married him four years later, sold her place in Jessamine County, and moved to the outskirts of Berea, about fifty miles away in Madison County.

## Tim Gets Married

By then, Tim had already settled in Berea where so many of his friends lived. There, he met Jane Post when, having given up competitive fencing, he enrolled in her Tai Chi class. (Fencing had helped put Tim through college, and he loved the sport. But it had also been an expensive hobby. He had fenced in an international competition in Germany and reached most of his goals).

Tim and Jane celebrated their union with
family and friends in 1995 at a large
gathering in their mountain hollow.

Jane was a self-sufficient, independent young widow with a sixteen-year-old daughter. Potter, shiatsu massage therapist, martial arts teacher, capable with chain saw and garden hoe—she's a gal of many talents. About five feet three tall, of sturdy build, and with long thick curly black hair, she's also beautiful and is a fabulous cook. She has become like another daughter to me.

Tim and Jane were married in 1995 amid a gathering of friends and family in the mountain holler where they had recently bought an early 1900s log cabin and over two hundred acres of forest. They became organic farmers and have developed a business selling their produce, eggs from their own chickens, home-baked goods, and the mushrooms they cultivate and also gather from the wild.

In 1997, they bought Papillon (they call him Pappy), a mellow white Percheron stallion who became Tim's logging horse, supplies fertilizer for their garden and fruit trees, and gives a medieval aura to the farm. ("Papillon" is French for "butterfly.")

Still my *SNEWS* partner, Tim ran the business end of the magazine from Berea, went on road trips with me, and came over to the farm for a few days during deadline week for every issue. But I could tell this was all getting to be too much for him. With no enthusiasm for going solo albeit with Jeff's capable intermittent help, I was by then ready to call it quits myself, find a buyer for *SNEWS*, and start a new chapter in my own life.

# 38

## SELLING *SNEWS*

So in the fall of '98, I hired a company to do a professional analysis of *SNEWS* and establish a selling price. They assessed its value at $120,000, and I sold it for less than that (but still a great price) to Oregon sweep Jim Gillam. He was the ideal buyer. A longtime sweep and *SNEWS* subscriber, he was technically oriented and had already written a handful of good articles for the magazine. Plus I knew and liked him.

I purely loved the idea of *SNEWS* going "back to the future," being published once again in Oregon where it had been hatched.

My last *SNEWS* was the January-February '99 combination issue. Jeff had this to say in an article I asked him to write for that final issue:

### Jeff's Parting Words

After 16 years, I have been given the "pink slip" from my job as Technical Advisor to *SNEWS*. (So much for job security!) It's my own fault—I introduced Jay to *SNEWS* in the first place, and a few years later when it came up for sale, I encouraged her to buy it.

I certainly will not miss the income, as I was not paid (although I have been accused of that, and worse). But I did receive a free subscription, sent first class, and later on, a fax machine!

I won't miss the phone calls with Jay at 6:30 a.m. as
I was trying to get out the door to go to clean chimneys,
or after 10:00 p.m. when I had finished spending two or
three hours on the phone returning customer calls. I won't
miss staying up until 1:00 or 2:00 a.m. writing articles for
*SNEWS* when I had not finished preparing statements for
work that I had done or sending proposals for covers for
chimneys I had climbed to measure.

And I won't miss frantic calls from Jay asking if I
have some "free time today to review articles before we
go to press?" (She's just too free-spirited to ever develop
and be able to stick to an actual production schedule!)

What I will miss is being part of the independent
magazine for Sweeps that keeps us all connected . . . The
sharing of ideas, experiences, and feelings . . . The mortar
which bonds us all together into one family.

It has been an honor to have my thoughts and words
printed in the pages of *SNEWS* and my reward is to have
a Sweep call me or stop me at a convention to express
appreciation. And I hope that I have been able to keep Jay
out of hot water on at least a few occasions . . .

$$* \quad * \quad *$$

In 1986, Jeff, still a bachelor, had bought a spread of lush woods
and fields near the Kentucky River. Two years later, he designed
and built a snug, great-looking house and called it the Sweep's Nest.
It was just a mile down the road from the little 1896 wood-heated
box cabin, originally the office for a sawmill, that he'd rented for
thirteen years for $50 a month.

He found someone to share his new place with him in 1994 when
he met Jaqui Linder—lovely widow, college teacher, thread-and-needle
artist, and kindred spirit. They have been together ever since.

Jaqui retired from teaching in 2005. She is now pursuing her
art career full-time, often tying it in with the healing arts and the
goddess culture.

As for Jeff, he left the sweeping life in July 2006. He and Jaqui do some traveling; he volunteers his services making exterior home repairs for the elderly poor through Repair Affair, is a community activist, mentors several young sweeps, and has rekindled his interest in photography. Like me, he still writes an occasional article for the new *SNEWS*.

He keeps his fields mowed and cuts and works up his own firewood. There's always a plentiful and well-seasoned supply of it neatly stacked in his woodshed. The Sweep's Nest has become the Rolling J Ranch or just the J&J.

I'm likely to see both of them at a few craft fairs every year in Berea and elsewhere. When I stopped by their place one day a year or two ago, there on the couch was a unique example of Jaqui's creative genius: a skinny long-legged cloth-doll replica of Jeff, right down to his own curly hair—salvaged strand by strand from the shower stall drain—plus wire-rim glasses, striped engineer's cap, leather gloves, and low-top lace-up boots.

All is well with my old friend Jeff.

# 39

# MY YEARS WITH THE CHIMNEY SWEEPS

I'm in love with a chimney sweep,
I love him a bunch, I love him a heap.
I keep his books, I answer his phone,
I wait for him when he doesn't come home.
There's black up his nose and black in his hair,
But I love him so much I don't even care.

It's a dirty job, but someone must do it,
To love a sweep and stick with him through it.

Hard-pressed to come up with a cover for the January-February '86 issue of *SNEWS*, I found a washed-out color slide I'd taken of Jeff climbing the metal roof of the cabin he rented in Nonesuch, Kentucky. It translated well into a black-and-white photo and worked for my cover.

The above poem, "To Love a Sweep" by Janice Wells, seemed a natural fit to use with it. Her husband, Frank, was a sweep in Puyallup, Washington.

I am full of good memories and nostalgia from my sixteen years with the chimney sweeps. Through *SNEWS*, I traveled to places

I'd never dreamed of visiting. I met sweeps from all over North America and a few from Germany, Great Britain, Sweden, and other far countries; and I spent an evening with sweeps in Hawaii, watching hot lava flow down the mountain and spill over the cliff, sizzling hot, into the sea . . .

For three days at one convention, I spent all my free time with Bil (short for Bill, he said) Wight, a British sweep I'll never forget. At a sweep convention in Oakland, California, I met Neal, a freelance writer and former sweep, who became one of my best friends. Once, I jitterbugged the night away with a young Canadian sweep and was so stiff and sore the next morning, I could hardly get out of bed.

Except for Jeff, Graham Wilder in Berea, and the Pete Looker / Terri Roben family in Ballston Lake, New York, the rest of my sweep friends are pretty much lost to me now—an occasional e-mail, a phone call to reminisce about "the old days," a Christmas card . . .

Tim told me once that in the company of sweeps, I "lit up like a Christmas tree!" With good reason. Among them, I found some of the best people I have ever known. In their "other lives," sweeps I met had been or still were teachers, musicians, bricklayers, firefighters, farmers, masons, carpenters, cooks, waiters, inventors, construction workers, housewives, secretaries, entrepreneurs, a baker (Doniphan, Missouri, sweep/baker Sheldon Zola's biscotti was to die for!), a freelance writer, an Alaskan bush pilot, a young handyman, a photographer, a private detective, and even a millionaire!

A sweep out West called himself High Lonesome. Countless other sweeps around the country experienced that same scary and exciting feeling of going at it alone early in their sweeping careers. It was not only lonely; it was right dangerous on those rooftops. It took courage, grit, agility, strength, and skill to persevere in all kinds of weather.

## A Bit of History

A young self-employed painter, carpenter, and fix-it man named Tom Risch in Wilton, Connecticut, was responsible for resuscitating this trade in America in the late 1970s. One day, he put on the top hat he found in an old trunk in the attic he was cleaning and danced about, singing, "Chim-chimeny, chim-chimeny, chim-chim-cheree!" He wondered aloud to the lady of the house, "Whatever happened to the chimney sweep of old?"

His curiosity aroused, Tom contacted the local fire chief, who explained the dangers of chimney fires. Then he talked at length to an old-timer who'd been a sweep. He did some further research, then bought the tools for his new trade. Soon, he could be seen walking sootily about town wearing a top hat, tails, black shirt and pants, and white gloves. He told folks he was cleaning chimneys to prevent chimney fires from burning their houses down.

"I was up at five, to my first job at seven or eight, women answering the door with rollers in their hair. The world was nonstop, and I just had to go!" He called himself the August West Chimney Sweep.

Tom developed and kept improving a sweep vac from an oil drum and leaf blower. He painted it red and teamed it with a sweeping manual and a few good brushes and scrapers. Then in 1977, he placed an ad for his how-to-do-it chimney cleaning kit in *Mother Earth News* (*TMEN*). This propelled a few hundred fledgling sweeps around the country into business.

*TMEN* got curious and flew out to Connecticut to do a story.

They ran a helluva good article in their January '78 issue, sending its tremors down through the years. With that big boost and some excellent marketing, Tom's kit took off, beginning for him an astounding career that launched an estimated ten thousand sweeps into this born-again trade.

Jeff Gitlin read Tom's ad and went to see him in Connecticut. "It was all pretty impressive to a young guy thinking of starting a chimney sweep business," he told me. But he wasn't buying. He went home and came up with own makeshift vac, plus some good brushes and scrapers. He soon bought a better vac with a stainless steel body. Jeff used it 'til he retired from sweeping in 2006 and says, "It always looked like new!"

As for Tom, he became somewhat of a businessman. He started wearing a coat and tie, bought a new suit in 1979, flew to Paris, drank good wine . . .

## The Army Cook

Thirty years earlier, John Chuha was a U.S. Army cook stationed in Germany after World War II. On his weekly four off-duty days in a row, looking for something to do, he started cleaning chimneys with German sweeps he met in a bar. He worked for them over the next four or five years in Landshut, Bavaria.

Out of the army and back in Whitaker, Pennsylvania, in 1952, he soon started his own chimney service and duct-cleaning business in the Pittsburgh area. "And that's all I've ever done," he told me happily.

He made smooth black leather stovepipe hats for himself, his company sweeps, and his wife, Aileen (who was the maid at a customer's house when he cleaned flues in Canada for a short time early in his career), saying they stood up to the weather better than a sweep's ordinary top hat or cap. No matter how hard the wind blew or how deep the snow, John would bundle up, clamp on his handmade hat, hop into one of his trucks, and go.

## The Millionaire

Al Palmer was once a millionaire in South Carolina. Then his big wholesale furniture factory's roof collapsed, and the walls caved in under a heavy load of snow. When the insurance company called it "an act of God" and refused coverage, Al was ruined.

He took a shot at being a photographer and private investigator, work he described as 95 percent drudgery, 5 percent panic, and downright sordid.

After that, the independent, offbeat life of a sweep appealed to him. So he learned the basics of the craft at the August West Chimney Sweep school in Connecticut, entered the trade at fifty-one, and never looked back.

Classy, courageous, and imaginative, Al knew how to get good publicity. One of his first jobs, for which he collected $4,500, was scrubbing away the creosote from inside a huge 174-foot-high factory chimney as he dangled on a cable lowered from a hovering helicopter.

Over a three-day period, he scraped out enough soot and stuff to fill sixteen one-and-a-half-ton truck beds. You can bet the local newspaper sent out a photographer to chronicle this event.

He told friends and customers that he'd not been nearly as happy or useful as a business tycoon as he was after becoming a chimney sweep.

Fred Toldo.

## Best-loved Sweep in America

Pawcatuck, Connecticut, sweep Fred Toldo was a seventh-generation sweep who had apprenticed in Austria and Germany. He became the best-loved sweep in America and a mentor to fellow sweeps. Like a giant tree downed in a storm, he left an empty place against the sky when he died in 1993 at the age of seventy-seven, only a year or two after he retired from sweeping.

A few years later, the Massachusetts Chimney Sweep Guild initiated the prestigious Fred Toldo Award in his memory. It is presented annually to an outstanding member of their own large and active guild.

## Sweeping Women

A number of tough, competent women were also drawn to the trade. Such as Missi Escobar, the Hangtown Sweep out in Placerville, California, who first cleaned flues with her husband, then bought him out when the marriage ended in divorce. ("Families who sweep together keep together" was a sweep slogan that usually, but not always, held true!)

Mina Holland of Buford, Georgia, became one of most respected sweeps in the country. Another Georgia gal, Mary Ann Beaufait, took up the trade after she and her husband read that intriguing article in *Mother Earth News*. She even went on to serve one term as president of the National Chimney Sweep Guild. And many wives cleaned chimneys with their sweep husbands in the early years of their marriage.

## Lucky Dale, Storyteller

Tall lanky immensely likable North Augusta, South Carolina, sweep Lucky Dale Meisinger was a born storyteller. In a SweepsGoofs session at one chimney sweep convention, he told about sucking the customer's pussycat into his vac hose by mistake. The kitten leapt yowling from the room after Lucky Dale quickly turned off the vac and shook him out of the hose. This story became the subject of one of our *Grate Days* center-spread comic strips in *SNEWS*. It also made the *National Enquirer*, slightly garbled, with the cat coming out the vac's exhaust end.

He told another story about getting hit on the head by a bucket of bricks plummeting down the flue when the rope his son was holding slipped. It knocked Lucky senseless. A little later, this same son asked, "Home-Pop, how much you getting out of this job?"

"About $865."

"I wouldn't take a lick like that for under $1,000!" his son said indignantly.

Lucky Dale went home and crawled into bed. He didn't feel so good.

He claimed that his daughters didn't get married unless the son-in-law came to work for him. And his sons had a saying, "You can't kill Home-Pop."

He was a superior chimney service professional and fireplace rebuilder. He loved to barter and once swapped a few of his cows for a twelve-foot-diameter-by-thirty-five-foot-high silo. He moved it to his farm (a feat in itself) and turned it into a charming three-story, three-room apartment with a spiral stairway, heated by a woodstove on the first floor.

The grain chute for the silo was transformed into an insulated stainless-steel-lined chimney during a workshop at Lucky Dale and Patsy's annual Connemara ("refuge from a troubled world") get-together for sweeps.

Lucky Dale made great wine, having learned how from a pro, and gave it away bottle by bottle to friends, fellow sweeps, and me.

## The Poet Sweep

Writing poetry helped Sunbury, Pennsylvania sweep Ernest Houdeshell Jr. get through difficult times. "It's mostly therapy for when things get me down," he told me. "But it's also for special events." Such as his and his wife Sandy's wedding anniversary, or a son going away to boot camp, or the time he had to ground a daughter for serious infractions of the rules—all occasions that called forth the muse in a man rooted in his family and steeped in loving memories of a difficult childhood.

Here's a poem we ran in the October '96 issue of *SNEWS*. Ernie wrote it in September of '95 when the "crazy" season for sweeps was well under way.

### *Driven . . .*

The bills and worries hit their stride
Before the day's begun.
Chasing dreams and sleep, and love,

We're up before the sun.

Upon our desk the paperwork
And schedule for the day;
The mail to open, calls to make
And then we're on our way.

Clean out the van and load the stuff
We need to do our work,
While other people pull the strings
And we just dance and jerk.

A dream that does not end with sleep
Will greet the rising sun;
When others start the journey home,
Our work still won't be done.

We try to share our hope
With those who are closest to our heart,
And then we find ourselves alone;
This is the hardest part.

Through doubt and fear and blazing sun
Through rain and mud and snow,
We walk the housetops with our brush
Where only angels go.

To make a chimney safe, you see,
For those who live below.
And feed our family, pay the bills;
This is why, you know.

And now at half-past midnight hour
I lay me down to sleep.
And only dream tomorrow's flues;
I am a chimney sweep.

## The *Wanderschaft* Sweep

One of the *SNEWS* subscribers I met at sweep gatherings was Norman Lenz, who ran a chimney service company in Toronto, Canada. He regaled us with stories about his life in Germany during and after World War II.

From the time he was four years old, all he ever wanted to be was a chimney sweep. In 1942, at the age of fourteen, he started his rigorous two-year apprenticeship in a suburb of Berlin. At the end of each difficult day, he had to write an essay describing all his sweeping jobs. He also had a course of study to master.

Once, he got stuck halfway up in a four-story *steiger*, a "climber" chimney that had to be cleaned from the inside. When he screamed for help, his journeyman instructor climbed the flue under him and managed to push him all the way to the top where they both gulped some fresh air. He was Norman's brace on the descent as he finished cleaning the rest of the flue.

Sweeps in training were thoroughly schooled in the intricacies of all types of heating systems and in the many government regulations affecting their work. Germany was divided into districts; and once a sweep became a journeyman, he was qualified to work under a meister, the master sweep in charge of a district.

Norman had no use for Hitler. Drafted at seventeen and sent to the northwest of Germany, he and five other recruits with painful, bloody feet from ill-fitting boots were left behind when the troops were sent to the front. With the war coming to an end, officers in charge of the recruits deserted. So they did too after managing to get hold of their passports, traveling papers, bicycles, and food from the kitchen. Norman made his way back to his family on the outskirts of Berlin, enduring many harrowing adventures along the way.

Their lives became extraordinarily hard under the Russian occupation. His father was still a prisoner of war. Money was scarce, and there was no food in the stores. In the middle of one night, Russian military police rapped loudly on their door. Motioning with their machine guns, they asked for the *troubachist*, chimney sweep. Norman dressed quickly and went with them. His mother and sisters were crying, afraid they might never see him again.

But the Russians just wanted him to clean the chimneys and cookstove at their headquarters in city hall at night when the kitchen was not in use!

Norman was a journeyman now. Dressed in his sweep uniform, he loaded up his tools one day and, with an empty stomach, rode his bike to a gated community of three hundred houses where Russian soldiers were billeted. He got a job cleaning their flues. The soldiers watched him work, fed him a hearty meal at noon, and sent him home each day with food that helped his family survive.

Before immigrating to Canada with his whole family in 1951 when he was twenty-three, Norman lived by his wits in war-ravaged Germany. For several years, he traveled the country as a *wanderschaft*, a tradesman looking for work. He found a job in Stuttgart under Meister Kammerer, whose district included seventeen villages. For eight months, he lived in a four-room apartment with the Kammerer family, which included nine children. He loved both the work and his adoptive family.

Norman chronicles his life in a delightful book, *"Wanderschaft": Tales of a Travelling Sweep*, available on the Internet at http://www.lulu.com.

### The Entrepreneur

Young Bob Daniels, "Sooty Bob," was the only sweep in the Tulsa, Oklahoma, area for a while. Soon, he was also peddling chimney caps to fellow sweeps. A few years later, he started Copperfield Chimney Supply, which grew into one of the biggest supply houses in the nation and, to this day, sponsors a string of educational seminars and workshops for its sweep customers.

### Incident on a Hawaii Beach

In February of 1985, Sooty Bob picked up my tab for Copperfield's annual weeklong Sweeping Hawaii convention so that I could cover it for *SNEWS*.

After an early breakfast, every morning was crammed with seminars and hands-on learning. Most afternoons left attendees free to explore the island or hit the beach. The weather was glorious.

Back home in Kentucky, Illinois, Michigan, and Wisconsin, temperatures plummeted, numbing winds blew, snow piled up, water pipes froze, schools closed, street people were invited into community shelters, car batteries went dead, traffic stopped . . . while there on the beach at Hanauma Bay on Oahu island were all these chimney sweeps and me relaxing in the sunshine after a Sweeping Hawaii morning crammed with the nuts and bolts of the chimney service trade.

In my canvas beach bag that last afternoon of the convention were the negatives and prints from five thirty-six-frame rolls of film I had picked up just before heading for the beach. After going for a swim, I enjoyed drying off in the sunshine, watching the waves roll in and recede.

Suddenly, a big wave took me by surprise, swirled over my beach bag, and would have carried it back out to sea if I hadn't raced after it and snatched it away. My negatives and pictures were soggy wet! My whole photo coverage of the convention. The salt water would surely ruin them.

Hurrying back to my hotel room, I carefully rinsed off the negatives and prints, then spread them out on bath towels on top of the two double beds. With my hair dryer setting on low, I dried them out very slowly—close to two hundred pictures, and I saved them all. I soon mailed Sooty Bob an album full of duplicate prints.

Ten years later, Sooty Bob invited me and Tim, my *SNEWS* partner, to attend another Sweeping Hawaii convention at Copperfield's expense. Tim did most of the picture taking while I interviewed participants and took computer notes for writing up the seminars and extracurricular events on the islands.

The following Monday after a breakfast/lunch cruise, Tim and I were on our own until our departure the next day. The weather was perfect.

We rented a car and drove north to where the highway ended at an overlook. From there, we hiked down a steep, narrow pathway to the unpopulated black beach far below and spent hours enjoying the surf and sand. That evening, we drove muddy back roads to the isolated sanctuary where King Kamehameha's birthright and other rituals were performed long years ago. We ate a picnic supper there, all alone, and watched the sunset on the ocean.

Early the next day, we made our careful way on foot down the steep, "four-wheel drive only" road deep into Waipo Valley, and hiked along the valley floor to where we could see twin waterfalls spilling from a high cliff. Then we walked in the other direction until we reached the ocean. We ate our simple lunch and walked barefoot along a water-cooled black beach where the surf was high.

On our meandering way back to the hotel, we explored winding roads through island communities and lovely rural landscapes . . . and a few hours later, we settled into our seats for the long flight home.

Jennifer met us at the Blue Grass Airport. And it was *cold*, with snow on the ground. Tim changed from shorts and T-shirt into jeans and sweatshirt; we loaded our luggage into my red Suzuki Sidekick and headed for the farm. We talked nonstop, filling Jennifer in on our week in paradise.

About an hour later, with a cracking fire in the woodstove warming up the kitchen and crackers and bowls of hot soup on the table, we started settling back into life on the mainland.

### A New Fireplace for Jay

Another of many fond memories was the two-day Bellfires Workshop at my farm in the summer of '94. A crew of eighteen sweeps and masons replaced my old coal grate in the living room with a state-of-the-art modular masonry fireplace and insulated stainless steel flue-lining system donated by Sleepy Hollow Chimney Supply in Brentwood, New York.

A few days before the workshop was slated to begin, we made a startling discovery—the old living room floor under its composition board surface was completely rotten, except for the section we had replaced after our honky-tonk piano crashed through it twenty-four years earlier.

So in a marathon two days, Tim and Eddie (my son-in-law) gutted the floor right down to the ground and put in a new insulated subfloor. Then Eddie poured a new hearth. He leveled the hearth, packed up his tools, and went home just before the first wave of participants arrived and started unloading.

This was a crew of three from New York and Pennsylvania. They negotiated my farm lane in a rented '94 Dodge airport limo. Its last three rows of seats were replaced by fireplace components, smoke dome, chimney-liner system, and all sorts of tools and gear. During the course of the day, the rest of the workshop participants drove in or were picked up at the Lexington airport.

It was a great workshop. Chris Prior from Middle Grove, New York, wrote it up for *SNEWS*; and Tim snapped most of the fourteen black-and-white photos that accompanied his article. The cover featured a group shot of the crew and me.

They left me with a beautiful clean burning state-of-the-art fireplace for my living room.

## The Americanization of Andre

"I will always remember this place on the creek," twenty-four-year-old Andre Borjesson said as he hugged me goodbye. "I want to find something like it outside Stockholm."

I hated to see this lovable young sweep leave, but next on his schedule was a day in Berea with Graham Wilder. His visit had been too short. We'd had such fun, and Tim even took him partying one evening.

Andre was on a four-month visit to the States, working with sweeps around the country to find out how they do things here. He would be reporting back to his sweepers' guild in Sweden.

He had completed three of the five years of rigorous schooling required for certification status in Sweden where his father, Lars-Gunnar, was a master sweep in charge of a large district in Stockholm.

American sweeps had been working Andre pretty hard, so Tim and I had offered him a few days vacation at the *SNEWS* place. Late on that first evening, warmed by a fire in the woodstove on the living room hearth, Andre had sighed, looked heavenward, and said, "I didn't get any sleep at Yay's because she kept asking me questions." (Except for pronouncing a *J* like a *Y*, he spoke excellent English.)

"Why don't you speak Swedish?" he asked me once in frustration as he struggled to find the right word to explain something to me about the regulations under which sweeps in his country work.

In Sweden, he explained, the government regulates installations, inspections, and servicing of all heating equipment and flues. He was astounded that there were no such rules in America and that anyone could be a sweep.

(Actually, most of our "professional" sweeps, especially our *SNEWS* subscribers, had undergone training and certification programs run by private companies or by the Chimney Safety Institute of America set up by the National Chimney Sweep Guild. But this was not compulsory.)

Andre loved his time hanging out with us at the farm, walking in the woods, watching the horses, sleeping to the sound of the rushing creek, and eating hearty meals featuring my homemade bread and topped off with brownies and ice cream.

Before leaving, wearing his new *SNEWS* T-shirt, he said, "Yay, it must be wonderful, yes, to have your own magazine and work right here at the place?"

"Yes, Andre, it is. It really is. But I like to travel too. Someday, I may come to visit you in Sweden."

But I never did.

### Remembering Keith Williams

Were it not for *SNEWS*, I would never have known British journalist Keith Williams, one of the unforgettable people in my life.

Nick and I met Keith in Baltimore in 1988 at the Wood Heating Alliance Expo. He had come over to cover "the biggest solid fuel jamboree in the world" for England's *Solid Fuel* magazine. Pulled into a force field of our own, the three of us spent all our free time together over the next three or four days.

Sandy haired, quizzical, a marvelous storyteller, Keith was my contemporary. He bore an uncanny likeness in so many ways to my father, that complicated, literate, funny, earthy, and loving man who helped make my childhood years so special. He even looked like Daddy.

One stormy night in Baltimore, Nick, Keith, and I scurried across the street from our motel into the Marriott in the pouring rain, lingered for hours over a lovely dinner of salad and wine.

Keith was an unflappable connoisseur of wine. We had great fun that night, pointing to wine after wine listed on the menu and asking him to characterize each one. The vocabulary he drew upon to do so was awesome. Could he possibly have been familiar with so many wines, or did he (as we seriously began to suspect) simply dig deep into his imagination for some of those wonderful and tantalizing descriptions? We'll never know . . .

Keith grew up and went to school in Surrey, England. In his teens, he won a competition for his ability to identify German aircraft. The prize was a trip to America, where he learned to fly.

He came of age during World War II and was an RAF bomber pilot from 1941-46. Although war is not funny, he told some of the most hilarious war stories I've ever heard. One he entertained Nick and me with concerned his unexpected "vacation" somewhere in India.

It seems that his squadron was split in two, and the half that included him was sent to India. The other half was on its way to the Japanese theater of operation when Japan surrendered. In the excitement, the Ministry of Defence forgot about Keith's half of the squadron.

He and his crew spent many months thus abandoned. So they settled into the life of the town, made friends with the inhabitants—a few crew members even took up various jobs to ward off boredom—and had "a jolly good time." They also managed to carry out a few mercy missions, dropping food into remote areas where people were starving.

He married his sweetheart, Audrey, after the war and made his living mostly as a writer in the early years for the BBC (British Broadcasting Company).

In 1956, he and Audrey immigrated to California for six years, where Keith hosted a daily radio program in Los Angeles. Called *Window on the World*, it was a daily chat and interview program with an international flavor.

Back in England again, he authored several books and wrote on a wide variety of topics for the BBC and a number of different magazines. His books included *A History of English Newspapers*, a funny book about food, and *The Book of the Wood Stove*.

A dedicated wood burner in a country where just a tiny percent of the populace did likewise, he worked up his own firewood and cleaned his own chimney. He was considered England's expert on solid-fuel heating systems.

**Heartbreaking News**

I received a letter from Audrey in December of 1998. After a run to the Wilmore Post Office, I sat reading it in my car back at the farm. She was writing to tell me that Keith had died of liver cancer two months earlier. I sat there, stricken, and burst into tears. I cried and cried and cried. Despite the breadth of land and sea that separated us, he was my dear friend.

We had kept in close touch through long letters and an occasional phone call. We always thought we would meet again someday. Audrey told me he had loved *SNEWS* and eagerly awaited the arrival of each issue. He wrote many articles for it. Some of them were hilarious.

His address charmed me: the Old Barn, Mariners Cross, Cotleigh, Honiton, East Devon. The Old Barn was actually three sturdy old barns hooked together. The conversion had taken place before he and Audrey bought the property in '84. They added a fireplace and chimney in the drawing room.

In the spring of '98, knowing my love of horses and in an effort to lure me to Great Britain, he described the wild ponies that roam hundreds of miles of scrub grassland on the open moorland thirty miles or so to the west of where he lived in rural East Devon.

"Seemingly," he wrote, "they require no shelter, but only food in order to survive. Once each year there is a roundup to check on the numbers . . . The animals are not artificially bred . . . and date in an unbroken line possibly back to the Anglo-Saxons . . . The laws that protect common land protect them also so that there is no fear that they will ever be domesticated.

"They are quite tame and take a greedy interest in any cars passing through . . . So, if you park and open your car window, within a minute or so a great wooly head will be thrust in and great soulful eyes search round, while thick snuffling nostrils test for the scent of goodies . . ."

He described how, in winter, the beasts "loomed up out of the dense, frosty fog" and urged me to bring my camera. "You would get some extraordinary pictures!"

Audrey told me that Keith left behind great stacks of writings and notes, which she had started working her way through. He was even writing a profile of me and was up to page 19. I wondered what on earth he could possibly say that consumed so many pages.

According to *Solid Fuel* magazine editor, Jonathan Brind, "Keith was many things: a bomber pilot; a cookery competition organizer and cookery writer; a film, radio and magazine journalist—but most of all, he was an English gentleman . . . He loved traveling, good wine, good company and a good book . . ."

He was the sort of character you are much more likely to come across in a good book than in real life. The world and I are richer for the fact that he was here and poorer for his absence.

# 40

# MY LETTERS TO PIERRE

In October of 1996, I received a letter from Claire. Wonder of all wonders, she enclosed three letters I had written to Pierre long ago. I looked at them with disbelief . . . but they were real. She had found them a year earlier when clearing out family papers in New York before moving permanently to Ashfield. She told me the letters had been on Pierre when he died.

"I hope you won't be too upset when you read these, that's my only hesitation," she wrote. "But perhaps it will do you good. I know you would want to have them . . ."

These were letters written my freshman year of college in the spring of 1944. The first was handwritten on my roommate's stationery. My return address was 134 E. Foster Ave., State College, PA. The second and third letters were typed on two little V-mail forms. They were all addressed to the following:

> 2nd Lt. Pierre Birel Rosset-Cournand
> O.S.S. Detachment
> A.P.O. 887, c/o Postmaster
> New York, New York.

### Saturday, Apr. 1, 1944

Dear Pierre—Now that I'm all wore out from playing April Fools jokes on my poor unsuspecting friends, I'll settle down and do something constructive for a while.

It seems wonderful to be able to sit down and write to you again, Pierre.

I was so sure that something had happened to you, so sure that I'd never hear from you again that I almost started to cry when I got that letter from you yesterday.

Yes, friends are a wonderful thing to think about and hold onto, whether the road is hard and rocky or not. Please always be there and able to write back to me. And remember, we've got a date to go rowing in a couple of years—and swimming, and walking thru the woods. Remember that time we decided to take a shortcut up to your cabin, and I was sure we were lost? And when we finally got there I was so hot and out of breath and you looked just as cool and calm as when you'd started.

Sometimes you were crazy, like me, and sometimes you were serious and moody.

The kind of life you're leading now and the things you're doing are beyond my grasp. But no matter how far away you are, you're only six cents, a piece of paper and a few weeks off. I wish I had a picture of you, but I guess it wouldn't be possible for you to send one.

Can you tell me anything about what's happened since you left the states, and about your friends in the paratroops, or would the censor rip your letter into shreds and start cussing?

Did you have fun on your motorcycle, running people down and scaring little children? It wouldn't be as much fun as riding Nonnie—but it would be fun, and exciting.

It rained the other night, real hard and long. I couldn't resist the urge to put on an old shirt and my bluejeans and raincoat, and go for a long walk. I got soaking wet, but just being out there in the dark by myself gave me a wonderful feeling.

You don't get a chance to be by yourself much up here, and when you are it's kinda nice and you start to do a lot of thinking. My shirt was a brown and white plaid one. Sorta big for me (sound familiar?) and it made me think of Ashfield.

I liked you with bluejeans and that shirt on, and your hair all mussed up. (Did Gen. Giraud make you get a haircut?) And I thought about you and all the other soldiers over there. We have soldiers and sailors and marines here, too. Only these are soldiers with books instead of guns. They march around campus singing at the top of their lungs, laughing, joking. And then they stop laughing sometimes when they start thinking about leaving college and their books behind.

Tuesday Afternoon—This morning it was warm and sunny and everyone had Spring fever. This afternoon there's a blizzard raging outside. Gee whiz, I wish Mother Nature would make up her mind—here I am stranded with my spring coat and no kerchief or mittens.

I'm a complete wreck—mentally, physically and otherwise—because Sunday I hiked halfway up Mount Nittany. I never saw so many fences in my life. Once there were little brown rabbits with white tails bobbing up and down all over the place. We had to cross a stream on a log at one time and standing right out in the middle of it I suddenly lost my nerve. For a while there I thought I'd never see dear old Wylie Dorm again. But the Joneses always come thru, come Hell or high water. Sunday afternoon was beautiful, and it was the first time I've been really out in the country since I came to Penn State. It made me think of Ashfield.

Pierre, I lost Nonnie. He hurt his leg and had to be shot last month. He was a big part of my life for three years, and when I heard what happened it took all the feeling out of me. I'll never be able to put my arms around his neck and lean my head up against him again, or whistle to him and watch as he canters up the field from the pond. Besides his being mine, besides my loving him so much, I guess he was a sort of a symbol to me. A symbol of beauty and warmth and high-headedness, and life as I wanted it to be. I'd rather have given up my chance to come to college than lose him.

College is O.K. Sometimes it's wonderful, and sometimes it's awfully discouraging. I have a swell roommate this semester and we have a lot of fun together. But the studying around this house is nil—there isn't even a semblance of order—people are always tearing up and down the stairs screaming bloody murder. Our chaperon [housemother] is a frightened little thing with big brown eyes and a pathetic smile. Consequently, I never get any homework done and my marks make my hair stand up on end.

Write me a nice long letter if you can, and don't scare me again by waiting five months. Good luck, Pierre—come back for that chocolate malted.—Julia

### May 24, 1944
Monday night, 9 p.m.

Dear Pierre—This place has been busy as a black market for the past couple months. Gee whiz, anyway, there's so much to do and so doggone little time to do it in. I have a vague suspicion that I'm headed for the nuthouse, but please don't tell anyone—it would break my Mother's heart.

Now this campus finally lives up to the pictures in the catalogue. The only trouble is that this semester will be over in about three weeks, which means that there are only two months out of the whole year that the campus is the way I like it to look.

I'm taking 5th year French now, mais *je hate le maitre*! He's real temperamental and insists that all the French Grammar books are wrong, but he, of course, knows everything. Grrrr! I'm scared of him. He stands up in front of us, points his finger at someone (usually me) and yells "STUPIDE" at the top of his lungs. Mon Dieu, ces Francais sont terrible.

Look here, young man, if you can write to me I wish you would. Because it's not much fun wondering and wondering if you're still O.K. and raring to go. Did you get my other two letters?

I wanted to go to college thru the summer, but I can't on account of because Pop is running out of money for the time being; then I wanted to get a job, but I can't, on account of because Pop says NO and I'm not 18 yet.

(Continued on Page II) So long for now, Julia

*(Page 2 had to be typed on another V-mail form and mailed separately.)*

Hi again—"A kindergarten teacher smiled pleasantly at the gentleman opposite on the trolley car. He did not respond. Realizing her error, she said aloud, 'Oh, please excuse me. I mistook you for the father of two of my children!' . . . She got off at the next corner."

This semester is kinda queer. My roommate and I like eathother, but we're always fighting like Hell; studying just doesn't seem to agree with me, and therefore I do as little as possible; I expect a 95 in an exam and get a 50, or expect a failure and get a 98; one day is like the 20th of January and the next is like the 8th of August. Well, it'll soon be over . . . Then, "ASHFIELD HERE I COME!."

I guess you must miss your music an awful lot over there, but then you can always sing and that helps. Are you still planning to go to college when you come back? Maybe it isn't so far away now, but there isn't much way of telling.

This dorm's a madhouse! The chaperon that's supposed to be running it is a poor pathetic little woman that's afraid of her own reflection in the mirror (not that I blame her). Oh well, who wants to study anyway?

Boy, it's amazing the way I can write two whole pages about practically nothing. Do you remember Malcolm Clark at Ashfield? My sister is contemplating marrying him.

Yipe! Old Main is striking ten. Goodnight, Pierre—Julia

*All these years later, I wish they had been better letters.*

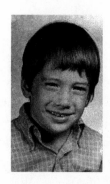

# 41

# SCOTTY, NIGHT VISITOR

Although it doesn't happen often, Scotty has come to me through the years in dreams, so in the flesh real that I am astounded. This gives me a sense that his spirit hovers nearby, always, to comfort me.

The first time he came back to me, glowing with life, his face was crumpled up and wet with tears. "Lisa hit me!" he whimpered. I held him tightly in my arms to comfort him.

"Oh, Scotty, brothers and sisters hit each other sometimes. And they say mean things to each other sometimes, but they always love each other. That's just the way brothers and sisters are! Now let's go find Lisa."

So I took his hand, and we went looking for tempestuous, tenderhearted Lisa, who was already feeling awful about being so mean to her little brother. When she saw him, she ran to him with a big hug, and she cried.

I came across another dream I wrote up in one of my journals:

> I crawled in bed, wiped out by my day, at 7:00 last
> night, listened to the first half of a Terry Gross interview
> on NPR and drifted off to sleep. I woke up a few times in
> the night, went right back to sleep, and between 1:30 and
> 3:00 a.m. I was with Scotty again. Just the two of us in a

house I didn't recognize. I remember thinking "the houses in our lives don't matter that much; it's the people in our lives that grab and hold us."

Scotty . . . fresh-faced, barefoot, full of love and sweetness. He must just have arisen from a nap and his clothes were soggy. "Well, let's pull these things off," I said after a hug, "and let's find you some dry clothes!"

"I know," he said, "why don't I take a bath?"

"Oh, that's a wonderful idea!" and I stated filling an old-fashioned claw-foot bathtub that materialized . . . Then he was getting into fresh clothes—a white undershirt, than a little blue cotton loose-weave sweater over shorts . . . We were talking, about what I don't recall, enjoying each other. And here I was with my dear little love again. If I linger any longer with this, my joy will turn again to sadness . . .

I try not to grieve, try not to miss my lost loves so much, try to BE HERE NOW. But here I am in tears.

This next journal excerpt I found is not about a dream, just a memory I put down:

When I was picking blackberries this morning, I remembered once taking the kids berry picking with me at a pick-your-own place—Jennifer, Joel, Lisa and Scotty, who was perhaps three-years old.

Scotty was just the right height to spot big, juicy red raspberries the rest of us couldn't see under the leaves. He'd be so excited: "There's one! There's one!" and he picked his little yellow plastic bucket full. Then as we were leaving the berry patch, he tripped and spilled out all his berries. He was so upset, but I hugged him and we all picked his berries up off the ground together, and soon he had a full bucket once more . . .

Oh, Scott my little love!

In his short lifetime, Scotty had a number of brushes with death, the most serious one being the day he almost drowned at the Windmill Swimming Pool, a few miles from us on the Nicholasville Road.

Bob was taking the children swimming, and I instructed Jennifer to keep suntan oil on little Scotty, who was very fair-skinned and burned easily. They came back earlier than usual that day with a frightening story to tell: Scotty went missing, and Bob found him lying on the bottom of the pool, his eyes wide open. He brought his limp body up to poolside and was able to revive him with artificial respiration. It was a terrifying experience for all of them.

About a year earlier, we took the whole family for a few days' vacation at General Butler State Resort Park where Doug was just finishing up band camp. Bob and the kids went swimming one afternoon while I watched them from shore, my belly big with Timmy, who was due in a few weeks.

As I watched, Scotty, who had been standing in the water next to his daddy, suddenly slipped under the water and disappeared. I screamed at Bob three or four times before he heard me. Alarmed, he reached down into the water and pulled Scotty out.

Another time, when Scotty was just a toddler, I was to meet Bob and the kids out at the building site for our new house in Jessamine County. When I arrived, a distressed Bob was sitting under a tree, holding Scotty, who had been wandering happily through the house and fallen into the stairwell hole. Luckily, he bounced off the landing halfway down and fell onto a bag of cement instead of hitting the concrete floor. Although a little banged up, he was basically okay.

Then there was the day I made a quick trip to town for something and returned to find Scotty on the kitchen couch, with Jennifer, Lisa, and Joel hovering close by. His face was bruised, his pants torn, and his knees bloody. He was crying, and he looked up at me accusingly. I knelt down, put my arms around him, and said, "Oh, Scotty, what has happened here?"

He had wanted so much to go with me that he had run after me, hollering. He climbed onto the rear bumper and was standing, holding on to the top of my Travelall, as I started up our circular driveway. I didn't see him or hear his voice over the roar of the engine. As I picked up speed, he fell off and sprawled on the gravel, skinning up his knees and face. The other children, who had watched in horror, ran down the driveway and brought him home.

## The Accident

Here now is the story of that terrible night when Scotty's life ended, as best I could piece it together many years later from several different accounts.

Bob had taken the boys for an evening ride on the deserted farm across the road. Timmy was in front of Bob on Rocket and Scotty, in front of Joel on Misty. Scotty, who was always thirsty, had hung his metal canteen on a tree on the far side of Ashgrove Pike, for it was bothersome carrying it on the horse. He planned to retrieve it on the way home.

They explored the old farmhouse, after which they rode around the farm some more and then headed for home, forgetting about Scotty's canteen.

Somehow, he ended up alone and on foot on the far side of Ashgrove Pike after going back to retrieve his canteen. He was waiting for a car to go by before he could cross the road, but on a blind hill, the car forced a motorcycle coming the other way off the road.

It hit a tree and careened into Scotty. It struck him with great force, flinging him into the metal railing of the bridge. He was killed instantly from a head injury. The motorcyclist was a neighbor boy who had been giving his young sister a ride on his bike. They were both hurt but recovered from their injuries.

Back at the house, the phone rang. Lisa answered it, hearing an unfamiliar voice say, "Are your brothers and sisters home, or do you know where they are?" Lisa said, "I think so!" and heard a police siren in the background. She ran outside to where her father and Joel were fooling with the horses and called out, "Where's Scotty?"

He hadn't come home yet, and Bob sent Joel to look for him. Joel returned on the run, saying, "Dad, something's happened down by the bridge!" Bob walked down to the bridge with dread in his heart, pulled back the white sheet, and found his little boy dead.

When I wanted to have a memorial service for Scotty, Bob would not hear of it. I did not have the will to proceed on this without him. He arranged to have Scotty cremated and kept his ashes for years in a metal can on a shelf in the kitchen/family room.

It would be twenty-three years before our family reached closure on Scotty's death. We held a memorial service at Bob's place, the only home our little boy had known. We shared our memories and pictures of him. Then we planted a little maple tree in the front yard close to the house. We each scooped up a handful or two of his ashes to mix with the dirt shoveled in around it, and we buried his dented-up canteen there too.

I am grateful for all the times I stopped what I was doing to read a book to Scotty or pack a lunch and take him on a walk down through the woods for a picnic by the creek. For the flowers we picked and the songs we sang together. And for all the happy memories I have of him.

Once, just a week before he left us, I found him painting the figure of a little boy on a deep red background on a large triangle of brown wrapping paper. "This is for a kite," he told me. A drip of white paint looked like a tear on his little boy's cheek.

"I just love it, Scotty! If you let me have it instead, I'll buy you another kite," I told him. He thought seriously about my offer, then said, "I'll give you three days!"

I found a new kite for him right away, and he gave me his painting. A few years later, I had it mounted and framed. It's one of my favorite pieces of artwork.

That spring, he often asked me, "Mom, when will I be seven?" His birthday would be on the fifth of July, and he could hardly wait.

And there was a movie he wanted so badly to see, the story of a bear's life, starting when he was a newborn cub. "Mom, could you take me so see it?" he begged me several times and later on, "Do you have a friend who could take me to see it?"

How I wish I had dropped everything and taken him to that movie. I didn't know our time together was running out.

I try not to think of his life as being cut short, but instead of what a good life it was—secure and full of joy.

As I kissed Scotty's soft cheek and tucked him into bed one night in the room he shared with Joel and Tim, I told him, "I love you so much."

"Huh," he said, looking up at me in surprise, "I thought you loved Timmy!"

"Oh, Scotty, mothers have room in their hearts for all their children," I said. He smiled serenely and dropped off to sleep as I sat there by his bed.

All through the years, Scotty has remained as real to me as Pierre. The sorrow never recedes. I told Jim Russell once, "I'll never get over it!" And he said, "Maybe you're not supposed to."

Scotty and Dandy.

# 42

# LEAVING THE JESSAMINE CREEK

After thirty-one years raising kids, horses, big gardens, chickens (and even hogs one year), working at the University of Kentucky for nine years, freelancing for five, and publishing *SNEWS* for sixteen . . . after all this, I sold my little farm on the creek, packed up, and vamoosed.

Both the farm and *SNEWS* sold for more than I could ever have imagined. All this left me with enough money to buy and remodel another house and put the remainder into a small investment portfolio I had started a few years earlier. I wasn't going to end up as a bag lady after all!

So was it hard to leave the beloved home place?

*No*! By the time I finished sorting through all that stuff and nonsense, recycled, threw away, sold, or gave away *tons* of junk and accumulated possessions, driving out the lane with that last load of my belongings proved to be *the great escape*.

Mostly, I would miss KZ. I had been diagnosed with osteoporosis and urged by my doctor to give up riding. "A fall could be catastrophic," she said. Sunshine Kyzyl was now twenty-four years old. He had been my companion on countless trail rides, adventures, and campouts in the valleys, mountains, forests, and wilderness areas of Kentucky and northern Tennessee. It was hard to give him up.

The day Lisa and I moved him to Lisa and Tommy's farm in Clark County, I drove the truck and horse trailer halfway out the rocky farm lane. Lisa led him to me, and we loaded him. Prancing along beside Lisa with head up and ears working, he looked like a young horse going eagerly to the races.

I ride him in my dreams, hear the cadence of his hoofbeats, feel his muscles working under me.

It was hard saying goodbye to Janice and Charlie Miller too. They are the folks who bought Jen's farm and quickly populated it with goats, chickens, and a Scottish Highland cow. Janice is an artist, a lover of books, and an enthusiastic dealer in antiques and country-living odds and ends. We had become such good friends, were always loaning books to each other, and visiting back and forth.

## Destination, Berea

With Jennifer and Tim both living in Madison County now, I decided this was the place for me too! So I moved to the outskirts of Berea one year after Jen sold her log house to the Millers and married Dave Zurick.

The first time I visited Berea was nine or ten years earlier. My old high school chum Anne Alevizon Mitchell had called to tell me she'd be in Berea with an elderly hostel group and wondered if I could meet her there. Yes yes! We had dinner at the Boone Tavern, spent the night there, had a great visit, and attended an amazing Body Recall class on campus the next morning.

Body Recall is an exercise program developed in the late 1970s by Dorothy Chrisman, a physical education teacher at Berea College for many years, and she was there to lead the class. When the ninety-minute session was over, she told us, "You have exercised every muscle in your body!" Back at my farm the next day, I woke up with a tingling sensation all over my body.

Located in the foothills of the Appalachians, Berea is both a college town and a center for writers, craftspeople, and artists. There's a great bookstore on Chestnut Street and a fine public library. Many of Berea College's lectures and concerts are open and free to the public too. I have found kindred spirits here.

Tim and Jane live just three miles away in their mountain holler. When I stopped there at sunset one day, after driving in their long narrow lane through the forest, Tim was coming down the steep mountain path riding Pappy bareback and holding a bag of freshly picked wild mushrooms. My mind's eye holds on to that image.

Jennifer, whose handmade baskets have become expensive collectors' items, lives seven miles from me with her husband, Dave, in their passive-solar and wood-heated cottage. It's located on Wolf Gap Road, off Red Lick Road just a few miles beyond Tim and Jane's place.

Dave is a fine-looking and personable prince of a fellow, a dandy "papa" to Jennifer's grandson Andrew. (Andrew is the son of Ezra and Crystal, now separated.) Jen often accompanies Dave on his journeys and has been to Nepal, Hawaii, Mexico, and other far places. They were in Thailand when the tsunami roared ashore in January of 2005, were just by chance safely on the other side of the peninsula that day.

At the time I moved to Berea, she and Dave were halfway across the world in Nepal. In a letter home, Jennifer described the first half of a two-week trekking adventure in the middle Himalayan mountains where she and Dave stayed in homes of the villagers in tiny settlements strung out along the steep rocky trails.

In another letter, she told about riding an elephant across a wide shallow river and into the jungle on a safari to see wild animals.

## My New House

My property outside Berea includes woods, lovely big hardwood trees, a wet-weather pond, and a small A-frame house with a view of the Appalachian hills. One end of the long, wide porch that stretches across the back of the house now serves as my woodshed. This little cul-de-sac neighborhood of four families is a friendly one. We try to look after one another.

Remodeling included laying up a masonry heater at the center of the house, adding windows, and installing poplar flooring. My three-year-old great-grandson, Andrew, trotted through the house and declared, "It's very colorful in here, Mama Jay!" I had transformed the interior with a dazzling new paint job.

A spiral stair beside the masonry heater leads to a narrow balcony. I've turned this space into a children's library with a large selection of books, a beanbag chair, skylight, and framed pictures from *Pinocchio* and *The Hobbit*. Neighborhood kids check out the books or climb the winding steps to sit and read a while.

Open the door off this space, and you're in my "writing place"—a small room with its own half bath and a tiny outdoor balcony. Two new skylights add fresh air, natural light, and a view of the ever-changing sky.

### My Own Masonry Heater!

Three and a half months before I moved, an international volunteer crew of fifteen stove masons and wannabes constructed my new heater during a five-day workshop. My old friend Jerry Frisch, the current MHA president, custom designed my hybrid fireplace-heater and led the workshop.

I knew most of the attendees. Five of them stayed with me, camping out in the backyard or sleeping on mattresses in the house. I retired each night to a mattress up in my writing place at the top of the house. We went to sleep loudly serenaded by tree frogs and woke up to the crowing of roosters from nearby farms.

I fixed breakfast every morning for the guys who stayed with me and lunch for the whole crowd. On the last evening, we gathered at Jen and Dave's place on Wolf Gap Road for a take-out pizza dinner.

Most of the heater-building materials, including the bake-oven door, were donated by wood-heat industry companies. The firebox door was designed and manufactured by Canadian stove mason Norbert Senf, who attended a few days of the workshop.

My custom-designed handmade heater cost me about a third of what it would have otherwise, and that money was donated to the MHA treasury. We all had a great time. I took lots of pictures, wrote up the workshop, and sold my article to *SNEWS*. Editor Jim Gillam devoted six pages of his September 2001 issue to "A Masonry Heater for Jay" and ran thirteen of my photos with it.

### Nannette

My old friend Nannette Prata lived with me my last year at the farm. We had met during our hippie days in the early 1970s, and she lived with us at the farm during her first semester of nursing school at UK before she married.

Once her children were grown, she had *finally* left her husband and, the timing being just right, took care of Jen's place for a month while she and Dave were on their honeymoon. Then she moved in with me, the perfect solution of an interim place for her to live.

Now a registered nurse, and with a constitution of iron, Nannette had for many years been working the twelve-hour weekend night shifts at the University of Kentucky hospital, plus various shifts during the week. She was a great hand at splitting firewood and helping with other work around the place. We shared expenses and became close friends. We had such good times together, tackled *big* projects, and had great fun flexing our woman-power muscles.

One summer day, we built a hefty water gate. The challenge was to replace a neighbor's puny water gate. It washed out time and again when the creek was running high, letting his cows and horses through the gap onto my farm when the creek was low again.

We stretched heavy cable between two sturdy trees, one next to the cliff, the other at creekside. Using strong wire, we threaded it through five or six heavy wood pallets in tandem, securing them to the cable. My theory was that the thundering rush of high water would lift the pallets, letting water and brush through. Then the pallets would drop back down into place as the water flow subsided and keep the livestock from escaping. It worked, and it lasted for years!

Another project involved adding insulation to the attic floor above the kitchen and family room. Starting early one morning, we carefully ripped up the floorboards, put down heavy brown paper between the rafters, and poured loose insulation on top of it. Then we nailed the floorboards back down. Hot, sweaty work, much of it in awkward and constricted places. Not fun.

I don't know how I could ever have moved without Nannette. She was a strong and tireless ally in helping me go through and get rid of things, then fill cardboard boxes with what I was taking with me. We cleaned out the barn and filled my truck many times to haul stuff to the town dump and unload it.

I hired a moving company to transport furniture and filing cabinets. Tim and his friends helped move the rest of my belongings, using their pickup trucks.

## The Day I Left

On September 11, 2001, I moved my last carload of worldly goods and two cats—MacAttack and his own ancient Mama Cat—to Madison County. Jen had left Mama Cat behind with Janice and Charlie, but they had two dogs, and Mama Cat wasn't happy there. So she ran away and was seen no more . . .

Until almost a year later when Nannette and I were taking a walk on the back of the farm. We heard a loud, plaintive meow, and Mama Cat emerged from the woods along the creek. Acting *really* glad to see us, she meowed two more times, rubbed against our legs, and followed us home. She looked great, no longer a scrawny old wreck. She and Mac would become friends at last and live out their lives on my safe gated back porch in Madison County.

That morning, as I made my last run to the Wilmore Post Office before heading for Berea, I switched on my car radio. An airplane had just smashed into the first Twin Tower at the Trade Center in New York City. By the time I arrived back at the farm, another airliner packed with passengers, among them a little three-year-old boy traveling with his daddy, had hit the second tower.

# 43

# SUMMER OF LOSS, 2003

*Losing Pauline, Reading My Diary to Claire, and a Week with Eva*

"If you want to see Pauline, you'd better come soon!"

It was the spring of 2003, and that was Malcolm's voice on my answering machine. I had just returned from MHA's annual meeting and workshops in the North Carolina mountains and was checking my messages.

Two weeks later, Lisa and I were on a plane headed East.

Pauline had been diagnosed with Alzheimer's a few years earlier, and Malcolm had devoted himself to taking care of her. However, she had of late become increasingly disoriented and frail. After she fell at home, suffering a painful and debilitating stress fracture of the spine, Malcolm realized he could no longer provide the round-the-clock attention she needed. He made the heart-wrenching decision to allow the State's long-term care system to take over.

The day we arrived, Malcolm took us to see her. She was asleep in her hospital bed, and he woke her up gently. Right away, she saw Lisa and greeted her fondly. Then from the other side of the bed, she heard my voice, so much like her own, turned, and reached out her hand to grip mine. "I thought you would *never* get here!" she said.

Back in Apple Valley that evening, Malcolm said in despair, "I've lost her, I've lost her!" She was the love of his life, and now she was in a nursing home.

Lisa and I stayed for a week and went with Malcolm every day to visit Pauline at Charlene Manor, the long-term care facility only thirty minutes or so from Apple Valley. Malcolm would sit morosely in his chair during the whole visit, and one day, Pauline remarked, "Look at Malcolm's face!" Not knowing how to describe it, she made a terrible grimace. Lisa and I started laughing.

Another time, when Lisa was being too solicitous, Pauline looked up at her mischievously and said, "Yes, Mother!"

Malcolm tacked an article about Pauline up on the wall by her bed one day, a feature story with pictures of her with the Tennessee walking horses she bred, raised, and trained. "I want people to know she's not just a sick old woman. She's somebody who has done important things in her life!" he said.

After we came back to Kentucky, Malcolm and I kept in close touch by phone. "She keeps asking me when I'm going to take her home," he told me. "One time, she wanted to know, 'Do I have to stay here until I die?' I didn't know what to tell her!"

Sometimes when Malcolm was about to leave, she would reach up, take hold of him fiercely, and say in a strong voice, "You're *not* going! You're *not* going!" It almost broke his heart.

But he soon pulled himself up out of despair and adjusted to a new routine. He would see Pauline through these last months or years. Every morning, after his shower and breakfast, he drove the seventeen miles to Charlene Manor and spent the day with her.

Even when she appeared comatose, curled up in fetal position, he sensed that she knew he was there. He came to realize that the sound of his voice was what sustained her in this alien place.

So he got into the habit of settling back in his chair by her bed and telling the story of their marriage to whoever would listen: how they had first met, the city girl and the farm boy; how he courted her in a horse-drawn surrey; their three remarkable sons; the countless adventures and happenings in their long years together. Sometimes Pauline roused and, in a lucid moment, corrected him or added a recollection of her own.

As time went by, she became so weak that she couldn't manage getting out of bed by herself or even walk a few steps unaided.

Phillips visited her one afternoon and found her sitting quietly with several other patients at the end of the hallway by the window. When he walked over and greeted her by name, she looked up at him, puzzled.

"Are you my uncle?" she asked.

"No, I'm your brother Phillips," he said gently.

When he wheeled her back to her room, she sat on the edge of the bed; and he settled into her wheelchair, facing her. She looked at him a long time, then said, "You are a good man." The last words she ever spoke to him.

Now after only three months at Charlene Manor, Pauline took matters into her own hands. She was my sister—practical, clear-eyed, unsentimental. I believe the fact that she didn't recognize her own brother propelled her into action. Frail as she was, she summoned the will and the strength to keep climbing out of bed in the night. Once, she tottered down the hall as far as the nurses' station. Finally, she fell and broke her hip.

Her living will determined that she be kept as comfortable as possible and allowed to let go within a few days' time of a life that was slowly being robbed of its essence by *The Long Forgetting*.

She had lived the life she'd dreamed of as a young girl. Now it was over, and she did not intend to stick around.

When Pauline died, I went home to attend her memorial service, as did Lisa and Jennifer. They flew back to Kentucky after a few days, but I stayed on to spend a few weeks with Malcolm.

Pauline's loss was devastating for us both. She and Malcolm had been married for almost sixty years. Their farm had become the home place I came back to year after year. I thought of Malcolm as "my other brother."

The memorial service was held in the Congregational Church, next to the Page place on Main Street. That's where I'd first met Pierre in the summer of 1941 when I was fifteen. I danced a waltz with him, both of us shy and almost wordless.

The night before the service, some of us drove up to the village to help with food preparation at the church. Noticing that a car was parked in the Pages' driveway, I slipped over there, hoping to find my old friend Sidney.

Years ago, we had played Kick the Can at the Page place in the early evenings, went to parties and get-togethers there, danced to records such as "The Story of a Starry Night," "Deep Purple," and one that went, "Bluebird, have you anything to say to me, can you tell me where my love might be? Is there a garden in the mist where someone's waiting to be kissed . . ." Pauline and I had both dated Sid and enjoyed his friendship. He became an officer in the navy during World War II, sent me his picture, and I wrote to him.

Now there he was, walking slowly toward me in the driveway! White haired, a little bent over, solidly built, he smiled at me in recognition. He spoke with tremendous difficulty, suffering from some serious malady, but his eyes were keenly aware. He had not heard about Pauline's death and was saddened by the news. I invited him to come to the service the next morning, and he did.

Before we parted that evening, he reached out to cup my face in his hands and said, so very slowly, "You . . . are . . . beautiful . . . Julia." I felt like crying.

\*      \*      \*

Malcolm and I were a comfort to each other during the next two weeks. We fixed our meals together, making forays into the garden for fresh vegetables and up into the orchard to pick blueberries and peaches. He baked delicious spelt bread in the bread maker from Pauline's recipe.

And we talked about Pauline, whose essence seemed to permeate the house. We almost expected her to walk into the room at any moment.

Reminiscing about their early years together, he said, "She changed me completely, and I didn't even know it!"

"I grew up smug and narrow-minded here in the valley," he explained. "We thought country people were better than city people, plain folks were better than rich people, that Negroes and Jews and foreigners were inferior. But Pauline gradually knocked all that right out of me.

"She never preached at me or scolded . . . I suppose it was just her own example that did it, the way she reacted to things and related to people."

He was particularly proud of the fact that "all three of our boys grew up without a shred of prejudice."

At last, I understood Pauline's long hesitation before accepting Malcolm's marriage proposal. She was wise enough to see what might be ahead for her if she became a member of the Clark family of Apple Valley. Impatient with her seeming reluctance to marry the man she loved, I remember stamping my foot and saying hotly, "If you don't marry him, I will!"

When I told Malcolm this, he shouted with laughter, saying, "What a catastrophe that would have been!"

## Reading My Diary to Claire

Toward the end of my stay in Apple Valley, Claire invited me down for the evening and to spend the night. This time, I brought my tattered diary with me. After supper was over, the dishes cleared away, and the kitchen set to rights, we settled down across the dining room table from each other. By the light of a kerosene lamp, fortified by a bottle of wine, I read my diary to Claire.

It was the first time in all these years that I had shared it with anyone.

Listening to myself read, I was sixteen again. How very young I was . . . how caught up in the spell of this exciting fellow who turned up at D.O.'s party that September evening and a few hours later was carrying me home perched sideways on the bar of his bike as we hurtled down the dark, wet night.

My long hair flying in his face must have made visibility difficult. I was surely uncomfortable, but I don't remember that. I only remember being entranced, my face wet from the rain, feeling safe with him, aware of the heat radiating from him, loving the lusty sound of his voice as he sang.

Claire and I drank the whole bottle of wine, then paused about halfway through the narrative while she opened a second bottle. Briefly, that broke the spell, but then we were back into the story full tilt.

I took these pictues of Malcolm and of Pauline with her
walking horse stallion Ike in 1981.

Both of us were emotionally drained when I closed my diary. We had spent three hours caught up in the past. I think Claire came away with a sure sense at last of the vitality and persona of the brother she had never known. And my heart ached all over again at losing him.

When I read her the part about going to see Pierre's family, Claire said, "You should have come back! My mother would have treasured you."

But I didn't know that.

## Goodbye, Eva

Eva Horton had been urging me to spend a month with her, but a week was all I could manage that summer. Malcolm drove me in to Greenfield to catch a bus to Portland, Maine. Since my last visit, Eva had bought a third mansion on Victorian Terrace and was in process of renovating it, dividing it into charming upscale apartments for bed-and-breakfast weekends or longer stays.

Although her cancer was in remission, I sensed that I would soon lose her. We went to art exhibits, craft fairs, flea markets, and the grocery store and stayed up talking late into the night. At a huge flea market, she found a Chagall poster for $2 and couldn't believe her good luck!

We celebrated my seventy-seventh birthday eating lobster and drinking wine at sunset on her deck after having salad and wine at a boat turned restaurant while our lobsters were being cooked. She gave me a journal in a tooled leather jacket and encouraged me to write in it every day. I've done so ever since.

I was up at dawn each morning to take a long walk, then do my exercises on her deck. After writing in her own journal, the habit of a lifetime, she would descend the stairs from her third-floor apartment and burst exuberantly into the kitchen-sitting room, ready for the breakfast we fixed and ate together. Then after she met briefly with her staff, off we would go to wherever. The weather was spectacular day after day, and she had plenty of energy for our adventures.

One evening, she went to bed early, leaving me with a stack of her journals. I read them far into the night. I found the following entry on the March 3, 1998, page of her journal: "When I was married [to Toby], I had forgotten that I am smart, I am beautiful and I have choices. Now I know."

I also read her February 20, 1998, entry, telling about meeting me in Cambridge after the National Chimney Sweep Guild convention I covered in Boston.

> And here we are at the Hyatt Regency in Cambridge. Room with a river view, 8th floor. The sun is rising over the city, the hum of traffic is constant, crows and gulls fly over the river—rowing crews practicing on the river . . . I used to come to this hotel 20 years ago, doing stove business—good memories!! Lots of them.
>
> My friendship with Jay is a gift. She is remarkable, fun, inspiring and warm. We dined elegantly in the rotating restaurant on the 16th floor . . . talked and talked . . . and as we tucked in, Jay said, "I can't figure out men, can't figure out women, so I'm gonna brush my teeth and go to bed . . . My horse makes more sense!"

Eva died the following January. A photograph of her sits here on my desk, watching over me. Gazing at her picture, I sometimes find myself talking to her, telling her what's happening in my life. I shall miss her always.

After that wrenching phone call from Eva's daughter, I threw myself into writing a feature story about her for *SNEWS* because writing is one of the ways I'm able to process and endure my grief.

On a tight deadline, I labored over it all week, finishing up on a Saturday night and faxing it to Jim Gillam.

Then I headed for Tim and Jane's place, which my "surprise" granddaughter, Susan, (Doug's daughter) and her birth mother, Mary, had managed to find in the dark. They had just driven down from Cincinnati to meet the Berea Hensleys. (Susan and her husband, Ken, wouldn't meet Doug, Heather, and Susan's half-brother, Rowan, and half-sister, Julia, in Sooke, British Columbia, until spring. It would prove a happy time for all of them.)

The next morning at my house, Jennifer, Susan, Mary, and I sat around marveling at how a whole new branch of the family had ensued from what Mary characterized as "a roll in the hay" so many years before.

The baby pictures Susan brought with her looked a lot like Doug's, and now she had mannerisms and facial expressions that mimicked his! It was quite amazing. "Well," Mary said, "I think she looks like me too!" Which she does. Mother and daughter are both dark-eyed, dark-haired beauties.

Doug would meet his grandson Zachary, almost four, the following summer in Berea at a Hensley family reunion. There were twenty-four of us, including my friend Nannette from Lexington, who brought along Annabelle, her three-year-old granddaughter. Belle and Zack were inseparable.

## Another Sad Goodbye

Eva was not the only friend I lost in 2004. Back on Staten Island, New York, Anne (Smith) Falevsky had been battling ovarian cancer for several years. In the fall of 2003, her condition worsened. Over the winter and spring, I talked to her often on the phone, both of us full of memories of our childhood together, our teenage adventures and romances in Bay Ridge and Ashfield.

She, Libby Shannon, Anne Alevizon and I had attended that last year of high school together at Fort Hamilton High, then went our separate ways, off to college, jobs, wedded bliss (or not!), and motherhood.

On a Saturday morning in May 2004, Anne's husband, Harlow, called, waking me up. In tears, he told me that Anne had died the night before.

Knowing she was bedridden and starting to leave us, I had called her a few days earlier. It was to be our last conversation.

"It's strange, Julia, so strange," she said. "I'm not in any pain . . . I just keep slipping in and out of sleep . . . poor Harlow . . . it's so strange . . ."

All through the years, her voice had always sounded the same, calm and forever young, just as it had in high school. This time, it was different. Dreamy. Hushed. Fading away.

After talking to Harlow, trying to comfort him, I wandered through the house, aching to reminisce with someone else who had loved Anne. I dialed Libby's number up in Wyandotte, Michigan, and left a message on her answering machine. I ended up going over to Jennifer's and hanging out with her while she transplanted some flats of flowers into her garden.

Libby returned my call a few evenings later. At first, we talked a lot about Anne. Libby described her as "serene."

I'd been out of touch with Libby since she wrote an article for *SNEWS* in the 1990s, describing her frightening experience with long-term carbon monoxide poisoning from a faulty gas furnace in the old house where she had raised her kids. She is an excellent writer.

At seventy-seven, she was still spunky, determined, and working full-time. She was to travel shortly to a Qigong workshop in Minneapolis, with the goal of learning it well enough to use it in some meditation counseling work she was doing. She was living out of one room in a retirement complex, having had a hardscrabble life since her divorce years earlier.

(A few years after our conversation about Anne, Libby's old high school sweetheart, Roy, now a wealthy widower, contacted her. They found that they were still dear to each other, and her life began to change.)

Talking to Libby triggered my memories of Anne. She was not athletically inclined—never interested, like me, in softball, basketball, horseback riding, skiing, roller-skating, ice-skating, and other sports. But oh, she could dance!

Her last two years of high school, she dated Earl. He was never her "boyfriend," she insisted, but she enjoyed his friendship; and he was a brilliant dancer who coached her on all the latest steps.

She piled up a big record collection—Frank Sinatra, Glenn Miller, and all the hits of the day. On many a Saturday afternoon, I rode my bike to her house, and we listened to them on her record player. We sang all the lyrics and cavorted around the living room, and she taught me to dance, especially to jitterbug, which was all the rage. What fun it was!

In Ashfield, we walked downstreet to the dance at the town hall on Saturday nights, wearing our colorful broomstick skirts and peasant blouses. We always found partners. Soon out of breath and soaked with sweat, we square-danced, jitterbugged, polkaed, and waltzed across the floor. She was with me the night I met Art Smith, the summer Malcolm and Ralph Townsley ran the dances.

I still remember Malcolm's lively New England twang riding skillfully atop the music, "The head two gents step forward and by their ladies stand. The side two gents step forward, and all join hands. Bow to your partners, ladies. Bow to your partners, all, and promenade the hall!" as he led us through the square dances. "Swing your partners, then hand in hand, take her to the promised land!"

Then there were those lazy, hazy days of summer when Anne and I spent whole afternoons floating around our pond in black inner tubes, sometimes sighting the fearsome turtle (probably harmless) that sent us paddling wildly for the shore.

I have a favorite snapshot of Anne at seventeen or eighteen, one I took with my old box camera as she stood on the sidewalk in front of her house on Eighty-ninth Street in Bay Ridge. She was tall and slim, with long blond hair, beautiful without makeup, and—Libby was right—serene.

# 44

# GATHERINGS OF THE CLANS, 2005

## *Uncle Dave and Malcolm Leave Us*

Dave told me once that when it came time for him to die, he did not intend to linger. And he didn't.

My cousin Liz called Monday afternoon on May 10, 2004, with the news. Her dad had died at ten that morning. He was ninety-four. He'd been fine on Friday, became congested and confused over the weekend, and was hospitalized. The diagnosis: pneumonia. They had not expected him to die, and Isabel was in shock that he was so suddenly gone.

He and Isabel had been content and happy at their Heritage Village retirement complex outside Morgantown, West Virginia, where they had their own apartment with a small balcony off the living room. Dave planted and tended his own vegetable garden there and took long walks every day through the countryside.

The Joneses clan gathered in Morgantown on June 14. Lisa, Jennifer, and I had driven in from Kentucky for this high-spirited, soul-feeding weekend. In our hotel room, we three crashed; and they, who had done all the driving, went right to sleep. Almost immediately, the phone rang. It was my cousin Wayne, Harry and Minnie's son, calling from a few rooms away. "Everyone's here in 2004. Come on over!"

I staggered down the hall, barefoot and groggy. "Everyone" included Wayne and his wife Marilyn, their daughters Janet and her

sister Sally's toddler Henry; Wayne's sister Janet and husband Nick;
my California cousins Cathy, her brother David (who looks like his
father, my Uncle Russ) and his wife Susan.

Nick has been one of my favorite people ever since I met him
at our Estes Park, Colorado, family reunion in the 1970s and
hiked up a mountain with him and my California cousin Dave.
A lanky lovable six feet four, Nick was "married to the Union."
Consequently, he wasn't home much through the years; but Janet
said that when he was, he made up for it. Their three daughters
adored him. What fun it was to see them all again! How I always do
enjoy my Jones kin, the offspring of my father's four brothers.

Phillips and Ereda had arrived earlier but were conked out in
room 202. Uncle Dave's other children—Liz, Ellen, Sally, and
David—were busy attending to last-minute details or were with their
mother.

## A Time for Remembering

We gathered at the Heritage Village chapel where my cousin
Sally had put on display many photos from her father's life. There
was a wonderful one of him water-skiing on Cheat Lake, also a
portrait from his college years, and a later one with a beard and long
gray hair. We looked at pictures and visited with Isabel before the
service started.

What followed was a grand celebration of Uncle Dave's life
and times. We all had our stories to tell. One after another—family,
friends, colleagues, neighbors from the village—we came forward
to share our memories.

My favorite story was one his son David told us. Uncle Dave
was an opera lover and listened to many a Saturday broadcast
of the Metropolitan Opera. David was an avid baseball fan and
remembered watching many a Saturday afternoon game on a muted
TV with an opera blaring forth from the radio in the next room.

I described Uncle Dave's summer visits to Ashfield in the 1930s
and our adventures together and how once I suddenly right-angled
my galloping horse into a wood road, and his horse almost dumped
him as she scrambled over a stone wall, trying to follow.

Also, I told about that day in a Chicago hospital when I was twenty-three, and he performed some minor surgery on me. Under local anesthetic, I closed my eyes and tried to be brave. Afterward, his surgical nurse told me he turned the operation over to another doctor midway through. She said she'd never seen Dr. Jones do that before.

Later, I asked him what it was like cutting into a family member and if it wasn't hard to do. "No no. Nothing to it," he said. I never did tell him I knew he'd copped out.

The sharing went on an on, causing both laughter and tears. I think it meant a lot to Isabel to have us all there, remembering together.

There were also many fond letters and e-mails from former students. Dave had been quietly passionate in his teaching of gross anatomy to medical students. Again and again, they had chosen him as their favorite teacher. One year, they presented him with a wonderful carving of him water-skiing, hair and beard flying in the wind.

His medical practice was primarily limited to his students and their families—he had delivered their babies, seen them through difficult times, and knew them far better than most college professors know their students.

Afterward, some of us walked up the hill to see the tree planted in Uncle Dave's name, with a bench and commemorative plaque nearby. Cameras were clicking, and I noticed my cousin Sally had an interracial boy with her about the same age as Henry. We hadn't heard that story yet! (He turns out to be my cousin Sally's daughter Jennifer's lovable illegitimate son, Darrien. Sally has taken on much of the responsibility for his care.)

Dave and Isabel's marriage had been a compatible, enduring one. Through the years, Isabel had also become quite fond of my children. Finally, I think, she forgave me for my youthful insensitivity and even became rather fond of me too.

Once, Dave commented to me that he thought a man ought to be able to live peacefully together with both his wife and mistress in the same house. "So, Dave," I said, "does that mean that if Isabel had a man on the side, he should be able to move in too?"

I can still remember the shocked, outraged look on his face at this suggestion. I laughed and laughed at him.

## My Week with Malcolm

Malcolm died quickly and unexpectedly in the spring of 2005. I was glad that I had been able to spend a week with him in August of 2004 after covering a ten-day masonry-heater-building workshop in Vermont for the Masonry Heater Association.

This had been an intense assignment for me. I had just bought a new state-of-the-art computer, then had to learn how to use it, a borrowed digital camera, and Photoshop software in just a few weeks' time. Such things do not come easy for me!

After the workshop, one of the attendees—an old friend from my *SNEWS* years—drove me right to Malcolm's door.

At eighty-four, this frugal Yankee farmer had splurged on a six-wheeler runabout, a two-seater that gave him the mobility he craved. Within minutes of my arrival, he said, "Let's go!"

I fastened my seat belt and hung on like mad as we sped up the mountain and through the orchards at breakneck speed. After all, this was the same fellow who, in his younger days, competed in gymkhanas and chased wild heifers across rough terrain on his horse, Judy.

One day, Malcolm and I whizzed on down the Apple Valley road for a long visit with Martha Townsley, the widow of his lifelong friend Ralph. We also monitored progress down at the apple storage where Malcolm's son Dana maneuvered an earthmover with great skill while his own son, Silas, was at the wheel of a dump truck.

They were preparing the site for an addition to the storage and apple-processing facility, which would include a covered loading bay for two big semitrucks that carry the apples to market.

Malcolm had rebounded somewhat from Pauline's death and was content. There were still times when grief and loneliness overtook him, but life was essentially good there on the farm where he was born and spent most of his life.

"I have my boys," he told me. "There's always something interesting going on, things for me to do. I have this place and no money worries . . . And I love talking about Pauline."

He had acquired quite a reputation as a storyteller and never tired of relating the happenings and adventures of their life together.

## The Memorial Service

Like Uncle Dave, Malcolm did not linger.

"I just want to be with Pauline," he said shortly before succumbing to heart failure less than a year later. I went home to Apple Valley for ten days for the gathering of the clan and to help go through his and my sister's belongings.

For the memorial service, his three sons had put together, and Dana narrated, a computer-generated slide show of the Clark family history there in the valley. They used old pictures from family photo albums, including a black-and-white close-up I'd taken of Malcolm in 1981, which was printed on the program and used to introduce the slide show.

My own favorite picture that day was one I'd never seen before of Pauline and Malcolm sitting on the Clark farm's first tractor. It was taken the first year of their marriage, and Pauline was holding a kitten.

At the end of the slide presentation, people were invited to share their memories. I found myself telling about the time Malcolm asked me to ride Judy for him at a gymkhana he couldn't attend. He wanted me to prevent his archrivals, Arnold Goodyear and Whitey Streeter, from amassing points toward a special trophy awarded each year. I was eighteen, home from college for the summer.

The big-ticket event was the potato race, which ran four heats with four competitors each, then a final heat to determine the champion. A box nailed to four posts at the far end of the course contained four potatoes. The starting-line posts had empty boxes. We raced to the far end, wheeled around the post, grabbed a potato, galloped back to the starting line, and plunked it into the box there. We repeated this process three times. I was the only girl competing.

I won my heat. Arnold and Whitey won theirs. Then with pounding heart and flushed face, I won the final heat. A slip of a girl on a great horse! The spectators went wild, and I'll never forget it.

## Evening at Pauline and Malcolm's

That evening, sons, daughters-in-law, grandchildren, and I gathered at Pauline and Malcolm's. Their son Brian read aloud from the stack of farm diaries Malcolm had kept day after day, year after year. It was crammed with such things as "fixed the tractor," "took the Jamaicans to Greenfield for groceries," "shod Pauline's horses," "apple picking started," "heavy rains washed out the valley road," "a freeze predicted" . . .

Now and then, he inserted a cryptic "Dana married," "Aaron married," and, finally, "Brian married Susan." Colleen and Jackie were outraged that Susan was the only wife whose name Malcolm mentioned.

We cried, and we laughed. It was a time for remembering, for being grateful for the lives Pauline and Malcolm had lived together on this thriving five-generation Clark farm. With Malcolm's death, I felt that an era in my own life had ended. But everyone made me feel like a member of the Clark family, and I hope to keep returning to Apple Valley.

Before catching a plane back to Kentucky, I spent a day and a night with Claire, plus two lovely days in Amherst with Phil and Ereda.

## A Visit with Claire

Claire was by then a permanent resident of South Ashfield. But off-the-grid living year-round at her isolated place is not always easy. Although the county did some long-needed repair and maintenance work on Bird Hill Road and keeps it snowplowed for her, the winters are still a challenge. Claire finds it helps to take a few trips in the dead of winter to visit friends in New York City and elsewhere.

She is busy in the fall of the year, raking leaves or high up on a ladder cleaning out gutters or carting load after load of firewood to the house and stacking it in the cellar as winter approaches. Through the years, she has gradually been repairing and repainting all the rooms, redoing old plastered ceilings . . . endlessly determined and productive.

In the evenings, she can often be found curled up in a chair, reading a novel or the latest Sunday edition of the *New York Times*. Since having solar panels installed to supply electricity to the house in 2003, she no longer needs to read by the light of a kerosene lamp.

After selling her apartment in Manhattan, Claire still had many photos, papers, and other paraphernalia from her family's past to sort and organize. The evening of my visit, we looked through boxes of old pictures together and found some of Pierre—excellent black-and-white proof sheets of studio pictures taken on his furlough before going overseas and even a few snapshots of him at seventeen or eighteen.

The only picture I'd had all these years was a small close-up portrait of him that his mother sent me. With the billed officer's cap sitting low on his forehead, covering his hair, it didn't look much like the Pierre I'd known, except for those dark eyes.

There were many fine proof-sheet poses of him with his three sisters. I especially loved several of him with little Claire . . . Studying these photos, I began to have a sense of the man Pierre was already becoming following his months of training at Fort Benning.

We also found copies of Pierre's memorial service program and the roll-of-honor page about him from a Phillips Academy publication. We gathered all this up for me to take back to Apple Valley where Aaron would scan them into his computer and burn a disk for me.

Pierre's Phillips Academy yearbook has never surfaced.

Claire built a fire that evening. It drew well and threw out lots of good heat. We pulled our chairs close, sipped wine, and visited long over our salad and toasted English muffins. I slept in Pierre's old room that night. It took me a long time to go to sleep. I felt his presence and did not want to give that up.

## A Devastating Dream

Two nights later, at Phil and Ereda's, I had a terrible dream. The setting was somewhat like my farmhouse on the Jessamine Creek, but not quite. I looked out a small narrow window to see two men coming across the yard, supporting Phillips between them, his head down and knees wobbly.

I rushed out the front door just in time to see them ease him to the ground. He huddled there in a fetal position, arms across his chest, and glanced up at me with stricken eyes.

"Has anyone called a doctor?" I asked as I bent over him.

One of the men was Dana. He looked at me sorrowfully with an expression on his face that signified "Too late."

I awoke into darkness and lay there in great distress. After a while, I started to cry and thought about Pauline and Malcolm and Uncle Dave. And Pierre and Daddy and Scotty and Eva. "They're all gone from my life now . . . they're gone . . ."

At six thirty in the morning, while I sat in the living room of the quiet house, I saw Phillips, sound and whole, pass by in the hallway in his underwear. Soon, he would be taking Ereda to her morning swim session, then return, and eat breakfast with me.

After a short walk in the cold morning air, I started packing.

### An Accident in the Clark Orchards

The summer following Malcolm's memorial service, Dana and Colleen's daughter, Naomi, had a four-wheeler accident up in the orchard one late-July day. A beautiful, athletic, high-spirited girl of twenty, she was chasing her brother, Silas, on his motorcycle up through the orchards when it happened.

They were having a great time until Silas suddenly bounced through a ditch they didn't know was there. He managed to keep his bike upright, but Naomi's four-wheeler hit the ditch and overturned. Although wearing a helmet, she suffered a broken back, leaving her paralyzed from midchest down.

With injuries similar to the ones that had left her uncle Aaron in a wheelchair a generation earlier, Naomi was at first devastated. She was between jobs and had no health care insurance. Then with her parents raising money from family and friends to make long-term rehab available, she resolved to go through whatever it would take to enable her to reach her first goal of riding her horse again.

Naomi was soon in outpatient therapy five or more hours a day at the Neuro Institute in Phoenix where they specialize in spinal cord injuries, brain injuries, and strokes. She has kept us all posted on her progress with long and frequent e-mails and accompanying pictures.

The rehab she is required to do is hard, it's painful, it's full of triumphs and setbacks. I am amazed at her courage, perseverance, and impressive upper body strength.

At the end of every e-mail is this quotation: "The only disability in life is a bad attitude."

My Uncle Dave.

# 45

## STOPOVER IN SARATOGA SPRINGS

### *The Story of a Chimney Sweep Family*

On my way to Ashfield for Malcolm's memorial service, I had stopped over in New York State to spend a few days with the Pete Looker family, old friends from my *SNEWS* years. I flew into Albany, arriving around nine in the evening.

Pete usually met me at the airport. One time, in July, he was wearing a top hat and shorts; and on the way to retrieving my luggage, talking a mile a minute, we discovered we were holding hands.

So now I scanned the crowd, looking for a man of medium height, with a strong muscular build, shaggy brown hair, a full beard, glasses, and gentle blue eyes. He has always reminded me of my son Doug—his temperament, quiet intensity, tenacity, and great sense of the ridiculous in our lives and the world.

"Pete is a very stubborn guy and has taught me the value of the tortoise, him, and the hare, me," his wife, Terri Roben, told me once. And it was she I now spied coming toward me at the airport. We hugged each other, walked to the baggage claim area, and pulled my suitcase from the carousel.

"You're one of Pete's favorite people," Terri volunteered as we walked to the parking lot. "He's taking tomorrow off to spend the day with you."

Driving into the outskirts of Saratoga Springs, Terri said, "Pete's still waging peace wherever he goes." She slowed down and pointed to Pete's dark green sweep van where it was parked at a big intersection not far off the interstate.

## Waging Peace

Painted in large white letters on the back of it were these words: An Illegal War, Based on Lies, and in even larger letters, BRING 'EM HOME.

Terri explained that he leaves his van in a conspicuous parking place after work every day and rides his bike home. He changes the message every month or so, using his van like a traveling billboard. Thousands of people see it every day.

Low-key, cheerful, and friendly, he waves at people as he drives about town. Terri keeps expecting people to splatter his van with rotten eggs or tomatoes, but it has only happened once. When the family went to Europe for a month one year, he left his van in a 24-7 parking space. "A friend watched it and washed off the eggs, hopefully from happy free-rangers," Pete said.

Other van messages have included the following:

> Try Peace, Not Empire.
> 100,000 Iraqi Dead—Enough?
> Is War Insane?
> If You Love the Troops, Bring Them Home!
> WHY IMPEACH? War Crimes—Torture—Corruption—
> Treason.
> (with check marks next to each answer)

"My effort is toward provocative questions," Pete explains. "Although sometimes I just vent—being a venting professional!"

Off duty, wherever he goes for a few hours each week—shopping at the grocery store, waiting for a bus, running errands—he's been known to wear a George W. Bush mask and carry a sign on his back that says Kick Me or Untax the Rich or

Impeach Me! Sometimes he dons a jester's cap and a sign saying Join Fools for War.

"Just having a little fun," Pete says, "and hopefully, leaving the world a better place."

He and Terri like to quote a Quaker proverb: "Let us take the risks of peace upon our lives, not impose the risks of war upon the world." And he lives by the Buddhist mantra of "Think globally, act locally."

Pete was at their small frame house when Terri and I got there. As we sat up late talking, three cats bounded happily about the living room. When I had last visited them in this same house in 2001, we were surrounded by boxes, with only some kitchen stuff, bedding, and a few clothes having been unpacked. They were in the process of moving from a rental house—something they hadn't mentioned to me, afraid I might not come.

The next morning of my 2005 visit, Pete and I had a great time on a walking tour of their working-class neighborhood of small well-cared-for houses and yards. Many of the garages had been turned into workshops or guest quarters, and it was fun seeing the different results.

Pete and Terri enjoyed living in this neighborhood. They had put down roots here and made new friends. They liked what Saratoga Springs, the city with a small-town flavor, had to offer. And they liked being able to walk or ride their bikes in so many places. So after Caitlin went off to college three years earlier, they had stayed on instead of returning to Ballston Lake as planned.

But fate was about to intervene.

**The Right Thing . . .**

"Sometimes you reluctantly do what you believe is the right thing," Pete told me. "Like buying a house in Saratoga Springs. But then it turns out to your great advantage." And he went on to tell me of the big change about to take place in their lives.

A developer was buying up all the properties in their neighborhood, planning to replace them with expensive condos.

Now Pete and Terri decided they would move back to Ballston Lake after all.

At noon, we meandered across a nearby park to their food co-op for a delicious and hearty vegetarian lunch in the cafeteria. The day went quickly as we caught up on one another's lives.

## What Terri Does

Terri had left for work right after breakfast. She's self-employed as a guitarist and singer who writes many of her own songs. One of her commitments is working with children in the schools and elsewhere, teaching them about recycling, healthy foods, peace, and living a worthwhile life from the heart. She particularly enjoys her sessions with preschoolers and their caretakers—mostly moms and sometimes dads and grandparents.

Once in the early 1980s, Terri was invited by the organizers to sing with guitarist and civil rights and peace activist Pete Seeger at a statewide labor rally in Albany, which she loved doing. She also spent time as a Pete Seeger volunteer, doing such things as peeling potatoes with him at peace conferences and festivals.

"He bought several copies of my *Riverwalk* album and asked me to send him a copy of my song 'A Great Capacity,' which is on my new CD," Terri told me. Her family CD, *Riverwalk and Other Songs*, as well as *The Path We Make* CD are both available at http://*www. terriroben.com*.

In late afternoon after Terri got home, she and Pete showed me some videotapes of Caitlin dancing. She was away at Bennington College in Vermont. Dance is her passion; and she was a delight to watch—petite, five foot two, graceful, long blonde hair, a lovely face.

It made me ache to see her again. The summer before, she had participated in a dance program in Italy and would be going there again in a few months.

## The Moon and River Café

After watching Caitlin's videos, we went to the Moon and River Café in the historic Stockade district of Schenectady for the rest of the evening. It was a small and cozy place, with tables to seat maybe eighteen people and a jar for donations to pay the musicians. This was one of Terri's weekly gigs. She performed solo and also in a trio of musicians.

Most of the songs she sang were her own. With her curly reddish brown hair, expressive face, and top-of-the-line talent, she captivated her audience. I requested "Friends and Lovers," a song about her and Pete that never fails to bring tears to my eyes. (She has since renamed it "The Way of Love," and it is one of the selections on her most recent CD.)

She had not sung it for a while, and Pete quietly thanked me. The chorus goes like this: "My lover, my friend, darling we were meant to be; lovers and friends, setting each other free." Another song I requested was "Sirens of Emergency," inspired by Pete's five years as a volunteer firefighter, telling what it was like waiting for him to come home safely from a fire.

In the mid-1980s, their own house in Scotia-Glenville burned down due to faulty *new* wiring. They lost just about everything, including all Pete's copies of *SNEWS* (his favorite magazines were *SNEWS* and *Utne Reader*). We gave him a complete set of back issues to replace them.

## Road Trip

I packed my bag the next morning, expecting to take a bus to Amherst, Massachusetts. But at breakfast, Pete announced that he was going to drive me there instead, detouring to Bennington College along the way to see Caitlin!

It was a beautiful road trip on a cool, sunny late-April day up through the kind of hill country I love, with the trees in process of leafing out.

Caitlin was waiting for us in the lounge of her dorm and gave us a walking tour of the campus. We visited all the classroom buildings too, and I thought what a great college this would have been for Stephani. Jen and Lisa would have loved it too.

It would, in fact, have been a fine choice of college for me!

The curricula included ballet, African and modern dance, theater arts, sculpture, all the fine arts, music of all kinds, dance, photography, literature, marine biology, political science, writing, journalism, film, languages, etc.

On our way once more, toward Brattleboro to pick up Route 91, we stopped for lunch at a roadside deli. We sat out in Terri's '95 Subaru, eating our tasty organic veggie sandwiches and talking.

Beyond our car windows as we hit the highway again were mountains, a few trees leafing out, a sprinkle of rain; but the weather was mostly cloudy, the sun appearing now and then. It was a magical road trip, and I couldn't think of anybody I'd rather be spending the day with.

We stopped in Apple Valley at the Clark farm where nobody seemed to be around. We could hear men's voices and the buzz of equipment running somewhere. It started to drizzle as we walked up through the orchards. I had told Pete so much about my sister and Malcolm and this farm. It was a treat to show it all to him at last.

After that, we drove the three miles up the mountain to Ashfield, passing the Big Pond at the edge of the village where Pierre and I had spent so many hours together.

On Main Street, I pointed out the town hall where I went square-dancing on Saturday nights, the library where I tied my pony to the hitching post in front, the church where I was married, the Page place where we played Kick the Can, had parties, and danced to records, and where I first met Pierre.

We turned off Main Street by the watering trough, now planted with flowers, and drove up South Street to the Place. We gazed at the rambling house, red barn, apple orchards, and pond that held so many memories for me. Then we walked slowly down the rocky, tree-shaded lane.

We arrived in Amherst in time for dinner with Phillips and Ereda, after which Pete headed for the Massachusetts Turnpike and drove on home to Saratoga Springs only two hours away.

**Early Memories**

I first met Pete and Terri at a sweep convention in the mid-1980s. One evening, Terri played her guitar for a group of us and sang a song she'd written about cleaning chimneys with Pete.

In the late 1970s, Pete had a job working with adults with developmental disabilities at Letchworth Village in Rockland County but felt the need for some more physically demanding part-time work to give balance to his life.

On Christmas night in 1977, he had a chimney fire in the "shack" (that's what Terri called it!) he lived in and heated with a woodstove. It scared the hell out of him. Soon after that, he read the January '78 *TMEN* article, visited Tom Risch in Connecticut, and bought one of his chimney-cleaning kits. He started practicing on his friend's chimneys, made some mistakes, learned a lot, and then hung out his shingle, so to speak.

Pete and Terri met in 1978. In 1980-82, they both worked at the Oswald D. Heck Developmental Center, a State institution in Schenectady that housed clients with various disabilities. Pete was union president there for two years. He was also a part-time sweep, he and Terri were living together, and she cleaned chimneys with him for a year just to help him out. (Pete likes to tell people, "Terri and I swept together before we were married.")

"But I only did that for a year," Terri told me. "Because we were working together full-time and part-time, and it was our first year living together. We were suffocating with no time apart. After that year, I told him to find a new partner and let me do the phone and scheduling work."

They were married in 1982, and Caitlin was born in 1984. Terri's song "Sleep" on her *The Path We Make* CD brings back vivid memories of my own struggle to get enough sleep with a new baby in the house.

Once she got her motherhood role under control, she continued developing her part-time professional career as a musician. She still kept the books and did the scheduling for Pete, whose sweep business had become a full-time job.

**A Sweep Family Weekend**

In the mid to late 1990s, I often made it to the New York State guild's annual sweep family summer weekend and workshops at Chris and Ingrid Prior's fifty-three-acre spread outside Middle Grove. Pete would meet me at the Albany Airport and take me to his family's three-acre homestead in Ballston Lake where I would tiptoe into the small bedroom I shared with Caitlin and crash.

Pete and I were off to the Priors' the next day, arriving in time for the noon meal, which officially began the weekend for anywhere from one hundred to 150 people. Terri and Caitlin usually came later in the day.

It was an exuberant weekend of meeting new sweeps, seeing old friends, swimming, walking in the woods, taking copious notes and pictures for *SNEWS*, and eating great food on long tables under a huge canvas canopy. Kids were racing about, jumping in the pool, and renewing friendships made in earlier years.

One year, Pete, seven-year-old Caitlin, and I shared a tent for the whole sweep family weekend—Terri never did like camping out. The next year, Pete brought along two small tents, and we pitched them side by side on a hilly site in the woods. A hellacious storm roared in during the night and flooded out all the campers on low ground. Hunkered down in our tents, we listened to the rain and the shouts of dismay and stayed high and dry.

As always on the last day, we watched Chris's top-burn fire far into the night. He carefully built it up, using half a cord of wood or more, then lit the cedar shavings at the top with one match. The fire would travel downward and burn for many hours. We had to keep moving our chairs back as the fire grew hotter and hotter while some moms and dads slipped quietly away to their tents or campers with sleepy children in tow.

In 1999, the whole family, including Caitlin and her best friend, Emily, came to see me at my farm on the Jessamine Creek; and I took them for a good visit with Tim and Jane fifty miles away in their mountain-hollow farm outside Berea.

Tim knows Pete and Terri from our *SNEWS* years, and Jane first met them when she attended one of the New York guild's sweep family weekends with Tim and me. She even set up her massage table there and had a few grateful sweep customers.

## Caitlin's School

The Lookers had moved to Ballston Lake in 1994 so Caitlin could catch a bus to her Spring Hill Waldorf School in Saratoga Springs fourteen miles away, ten miles closer than their previous daily commute by car from Scotia-Glenville where they had built another house after the first one burned down.

The family spent so much time in Saratoga Springs in connection with the school, which is run by teachers and parents, that they finally moved there in 1999. Caitlin attended Spring Hill for ten years and graduated in 2002.

The school offers kindergarten through twelfth grade, with a student body of about 250, including sixty-five in high school. Eurythmy, one of its unique features, is part of the weekly life of every student. It is a movement discipline developed by Rudolf Steiner for learning body awareness and expressive ways to communicate poetry and music. "Eurythmy was very appealing for Caitlin's natural dance instincts," Terri told me.

American history classes in the eleventh and twelfth grades used a textbook by historian and peace activist Howard Zinn. This came about due to Pete's suggestion as a member of the school's board of directors. Zinn's grand and enlightening book is titled *A People's History of the United States*. First published in 1980, it is authentic history, not what most of us were exposed to in school!

Zinn tells America's story from the viewpoint and often in the words of our country's women, factory workers, farmers, Native Americans, immigrants, the working poor, and African Americans. This is the history I had been made aware of in bits and pieces by my father, who was familiar with the real story of America and its people.

Pete, Terri, and I have some of the same heroes: Howard Zinn, Dennis Kucinich, Pete Seeger, Joni Mitchell, Gloria Steinem, Oprah . . . to mention just a few. "Anyone," says Pete, "who has devoted their lives to making the world a better place." (He told me he even has my son Tim and me on his list.)

To my own list, I would add at least six more:

- Terri Roben and Pete Looker
- A. A. Milne of Christopher Robin and *Winnie-the-Pooh* fame. He also wrote *Peace with Honour* in 1934, exposing the myths of war. Simply written and profound, it should be required reading for every schoolchild, politician, world leader, and the rest of us. (I paid fifteen cents at a yard sale for my copy.)
- Oral historian Studs Terkel, whose books include *Working* and *American Dreams: Lost and Found,* has taught me much about other people in this country—their lives, their work, their hopes, and their dreams.
- Jim Hightower, former secretary of agriculture in Texas who now edits the *Hightower Lowdown*, a dandy populist monthly newsletter
- And closer to home, Tom Gish, courageous longtime editor of the *Mountain Eagle* weekly newspaper in Whitesburg, Kentucky. He and his wife, Pat, crusade untiringly for mine safety and better lives for coal miners and their families and against the powerful coal companies whose strip-mining and mountaintop-removal practices do so much harm to the people and the environment of Appalachia.

Soon after my visit, Pete and Terri sold their house and land in Saratoga Springs for a big profit and moved back to Ballston Lake. The sale money made it possible for them to travel that summer to six European countries and see Caitlin dance in Italy on a mountaintop stage in a medieval village. Then Caitlin returned to the United States with them, traveling through France on the way.

Back home again in Ballston Lake, they started the improvements they'd dreamed of making—building an Amish shed with solar panels for generating household electricity, insulating their house, and planting fruit and nut trees around the property.

I can hardly wait for my next visit.

# MAC GOES MISSING

One day in the late fall of 2005, MacAttack, my seventeen-year-old back-porch cat, went missing. He was not waiting by the kitchen door as usual for his breakfast. It had been a cold, windy, rainy night. I looked under the thick cardboard box with a door cut into it that covers his cozy sleeping pad. No old yellow cat with big green eyes was curled up there asleep.

I could not find him. In the way of all cats, had he known his time had come and slipped away to die, the way Mama Cat had a year or two earlier?

The last time I saw him, my artist friend Holly Van Meter had come for a visit. We found Mac under his box, and he crawled out sleepy eyed to spend a little time with us. He always did love company.

Two weeks after he went missing, he came back. I found him stretched out on the colorful fall leaves near the back porch. His body was still warm, his unseeing emerald green eyes wide open. He had come home to die. But where had he been?

Tenderly, I carried him into the house and called Tim. "I found Mac. Can I bury him over at your place?"

"Come over around five o'clock," Tim said. After he and Levi Gordon finished up some carpentry work, they would help me pick a good spot for Mac's grave.

When I got to Tim's place, he and Levi had already dug Mac's grave by the edge of the woods. They both hugged me close.

Levi is very tall and lean, with long hair, a long beard, and a gentle nature. He is a fine carpenter, jack-of-all-trades, woodsman, and reliable friend. With his wife, Bluebird, he turns up at most of our community work parties and potlucks. And whenever the guitar pickers among us start strumming, Levi pulls out his pennywhistle and joins in the music making. Introducing me to a newcomer once, Levi said, "Jay is everybody's mother."

Several of those work parties a few years ago were at Levi and Bluebird's where they were finally able to build their own grand house for the family, with the help of their friends, after years of living first out of their van and then in a school bus.

After Tim laid Mac in his little grave, I told Levi Mac's story—how he was actually MacAttack II and how I had rescued his daddy after seeing the tiny yellow kitten almost get hit by a truck on a country road. I drove back and found him hunkered down in the weeds. When I picked him up, he sank his teeth into my thumb. I thought he was wild, but he had just been frightened.

We named him MacAttack. When he grew up, he chased dogs and cats, except Nick's Trampas, off the place. He also disappeared for months at a time, then came home to recuperate from his tomcatting. A blasto infection did him in when he was about seven.

But before he died, he sired a litter of Mama Cat's kittens up at Jennifer and Eddie's. One of them was his spittin' image, little Mac. We had him altered so that he wouldn't periodically run off and leave us the way his daddy had.

Because he could never behave himself in the house, Mac became our barn cat. He chased dogs and all other cats out of the yard. He liked to accompany me partway on my daily walk out the lane, then hide in the underbrush and leap out at me in a surprise attack as I walked back.

In his old age, he became wary of dogs and was content with Mama Cat on the back porch in a neighborhood where the dogs outnumber the people.

After I told Mac's story, Tim shoveled dirt into the grave and found a rock to mark it. Levi played several farewell tunes for Mac on his pennywhistle, and that's what I remember most of all.

One early morning, a few weeks before Mac left me, I was doing my Qigong exercises out on the back porch. Thunder rolled, rain beat down on the metal roof, roosters crowed in the distance as the sky changed colors . . . and close by came the loud, contented purring of a cat.

He had been such an everyday part of my life . . . How would I manage now without my old friend?

# 46

## REMEMBERING ERNIE JORDAN

Bob called me one day in January of 2006 to say that he'd heard about Ernie Jordan's death just in time to attend his memorial service. He had saved a program for me and would put it in the mail. He told me that all five of Ernie's children spoke about him at the service "eloquently."

The news saddened me and brought back vivid memories of Ernie, a man with a big heart and a big mission in life. With a doctorate in education and a specialty in marriage counseling, he worked for the Comprehensive Care Center in Lexington. He was our marriage counselor there for many years.

He also held a series of counseling session for all our kids. I was not privy to these meetings, except for the one he scheduled with the whole family at our house. When he asked the children why they thought their father loved their mother, they said the following:

"Because she's beautiful . . ."

"Because she's kind . . .

". . . and funny!"

When he asked them why they thought their mother loved their father, one of them said, "Because he's handsome." They tried hard to come up with some other reasons but couldn't.

I don't think the kids ever realized how much their father loved them.

Because Bob didn't always make it to our marriage counseling sessions—he had an emergency call, or he "just forgot"—I spent a fair amount of time alone with Ernie, getting acquainted. He was married to Dot, and they had four daughters and one son.

During World War II, Ernie was an airplane mechanic for the navy. Afterward, he liked to help people fix their cars. Also a serious gardener, he grew a whole backyard full of vegetables, but his pride and joy was a large ever-bearing red raspberry patch. Once, he picked a quart of them for me.

He was hungry to travel, to see firsthand how other people in other countries lived, related to each other, and raised their children.

I kept in touch with Ernie through the years, visiting with him by phone and sending him all my annual family letters.

When I visited our local library and found his obituary in the Lexington paper, I learned some more about my old friend. The article started out, "Dr. Ernest Edson Jordan left this world for his next adventure on Monday, Jan. 16, 2006. Helping others was the theme of his life."

He worked with the Navajo Indians in Arizona and New Mexico before earning a master's degree in public health at Berkley. In retirement, he and Dorothy, "his partner in adventure for fifty-six years," served in the Peace Corps, first in Paraguay, then in the Solomon Islands.

Below Ernie's picture on the cover of the memorial service program were these two quotes: "Where there's a will, there's a way!" and "Use it up, wear it out, make it do, or do without." On the inside cover are the words to a song included in the service, "If I Had a Hammer."

According to the program, each of his children talked about one of the tools in Ernie's personal bag of tools: character, communication, service, ingenuity, and learning.

Ernie had accumulated and used so many tools that his family didn't know what to do with them. So upon leaving the church after the service, every person there was given one of the tools from Ernie's vast collection. The words to a poem by R. L. Sharpe were printed on the back of the program:

## A Bag of Tools

Isn't it strange
That princes and kings,
And clowns that caper
In sawdust rings,
And common people
Like you and me
Are builders for eternity?

Each is given a bag of tools,
A shapeless mass,
A book of rules;
And each must make—
Ere life is flown—
A stumbling block
Or a stepping stone.

# 47

# A BRIEF HISTORY LESSON

## *Charles de Gaulle and the Fighting French*

In November of 1943, after officer training in Fort Benning, Georgia, Pierre Birel Rosset-Cournand joined General Charles de Gaulle's Free French Army as a commando paratrooper.

De Gaulle was the brilliant young commander of tanks in the Fifth Army. He had fled to England three years earlier after France's premier, Marshall Henri-Philippe Pétain, signed an armistice with Germany. De Gaulle himself would not surrender. Instead, he established his own headquarters in London and set about gathering up patriots under the banner of his Free French Army, often referred to as the Fighting French.

In 1939, France's army had been as strong as Germany's, and few in France believed the Germans would dare to attack them. However, when German forces did attack France in September of that year, they invaded through Belgium, bypassing the formidable Maginot Line and coming through the Ardennes forest, which had been considered impenetrable.

Once a heroic World War I general, Pétain was now a feeble old man in his eighties who had lost the will to fight and soon capitulated to the enemy. He signed an armistice with Germany and set up a collaborationist government. Such was his message to a shocked citizenry on June 17, 1940.

The war was officially over, and the Germans marched triumphantly into a submissive Paris. But from his headquarters in London, de Gaulle had soon become a force to be reckoned with in opposing the new order in France. He not only loved his country fiercely, but had the ambitious goal of becoming the after-war premier of France.

On June 18, 1940, de Gaulle addressed the French people by radio from London. He assured them the war was not lost and that eventually "victory will be ours!" He said that the flame of French resistance must not die. The news spread quickly.

## Resistance Movement Takes Root

But long before many citizens even knew who de Gaulle was, they had plunged into Resistance activity individually and in secret groups under diverse and courageous leaders. The honor of France was at stake! They set up escape networks for war prisoners and Jews, with safe houses, transportation, fake identities. They sabotaged railways and German military installations, factories, troop transports, airfields, and missile sites.

Politically right, left, and center, these Resistance fighters from all walks of life learned to trust each other and work together. Women as well as men were active in the underground, from the peasant girl who worked as maid for a Resistance fighter and once saved him from certain death to Marie-Madeleine Fourcade, the beautiful well-educated Parisian mother of two who became leader of the most powerful Resistance network in France.

When Gestapo officers arrived to search the house, the Resistance fighter's maid risked her own life by hiding his illegal shortwave radio and paraphernalia in the large pocket of her apron under a mess of fresh green beans. As for Marie-Madeleine, she was once captured by the Nazis and avoided torture and death by slipping away from them. Holding her clothes in her teeth, lubricated by her own sweat, she squirmed out of a small high window in her cell, avoided the guards, and escaped into the countryside.

Many hundreds of Resistance fighters paid with their lives for their activities. They were betrayed, captured, tortured, killed, or sent to concentration camps in Germany. The Nazis went to extreme and brutal lengths to crush the underground movement, swiftly executing citizens known to have helped the Resistance, sometimes massacring the inhabitants of a whole village.

By the end of 1941, there were so many diverse groups, so much duplication, so many networks that it became obvious that they needed to be unified inside France and also linked with de Gaulle's Free France headquarters across the channel.

De Gaulle set about organizing the Resistance movement in northern France, above the demarcation line that separated German-occupied France from the southern half of the country. Resistance forces in the south reported to the Allied command in London although they too felt de Gaulle was their true leader.

## The Maquis

Then there were the Maquis, refugees from the German draft in the winter of 1942-43 to secure forced labor to ship back to Germany. These French youths fled into the countryside by the hundreds and thousands, hiding out in the mountains and the forests.

The Resistance and ordinary French citizens did their best to get food, shelter, and clothing to them. Supplies also came through Alliance parachute drops. Add weapons, ammunition, explosives, radio transmitters, and training to that list; and the Maquis became an effective Resistance force. They were even granted official military status as French Forces of the Interior (FFI) by General Dwight D. Eisenhower.

## De Gaulle and Giraud

Churchill and Roosevelt did not like or trust de Gaulle although they respected him and gave him grudging assistance. The British and American forces privately planned to occupy France themselves after the war.

On the political front, the British and Americans decided to back General Henri-Honoré Giraud. He outranked de Gaulle by two stars, had a fine World War I combat record, was fearless, and very ambitious. This counterproductive political infighting went on throughout the war.

After Eisenhower's second Allied assault on French North Africa was successful in May of 1943, a provisional government was set up there with de Gaulle as president and Giraud as military commander in chief, something the French Resistance forces had insisted upon in a highly publicized report though their spokesman, Jean Moulin.

It was during this brief partnership of the two generals who didn't like each other that Giraud traveled to New York City, recruiting Pierre and other young men to train and serve as officers in the Free French Army.

## The Liberation of Paris

The Allied landing on the beaches of Normandy in June of 1944 signaled the beginnings of the liberation of France. As the war came to a hard-fought close that summer, de Gaulle visited Eisenhower in the field and pressured him to allow the liberation of Paris to be accomplished by a Free French Army division under Eisenhower's command.

At first reluctant, Eisenhower finally agreed to this. As head of all the Allied forces in Europe, he knew full well how essential the Free French Army Divisions under his command, as well as the underground Resistance fighters, had been in turning the tide of the war. Without their assistance, including action by small commando units such as Pierre's, Britain, that tiny courageous kingdom across the channel from France, might well have gone down in defeat.

Thus, it came about that on August 25, 1944, French General Leclerk's forces on three fronts—under de Gaulle's orders and the tricolor flag of the republic and backed up by a battle-hardened American division—liberated Paris.

Pressured by both Swedish Consul Raul Nordling, the key intermediary between the Germans and the French, and Pierre Taittinger, the Vichy-appointed mayor of Paris, Major General Dietrich von Choltitz surrendered to General Leclerk rather than retreat from the city, blowing it up behind him as ordered. The city has been meticulously wired with explosives for the carrying out of such a plan.

Von Choltitz was a cruel man who had already destroyed whole cities and their populations without a shred of sympathy for his victims. But why destroy this great city and kill hundreds of thousands of people in the last days of a war already lost and be forever remembered and vilified as the German officer responsible? His decision not to do so was a gigantic act of insubordination to his führer.

The installation of General Charles de Gaulle as the premier of France took place in Paris the following day, with the bullets still flying.

The liberation of the whole of France, except for a few isolated pockets of German resistance, took place by the end of August. It was facilitated by units of de Gaulle's Fighting French and the Maquis.

Pierre was killed in one of those isolated pockets of resistance. He and his men had parachuted into the Belfort Gap area to help a group of French soldiers break through the German panzer division surrounding them. It was September 15, 1944.

---

**My information sources:

David Schoenbrun's *Soldiers of the Night: The Story of the French Resistance*, published in August 1981, is a gripping account by an American intelligence agent and war correspondent who was there and knew many of the resistance fighters.

Ian Wellsted's *SAS with the Maquis: In Action with the French Resistance, June-September 1944* is a firsthand reminiscence by a member and then leader of an SAS (Special Air Service) unit from England that parachuted into occupied France. It was written from extensive notes he took at the time.

***For those wishing to know more about the French Resistance, there is the highly acclaimed recently remastered black-and-white

1969 film *Army of Shadows*. The original film was directed by Pierre Melville, himself a former Resistance fighter. The film is a stark minimalist look at what it meant to forsake all else and dedicate one's life to the cause. It is now available on the Internet and elsewhere as a DVD.

For people who love to read, I also recommend the book *Army of Shadows: A Novel of the Resistance* by John Harris. Published in 1979, it has no connection to the film of the same name. It is instead the gripping story of two English servicemen, the sole surviving crew members of a bomber shot down at night over France. They melted into the life of a rural community, were supplied with new identities, worked on a farm, and played important roles in the Resistance. A believable love story is included.

Also not to be missed is *Suite Française*, Irène Némirovsky's long-lost manuscript, published in the United States just this year (2006). Hidden deep in the French countryside, Némirovsky, already a well-known and beloved author, started writing this last book in 1940. Her two-part tour de force is fiction, but it holds up an uncanny mirror to the times. Part 1, *Storm in June,* tells about families and individuals caught up in the exodus from Paris on the eve of the Nazi occupation in June of 1940. Suddenly, whether poor, middle class, or wealthy, they were all refugees spilling out into the French countryside and very soon hungry. Part 2, *Dulce*, tells about life in the village of Bussy, occupied by the Germans.

When I finished reading Némirovsky's book, I wanted to know what happened next to all these people who had become so familiar to me. But this was not to be. The author's original plan had been for a five-part series; but she and her husband, Michel Epstein, both Jewish, were arrested by the Nazis and perished at Auschwitz in September and October of 1942.

When the Nazis returned for their children, seven-year-old Denise's schoolteacher hid her, then collected her little sister too, and facilitated their escape with the aid of the family's friends and relatives.

Denise had seen her mother endlessly writing, using black ink and tiny handwriting to save ink and paper. In order to have a memento of her mother, she put the leather-bound notebook of her writings in her suitcase before they fled. This went with the two little girls from one perilous hiding place to another. They thought it was a diary but found it too painful to dip into it after the war.

Many years later, Denise decided to copy it before giving it to the Institut Mémoires de l'édition Contemporaine where documented memories of the war were preserved. Using a large magnifying glass to help her decipher the tiny writing, she painstakingly typed out the whole book, soon discovering that she had a masterpiece on her hands.

She sent this typed manuscript to the publisher Denoel. In 2002, sixty-two years after the author's death, her book was published in Paris. Two years later, it was translated into English and published in the United States.

Denise's sister, Elisabeth Gille, died in 1996 and never read her mother's book. But she herself wrote *Le Mirador* (*The Watchtower*), a very fine imagined biography of the mother she never had a chance to know, for she was only five when Irene Némirovsky died.

# 48

# IMAGINING PIERRE IN FRANCE

*This chapter is the result of my wondering and agonizing all those years ago about what was happening to Pierre in France. I remember hearing stories about the French Resistance fighters, but this did not all come vividly alive for me until just recently when I read those two authentic memoirs by David Schoenbrun and Ian Wellsted.*

Remembering the courageous people and tumultuous events I encountered in these two remarkable books, I wondered anew about Pierre's experiences during those last ten months of his life.

How much did he manage to see of the country he had known in his childhood and on a few return visits? Aged chateaus, old-style houses with round towers and tile roofs, little gardens burning with color everywhere, winding roads, lovely old churches, mountain villages, ancient castles with their crumbling parapets and towers . . . Did he also see villages reduced to a vast expanse of rubble and a church spire, destroyed by the Nazis in retaliation for help given to the Resistance fighters by one or more of its citizens?

I wonder what it might possibly have been like for him on a commando mission—this boy grown into a man I would never know. Pierre in paratroop gear—perhaps with shaggy hair and a few weeks growth of beard—heavily loaded, being dropped with his small group of men to float down into a torch-lit clearing at night in mountainous territory . . .

Resistance fighters they may have encountered had camps in the mountains and used local people as informants about the whereabouts and activities of German soldiers in the region. These were farmers, farmers' wives, townspeople, pretty girls on bicycles, or young boys who could scurry through the forest and along the trails with messages. All of these everyday patriots, deep in German-occupied territory, risked their lives to help the Resistance forces prevail.

Into the midst of all this came Pierre and his men. While they scouted the possibilities of their assignment, did they establish an esprit de corps with one of those small bands of Resistance fighters? Or were they quickly in and out again? And how did they escape after accomplishing their mission? Was there a pickup point on a mountain clearing where a plane swooped in under the cover of darkness, quickly spirited them on board, and took off again?

Did Pierre think of me sometimes? Did he ever reach into his pocket, pull out the letters from me, read them by flashlight or firelight, then carefully fold them and put them away?

These questions must go forever unanswered . . .

# 49

## REMINISCING

All my working life, I have made my living as a writer, but *Rowing Backwards* is the most essential project I have ever undertaken.

I remember how Pierre described his last few hours at his cabin in the forest, "drinking cheap whisky, dropping a tear or two on my books, records, and writings . . . and thinking of the bright new world I might return to with its colossal lakes."

I have often wondered what books he read, what he included in his writings, what his deepest thoughts and longings were about life and love and friendship and war . . .

He does not come to me in dreams, the way my Scotty does. But to this day, in times when I am deeply alone, I can conjure him to me, look into those dark eyes again, smell him, feel the heat radiating from his body, hear his voice and his laughter, evoke his intense presence. And I am sixteen again. Linking yesteryear to today, he stays doggedly with me through all time.

He was my confusing, wildly exciting first love in those sunstruck July days of my awakening womanhood.

He was my first love, and I failed him, sending him off to war without even a kiss or without telling him how much he meant to me and how much I longed to break through the bonds of my foolish inhibitions. But I think he must have known, must have sensed my turmoil, my deep affinity for him.

Ours is a coming-of-age story, but as the much-loved leader of a band of commandoes dropped behind enemy lines, he grew up so much faster than I did in my sheltered world thousands of miles from German-occupied France. If he had survived the war, I am sure he would have found me older and wiser about life and human relationships but still untouched by the kinds of experiences that honed his own character and outlook . . .

He was my first love . . . but Bob Hensley was to become the love of my adult life, the father of all my children, my link to future generations. It was my resolve after Pierre's death to become a self-sufficient, independent woman that empowered me to complete college, postpone sexual fulfillment, and find my calling before meeting and marrying Bob, who embodied many of the qualities I had so admired and loved in Pierre.

I cannot change the past, but if I were offered another chance in an alternate world where a war did not part us, it is Pierre I would return to and strive with all my heart to establish a new honest relationship and build a life together . . . beginning with that trip around the world.

This memoir is a salute to our young lives, to the one I went on to live and his that was cut short.

Pierre and Claire in November, 1943 before
he was shipped overseas.

# 50

# SOLACE

A long time evolving on the back roads of my mind, this book was begun in 2003, the summer of my seventy-seventh year. It has been and still is a challenging life journey, full of family and friends, good books to read, worthwhile work and causes to absorb me.

It was Pierre whose death set my feet upon the stepping stones that have finally brought me to this time and place.

I am still full of memories of Pierre and the life-changing sorrow of his loss. Herewith, after a dreamless night, I rewrite two pieces of our long-ago past together to give me solace from a few deep regrets. Sentence after sentence flow onto my computer screen full-blown, as if by magic.

*First, I tinker with the July 15, 1943, entry in my diary, starting with where I jumped down off the ladder from Pierre's tree house:*

### July 15, 1943

. . . He caught me and we stood there, his hands at my waist, mine resting on his shoulders. He looked directly into my eyes, like that day at the Ashfield cemetery, as if it was a challenge. And I suddenly reached up to pull his head down for a light goodbye kiss. But, quick as a cat, he had one hand tangled in my hair, keeping my mouth against his, while his other arm pulled me close.

It was a long, deep coming together that set our hearts to wildly beating. Which was his heart? Which was mine? Afterwards we stood with our arms locked around each other, our hearts still thudding against each other's ribs. He let out his breath with a deep groan, and tears spilled down my face. We stood thus for a long time. I finally blotted my hot, wet face against his steaming shirt.

At long last, we walked reluctantly down the path through the woods to where Pauline awaited us with the horses, saddled and ready to go. She shot us both an odd, startled look.

We rode in silence along Bird Hill Road, then along the shoulder of the highway up the mountain to the village, my thoughts in turmoil. I did not know a kiss could be like that. No wonder I had been so afraid to chance it.

*I also change the part about his furlough, which brings us to a Friday evening in mid-November 1943 at my freshman dorm in town at Penn State.*

I came in from a date that night to find my roommate Doris waiting up for me. "Someone named Pierre was here to see you, and he has a French accent . . . Jay, he is so good looking!"

I was flabbergasted, and spent a restless night. He returned early Saturday morning. I came slowly down the stairs and when I reached out to him, he caught both my hands in his. We stood there speechless, searching each other's face. He seemed taller, older, an intense dark-eyed stranger. He wore jeans, boots, a warm flannel shirt open over a khaki shirt.

We left his motorcycle in the back yard and started to walk the four or five blocks to The Corner Room for breakfast. A company of Marines marched by us in formation on their way to campus, singing in cadence at the top of their lungs.

Looking sideways at them, Pierre reached out and laced the fingers of his left hand through those of my right hand. His warmth traveled through me, set my pulse to racing, and my face felt hot. He stopped, raised his hand, looked down at my fingers clasped in his and said, "Ah, Jezebel, where are your long red nails?"

"Gone for good," I told him, laughing. I was his Jezebel again and he was my Pierre, worth that whole company of Marines to me. I matched my stride to his as we walked on.

My mind in disarray, I could choke down little breakfast. But he ate heartily—hot cereal, ham and eggs, orange juice, buttered biscuits and coffee. By noon I would be starving!

He pushed our dishes to one side, spread a map out on the table and traced for me the highways and byways he had traveled from Ft. Benning, Georgia in the past two days—across mountains and valleys, through cities and towns, over rivers and farmland. It had been a long road trip!

"Where are you staying?" I asked. Carefully refolding his map, he paused and pointed to the ceiling. I remembered then that there was a hotel over The Corner Room.

"I'm leaving early Monday morning. Let's get your homework out of the way, and then we can do what we want . . . I brought a helmet for you."

Back at Wylie Dorm, I collected my books and notebook. He placed a helmet and goggles carefully over my head, adjusted them and fastened the straps under my chin, his face close to mine. Then he donned his own, pulled on a pair of black leather gloves and climbed aboard. Keeping his left foot on the ground as he balanced the weight of the bike, he looked back at me and said, "Well?" I flung my leg over the seat behind him and wrapped my arms around him.

I'd never been on a motorcycle. This thunderous, vibrating machine would give us a far different experience from that headlong bicycle ride in the dark down Norton Hill on Steady Lane one rainy September night.

I closed my eyes and held on tight.

We sped up to the library on campus, where we tackled my assignments for Monday. He practically dictated four or five pages of a history report to me, making sense of my scattered notes, including some of his own perceptions. The rest of the assignments were easy—he leaned back and smiled, watching me bent over my books and papers with flushed face as I tried to ignore him.

By one o'clock, after a tour of the campus, we were back at
The Corner Room, where Pierre ordered a big picnic lunch to go.
We straddled our iron steed and took off for farm country in the
wide Nittany Valley beyond the town of State College. This was an
exhilarating cross between riding a horse and flying!

It was a cool, sunny afternoon. Lush autumn-tinged countryside,
pastures, farm animals and farm buildings rushed by us on both
sides and stretched out ahead. Finding a shady hideaway by a stream
some distance from the dirt road we'd traveled, we lit into a hearty
lunch of fresh apples, thick ham and cheese sandwiches and cookies.
Pierre opened a bottle of white wine with a fancy French label and
poured it into two paper cups.

Me: Pierre, it's against the rules to drink alcoholic beverages at
Penn State.

Him, laughing: Don't they have secret bars at all the fraternity
houses?

Me: Yes . . . but it's still against the rules, and I don't drink!

Him: Well, it's okay now—you're not on campus. Be adventuresome!

So, I sipped a little from my cup, coughed, pretended to be
strangling, screwed up my face and stuck my tongue out at him.
Shaking his head in mock disgust, he drank his own cup of wine,
and mine, too. Raising his cup to me, he said, "C'est dommage!
This is very fine wine."

We talked and talked. I brought him up-to-date on happenings
at Ashfield, which included my sister's meeting Malcolm. I told
him about my new friends at college and described a few of
my subjects—especially my short-story writing class—and my
*formidable* French professor. But I said not a word about freshman
orientation.

He told me a little about his officer training, and about the
horrible things that were happening to citizens of France under
the German occupation. As the afternoon wore on we became
completely at ease with each other. It seemed we could talk about
almost anything, just like in the old days.

"Pierre . . . we had a freshman orientation class on the birds and
the bees with a woman doctor a few weeks ago," I said, intending

to make light of it. But my face grew fiery hot and I blurted out, "There's a lot I still don't get, and it all sounds dreadful . . . really scary!"

I sat there, mortified . . . and, startled, he just looked at me. He began to say something, then shook a cigarette out of its pack and kept busy lighting it for a long time. After a few minutes, he snuffed it out on the ground. Then, with a glint in his eye, he stood up, bared his teeth, made his hands into menacing claws and growled.

"Cut that out!" I yelled. "You're not funny," and I heard his laughter as I turned and fled. He ran after me, caught me and put his arms around me.

"Don't laugh at me," I pleaded against his shoulder. "I'm serious!"

"What else can I do?" he said. "I don't dare kiss you!" And he was still laughing.

After awhile he said, "It will be dark soon, it's getting cold, and I'm hungry. Let's go!"

He kissed me quickly on the cheek and took my hand. We walked back to the motorcycle and gathered up our stuff. He put on a black windbreaker, turned up the collar, pulled out a warm flannel shirt for me and buttoned it up under my chin as if I were a little kid! Then we put on our helmets and goggles and climbed aboard. "Snuggle up," he yelled as the motorcycle came noisily alive, and we bounced over uneven ground to the road.

The sun was going down as we roared into town. We grabbed a hamburger and milkshake at the drugstore and ended up at Autoport a few miles outside town, dancing to the jukebox tunes—my very first time there.

I was a great jitterbugger, but Pierre didn't have a clue. The night I first met him at one of Sidney Page's parties, we danced to the music of the Blue Danube Waltz, which he knew how to do. We'd both been shy and uncomfortable and said very little to each other. Now I set about determined to teach him how to jitterbug and we had a hilarious time. He was quick to learn and we flung ourselves across the floor, our boots stomping out the rhythm.

It was a crowded Saturday night. Students and military cadets I knew greeted me, but their faces fuzzed out and it was all like

SOLACE

a dream. The slow dances were pure magic—"This is the Story of a Starry night," "Long Ago and Far Away," "Deep Purple," "Skylark"—all the familiar old tunes we'd heard at Mike's place and at Sid's and D.O.'s.

Pierre kept an eye on his watch and made sure to deliver me to Wylie Dorm on time. We decided to go hiking the next day and he bestowed on me a gentle goodnight kiss—acting as if I were made of glass!—and left.

I was deep asleep Sunday morning when he arrived downstairs. Doris had to drag me, protesting, out of bed. Groggily, I pulled on socks, hiking boots, jeans and long-sleeved denim shirt, slung Pierre's warm flannel shirt over my shoulder and started down the stairs with unkempt hair and flapping boot laces. Pierre looked up at me as I came and smiled. "Good morning, sleepy head! Let's be off."

Up to The Corner Room on his motorcycle, and this time I ate almost as much as he did. They packed a picnic lunch for us and we headed for the hills. We hiked all morning and afternoon, up through woods and fields, over fences and across streams. It was a gorgeous day on the mountain, with a cool wind blowing and little brown rabbits with white tails hopping about here and there.

Late in the morning we climbed into the branches of a big tree and wiled away an hour or more playing pirates. Our imaginary Jolly Roger flag flying high, we searched the vast and churning seas around us, looking for hapless ships to attack—which started Pierre on his repertoire of rollicking Gilbert and Sullivan songs.

I was exhausted from all that dancing the night before, plus our morning's hike and not nearly enough sleep. Pierre was in so much better shape than I was, fit and strong, ready for anything. Did he never grow weary?

We ate in the shade of our pirate ship, sitting on the blanket he spread out for us. He had stowed away our lunch, a bottle of wine, the blanket and a book of poetry in his knapsack. He knew Robert Frost was one of my favorite poets.

After we ate, I collapsed on the blanket. Propped up on one elbow, Pierre began reading to me, his French accent at odds with the author's New England twang.

I closed my eyes. "I love Robert Frost," I mumbled. "I love your voice . . . when I was little Daddy used to read lots of poetry to me . . ." I dozed off in familiar territory . . . *I'm going out to fetch the little calf that's standing by the mother. It's so young. It totters when she licks it with her tongue. I sha'n't be gone long. You come too. And, Something there is that doesn't love a wall, that sends the frozen-ground-swell under it, and spills the upper boulders in the sun . . .*

I awoke to find Pierre gazing at me over his closed book. I thought suddenly of our scrappy times together in the rowboat.

"You slept a long, long time," he said. ". . . and you snore."

I sat up, indignant. "I do not! You made that up! Besides, people in glass houses shouldn't throw stones—you probably snore, too!"

"Peut-etre," he laughed, "Who knows?" Then he stood up and opened both arms to me: "Come, Cherie, stay with me tonight and find out for yourself!"

I knew he was just teasing, but this went too far. I retorted crossly, "I'm a college girl and I sleep alone at Wylie dorm every night!"

He laughed at me. Then, suddenly serious, he said, "Ah, but if you could do as you please, you would stay with me!"

I jumped to my feet, faced him, and found myself answering, "Peut-etre! Peut-etre!" For he was at that moment irresistible, and our time together was running out.

Shocked by my own boldness, I took refuge behind our pirate tree, then leaned out to one side and peered at him. He stood there intoxicatingly male in the late afternoon sun, put his hands on his hips and growled. I started laughing, and with that glint still in his eyes, he did, too.

We soon headed hand-in-hand back down the mountain and found his motorcycle where we'd hidden it in the woods. As we got ready to pack up, I said, "Where's that spectacular French officer's hat you told me about?"

"Right here!" He pulled it out of his pack on the motorcycle and adjusted it over a mock-fierce face. It sat low on his forehead, hiding his thick, short-cropped brown hair.

"You look like one of those little Foreign Legion wooden soldiers my brother used to play with," I said. And then I shouted at him, "But I know this is for real, and I can't bear for you to leave me and go off to war!" His face contorted briefly as he pulled off his hat and turned away.

We ate supper at The Corner Room, left his motorcycle at the hotel and walked for hours, hand in hand, along dark streets dimly lit at intervals by street lamps. We came finally, reluctantly, to Wylie Dorm. I was dead tired and I had an 8 o'clock class Monday morning. But I did not want this day to end. We finally said our goodbyes in a cold drizzling rain at the kitchen door.

"Thank you for coming, Pierre, even when I'd told you not to. Thank you for helping me with my homework. Thank you for two wonderful, wonderful days!"

We stood there in the darkness with our arms around each other. I sobbed, and he was very quiet. Then he started singing softly in his wonderful deep voice, "I polished up the handle so carefully that now I am the ruler of the Queen's Navy!" He kissed me, fiercely and then tenderly. I matched his tenderness with my own, my fierceness squelched by the birds and the bees. I had begun to comprehend, at last, the powerful forces that bound us.

He stepped back, raised his hand in a half-salute, said, "Te Quiero!" and I whispered the same words to him. "Listen for me, I'll come by about sunrise." And he was gone, running through the rain.

I lay awake all night and into the early morning hours. At last I heard him thunder by, and cried out his name, waking up a startled Doris.

He traveled across Pennsylvania and into New York Sate, on to New York City and Manhattan, where his family waited. It was another long road trip. The next I knew he was overseas.

                         *       *       *

I have read these two pieces of pure fiction again and again until they have become as real to me as the rest of my narrative. I am at last content.

\*     \*     \*

The storyteller in Amy Tan's novel of China *The Hundred Secret Senses* says the following on the last page: "Believing in ghosts is believing that love never dies. If people we love die, then they are lost only to our ordinary senses. If we remember them, we can find them anytime with our hundred secret senses . . ."

I know this to be true. I am certain there is a spirit world to which some of us have access, for Pierre has remained a part of my life for generations. Has he received word in the spirit world that I altered a few things in our history together, giving us both at last the gift of my honest self? Perhaps he has found Scotty, my little lost boy, and they are both waiting for me there in the spirit world.

Islam's prophet Mohammad reportedly once said that there are no old women in the hereafter, for they are all young again.

Tommy and Lisa in summer of 1983.

My brother Phillips and me in 1981.

Doug with Rowan (left) and Julia.

Ezra and Stephani grew up together.

Tim at 22.               Allie at seven.

Jane, Pappy and Tim.

# 51

# THOUGHTS UPON TURNING EIGHTY

### *Plus an Update on Family and Friends*

Life in Madison County, Kentucky, is good. This beautiful rural county and the many kindred spirits I have found here among writers, artists, craftspeople, musicians, organic farmers, and others feed my soul. I've joined a small Unitarian Fellowship of diverse and worthwhile people in nearby Richmond and look forward to their eclectic Sunday programs and other get-togethers.

Since Tim and Jane's barn-building weekend workshops a year before I moved to Madison County, there have been countless other "garden parties" and potluck gatherings among their wide circle of friends. I happily document many of these with my digital Kodak camera and a Photoshop computer program that enables me to crop and work with them to my heart's content.

We have built indoor and outdoor cob ovens—these are domed bake ovens made from layers of various mixtures of clay, water, sand, straw, and manure. We have put in gardens, helped build a house, dig a pond, tear down an old house, and more. A garden party at my house a few years ago left me with new plantings around the house and raised gardens for vegetables, berries, and flowers.

In a more-recent family potluck and workshop, we planted new shrubs and trees in my yard. We also harvested and cut up a pickup load of firewood from my woodsy pond area where the local utility company had mistakenly cut down twenty-five of my trees. (They contritely wrote me a big check for the damage!)

Tucked in among these activities, I'm reading scads of books, working on my own book, spending time with friends and family, attending free concerts and art shows in Berea, keeping up with friends and relatives around the country, and taking care of my place. I carefully build and light off my top-burn fires in late fall and winter from a good supply of seasoned wood stacked on my back porch.

## Living with Chaos

All my life, I have battled against my disorderly ways—from the Fibber Mcgee closets and drawers of my childhood to my inscrutable filing "systems." I still live in a certain amount of chaos. It is said that writing is the process of bringing order out of chaos, so this may be all that has saved me.

My health is otherwise excellent. After my last annual checkup disclosed that all systems were go, my doctor told me, "You have the heart of a twenty-five-year-old!" That's good to know.

I eat well and take a carefully chosen handful of food supplements every day. I stay fit and strong from daily walks and an exercise routine that keep my back, neck, and thrice-dislocated right shoulder from giving me trouble—unless I carry in too heavy a load of firewood, and then my body quickly lets me know!

## Tim's Mushrooms

My children's lives too are moving right along.

Tim and Jane have developed a thriving business selling their own organic produce, eggs, home-baked goods, and mushrooms. As an integral part of this, they have established a food-distribution network that allows them to sell other local organic farmers' produce as well. I am one of their regular customers.

Tim has evolved into an expert on growing mushrooms and gathering them from the wild. He not only sells his mushrooms to upscale restaurants, but also offers hands-on workshops on the subject.

These are held at his and Jane's farm in the holler in the spring of the year. They typically start with Tim's introduction to mushroom culture—a question-and-answer session in one of his inoculated-log gardens, followed by a hearty brunch prepared by Jane back at the cabin.

After that comes a training session out at the barn on inoculating logs with mushroom spore. This is followed by a vigorous hike up the mountain to enjoy the wildflowers, look for wild mushrooms, and learn another method of cultivating them by sandwiching mushroom spore mixed with sawdust between the top of a tree stump and a slice of the tree. Along about midafternoon, Jane offers a lesson on mushroom cookery.

Later, Tim demonstrates still another way to grow mushrooms by mixing the spore in sawdust with wood chips and dirt, spread out and then covered with leaves. Last of all, as the sun slips early behind the mountain, comes a dinner of salad, homemade pizza, and berry pie. Jane bakes her pizzas and pies in their outdoor cob oven, constructed in an earlier garden party at the farm.

Participants head home in the semidarkness, each with a mushroom log of his or her own, a log formerly inoculated by Tim.

## Doug and Heather

For two years in a row, Doug's Continuum Consort made trips to Korea. The first year's purpose was to present a program of works by contemporary Korean and Canadian composers for the Pan Music Festival. The Continuum Consort was the first Canadian ensemble ever invited to participate.

The second year, they performed a program of works composed for them by contemporary Canadian and Korean women composers in the Delos composers' collective. Everywhere, they played to sold-out crowds. They also did several lecture-concerts at universities outside Seoul where one student translator told Doug he was the ideal man for the Korean woman.

"She must have been joking!" Doug concluded.

A good share of their expenses for these trips was paid by government-subsidized Korean composers whose music they played, as well as by the British Columbia Arts Council.

Back home on Vancouver Island, Doug still teaches at the Victoria Conservatory and a girls' school in Victoria. His specialty is classical guitar and various lute-type instruments ideal for playing the early music he loves. He also plays several classical Persian instruments and teaches same to private students, the children of local Iranian families. His ability to speak Farsi is a big asset here.

Doug and Heather's offspring are warmly open to life and people. Rowan, eleven, is an expert on trains and on building Harry Potter's Hogwarts school complex and no end of his own designs of locomotives and other things from thousands of little Lego pieces. He also plays a bit of fiddle and violin and belongs to the Victoria Children's Choir, a choral group with a regular schedule of concerts. (In another two years, he would be selected by Pacific Opera Victoria for a part in their spring 2009 production of *The Magic Flute*!)

Julia, eight and a half, has a stack of medals and trophies from her four years as an Irish dancer. She fell in love with this style of dancing when she was five. Now she no longer wants to compete and just dances for the fun of it. A serious musician, she has taken violin and fiddle lessons for many years, but also plays piano and guitar for fun.

Rowan likes—and Julia (my namesake, remember?) is crazy about—riding horses. They both enjoy those frequent family walks in the forest and bike rides on the island's scenic Galloping Goose Trail a few miles away.

I try to visit them for two weeks every few years when I accumulate enough miles on my credit card for a free round-trip flight. I always have a great time living their everyday lives with them and their friends, many of whom are the parents and children in their homeschooling group.

Doug and Heather are gradually turning their three-level house in the country into a work of art with the help of their artist and artisan friends. For this, they barter their own services as guitar instructors.

Doug's daughter Susan, husband Ken, and son Zackary visit Doug's family periodically on Vancouver Island and live close enough, in Cincinnati, for the rest of us to see them now and then.

## Jennifer and Dave

Jen continues with her basket-weaving career, teaches workshops, and has juried into the prestigious Smithsonian Craft Show two years in a row. Her baskets have become collectors' items and command high prices.

At home, she grows an amazing array of flowers and a vegetable garden that produces a bountiful harvest every year. In her husband Dave's latest book, the *Illustrated Atlas of the Himalaya*, is his picture on page 139 of Jennifer riding an elephant in the jungles of Nepal. Featuring his magnificent photographs, this large-format book draws on Dave's twenty-five years of travels and research in the region.

Jen accompanies Dave on some of his trips and their grandson Andrew, Ezra's son, spends many weekends with them.

As for Ezra, he is a whiz at computers, and the rest of us often call on him for help. He has many construction and home-maintenance skills and also earns good money on occasion with his chain saw, clearing out and cutting up storm-damaged and downed trees. I always look forward to seeing him and his dynamic, lovable live-in fiancée Nicole at our family gatherings.

## Lisa and Tommy

Their oldest son, Josh, nineteen, is on his own in California where he works at a Mammoth Lake ski resort in winter and as a tile-laying apprentice in summer. He lives with his sweetheart, Rachael Santos. We don't see them very often.

His sister, Hannah, a seventeen-year-old beauty at this writing, has won many local singing contests. With her lovely voice and great stage presence, she is the darling of Clark County. She is working toward moving out of the family home, renting an apartment in Lexington with her best friend, finding a job, and producing her own CDs.

Elijah, now thirteen, will soon be the only chick left in the nest. He's an enthusiastic reader and computer gamester.

Tommy, retired firefighter, is a Civil War history buff, takes part in battle reenactments, is an avid motorcycle rider, undertakes many building projects on their farm. Despite his battle against

Jennifer, rolling up freshly harvested
bark. She gave me one of her handmade
baskets at my 80th birthday party, below.

rheumatoid arthritis, he manages to raise and tend a big fruit and vegetable garden for the family, plus a pick-your-own strawberry patch money raiser. Every spring and summer, he runs a lawn-mowing and garden-tilling service.

Lisa cleans people's houses four or five days a week, loves her customers, and plays her magic flute for her church and special events elsewhere. She and Tommy often hop on his motorcycle and roar off to various adventures and campouts.

Lisa recently earned a nurse's assistant certificate that qualifies her to be a home-care worker, something for which she is well suited by her temperament and loving, compassionate nature. She is also training and riding her own horse.

She accompanies Jennifer two or three times a year to big events such as the Smithsonian and Philadelphia Museum of Art shows and helps her in her booth. They both treasure this sister time together.

## Update on Joel

For years, Joel ran his own home renovation and repair business in Fort Pierce, Florida, where he lived with his wife, Nancy, and their daughter, Emy, now in her teens. In October of 2004, they lost their little eleven-month-old son, Boo, to a rare and incurable malady, Gaucher's disease, diagnosed when he was about five months old.

Joel, who adored his only little boy, faced this terrible loss with uncommon courage and resilience. "We all go into this world, and we all leave this world," he said. "And we never know when it will be. We are going to love him and take care of him as long as we have him."

Little Boo died in his daddy Joel's arms after opening his eyes wide and looking up at him intensely. "Say hello to God for me," Joel said and promised Boo he'd be with him again someday. At the memorial service, Joel played his guitar and sang songs he'd adapted just for Boo and had sung to him often.

Since then, Joel's business has bottomed out, people are leaving Florida in droves, his home is being foreclosed, and he and Nancy have separated.

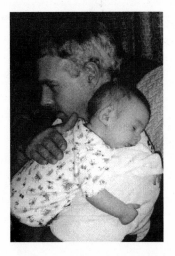

Joel with his son Shane.

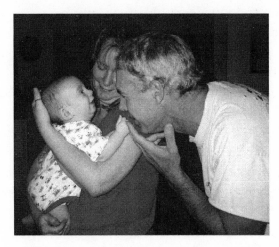

Shown with Nancy and Joel, little "Boo"
was surrounded by love during his short life.

But Joel is a survivor, come what may. He loves Kentucky and will move to Berea soon where he'll find there's a big demand from our family and friends for his fix-it and carpentry services.

Joel's daughter Allie, now twenty-three, moved back up from Florida to Lexington a few years ago to attend college and be nearer the Kentucky branch of the Hensleys. Her longtime sweetheart, David DeAtley, whom we like *so* much, is now serving his second tour of duty in Iraq.

## Stephani

My stepdaughter (sort of) Stephani and her husband, Jamie Middlestetter, whom she met on the Internet a few years ago, live out in Rancho Cucamonga, California, where she has a job working with children and is involved in one amateur theater production after another.

Steph's dad, Nick, still in Phoenix, is no longer involved in the theater scene there. When I asked him why by phone a few years ago, he said, "Because I can't handle two addictions at once!" He's a real estate agent and loves it. He married another real estate agent, Julie, and Steph reports that he's a good grandpa to Julie's passel of grandkids. He's now working on his own memoir.

## Linda's Next Book

In 1994, Linda Kanzinger, who lived with us at the farm off and on in the 1970s, moved into her own house in a predominantly black community in Portland, Oregon. Since then, a gentrification of the neighborhood has triggered her exceedingly well-researched new book-writing project, *We Are Talking About Our Whiteness Now*.

In addition to her writing career, Linda spends a lot of time at Timber Valley, Washington, where she owns seven acres of forest land and camps from the back of her Nissan truck. She's a passionate organic gardener—veggies, fruit trees, berry bushes—both in the city and out in the woods.

Although I miss seeing her on a regular basis, we keep in close touch. I have visited her in Portland four or five times, most recently in 2003 when I became acquainted with some of her intriguing black friends and neighbors.

**Naomi's Life**

Out in Phoenix, my great-niece Naomi is still undergoing rehab, making slow progress. She was flown to Germany recently for stem cell surgery.

Once, she e-mailed us a picture of herself skydiving, strapped on to an experienced skydiver. Another time, at the wheel of a handicap-equipped race car, she competed in a race; not long after that, she won a race on her own special bike, without even training for it. Her folks, Dana and Colleen, have bought her a car; so between that and her bike, she really gets around.

Of all the pictures she has e-mailed us to document her workouts and activities, my favorite is the one of her on Stroller while back home in Apple Valley for a visit. Once helped into the saddle, she had an exhilarating ride.

Stroller is the handsome chestnut gelding my sister raised from a mare she bred to her walking horse stallion, Ike. After training and riding Stroller herself for several years, she gave him to Naomi, who had worked at a horse-training facility and was a good rider.

(Gazing into Naomi's crystal ball, we glimpse her falling in love and moving in with Bryce, a paraplegic with a similar upbeat attitude toward life.)

Naomi has goals; she is ambitious. She plans to enroll at Arizona State University, study hard, and become a psychologist. I do not doubt that, whether she ever fully recovers or not, she will go on to do something grand in the world.

**News from Apple Valley**

Next time I'm "back home" for a visit, I expect to stay at Pauline and Malcolm's, but it won't be the same. By then, the house, built circa 1945-48, will have been gutted and completely remodeled by their son Brian and his wife, Susan. With Brian taking early retirement from IBM in Minnesota, they will soon move their family to Apple Valley where Brian plans to continue his three-way partnership with Dana and Aaron in their Clark Brothers Orchards business.

I haven't been back to those parts since Malcolm's memorial service in 2005. I'll finally meet Dick Lilly, who has been such a help with my book via e-mail and telephone. And it will be fun to get reacquainted with his mother, Ann, whom I once I took for walks and picnic lunches in the woods below our pond when she was a little girl.

Pierre's sister Claire and I have been writing to each other, and it will be wonderful to see her again. She was one of my readers for the first draft of my memoir, and I hope to have a copy of the published book for her when I visit.

## Candy's Ordeal

In the spring of 2005, my horse-trainer friend Candy Kreigh Haasch called me from a rehab hospital in Wisconsin. She had suffered an aggressive brain tumor and was partially paralyzed following surgery to remove it. She went through a grueling rehab process, and over the next few years, she had to learn to ride all over again.

She told me the whole experience has made her a better teacher. It reminds her of what her students go through when they're first exposed to horses and learning how to ride them.

Although not yet 100 percent healed, she has started fox hunting again.

She and her husband Jim now own a farm in Missouri. In addition to her horse activities, she holds down a full-time lab-technician job at Barton County Memorial Hospital in the nearby town of Lamar.

Whew! I have so many fantastic friends. I wish I could include more of them in this memoir.

## Howard's Accident

A few years ago, my old friend Howard Aldous was skiing at the heli-ski resort he and his brother Pat owned in the mountains of central British Columbia. It was the last run on the last day in the season. He hit a patch of ice under the snow, lost control, and found himself in a free fall off the mountain, plummeting a long way down.

Seriously hurt, he was flown to a hospital in Vancouver for extensive surgery and rehab. He will never completely recover from his injuries, but he can walk again.

Meanwhile, he had prospered financially. "Howard never dreamed he'd be rich," Donna told me. They have moved to Vancouver where they live in their high-ceiling, spacious, welcoming, and beautifully decorated house in an upscale mountainside residential area overlooking Lions' Gate Bridge, English Bay, and the city. Donna says it's the first place they've ever lived where Howard doesn't feel he's too big for the house.

Wealth hasn't spoiled them. They are still the same dear people as before. When I visited them recently, they were in the midst of a family reunion, including a fortieth birthday party for their older son, Kent, a fine-looking very tall fellow who reminded me of Howard at his age. We spent a lot of time together.

Both sons, airline pilot Kent and attorney/musician Pat, married late; and Donna feared she and Howard would never have grandkids. But now they have three, a lovable little girl and a set of lively twins.

As for me, Donna said, "You haven't changed!"

## A Memory from My *SNEWS* Years

Looking back on this period of my life, one event in particular stands out. It happened at the last sweep gathering I attended before selling *SNEWS*—the Northeast Regional Expo held in Buffalo, New York, in January '99 within sight of the mighty Niagara Falls.

It had been a difficult convention. Tim wasn't with me, and I missed him terribly. *That's okay*, I said to myself, *I can do this. So Tim's fencing in Mexico, can't run interference for me, carry the heavy stuff, set up the SNEWS booth, remember people's names, handle subscription orders, take lots of pictures, make things run smoothly . . . I can do this without him!*

It was a refrain that was to replay in my head all week—*I can do this!* When my flight to Buffalo was cancelled at the last minute, when my computer quit before the first seminar, when my camera failed me too, and when I started to panic as the time for the Qigong seminar I'd promised to do drew near . . .

Coping without my laptop, I filled a purple "fat lil' notebook" (four-by-five-inch spiral) with my handwritten notes, day after day. I borrowed a camera, learned how to use it, and took a slew of pretty good pictures.

Finally, it was time for the Saturday night banquet and awards program that wound up the expo. Whew! Sweeps from the big Massachusetts guild, of which I was an honorary member, insisted I join them at one of their tables.

After dessert, I sat there writing up the goings-on as the state guild president, Judd Berg, at the podium reminisced about the late Fred Toldo, "America's best-loved sweep," and then introduced the current Fred Toldo Award recipient: "Our honoree, who knew Fred Toldo as a gentleman and as an advocate of sweep education, has invested blood, sweat, and tears to help raise us to dignity by quenching our thirst for knowledge and making us feel as one great family . . . Jay Hensley!"

Stunned, my face growing hot, I dropped my pen, got to my feet, made my way through a standing-ovation crowd to the podium, and gave Judd a big hug. I was immensely honored, elated, and close to tears. The first words out of my mouth were, "Wait 'til I tell Tim!"

Judd presented me with an exuberant sweep-on-the-roof award plaque by Eva Horton. In the background, the band would soon be playing Louis Armstrong's "What a Wonderful World."

## A Spectator Bird

Concerning the national and international scene, I have now withdrawn from the fray, no longer march in peace parades, and am extremely selective in my petition signing. I let my bumper stickers speak for me: War Is Not the Answer! and Peace Is Patriotic.

I have become, for the most part, a watcher in the woods, a spectator bird like the elderly man in Wallace Stegner's book by the same name.

Even so, appalled by the havoc and misery our current president and his cronies have caused in the world with their illegal, mismanaged, and costly Iraq war based on lies, I have joined the groundswell of citizens demanding a Bush/Cheney impeachment. The solution is there, right in our own constitution. And although we have a somewhat dysfunctional Congress, we still must make our voices heard.

If our representatives and senators were to impeach Bush, they would be deeply admired in this country and around the world. (I wrote to many of them on both sides of the aisle about this, but they have chosen to ignore my advice.)

In the rush to war, with the majority of our media playing dead and the steady beat of the patriotism drums sounding in the background, only a handful of people dug in their heels and urged caution. One of these was Senator Byrd. He was so outspoken, so courageous, so impassioned, so on-target in his opposition to this ill-conceived preemptive strike. Why did so few people listen?

### A Volunteer Army Betrayed

In February of 2005, I read an in-depth feature story in the *Lexington Herald-Leader* that told the story of an American soldier who took refuge in Canada rather than return to Iraq after a Christmas furlough.

He had been in the thick of the fighting, had been wounded, and was then awarded a Purple Heart medal. Given license to kill innocent Iraqi civilians who get in the way of military action, he could not force himself to do so. He felt betrayed, that he was serving in Iraq under false pretenses.

Would Canada allow him to stay and build a new life there? His wife and four-year-old daughter were still living in the United States, awaiting the outcome of his defection. (By this time, 5,500 other servicemen and women had gone AWOL.)

There is now an effective independently funded organization, Citizen Soldier, that provides legal aid, psychological counseling, and other assistance to service personnel with similar stories.

### A New Vision

We inhabit a world that is both beautiful and terrible, a world scarred by war, hatred, poverty, ignorance, greed, and seemingly endless acts of terrorism. But there also are capable organizations and individuals—writers, teachers, statesmen, and ordinary people of all races and religious and political persuasion—who are working doggedly for peace and understanding among nations.

Now building momentum in the land is an exciting new vision of a Green economy based on alternative energy. It promises millions of new jobs, more sustainable housing, and simplified lifestyles.

It is very doable. It holds the key to managing the global economy and solving the global environmental crisis that affects the food we grow, the fuels we use, the future of our forests, and the fate of our planet. We seek gifted and tenacious leaders to help us make this happen.

## Criticism from an Old Friend

My lifelong friend Anne Alevizon Mitchell is turned off by what she calls my "extreme political bias," lack of tolerance for other opinions, and disrespect for my government. She reminds me that "history is rewritten over and over again as more facts and truths emerge, so let us have a little skepticism about who knows all the answers."

And she says, philosophically, "War is terrible, and war is inevitable until human beings are far more evolved. It was written two thousand years ago, 'Only the dead have seen the end of war.'"

I fear that she is right, but hope springs eternal . . .

Anne retired from her librarian job at SUNY after twenty-seven years and enjoys her life at Wake Robin, a retirement village in Shelburne, Vermont, close enough for frequent visits from children and grandchildren.

I last saw her here in Kentucky just a few years ago during a family reunion in Moorehead where her son Steve is an obstetrician. He married MyLe, a lovely Vietnamese girl, who is a great cook of dishes from the land of her birth. They have two daughters who look much like their mother to me.

Three of Anne's children were there, plus a passel of grandkids. Mitch came too. He almost always turns up at family reunions and stays active in his sons' and daughters' lives. He now lives in Kentucky, not far from his son Steve.

Out in San Diego, Anne's sister Rita, still confined to a wheelchair, worked for a while at a part-time editing job for a local newspaper, joined various groups and causes, and became a bridge master. Over the years, she particularly relished the time she spent with her bridge-playing friends. But despite a number of surgeries, her physical condition deteriorated; and after careful planning, she ended her life, all alone, with an overdose of barbiturates in 1987.

**And Now I Am Eighty!**

My brother, Phillips, and his wife, Ereda, came to my eightieth birthday celebration in the late summer of 2006 at Jennifer and Dave's place. Phillips had just celebrated his own seventy-sixth birthday. After a call from Lisa urging them to come, they drove all the way from Amherst, Massachusetts, to surprise me.

Phil is rail thin but copes cheerfully with severe rheumatoid arthritis. He and Ereda still go out dancing every week and take off at least once a year for a guided tour of some far country. A few months later, Ereda mails us all a copy of her meticulous and entertaining day-by-day diary of their trip.

Bob Hensley came too. Since retiring, he has sailed his thirty-six-foot sloop to France and back, has become a fine potter and ceramist, and is taking nonstop a wide variety of Donovan courses for seniors at UK. He and his wife, Cathy, are part of my extended family. We see them at most of our family gatherings, and I would not want to be without them!

My old friends Nannette, Peg Taylor, and Vicki Johnston also attended my birthday party.

Whenever I have a doctor's appointment, a session with my financial advisor, or business of any kind in Lexington, I arrange to stay overnight with Nannette or at least meet her somewhere for a lingering breakfast or lunch.

(In Nannette's crystal ball, we watch as she soon meets Tim Benincasa, the love of her life, at a small art show in Lexington and marries him a year later. We see that he is a dandy fellow, open-minded and fun-loving, a successful self-employed engineer, entrepreneur, and business consultant.)

As for Vicki, after teaching art in the public school system for
many years, she now earns her living as an artist, jewelry maker,
and craftswoman. I see her most often these days at Peg and Tim's
annual Derby Day party and other gatherings at Good Spring Farm.

After Peg retired from her career as an educator a few years ago,
she renovated the old farmhouse where her husband, Tim, grew up
and turned it into a bed-and-breakfast. It is only a stone's throw
from their log house.

Despite its location way back in the boonies, her venture has
been a big success. Farmhouse Inn on Good Spring Farm: doesn't
that have a good ring to it? Kentucky writers Wendell Berry and
Gurney Norman were her first guests.

Peg wrote the following eightieth-birthday letter to me. Her note
card featured a picture of the front porch swing on their log house in
McCreary County:

> Dear Jay, Dear Friend . . . We haven't known each
> other all 80 years, but we are sister-like in our friendship,
> and it seems we've known each other forever.
>
> Imagine yourself with me on the swing, roses in
> bloom, as we "swing" into the rest of our lives. Telling
> stories, comparing notes, remembering adventures with
> Vicki, our kids, horses, men—the whole gamut—We've
> been there.
>
> Congratulations on reaching this milestone, only
> fourteen years ahead of me! Your "joie de vivre," nerve,
> enthusiasm, pick-yourself-up-out-of-the-dust guts and
> humor will keep the rest of us on our toes. Keep on
> keeping on—and many happy returns.
>
> With love and admiration—Peg

Not long after my birthday celebration, I visit Peg and Tim at
Good Spring Farm and join a potluck gathering of their close friends
and neighbors I've come to know through the years.

The following evening, Peg and I cage for deportation three
superfluous, troublesome roosters who have been beating up on

the hens. She ventures into the chicken house with a flashlight. I wait outside in the dark with an open cage. There is much loud squawking; then Peg reappears with a rooster hanging upside down from her fist. We plop it, headfirst and protesting, into the cage; then on to the next rooster. (Peg says my reenactment for Tim later on is even funnier than the real thing.)

Very early the next morning, Jill, their exuberant border collie, leaps up onto my bed on top of me to greet the day.

"Get off me, you big horse!" I yell, startled awake. A bit later, I hear a rooster crow, glimpse the faint beginnings of the sunrise from my upstairs window, hustle into my clothes, and dash out into the frosty morning air. I trek across muddy pastures toward the east, then perform my ritual Qigong and Tao exercises as the rising sun pulls the day alive.

Overcome with the wonder of it all, I fling my arms wide and shout, "Great Spirit, grant me many more years of this good life and these good people!"

Get Published, Inc!
Thorofare, NJ 08086
28 December, 2009
BA2009300